EVENING
BY EVENING

CHARLES H.
SPURGEON

BRIDGE
LOGOS
FOUNDATION

Alachua, Florida 32615

Bridge-Logos
Alachua, FL 32615 USA

Evening By Evening
by Charles H. Spurgeon

Copyright ©2005 by Bridge-Logos

Printed in the United States of America.

Library of Congress Catalog Card Number: 00-105-360
International Standard Book Number 978-0-88270-877-5

Scripture quotations in this book are from the *King James Version* of the Bible.

Unless otherwise indicated, Scripture quotations are taken from the *New American Standard Bible.* © 1960, 1962, 1963, 1968, 1971, 1972, 1973, 1975, 1977 by The Lockman Foundation. Used by permission.

G163.318.TB.m909.35230

My soul shall be satisfied as with marrow and fatness:
and my mouth shall praise Thee with joyful lips:
when I remember Thee upon my bed, and
meditate on Thee in the night watches.
Psalm 63: 5-6

"Brethren, it is a good thing to be under the sound
Word of God."
– Charles Haddon Spurgeon

Contents

Charles Haddon Spurgeon

1834–1892

From Boy Preacher to Prince of Preachers, Charles Haddon Spurgeon moved tens of thousands to trust Christ for their eternal salvation and left a treasure trove of sermons and writings that continue to move and touch his readers. And Spurgeon did all through great infirmities and trials, living humbly even as he became a world-renowned celebrity.

The 15-year-old boy entered the Primitive Methodist Church amid a howling snowstorm that had kept him from reaching his intended church. The unusual English storm also kept the preacher from reaching the church. Only a handful of hearty believers made it, and the young lad, Charles, joined them in the service with singing.

Charles describes the events this way:

> At last, a very thin looking man, a shoemaker, went up into the pulpit to preach … He was forced to stick to his Scripture text, for the simple reason that he had little else to say. The text was, "Look unto me, and be ye saved, all the ends of the earth" (Isaiah 45:22).
>
> When he had managed to spin out 10 minutes or so, he was at the end of his tether. Then he looked at me under the gallery, and I daresay, with so few present, he knew me to be a stranger. Just fixing his eyes on me, as if he knew all my heart, he said, "Young man, you look very miserable." Well, I did, but I had not been accustomed to have remarks made from the pulpit

on my personal appearance before. However, it was a good blow, struck right home. He continued, "And you always will be miserable—miserable in life, and miserable in death—if you don't obey my text; but if you obey now, this moment, you will be saved." Then, lifting up his hands, he shouted as only a Primitive Methodist could do, "Young man, look to Jesus Christ. Look! Look! Look! You have nothing to do but to look and live."

I saw at once the way of salvation ... I had been waiting to do fifty things, but when I heard the word, "Look!" what a charming word it seemed to me! Oh! I looked until I could almost have looked my eyes away. There and then the cloud was gone, the darkness had rolled away, and that moment I saw the sun; and I could have risen that instant, and sung with the most enthusiastic of them, of the precious blood of Christ, and the simple faith which looks alone to HIM ...

> E'er since by faith I saw the stream
> Thy flowing wounds supply
> Redeeming love has been my theme
> And shall be till I die.

God's hand was in a snowstorm, an absent preacher, a faithful little shoemaker, and an aptly spoken word. And He brought forth the salvation of a man who would see tens of thousands of souls converted under his ministry, and tens of millions influenced by his writings that are reprinted and absorbed by Christians to this day. Once in the Kingdom, God lit a fire in Charles that would light the way for millions of people.

The bedraggled 15-year-old boy who heard the word of the Lord that day and looked up to see Jesus was Charles Haddon Spurgeon, often called the Prince of Preachers, a teacher and man who lived the Word and was used by God.

Young Beginnings
Spurgeon's Christian roots can be traced back to persecuted Dutchmen who fled to England centuries earlier only to find

different persecution. Job Spurgeon was imprisoned in 1677 for six years and had all of his belongings confiscated for attending a worship service not sanctioned by the Church of England. A few years after being released from prison, he was sent back for the same offense.

Spurgeon's father and grandfather were both strong Christians and Congregationalist ministers.

Into this godly heritage, Charles Haddon Spurgeon was born June 19, 1834 in Kelvedon, Essex, England—the first of 17 children. Interestingly, as an infant, he was sent to live with his grandparents and stayed with them until he was six years old. There, he was given a complete youngster's understanding of Scriptures, and by age six he had learned to love John Bunyan's classic *Pilgrim's Progress*.

Back with his parents, he grew up in a home with strong Puritan teachings and faithful, restrained lives to match. There was no known hypocrisy in his parents' lives. And the Spurgeons did not allow it in their offspring. By outward standards, he and his siblings were exemplary children.

Little Charles once lost his pencil and decided to buy one at the store on credit. When his father found out, he gave him a lecture on the sins of debt that he never forgot.

> I was marched off to the shop like a deserter marched into barracks, crying bitterly all down the street and feeling dreadfully ashamed, because I thought everybody knew I was in debt. The farthing was paid amid solemn warnings, and the poor debtor was set free like a bird out of a cage.

Spurgeon spent some time at a boarding school, and here we see a flash of his occasional fieriness. When he first started there, he knelt to pray before going to bed and was pelted by other boys with slippers and other items. He arose and struck at the mocking boys to his right and then to his left. After several were knocked down, the others stopped and stayed still. Then he knelt back down and returned to his prayers. He reported not being interrupted again.

From his earliest days, Spurgeon struggled with the sin in

3

his life. Although his sinfulness might appear small from the outside, it weighed heavily on the boy's heart. No doubt at least part of this reason was all the talk and teaching in the home of fallen nature. In addition to Scripture, Spurgeon was reared on the writings of John Bunyan and Richard Baxter, making him keenly aware of the soul's struggle with sin. He had a sharp sense of the justice of God.

> Sin, whatever it might be to other people, became to me an intolerable burden. It was not so much that I feared hell as that I feared sin, and all the while I had upon my mind a deep concern for the honour of God's name. I felt that it would not satisfy my conscience if I could be forgiven unjustly, but then there came the question, how could God be just and yet justify me, who had been so guilty?

During that cold Sunday morning in January 1850, Spurgeon was making his way toward his own church, but the fateful snowstorm forced him to the Primitive Methodist Church where the faithful cobbler showed him the way to salvation through the words of the prophet Isaiah.

Spurgeon, of course, knew the Gospel well from his upbringing, but God chose to use a vehicle outside his family to draw him to His Son. It was the longing of his heart, and Christ filled it.

> I do from my soul confess that I was never satisfied till I came to Christ ... Since that dear hour when my soul cast itself on Jesus, I have found solid joy and peace, but before that all those supposed gaieties of early youth, all the imagined joy and ease of boyhood, were but vanity and vexation of spirit to me. That happy day when I found the Saviour and learnt to cling to His dear feet was a day never to be forgotten by me, an obscure child, unknown, unheard of. I listened to the word of God, and that precious text led me to the Cross of Christ.

Spurgeon attended Oxford for a while. However, because he

was not a member of the Church of England, he was not allowed to earn a degree. But he studied diligently, and his keen mind was obvious. And he was free to preach as he desired, taking part in street preaching.

Spurgeon was never able to keep his joy and the basic message of the Gospel to himself. It spilled out of him naturally. Almost immediately, he set out as a servant of God, putting his hand to the plow and not looking back. There was nothing too small or trivial; he only wanted to do God's will. The Lord began him small, found him faithful, and in a stunningly short time, brought him to great things.

> The very first service which my youthful heart rendered to Christ was the placing of tracts in envelopes, and then sealing them up, that I might send them. I might have done nothing for Christ if I had not been encouraged by finding myself able to do a little. Then I sought to do something more, and from that something more, and I do not doubt that many servants of God have been led on to higher and nobler labours for their Lord, because they began to serve Him in the right spirit and manner.

His spirit was to share Christ in any way he could—writing verses on a scrap of paper and leaving it for someone to find.

> I could scarcely content myself even for five minutes without trying to do something for Christ.

Nothing could stop him.

> It may be that in the young dawn of my Christian life, I did imprudent things in order to serve the cause of Christ, but I still say, give me back that time again, with all its imprudence and with all its hastiness, if I may but have the same love to my Master, the same overwhelming influence in my spirit, making me obey my Lord's commands because it was a pleasure to me to do anything to serve my God.

Deceived Onto the Path of Greatness

Spurgeon was actually tricked into his first sermon. James Vinter, who headed the Local Preachers' Association in Cambridge, heard of Spurgeon's success giving the closing address after Sunday school. Vinter invited Spurgeon to accompany a man to the village of Teversham where he was to preach. Enroute, Spurgeon said he would be praying for him, and the man stopped in surprise. He had never preached, he said, and never intended to. He assumed Spurgeon was preaching and suggested that if he were not, they should turn back.

Spurgeon realized he had been tricked, but he decided to give a message anyway, even though he was completely unprepared and had never preached. He chose the Scripture "Unto you therefore which believe He is precious" on which to preach, and God greatly blessed the 16-year-old. When he finished, a woman's voice piped up and asked, "Bless your dear heart. How old are you?" Spurgeon very solemnly replied, "You must wait till the service is over before making such inquiries. Let us now sing."

And so the boy preacher was launched at age sixteen.

Within eighteen months of his conversion, Spurgeon was made pastor of the small Waterbeach Baptist Chapel.

He said he became a Baptist because of studying the New Testament in Greek. "According to my reading of Holy Scripture, the believer in Christ should be buried with Him in baptism, and so enter upon his open Christian life."

Spurgeon's mother once proclaimed, "Ah, Charles! I often prayed the Lord to make you a Christian, but I never asked that you become a Baptist."

Spurgeon with a smile responded quickly, "Ah, mother! The Lord has answered your prayer with His usual bounty, and given you exceeding abundantly above what you asked or thought."

England was in a state of considerable spiritual darkness, with corruption and apathy in the Church of England. While there were firm remnants of Christianity, the overall picture was dismal. The Rev. Desmond Morse-Boycott of the Church of England wrote:

England was a land of closed churches and unstoled clergy ... The parson was often an absentee, not infrequently a drunkard ... The rich went to church to doze in upholstered curtained pews fitted with fireplaces, while the poor were herded together on uncomfortable benches.

The small town of Waterbeach was in a similarly, spiritually dilapidated state. But God was with the 17-year-old pastor, and the work of Charles Spurgeon began to bear fruit almost immediately. The thatched-roof church was soon crammed with people, and some men who were the lowest and most noxious in the village became great blessings in the church.

Many of the villagers helped out their young pastor with his needs, knowing that the tiny amount of income he was provided could not support even such a modest lifestyle. Spurgeon was determined to stick it out as long as God desired it. He seemed to want little for himself and truly delighted in the changed lives of those in the village.

I can testify that great numbers of humble country folk accepted the Saviour's invitation, and it was delightful to see what a firm grip they afterwards had on the verities of the faith. Many of them became perfect masters of divinity. I used to think sometimes that if they had degrees who deserved them, diplomas would often be transferred and given to those who hold the plough handle or work at the carpenter's bench.

This attitude toward the simple man remained with Spurgeon, a country boy himself, who remained comfortable and approachable by any class even when he became a worldwide name.

He spent three years in Waterbeach and although a mere teenager most of the time, the church and the village flourished under his care and ministering. He wrote:

It was a pleasant thing to walk through that place when drunkenness had almost ceased, when debauchery in the case of many was dead, when men and women went forth to labour with joyful hearts, singing the praises of the ever-living God.

New Park Street: Great Church, Little Preacher

In November 1853, the young man received an invitation to preach a Sunday service at New Park Street Chapel in London. New Park Street was famous among Baptists and Londoners and most Christians as a place of great godly influence and preaching in the 1700s. Spurgeon thought at first it was a mistake. Why would such a great church be interested in this little, country lay preacher?

But after he determined that the invitation was indeed not an error, he replied in sincere humility, informing them that he was only 19 and had never preached in a large church. He went on to say he had a prior commitment for the date they requested and offered December 11. The New Park Street deacons accepted.

New Park Street Chapel was symbolic of the decline in Baptist churches in England in the middle 1800s. The once vibrant church was a shell of its former glory. Few congregations in the whole of London topped 300 people, and all the talk was of the decline in church attendance. In fact, the Baptist denomination was divided on several issues.

Spurgeon arrived in London on a cold and dreary day, staying in a tiny little apartment where the other young men boarding there ridiculed him for claiming that he would be preaching at New Park Street. He felt completely alone, without a friend in the city. When he tried to sleep, it was torture in the cramped room with the cacophony of horses and cabs all night. He already hated London.

And yet he considered that perhaps God was in all of it.

When he arrived at New Park Street the next morning, he was in awe of the magnificent building, and wondered how such a sophisticated and perhaps critical congregation would receive him. But more surprises were in store. As the time of the service approached, the great chapel did not fill up. In fact, it was dotted with just a few souls. It felt practically empty.

Spurgeon rose and spoke on "Every good gift and every

perfect gift is from above and cometh down from the Father of Lights, with Whom is no variableness neither shadow of turning." Every thread of Spurgeon's preaching led up to the Cross. He did not preach on moral issues or anything in modern debate. He simply preached Christ crucified and let everything else fall as it may.

The people seemed unsure of the young preacher who knew Scripture so well and seemed to already have a vast wealth of knowledge and experience. But when the evening service came about, everyone returned and brought a good number more with them. He preached from Revelation, "They are without fault before the throne of God."

In one day, his future and the church's future were cemented together. He was invited to pastor the church. And while he could not accept immediately, and did not treasure leaving his flock in Waterbeach, he received peace from God to take the position.

Spurgeon Breaks the Mold

Spurgeon was not one to simply go with the flow. But he also understood the need for discipline and submission.

An example from his first months at New Park Street Chapel demonstrates this vividly. He was not truly ordained when he accepted the New Park Street pulpit. It was suggested there be a formal ordination service over which one of London's ordained ministers would preside. Spurgeon thoughtfully replied in a long letter to the deacons.

He opposed the ordination ceremony. His calling was from God, and he had already recognized his ministry. He objected to the concept of ministers passing on power from one to another and believed it was completely up to the local church. But, he was willing to submit to the church leadership if they felt his ceremonial ordination to be critically important: "It will be submission. I shall endure it as a self-mortification in order that you may all be pleased. I would rather please you than myself."

The ordination ceremony never took place.

Spurgeon also broke the mold of tradition by discouraging references to himself as "Reverend" or even "Pastor," and by discarding the long, black frock of ministers and wearing plain clothes. These changes were severely criticized by other ministers, who believed they ought to be set apart from the flock. Moreover, Spurgeon broke through the heavy academic style of preaching so in vogue. He chose instead to speak directly to his listeners in words that could not possibly be misunderstood.

But it was not the insistence on outward changes that brought people to hear Spurgeon; it was the message of Jesus Christ crucified and arisen, and the need for Him alone for salvation. And the people came and came. Soon, not only was the once nearly empty chapel filled, but the street outside was blocked on Sundays for the overflow crowd to listen to this very young man of God.

Soon it became evident that larger space was necessary. They turned to the Music Hall in the Royal Surrey Gardens. This was a huge step, because the building housed up to 12,000 people. Spurgeon and William Olney—the man who was instrumental in bringing Spurgeon to London—feared it might have been far too large and they would have looked silly. But where they were simply could not work any longer, so they pressed forward.

Terror, Flight, Disorder and Death

It was a disaster that first night in October 1856. The Music Hall was jammed to capacity, such as it never was with secular performances. But after a Scripture reading and prayer, the wicked had their planned moment. Someone shouted, "Fire!" and another shouted, "The balcony is giving way!" Several others shouted similar fears. A panic erupted among the people and as they pressed toward the doors, seven people were killed, trampled by others desperately trying to flee a perfectly safe building.

The British Banner wrote: "At the most solemn moment of the occasion, the wicked rose in their strength, like a whirlwind, sin entered, followed by terror, flight, disorder and death!"

It seemed clear to everyone that it was a staged effort by evil-doers to wreck the work of God—everyone except Spurgeon, who to the end of his life wanted to "hope there was no concerted wickedness."

Spurgeon, only 22 years old, was devastated. The burden of

it overwhelmed him. He became sick and was unable to preach for a couple of Sundays. But gradually his strength returned, and along with it his speaking became as powerful as ever. And the church was able to make good use of Music Hall afterward.

Eventually, however, a new building of their own was needed. In 1861, they built the Metropolitan Tabernacle, which still stands in London today. It was a huge structure that comfortably seated 3,700, with room for another 2,000 to squeeze in, which they normally did.

Charles in Love

Susannah Thompson was a "greatly privileged favourite" of William Olney, who was the lead Deacon and responsible for bringing Spurgeon to London. And so she saw Spurgeon preach his first three sermons at New Park Street Chapel.

Despite her Christian upbringing, she had never professed her faith in Christ, although she was very well aware of her need for the Saviour.

During a Sunday evening sermon about a year before Spurgeon arrived, the preacher spoke on "The word is nigh thee, even in thy mouth, and in thy heart," and the light dawned in Susannah's soul. She wrote:

> The Lord said to me, through His servant, 'Give me thine heart,' and, constrained by His love, that night witnessed my solemn resolution of entire surrender to Himself.

But she records that she grew cold and indifferent to the things of God, and was in such a state when Spurgeon took the pulpit.

Some of their early connections are shrouded in personal privacy that eludes history. But she writes that quite unexpectedly, Spurgeon gave her an illustrated copy of *The Pilgrim's Progress*, the John Bunyan book that had meant so much to him since childhood. He inscribed it, "Miss Thompson, with desires for progress in the blessed pilgrimage, from C.H. Spurgeon, April 20, 1854."

In June 1854, the two were providentially seated next to each other at a party. Spurgeon handed a book written by Martin Tupper to Susannah and asked about a quotation in it: "Seek a good wife of Thy God, for she is the best gift of His Providence."

She blushed slightly, then heard him whisper the question, "Do you pray for him who is to be your husband?" There was a pause, and then Spurgeon asked her if she would take a walk with him. In August, they were engaged and they married on January 8, 1856.

The home they made was modest, and they took care to avoid any excessive displays. Their homes in town and later in Westwood were seemingly open to everyone: to missionaries, preachers and visitors from around the world. And they gave generously to those in need. The estimates from a review of their accounting books found that they gave away about five times as much as they kept for themselves. That's more than an 80 percent "tithe."

The Spurgeon's twin boys—Thomas and Charles—were born September 20, 1856. They were tremendous blessings to their parents and became preachers and leading men of God themselves. But the birth left Susannah an invalid in her home for 15 years. Yet her joy and that of her husband did not diminish.

"She was a fine example of the triumph of sanctified will over physical suffering," J.C. Carlile wrote in *Charles Spurgeon, The Great Orator*. "Even in pain, she dictated many letters to other sufferers and helped bear the burdens of ministries of all denominations who had fallen on evil times."

Out of the money she saved in frugal housekeeping, she began the Book Fund, which financed thousands of books of Bible study for pastors around the world. She also found money for soup kitchens, clothing for the children of poorly paid village ministers, and the individual needs of untold numbers of people.

Despite her fragile health, Susannah proved to be the ideal partner for Spurgeon, loving and serving the Lord first and sharing a spiritual intensity that helped buoy him when he needed it. Despite her extended illness, she did not seem to be a major burden on her husband. On the contrary, she was his helpmate.

Prince of Preachers

Spurgeon brought a whole new method to preaching. He did not strive for the flowery speech of the humanists or the rhetoric of the High Calvinists. Nor did he muddle through, as did many of the rural preachers. He spoke simply and from the depth of his heart and his intellect, but it was not to impress man. It was to impress upon man the glory of God, the fallen sinning state of each of us and the salvation of Christ.

"His ideal was that of the fisherman," wrote Carlile, who was a student under Spurgeon. "He lowered his net to catch fish; he baited his hook, not for decorative purposes but to secure souls."

Spurgeon never took his eye off the Word. God's great truths defined everything for him, and they informed his preaching. He wanted to make people clearly understand him. There would be no fogs in his preaching.

"Sermons should have real teaching in them, and their doctrine should be solid, substantial and abundant," Spurgeon wrote. "The world still needs to be told of its Saviour and of the way to reach Him."

Spurgeon did not do much on the spur of the moment. Occasionally he gave sermons without preparation—such as his first one. But most of the time he was intent on always finding just the right words and meanings to make his point clear. He wanted to use illustrations to make the points from ancient Scripture real to his listeners. He was very willing to quote other great men of God, from Bunyan to John Knox to Richard Baxter. And so he labored over every sermon, always starting at the beginning—with prayer. In speaking to students at his Pastors' College, he put it very clearly to them:

> I frequently sit hour after hour praying and waiting for a subject, and this is the main part of my study; much hard labour have I spent in manipulating topics, ruminating upon points of doctrine, making skeletons

out of verses and then burying every bone of them in the catacombs of oblivion, sailing on and on over leagues of broken water till I see the red lights and make sail direct to the desired haven.

Unstudied thoughts coming from the mind without previous research, without the subjects in hand having been investigated at all, must be of a very inferior quality, even from the most superior men, and as none of us would have the effrontery to glorify ourselves as men of genius or wonders of erudition, I fear that our unpremeditated thoughts upon most subjects would not be remarkably worthy of attention at all.

Our sermons should be our mental lifeblood—the outflow of our intellectual and spiritual vigor; or, to change the figure, they should be diamonds well cut and well set, precious intrinsically and bearing the marks of labour. God forbid that we should offer to the Lord that which costs us nothing.

And there you have the heart of C.H. Spurgeon on preaching. Notice that it does not include anything other than what is driving the preacher to preach. There is nothing on methods or deliveries or services. Where is the heart of the man expounding on the Word of God? That was the question for Spurgeon.

When asked once about how he attracted so many people while other churches were dormant or dwindling, he answered:

I did not seek them. They have always sought me. My concern has been to preach Christ and leave the rest to His keeping.

That was his heart.

Although it would not be his style, Spurgeon could certainly point to the results of preaching Christ first and Him crucified, preaching from deep study and prayer, and preaching for the glory of the Lord and not the preacher.

The Tabernacle For a Growing Congregation

The church needed a new home, and although the Music Hall worked for a while, the leadership knew that they needed to build. Spurgeon's vision was for a Greek structure. He felt there were no sacred languages other than ancient Greek and Hebrew. He believed that a Christian church should not be a Gothic structure, but should be Grecian.

The Metropolitan Tabernacle was completed in 1861—the largest church in the world at the time, holding nearly 6,000 people. Predictably, Spurgeon was criticized for building such a monumental edifice. He was charged with puffing himself up and being ostentatious. It was also said that the money could have been better spent on the poor. But the charges of egotism and ostentation evaporated when the church opened and filled up twice every Sunday. And as for helping the poor, Spurgeon's personal giving and books open for review shamed any critic. The couple's 80 percent tithe put to rest the lie that he was making himself rich through the Tabernacle.

At one point, an American lecture bureau invited him to come to America to tour all major cities and give 50 lectures. They offered to pay all expenses, plus $50,000—which would be a quarter million dollars today. Spurgeon wasn't interested. Ever keeping his eye on the Master's will, he quickly replied, "I can do better. I will stay in London and try to save 50 souls."

He was comfortable, but given his position of worldwide prominence and influence, and particularly the sales of millions of his books, his lifestyle was very modest. He could have lived as a king, but lived *for* the King and allowed his riches to be stored up in heaven rather than on earth.

Winning Souls From His Knees

Spurgeon did not desire to take church members from other congregations; he wanted to get the lost into the Tabernacle and into the Kingdom. By always preaching Christ and salvation, he knew he never missed the opportunity for a lost soul to hear the Gospel.

The soul-winning ways of Spurgeon began where everything began with him: in prayer. The Tabernacle was known as a church that prayed. Spurgeon may have set the example for many in later years, but the leadership had made the commitment before he arrived. The remnant that sought him out were on their knees, paving the way. That critical resolution was never lost.

No doubt many people came to hear Spurgeon out of curiosity, but saved or lost, they all heard a Christ preached that captured them.

Bob Ross wrote that Spurgeon "plainly preached the Word, pressing the Law and the Gospel upon his hearers—the Law to convict and break the hardened, and the Gospel to heal the broken."

He loved God and he loved his fellow men. Here is how he concluded one of his sermons:

> He that believeth not shall be damned. Weary sinner, hellish sinner, thou who are at the devil's castaway, reprobate, profligate, harlot, robber, thief, adulterer, fornicator, drunkard, swearer … listen! I speak to thee as to the rest. I exempt no man. God hath said there is no exemption here. Whosoever believeth in the name of Jesus Christ shall be saved. Sin is no barrier. The guilt is no obstacle. Whosoever, though he were black as Satan, though he were guilty as a fiend—whosoever this night believes shall every sin forgiven, shall every crime effaced, shall every iniquity blotted out; shall be saved in the Lord Jesus Christ, and shall stand in heaven safe and secure. That is the glorious gospel. God apply it home to your hearts and give you faith in Jesus.

New Park Street went from 232 members when Spurgeon arrived to more than 5,000 about 10 years later. It was the largest independent congregation in the world—independent of denominations, but dependent on the King of kings. Prime Minister Gladstone, many members of the royal family, members of Parliament, and dignitaries from around the world visited the Tabernacle. But no matter who was in attendance, like Baxter and others before him, the message had to remain the same. All were sinners; all needed Christ or were condemned eternally. No one from the rag-tag orphan to the king escaped the equation.

People swarmed to him to hear the Truth. No numbers were kept, because Spurgeon did not use the modern altar call. He did not request a public decision. He simply quoted Scripture to believe in Christ and be saved. But even without the numbers, the fruits were quite clear. The growth of the church was primarily new believers. He planted several other churches in the London area, offshoots of the Tabernacle.

> From the very early days of my ministry in London, the Lord gave such an abundant blessing upon the proclamation of His truth that whenever I was able to appoint a time for seeking converts and inquirers, it was seldom, if ever, that I waited in vain; and usually, so many came, that I was quite overwhelmed with gratitude and thanksgiving to God.

Spurgeon's Legacy of the Pen
Spurgeon always loved to write. As a child, he planned his own magazine and wrote articles for it. This gift carried on until his death, leaving a godly legacy to future generations through both his preaching and writings.

From early on, there was such demand for the words he gave that his sermons were printed and distributed in England and the United States. The first ones were bound up and 500 printed. They disappeared so fast, more were printed until about 6,000 were distributed. Later more than 200,000 booklets with his sermons were printed.

Probably the most popular books he wrote were a little series entitled *John Ploughman's Talk*. More than 300,000 volumes were printed and sold very quickly. Subsequent printings added greatly to that number.

His writings encouraged lay believers and instructed ministers. But mostly, they were meant for the average man.

There was more that Spurgeon accomplished. In 1856 he started the Pastor's College with only one student. It grew steadily until about 100 young men were enrolled to become ministers of the Gospel. The College also housed the Stockwell Orphanage with boys' and girls' schools overseen by Spurgeon and supported by funds he helped raise.

He published a monthly magazine called the *Sword and the Trowel*, beginning in 1865, in which he essentially continued preaching Christ, but also touched on issues of doctrine within the church.

His autobiography lists 78 books he wrote and published, in addition to the sermons and the magazine.

Calvinist Without Apology

Spurgeon was an unapologetic Calvinist, in that he believed what Calvin believed. But he disliked the term, because it took the focus off the Saviour. He simply agreed with Calvin's theology, and believed that the Puritan fathers had come closest to Scriptural truth.

> We know nothing of the new ologies; we stand by the old ways ... Believing that the Puritanic school embodied more gospel truth in it than any other since the days of the apostles.

He defined Calvinism in its simplest terms this way:

> If anyone should ask me what I mean by a Calvinist, I should reply, "He is one who says, Salvation is of the Lord." I cannot find in Scripture any other doctrine than this. It is the essence of the Bible. "He only is my rock and my salvation." Tell me anything contrary to this truth, and it will be heresy; tell me a heresy, and I shall find its essence here, that it has departed from this great, this fundamental rock-truth, "God is my rock and my salvation."

The Protestant pastors were generally evangelical, but they were weak in their doctrine. And the result was clear in the lives of church members. Spurgeon wanted to set the church back on the rock-hard path of strong doctrine.

Spurgeon said,

My daily labor is to revive the old doctrines of Gill, Owen, Calvin, Augustine and Christ … The old truth that Calvin preached, that Augustine preached, is the truth that I preach today, or else I would be false to my conscience and my God. I cannot shape truth; I know of no such thing as paring off the rough edges of a doctrine. John Knox's gospel is my gospel. And that gospel which thundered through Scotland must thunder through England again.

In his day, however, not unlike today, there were elements from Hyper-Calvinists to Arminians who found fault with Spurgeon's doctrine. Knowing Scripture so well—he had much of it committed to memory—and knowing the writings of the church fathers intimately, he was able to aptly defend his doctrines.

But while willing to do it, he did not like the arena of battling other believers over issues of doctrine. He preferred the bottom line.

If I am asked to say what my creed is, I think I must reply, "It is Jesus Christ" … Jesus Christ, Who is the sum and the substance of the Gospel, Who is in Himself all theology, the Incarnation of every precious truth, the all-glorious embodiment of the way, the truth and the life.

He urged listeners, "Do not make minor doctrines main points," but stick with the theme of grace from God through Jesus. Yet he could discuss the most minute doctrines in great detail and earnestness, and they were apparently important to him.

Battling the Erosion and Corrosion of the Down-Grade

By the late 1880s, there was an insipid falling away from God's Truth that infected many churches, including the Baptists. Some ministers openly preached against the infallibility of the Bible, the deity of Christ and eternal salvation. Those few were censured by the Baptist Union. But many others did so more surreptitiously.

In the light of great scientific discoveries, these learned men began to question portions of Scripture or elements of the Trinity. They cast themselves as progressive and modern. Some found a new understanding in the theories of Charles Darwin, and pointed to what they felt were contradictions between Scripture and science—choosing science as their guide. Their congregations followed.

Carlile wrote:

> The pulpit was charged with silent surrender to the radical betrayal of the evangelical foundations of the Christian faith.

A blind eye was turned toward this apostasy within the Baptist Union and other denominations. It became known as the "Down-Grade" controversy.

Spurgeon at first thought it was an exception here and there. But he soon began to see a rapid spread of these ideas and was alarmed at the sudden infusion within his own denomination. Spurgeon was a very sick man by this point, and in fact, was only a few years from death. He likely knew it. And so there was no personal gain for him to enter into such a burgeoning fray at the end of his life. In fact, it probably taxed his failing strength.

Nonetheless, he felt compelled to defend the Gospel.

After a number of private conversations and correspondences with men he thought were reducing Scripture, and with S.H. Booth, the secretary of the Baptist Union, he brought the issue into the open in an 1887 *Sword and the Trowel* article. In the magazine, he issued a general warning to readers of the defection from the Truth that was riddling the Nonconformist churches.

Spurgeon laid out three charges: 1) The infallibility of Scripture from God was denied, 2) the way of salvation through Christ was not preached, and 3) hell was denied, as was any eternal punishment for sin.

It went right to the heart of the Gospel.

Just how deeply the unbelief had ensnared the church became obvious with the response. Many in the camp of science vigorously attacked Spurgeon over religion. He was also attacked through Christian publications and even the pulpit. And shockingly, at the next annual meeting of the Baptist Union, the issue was ignored. There was complete silence.

After repeated attempts to get the Baptist Union to confront the issue, Spurgeon felt he had no choice. He withdrew from the union. By unanimous vote, the congregation of the Tabernacle followed him. This was a blow to the union, as Spurgeon was by far the best-known Baptist preacher, and his congregation many times larger than any other. After several private attempts to get Spurgeon to return, the union passed a motion of censure against him—almost unanimously.

Booth claimed that Spurgeon had never brought the matter up with him. Spurgeon was stunned and was ready to produce the written documentation between Booth and him as evidence that the matter had indeed been thoroughly explored. But Booth insisted that those were private correspondences. As easily as Spurgeon could have proved his position and Booth's hypocrisy, he honored his old friend, and in spite of the betrayal, never revealed the letters. Without the proof, he undermined his own credibility. He also lost a friend. This was a painful split, because Spurgeon and Booth had been close for many years. To Booth's credit, Spurgeon knew he was trying to keep the controversy from blowing up and dividing the union. But it was unacceptable compromise for Spurgeon.

The censure passed by the Baptist Union was a deep wound for Spurgeon. But he had set out his path of defense of Scripture and would not turn back. He was absolutely militant about God's Word. But however strong his heart was in the matter, his body was not up to the battle. The controversy wore down his feeble frame even further, hastening the inevitable.

Suffering with Christ

Like so many great men and women of God, Spurgeon tasted of immense physical suffering. And much of his suffering was brought on by his zeal to push himself to the brink and beyond to do God's good will.

Arnold Dallimore wrote of the schedule that took its toll on Spurgeon's body:

Although he began full of youthful vigor he labored to such an extent that his health soon was drained. He preached 10 times a week on the average, often in places that were far removed from London. He oversaw his Pastors' College, his orphanage and almshouses, and bore the responsibility of raising the funds to keep them all vibrant and healthy. Every Monday he edited a sermon preached the previous day to prepare it for the press and each month he produced his magazine. He was also constantly producing books.

By the age of 30, he was already showing the signs of the stress. The painful disease of gout developed. Over the years, he would be in such agony that he was bed-ridden and unable to move. Many of his sermons were preached through obvious pain. He would use his cane and, with the help of church members, mount the podium to preach. Frequently, once he embarked upon the word of God, the pain seemed to dissipate, and he became animated and energetic until he was finished.

Spurgeon's views on his physical suffering are not those of many Christians today. He saw suffering as a gift from God. Without his suffering, he never could have been the comforting and sympathetic man that he was to the sick and downtrodden.

His son, Charles Jr., wrote:

> I know of no one who could, more sweetly than my dear father, impart comfort to bleeding hearts and sad spirits. As the crushing of the flower causes it to yield its aroma, so he, having endured in the long continued illness of my beloved mother, and also constant pains himself, was able to sympathize most tenderly with all sufferers.

Spurgeon knew this truth intimately.

> In the matter of faith healing, health is set before us as if it were the great thing to be desired above all things. Is it so? I venture to say that the greatest earthly

blessing that God can give to any of us is health, with the exception of sickness. Sickness has frequently been of more use to the saints of God than health has.

Spurgeon at Rest, at Last

In his last years, Spurgeon spent some wintertime in Menton, in South France, to help his ailing body. That is where he was in January 1892. He was very sick, yet he could not help but hold little services with just the handful of friends and family. He had spoken to the great throngs of thousands, but he would expound the word of God to any group, no matter how small.

Wilson Carlile was with Spurgeon in his last days, and it was clear that the Down-Grade issue was still on his heart.

> When he was dying at the East Bay, Menton, my wife and I went to his family prayers, which he took though in bed. He prayed for all the wandering sheep, concluding, "Thou, Lord, seest the various labels upon them and rightly regardest them by the mark of the Cross in their hearts. They are all Thy one fold."

Spurgeon crossed the River Jordan January 31, 1892, and entered into the loving arms of the Master whom he served so diligently on this earth. Typical of his humility and understanding of man's heart, he had left the request: "Remember, a plain stone. 'C.H.S.' and no more; no fuss."

He knew that a monument would be to him, and not to his Saviour. On his casket was this inscription:

> In ever loving memory of Charles Haddon Spurgeon, born at Kelvedon, June 19, 1834, fell asleep in Jesus at Menton, January 31, 1892. I have fought a good fight, I have finished my course, I have kept the faith.

Indeed he did.

By Rod Thomson

Rod Thomson is an award-winning journalist and writer in Sarasota, Florida, and the administrator of Hand to the Plow Ministries.

Illustration Portfolio

THE BIRTHPLACE OF CHARLES H. SPURGEON
June 19, 1834 in Kelvedon, Essex, England

REV. JOHN SPURGEON
father of C.H. Spurgeon

ELIZA SPURGEON
mother of C.H. Spurgeon

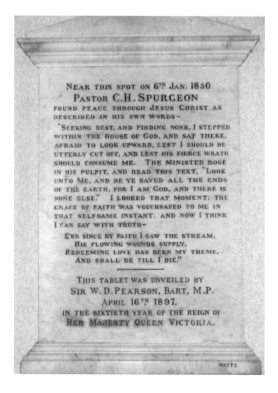

Near this spot on 6th Jan. 1850
Pastor C.H. Spurgeon
found peace through Jesus Christ as described in his own words –
"Seeking rest, and finding none, I stepped within the House of God,
and sat there, afraid to look upward, lest I should be utterly cut
off, and lest His fierce wrath should consume me. The minister rose
in his pulpit, and read this text, "Look unto Me, and be ye saved all
the ends of the Earth, for I am God, and there is none else."
I looked that moment: the grace of faith was vouchsafed to me in
that selfsame instatnt; and now I think I can say with truth –
E'er since by faith I saw the stream,
His flowing wounds supply,
Redeeming love has been my theme,
And shall be till I die."

This tablet was unveiled by
Sir W.D. Pearson, Bart, M.P.
April 16th 1897.
in the sixtieth year of the reign of
Her Majesty Queen Victoria

Above: The cottage where Mr. Spurgeon preached his first sermon at age 16. *Left:* Susannah Tompson became Mrs. Charles Spurgeon on January 8, 1856. Despite fragile health, she was a strong partner to her husband and his ministry. *Below:* The Spurgeons lived a comfortable but modest life at Westwood, and used the majority of their income to help ministers, the poor, and people in need.

WESTWOOD

THE NEW PARK STREET CHAPEL
Spurgeon accepted his first pastorate in December 1853,
at the age of 19.

MUSIC HALL IN THE ROYAL SURREY GARDENS
In spite of a disasterous beginning, the congregation used this
building as a meeting place for five years.

THE METROPOLITAN TABERNACLE
Above: Completed in 1861, the new home of the Park Street congregation was built in the Greek style. It was the largest church in the world at the time and held nearly 6,000 people. *Left*: Spurgeon sometimes needed to be helped into the pulpit because of the pain he suffered from gout.

STOCKWELL ORPHANAGE

Spurgeon oversaw and raised funds to support the Boy's
School and Girl's School at Stockwell Orphanage (*above*), as
well as the Pastor's College he founded (*bottom*).

THE PASTOR'S COLLEGE

THE SWORD AND THE TROWEL
Spurgeon published this monthly magazine beginning in 1865, in which he essentially continued preaching Christ, but also touched on issues of doctrine within the church.

Spurgeon in his study at Westwood, his family home.

Spurgeon's study at Westwood (*above*) contained more than 12,000 volumes. Mr. Spurgeon's work was enormous. Besides editing and furnishing most of the matter for his monthly magazine, *The Sword and Trowel*, since January 1, 1865, he wrote *The Saint and His Saviour*, *The Treasury of David, an Exposition of the Psalms* in seven octavo volumes; *The New Park Street Pulpit* and the *Metropolitan Tabernacle Pulpit*, which contains about two thousand of his weekly sermons from 1855 to 1889, making thirty large volumes. Also *Lectures to My Students, Commenting and Commentaries, John Ploughman*, the *Cheque Book of the Bank of Faith*, and various other publications.

Mark XVI. 14

This shows us the way in wh we must deal with
unbelief in ourselves, & in others. It is a sin
& should be treated as such. Jesus wd not have
upbraided had not this been the case.
In the case before us they had repeated
testimonies, from their own brethren, & backed by
his own word — but we have even more
guilt for we know him to be risen & yet doubt.

I. Let us consider its evil in itself
   Suppose some one doubted us.
   Think of who he is & what he has done.
   Consider his near & dear relation to us.
   The many times in wh we have doubted
   And upon the same matter.
   Where his promises forbade unbelief
   Despite our own declarations.
   What have we believed in preference?

II. Let us observe the evils wh it causes
   It grieves the Spirit of God.
   It causes distress in our own hearts
   It weakens us for action or suffering
   It depresses others.
   It leaves an ill impression con sinners
   It cannot but gender to bondage.

III. Let us reflect upon its sinfulness where
        it reigns
   It gives God the lie.
   It argues hatred in the heart
   It is the sign of utter moral death.
   It is the essence of hell.

SERMON NOTES
This one page of handwritten notes is all Spurgeon took
with him into the pulpit when he preached the sermon titled
"Unbelievers Upbraided."

33

January

We will be glad and rejoice in You
(Song of Solomon 1:4).

We will be glad and rejoice in You. We will not open the gates of the year to the sorrowful notes of the sackbut [medieval wind instrument], but to the sweet strains of the harp of joy, and the high sounding cymbals of gladness. "O come, let us sing unto the Lord. Let us make a joyful noise unto the rock of our salvation."[1] We, the called and faithful and chosen, we will drive away our grief, and set up our banners of confidence in the name of God. Let others lament over their troubles. We, who have the sweetening tree to cast into Marah's bitter pool[2] with oy, will magnify the Lord. Eternal Spirit, our effectual Comforter, we, who are the temples in which You dwell, will never cease from adoring and blessing the name of Jesus. *We* WILL. We are resolved about it. Jesus must have the crown of our heart's delight. We will not dishonor our Bridegroom by mourning in His presence.[3] We are ordained to be the minstrels of the skies; let us rehearse our everlasting anthem before we sing it in the halls of the New Jerusalem.[4] *We will* BE GLAD AND REJOICE—two words with one sense: double joy, blessedness upon blessedness. Need there be any limit to our rejoicing in the Lord even now? Do not men of grace find their Lord to be camphor and spikenard, calamus and cinnamon even now, and what better fragrance do they have in heaven itself? *We will be glad and rejoice* IN YOU. That last word is the meat in the dish, the kernel of the nut, and the soul of the text. What heavens are laid up in Jesus! What rivers of infinite bliss have their source, ay, and every drop of their fullness in Him! Since, O sweet Lord Jesus, You are the present portion of Your people, favor us this year with such a sense of Your preciousness, that from the first to the last day we may be glad and rejoice in You. Let January open with joy in the Lord, and December close with gladness in Jesus.

⇜ *January 2* ↝

Let the people renew their strength (Isaiah 41:1).

All things on earth need to be renewed. No created thing continues by itself. "Thou renewest the face of the year,"[5] was the psalmist's utterance. Even the trees, which neither wear themselves with care nor shorten their lives with labor, must drink of the rain of heaven and suck from the hidden treasures of the soil. The cedars of Lebanon, which God has planted, only live because day by day they are full of sap freshly drawn from the earth. Neither can man's life be sustained without renewal from God. As it is necessary to repair the waste of the body by the frequent meal, so we must repair the waste of the soul by feeding upon the Book of God, or by listening to the preached Word, or by the soul-fattening table of the ordinances. How depressed our graces are when means are neglected! What poor starvelings some saints are when they live without the diligent use of the Word of God and secret prayer! If our piety can live without God, it is not of divine creating. It is but a dream, for if God had begotten it, it would wait upon Him as the flowers wait upon the dew. Without constant restoration we are not ready for the perpetual assaults of hell, or the stern afflictions of heaven, or even for the strife within. When the whirlwind is loosed, woe to the tree that has not sucked up fresh sap and grasped the rock with many intertwined roots. When storms arise, woe to the mariners who have not strengthened their masts, or cast their anchors, or sought safe haven. If we suffer the good to grow weaker, the evil will surely gather strength and struggle desperately for the mastery over us. As a possible consequence, painful desolation and lamentable disgrace may follow. Let us draw near to the footstool of divine mercy in humble entreaty, and we shall realize the fulfillment of the promise, "They that wait on the Lord shall renew their strength."[6]

⤜ *January 3* ⤝

The voice of one crying in the wilderness, "Prepare ye
the way of the Lord, make his paths straight"
(Luke 3:4).

The voice crying in the wilderness demanded a way for the Lord—a way prepared in the wilderness.[7] I would pay attention to the Master's proclamation, and give Him a road into my heart, cast up by gracious operations through the desert of my nature. The four directions that follow in the Scripture must have our serious attention: *Every valley must be exalted.*[8] Low and groveling thoughts of God must be given up; doubting and despairing must be removed; and self-seeking and carnal delights must be forsaken. Across these deep valleys a glorious causeway of grace must be raised. *Every mountain and hill shall be laid low.* Proud creature-sufficiency and boastful self-righteousness must be leveled to make a highway for the King of kings. Divine fellowship is never promised to haughty, high-minded sinners. The Lord has respect for the lowly, and visits the deeply sorry sinner, but those who are lofty are an abomination to Him.[9] My soul, beseech the Holy Spirit to set you right in this respect. *The crooked shall be made straight.* The wavering heart must have a straight path of decision for God and holiness marked out for it. Double-minded men are strangers to the God of truth. My soul, take heed to be honest and true in all things, as in the sight of the heart-searching God. *The rough places shall be made smooth.* Stumbling blocks of sin must be removed, and thorns and briers of rebellion must be uprooted. So great a visitor must not find miry ways and stony places when He comes to honor His favored ones with His company. O, that on this evening the Lord may find in my heart a highway made ready by His grace, that He may make a triumphant progress through the utmost bounds of my soul from the beginning of this year even to the end of it.

ᴥ *January 4* ᴔ

And Joseph knew his brethren, but they knew not him
(Genesis 42:8).

Our heavenly father knows us. This was most blessedly perfect
long before we had the slightest knowledge of Him. "His eyes
beheld our substance, yet being imperfect, and in His book
all our members were written, when as yet there was none of
them."[10] Before we had a being in the world, we had a being in
His heart. When we were enemies to Him, He knew us—our
misery, our madness, and our wickedness. When we wept bitterly
in despairing repentance, and viewed Him only as a judge and a
ruler, He viewed us as His brethren well beloved, and He yearned
for us. He never mistook His chosen, but always beheld them as
objects of His infinite affection. "The Lord knoweth them that
are His,"[11] is as true of the prodigals who are feeding swine as
of the children who sit at the table. But, alas! *we knew not our
royal Brother*, and out of this ignorance grew a host of sins. We
withheld our hearts from Him, and allowed Him no entrance to
our love. We mistrusted Him, and gave no credit to His words.
We rebelled against Him, and paid Him no loving homage. The
Sun of Righteousness[12] shone forth, and we could not see Him.
Heaven came down to earth, and earth perceived it not.[13] Let
God be praised, those days are over with us; yet even now we
know only a little of Jesus compared with what He knows of us.
We have only begun to study Him, but He knows us altogether.
It is a blessed circumstance that the ignorance is not on His side,
for then it would be a hopeless case for us. He will not say to
us, "I never knew you,"[14] but He will confess our names in the
day of His appearing, and meanwhile will manifest Himself to
us, as He doth not unto the world.[15]

↘ *January 5* ↖

And God saw the light
(Genesis 1:4).

This morning we noticed the goodness of the light, and the Lord's dividing it from the darkness, we now note the special eye, which the Lord had for the light. "God saw the light"—He looked at it with satisfaction, gazed upon it with pleasure, saw that it "was good." If the Lord has given you light, dear reader, He looks on that light with peculiar interest; for not only is it dear to Him as His own handiwork, but because it is like Himself. "He is light."[16] It is pleasant for the believer to know that God's eye is thus tenderly observant of that work of grace, which He has begun. He never loses sight of the treasure, which He has placed in our earthen vessels.[17] Sometimes we cannot see the light, but God always sees the light, and that is much better than our seeing it. Better for the judge to see my innocence than for me to *think* I see it. It is very comfortable for me to know that I am one of God's people—but whether *I* know it or not, if the Lord knows it, I am still safe. This is the foundation: "The Lord knoweth them that are His."[18] You may be sighing and groaning because of inbred sin, and mourning over your darkness, yet the Lord sees "light" in your heart, for He has put it there, and all the cloudiness and gloom of your soul cannot conceal your light from His gracious eye. You may have sunk low in despondency and even despair, but if your soul has any longing toward Christ, and if you are seeking to rest in His finished work, God sees the "light." He not only *sees* it, but He also *preserves* it in you. "I, the Lord, do keep it." This is a precious thought to those who, after anxious watching and guarding of themselves, feel their own powerlessness to do so. Thus preserved by His grace, He will one day develop the light into the splendor of noonday and the fullness of glory. The light

⚛ *January 6* ⚛

Now the hand of the Lord was upon me in the evening
(Ezekiel 33:22).

In the way of *judgment* this may be the case, and, if so, it is mine to consider the reason of such a visitation, and bear the rod and Him that has appointed it. I am not the only one who is chastened in the night season; let me cheerfully submit to the affliction, and carefully endeavor to profit from it.[19] But the hand of the Lord may also be felt in another manner: strengthening the soul and lifting the spirit upward toward eternal things. O that in this sense, I may feel the Lord dealing with me! A sense of the divine presence and indwelling bears the soul toward heaven as upon the wings of eagles. At such times we are full to the brim with spiritual joy, and forget the cares and sorrows of earth, the invisible is near and the visible loses its power over us. Servant-body waits at the foot of the hill, and the master-spirit worships upon the summit in the presence of the Lord. O that a hallowed season of divine communion may be granted to me this evening! The Lord knows that I need it greatly. My graces languish. My corruptions rage. My faith is weak. My devotion is cold. All these are reasons that His healing hand should be laid upon me. His hand can cool the heat of my burning brow, and calm the tumult of my palpitating heart. That glorious right hand that molded the world can new-create my mind. The unwearied hand that bears the earth's huge pillars up can sustain my spirit. The loving hand that encloses all the saints can cherish me. And the mighty hand that breaks the enemy into pieces can subdue my sins. Why should I not feel that hand touching me this evening? Come, my soul, address your God with the potent plea, that Jesus' hands were pierced for your redemption,[20] and you will surely feel that same hand upon you that once touched Daniel and set him upon his knees so that he might see visions of God.

I have prayed for you
(Luke 22:32).

How encouraging is the thought of the Redeemer's endless intercession for us.[29] When we pray, He pleads for us. And when we are *not* praying, He is advocating our cause, and by His supplications shielding us from unseen dangers. Notice the word of comfort addressed to Peter—"Simon, Simon, Satan has desired to have you that he may sift you as wheat;[30] but"—what? "But go and pray for yourself." That would be good advice, but that is not how it's written. Neither does he say, "But I will keep you watchful, and so you shall be preserved." That was a great blessing. No, it is: "But I have prayed for you, that your faith fail not." We know little about all that we owe to our Savior's prayers. When we reach the hilltops of heaven, and look back upon all the way whereby the Lord our God has led us, how we shall praise Him who, before the eternal throne, undid the mischief, which Satan was doing upon earth.[31] How shall we thank Him because He never held His peace, but day and night pointed to the wounds upon His hands, and carried our names upon His breastplate! Even before Satan had begun to tempt, Jesus had forestalled him and entered a plea in heaven. Mercy outruns malice. Mark, He does not say, "Satan has *desired* to have you." He checks Satan even in his very desire, and nips it in the bud. He does not say, "But I have desired to pray for you." No, but "I *have* prayed for you: I have done it already; I have gone to court and entered a counterplea even before an accusation is made." O Jesus, what a comfort it is that you have pleaded our cause against our unseen enemies, countermined their mines, and unmasked their ambushes. Here is a matter for joy, gratitude, hope, and confidence.

I have yet to speak on God's behalf.
(Job 36:2).

We ought not to court publicity for our virtue or notoriety for our zeal, but at the same time, it is a sin to be always seeking to hide that which God has bestowed upon us for the good of others.[32] A Christian is not to be a village in a valley, but "a city set upon a hill." He is not to be a candle under a bushel, but a candle in a candlestick, giving light to all. Retirement may be lovely in its season, and to hide one's self is doubtless modest, but the hiding of *Christ* in us can never be justified, and the keeping back of truth, which is precious to us is a sin against others and an offense against God. If you are of a nervous temperament and of retiring disposition, take care that you do not too much indulge this trembling propensity, lest you should be useless to the church. Seek in the name of Him who was not ashamed of you to do some little violence to your feelings, and tell to others what Christ has told to you. If you cannot speak with trumpet tongue, use the still, small voice. If the pulpit cannot be your tribune, if the press may not carry on its wings your words, then say with Peter and John, "Silver and gold have I none; but such as I have give I You."[33] If you cannot preach a sermon from a mountaintop, talk to the Samaritan woman by Sychar's well.[34] Utter the praises of Jesus in the house, if not in the temple; in the field, if not upon the exchange; in the midst of your own household, if you cannot in the midst of the great family of man. From the hidden springs within let sweetly flowing rivulets of testimony flow forth, giving drink to every passer-by. Hide not your talent; trade with it; and you shall bring in good interest to your Lord and Master.[35] To speak for God will be refreshing to us, cheering to saints, useful to sinners, and honoring to the Savior. Silent children are an affliction to their parents. Lord, unloose all Your children's tongue.

⌁ *January 13* ⌁

The iron did swim (2 Kings 6:9).

The axe-head seemed hopelessly lost, and as it was borrowed, the honor of the prophetic band was likely to be imperiled, and so the name of their God to be compromised. Contrary to all expectation, the iron was made to mount from the depth of the stream and to swim, because things that are impossible with man are possible with God.[36] Only a few years ago, I knew a man in Christ who was called to undertake a task far exceeding his strength. It appeared so difficult that even the idea of attempting it seemed absurd. Yet he was called to do it, and his faith rose with the occasion. God honored his faith, unlooked-for aid was sent, and the iron did swim. Another of the Lord's family was in grievous financial straits; he was able to meet all claims and much more if only he could have realized a certain portion of his estate, but he was overtaken with a sudden pressure. He looked in vain to friends, but faith led him to the unfailing Helper, and lo, the trouble was averted, his footsteps were enlarged, and the iron did swim. A third had a sorrowful case of depravity to deal with. He had taught, reproved, warned, invited, and interceded, but all in vain. Old Adam was too strong for young Melancthon; the stubborn spirit would not relent. Then came an agony of prayer, and before long, a blessed answer was sent from heaven. The hard heart was broken; the iron did swim. Beloved reader, what is your desperate case? What heavy matter do you have in hand this evening? Bring it here. The God of the prophets lives, and lives to help His saints. He will not suffer you to lack any good thing. Believe in the Lord of hosts! Approach Him, pleading the name of Jesus, and the iron shall swim. You, too, will see the finger of God working marvels for His people. According to your faith, it will happen for you,[37] and yet again the iron shall swim.

◄ *January 14* ►

Beginning to sink, he cried, saying, Lord, save me
(Matthew 14:30).

Sinking times are praying times with the Lord's servants. Peter neglected prayer at starting upon his venturous journey, but when he began to sink, his danger made him a humble petitioner, and his cry, although late, was not too late. In our hours of bodily pain and mental anguish, we find ourselves as naturally driven to prayer as the wreck is driven upon the shore by the waves. The fox runs to its hole for protection; the bird flies to the wood for shelter; and even so the tried believer hastens to the mercy seat for safety. Heaven's great harbor of refuge is All-prayer; thousands of weather-beaten vessels have found a haven there, and the moment a storm comes on, it is wise for us to make for it with all sail. *Short prayers are long enough.* There were but three words in Peter's gasping petition, "Lord, save me." But they were sufficient for his purpose. Not length, but strength is desirable. A sense of need is a mighty teacher of brevity. If our prayers had fewer tail feathers of pride and more wing, they would be all the better. Verbiage is to devotion as chaff to the wheat. Precious things lie in small compass, and all that is real prayer in many a long address might have been uttered in a petition as short as Peter's. *Our extreme circumstances are the Lord's opportunities.* Immediately a keen sense of danger forces an anxious cry from us that the ear of Jesus hears. With Him, ear and heart go together, and the hand does not long linger. At the last moment, we appeal to our Master, but His swift hand makes up for our delays by instant and effectual action. Are we nearly engulfed by the boisterous waters of affliction? Let us then lift up our souls unto our Savior, and we may rest assured that He will not allow us to perish. When we can do nothing, Jesus can do all things. Let us enlist His powerful aid upon our side, and all will be well.

But I give myself unto prayer (Psalm 109:4).

Lying tongues were busy against the reputation of David, but he did not defend himself; he moved the case into a higher court, and pleaded before the great King Himself. Prayer is the safest method of replying to words of hatred. The psalmist didn't pray in a cold-hearted manner. He gave himself to the exercise—threw his whole soul and heart into it—straining every sinew and muscle, as Jacob did when wrestling with the angel. Thus, and thus only, shall any of us speed at the throne of grace.[38] As a shadow has no power because there is no substance in it, even so that supplication, in which a man's proper self is not thoroughly present in agonizing earnestness and vehement desire, is utterly ineffectual. It lacks that which would give it force. "Fervent prayer,"[39] says an old divine, "is like a cannon planted at the gates of heaven. It makes them fly open." The common fault with the most of us is our readiness to yield to distractions. Our thoughts go roving here and there, and we make little progress toward our desired end.[40] Like quicksilver, our minds will not hold together, but roll off this way and that. How great an evil this is! It injures us, and what is worse, it insults our God. What should we think of a petitioner, if, while having an audience with a prince, he should be playing with a feather or catching a fly? Continuance and perseverance are intended in the expression of our text. David did not cry once and then lapse into silence; his holy clamor was continued till it brought down the blessing. Prayer must not be our chance work, but our daily business, our habit and vocation. As artists give themselves to their models, and poets to their classical pursuits, so must we addict ourselves to prayer. We must be immersed in prayer as in our element, and so pray without ceasing.[41] Lord, teach us so to pray, that we may be more and more in supplication.

The Messiah shall be cut off, but not for himself
(Daniel 9:26).

Blessed is His name; there was no cause of death in Him. Neither original nor actual sin had defiled Him, and therefore death had no claim upon Him. No man could have taken His life from Him justly, for He had done no man wrong, and no man could even have lain Him by force unless He had been pleased to yield Himself to die.[42] But lo, one sins and another suffers. Justice was offended by us, but found its satisfaction in Him. Rivers of tears, mountains of offerings, seas of the blood of bulls, and hills of frankincense could not have been used to remove sin. But Jesus was cut off for us, and the cause of wrath was cut off at once, because sin was put away forever. Herein is wisdom, whereby substitution, the sure and speedy way of atonement, was devised! Herein is humility, which brought Messiah, the Prince, to wear a crown of thorns, and die upon the cross! Herein is love, which led the Redeemer to lay down His life for His enemies! It is not enough, however, to admire the spectacle of the innocent bleeding for the guilty. We must make sure of our interest. The special object of the Messiah's death was the salvation of His church. Have we a part and a lot among those for whom He gave His life a ransom?[43] Did the Lord Jesus stand as our representative? Are we healed by His stripes?[44] It will be a terrible thing indeed if we come short of a portion in His sacrifice. It would better for us if we had never been born. As solemn as the question is, joyfully it may be answered clearly and without mistake. To all who believe on Him, the Lord Jesus is a present Savior, and upon them, all the blood of reconciliation has been sprinkled. Let all who trust in the merit of Messiah's death be joyful at every remembrance of Him, and let their holy gratitude lead them to the fullest consecration to His cause.

And it came to pass in an evening-tide, that David arose from off his bed, and walked upon the roof of the king's house (2 Samuel 11:2).

At that hour David saw Bathsheba. We are never out of the reach of temptation. Both at home and abroad we are liable to be tempted by evil. The morning opens with peril, and the shades of evening find us still in jeopardy. They are well kept whom God keeps, but woe unto those who go forth into the world, or even dare to walk their own house unarmed. Those who think themselves secure are more exposed to danger than any others. The armor-bearer of Sin is Self-confidence. David should have been fighting the Lord's battles, but instead he tarried at Jerusalem and gave himself up to luxurious inactivity, arising from his bed at eventide. Idleness and luxury are the devil's jackals, and find abundant prey for him. In stagnant waters, noxious creatures swarm. And neglected soil soon yields a dense tangle of weeds and briars. Oh, for the constraining love of Jesus to keep us active and useful! When I see the King of Israel sluggishly leaving his couch at the close of the day, and falling at once into temptation, let me take warning and set holy watchfulness to guard the door. Is it possible that the king had mounted his housetop for retirement and devotion? If so, what a caution is given us to count no place, however secret, a sanctuary from sin! While our hearts are so like tinderboxes, and sparks so plentiful, we need to use all diligence in all places to prevent a blaze. Satan can climb housetops and enter closets. And even if we could shut out that foul fiend, our own corruptions are enough to work our ruin unless grace prevents it. Reader, beware of evening temptations. Be not secure. The sun is down, but sin is up. We need a watchman for the night, as well as a guardian for the day. O blessed Spirit, keep us from all evil this night. Amen.

ᗩ *January 18* ᖇ

He expounded unto them in all the Scriptures the things concerning himself (Luke 24:27).

The two disciples on the road to Emmaus had a most profitable journey. Their companion and teacher was *the best of tutors*: the interpreter—one of a thousand, in whom are hidden all the treasures of wisdom and knowledge. The Lord Jesus condescended to become a preacher of the gospel, and He was not ashamed to exercise His calling before an audience of two persons. Now, as then, He does not refuse to become the teacher of even one. Let us court the company of so excellent an Instructor, for till He is made unto us wisdom, we shall never be wise unto salvation.[45] This unrivalled tutor used the best of books as His textbook. Although able to reveal fresh truth, He preferred to expound the old. He knew by His omniscience the most instructive way of teaching. By turning at once to Moses and the prophets, He showed us that the surest road to wisdom is not speculation, reasoning, or reading human books, but meditation upon the Word of God. The best way to be spiritually rich in heavenly knowledge is to dig in this mine of diamonds, to gather pearls from this heavenly sea. When Jesus Himself sought to enrich others, He wrought in the quarry of Holy Scripture. The favored pair was led to consider the best of subjects, for Jesus spoke of Jesus, and expounded the things concerning Him. Here the diamond cut the diamond, and what could be more admirable? The Master of the House unlocked His own doors, conducted the guests to His table, and placed His own dainties upon it. He who hid the treasure in the field Himself guided the searchers to it. Our Lord would naturally discourse upon the sweetest of topics, and He could find none sweeter than His own person and work: with an eye to these we should always search the Word. O for grace to study the Bible with Jesus as both our teacher and our lesson!

☞ *January 19* ☜

Then opened He their understanding, that they might understand the Scriptures (Luke 24:45).

He whom we viewed last evening as opening Scripture, we here perceive opening the understanding. In the first work, He has many fellow-laborers, but in the second, He stands alone. Many can bring the Scriptures to the mind, but the Lord alone can prepare the mind to receive them. Our Lord Jesus differs from all other teachers. They reach the ear, but He instructs the heart. They deal with the outward letter, but He imparts an inward taste for the truth, by which we perceive its savor and spirit. The most unlearned of men become ripe scholars in the school of grace when the Lord Jesus by His Holy Spirit unfolds the mysteries of the kingdom to them, and grants the divine anointing by which they are enabled to behold the invisible.[46] Happy are we if we have had our understandings cleared and strengthened by the Master! How many men of profound learning are ignorant of eternal things! They know the killing letter of revelation, but its killing spirit they cannot discern. They have a veil upon their hearts, which the eyes of carnal reason cannot penetrate. Such was our case a little time ago. We, who now see, were once utterly blind; truth was to us as beauty in the dark—a thing unnoticed and neglected. Had it not been for the love of Jesus, we would have remained to this moment in utter ignorance, for without His gracious opening of our understanding, we could no more have attained to spiritual knowledge than an infant could climb the Pyramids, or an ostrich could fly up to the stars. Jesus' College is the only one in which God's truth can be really learned. Other schools may teach us what is to be believed, but Christ's alone can show us how to believe it. Let us sit at the feet of Jesus, and by earnest prayer, call in His blessed assistance so that our dull wits may grow brighter, and our feeble understandings may receive heavenly things.

☞ January 20 ☜

Turn away mine eyes from beholding vanity; and quicken Thou me in Your way (Psalm 119:37).

There are various kinds of vanity. The cap and bells of the fool, the mirth of the world, the dance, the lyre, and the cup of the dissolute: all men know these to be vanities. They are obvious. Far more treacherous are those equally vain things: the cares of this world and the deceitfulness of riches.[47] A man may follow vanity as truly in the counting house as in the theatre. If he spends his life in amassing wealth, he passes his days in a vain show. Unless we follow Christ and make our God the great object of life, we only differ in appearance from the most frivolous. It is clear that there is much need of the first prayer of our text: "Quicken Thou me in Your way." The psalmist confesses that he is dull, heavy, lumpy, and all but dead. Perhaps, dear reader, you feel the same. We are so sluggish that the best motives cannot quicken us, apart from the Lord Himself. What! Will not hell quicken me? Shall I think of sinners perishing, and yet not be awakened? Will not heaven quicken me? Can I think of the reward that awaits the righteous, and yet be cold? Will not death quicken me? Can I think of dying and standing before my God, and yet be slothful in my Master's service? Will not Christ's love constrain me? Can I think of His dear wounds, can I sit at the foot of His cross, and not be stirred with fervency and zeal? It seems so! No mere consideration can quicken us to zeal, but God Himself must do it, hence the cry, "Quicken *Thou* me." The psalmist breathes out his whole soul in vehement pleadings. His body and his soul unite in prayer. "Turn away mine eyes," says the body. "Quicken Thou me," cries the soul. This is a fit prayer for every day. O Lord, hear it in my case this night.

⚐ January 21 ⚑

He was sore athirst, and called on the Lord, and said,
Thou hast given this great deliverance into the hand of
Your servant: and now shall I die for thirst?
(Judges 15:18).

Samson was thirsty and ready to die. The difficulty was totally different from any that the hero had met before. Merely to satisfy thirst is not so great a matter as being delivered from a thousand Philistines! But when he was thirsty, Samson felt that this little present difficulty was more weighty than the great past difficulty out of which he had so specially been delivered. It is very usual for God's people, when they have enjoyed a great deliverance, to find a little trouble too much for them. Samson slays a thousand Philistines and piles them up in heaps, and then faints for a little water! Jacob wrestles with God at Peniel and overcomes Omnipotence itself, and then goes "halting on his thigh!"[48] Strange that there must be a shrinking of the sinew whenever we win the day. As if the Lord must teach us how small we are—how as nothing—in order to keep us within bounds. Samson boasted right loudly when he said, "I have slain a thousand men." His boastful throat soon grew hoarse with thirst, and he betook himself to prayer. God has many ways of humbling His people. Dear child of God, if after great mercy you are laid very low, your case is not an unusual one. When David had mounted the throne of Israel, he said, "I am this day weak, though anointed king."[49] You must expect to feel weakest when you are enjoying your greatest triumph. If God has wrought for you great deliverances in the past, your present difficulty is only like Samson's thirst, and the Lord will not let you faint or suffer the daughter of the uncircumcised to triumph over you. The road of sorrow is the road to heaven, but there are wells of refreshing water all along the route. So, you who are in trial, cheer your heart with Samson's words, and rest assured that God will deliver you before long.

☙ *January 22* ☙

Doth Job fear God for naught? (Job 1:9)

This was Satan's wicked question concerning that upright man of old, but there are many in the present day of whom it might be asked with justice, for they love God after a fashion because He prospers them, but if things go wrong, they give up all their boasted faith in God. If they can clearly see that since the time of their supposed conversion, the world has gone prosperously with them, then they will love God in their poor carnal way. But if they endure adversity, they rebel against the Lord. Their love is the love of the table, not of the host; a love of the cupboard, not of the master of the house. As for the true Christian, he expects to have his reward in the next life, and to endure hardness in this.[50] The promise of the old covenant is adversity. Remember Christ's words—"Every branch in Me that beareth not fruit"[51]—What? "He purgeth it, that it may bring forth fruit." If you bring forth fruit, you will have to endure affliction. "Alas!" you say, "that is a terrible prospect." But this affliction works out such precious results that the Christian who is the subject of it must learn to rejoice in tribulations,[52] because as his tribulations abound, so his consolations abound by Christ Jesus. Rest assured, when you are a child of God, you will be no stranger to the rod. Sooner or later every bar of gold must pass through the fire. Fear not. Instead, rejoice that such fruitful times are in store for you, for in them you will be weaned from earth and made ready for heaven. You will be delivered from clinging to the present, and made to long for those eternal things, which are so soon to be revealed to you. When you feel that you serve God for nothing at present, you will then rejoice in the infinite reward of the future.

☞ *January 23* ☜

We will remember Your love more than wine
(Song of Solomon 1:4).

Jesus will not let His people forget His love. If all the love they
have enjoyed should be forgotten, He would visit them with
fresh love. "Do you forget my cross?" says He, "I will cause you
to remember it; for at My table I will manifest Myself anew to
you. Do you forget what I did for you in the council-chamber of
eternity? I will remind you of it, for you shall need a counselor,
and shall find Me ready at your call." Mothers do not let their
children forget them. If the boy has gone to Australia, and does
not write home, his mother writes: "Has John forgotten his
mother?" A sweet letter returns to her, which proves that the
gentle reminder was not in vain. So is it with Jesus. He says to us,
"Remember Me," and our response is, "We will remember Your
love." *We will* remember Your love and its matchless history.
It is as ancient as the glory that You had with the Father before
the world was. We remember, O Jesus, Your eternal love when
You became our Surety,[53] and took us as Your betrothed. We
remember the love that suggested the sacrifice of Yourself, the
love that, until the fullness of time, mused over that sacrifice.
We long for the hour when it was written of You in the volume
of the book: "Lo, I come."[54] We remember Your love, O Jesus,
as it was manifest to us in Your holy life from the manger of
Bethlehem to the garden of Gethsemane. We track You from
the cradle to the grave—for every word and deed of Yours was
love—and we rejoice in Your love, which death did not exhaust,
and which shone resplendent in Your resurrection. We remember
that burning fire of love which will never let You hold Your
peace until Your chosen ones are all safely home, until Zion is
glorified, and Jerusalem is settled on her everlasting foundations
of light and love in heaven.

Martha was cumbered about much serving
(Luke 10:40).

Her fault was not that she *served*; the condition of a servant suits every Christian well. "I serve," should be the motto of all the princes of the royal family of heaven. Nor was it her fault that she had "much serving." We cannot do too much. Let us do all that we possibly can; let head and heart and hands be engaged in the Master's service. It was no fault of hers that she was busy preparing a feast for the Master. Happy Martha, to have an opportunity of entertaining so blessed a guest; and happy, too, to have the spirit to throw her whole soul so heartily into the engagement. Her fault was that she grew "cumbered with much serving," so that she forgot *Him*, and remembered only the service. She allowed service to override communion, and so presented one duty stained with the blood of another. We ought to be Martha and Mary in one; we should do much service and have much communion at the same time. We need great grace for this. It is easier to serve than to commune. Joshua never grew weary in fighting with the Amalekites; but Moses, on the top of the mountain in prayer, needed two helpers to sustain his hands.[55] The more spiritual the exercise, the sooner we tire in it. The choicest fruits are the hardest to rear. The most heavenly graces are the most difficult to cultivate. Beloved, while we do not neglect external things, which are good enough in themselves, we ought also to see to it that we enjoy living, personal fellowship with Jesus. See to it that sitting at the Savior's feet is not neglected, even though it is under the false pretext of doing Him service. The first thing for our soul's health, the first thing for His glory, and the first thing for our own usefulness is to keep ourselves in perpetual communion with the Lord Jesus, and to make sure that the vital spirituality of our religion is maintained over and above everything else in the world.

⇢ᴬ *January 25* ℱ

Do we then make void the law through faith? God forbid: yea, we establish the law (Romans 3:31).

When the believer is adopted into the Lord's family, his relationship to old Adam and the law ceases at once;[56] but then he is under a new rule and a new covenant. Believer, you are God's child; it is your first duty to obey your heavenly Father. You have nothing to do with a servile spirit. You are not a slave, but a child,[57] and now, inasmuch as you are a beloved child, you are bound to obey your Father's faintest wish, the least intimation of His will. Does He bid you fulfill a sacred ordinance? You neglect it at your peril, for you will be disobeying your Father. Does He command you to seek the image of Jesus? It is not your joy to do so? Does Jesus tell you, "Be ye perfect, even as your Father which is in heaven is perfect?"[58] Then not because the law commands, but because your Savior commands, you will labor to be perfect in holiness. Does He bid his saints love one another? Do it, not because the law says, "Love your neighbor," but because Jesus says, "If ye love Me, keep My commandments."[59] And this is the commandment that He has given unto you: "… that ye love one another."[60] Are you told to distribute to the poor? Do it, not because charity is a burden that you dare not shirk, but because Jesus teaches, "Give to him that asketh of you."[61] Does the Word say, "Love God with all your heart?" Look at the commandment and reply, "Ah! Commandment, Christ has fulfilled you already—I have no need, therefore, to fulfill you for my salvation,[62] but I rejoice to yield obedience to you because God is my Father now and He has a claim upon me, which I would not dispute." May the Holy Ghost make your heart obedient to the constraining power of Christ's love, that your prayer may be, "Make me to go in the path of Your commandments; for therein do I delight."[63] Grace is the mother and nurse of holiness, and not the apologist of sin.

All they that heard it wondered at those things
(Luke 2:18).

We must not cease to wonder at the great marvels of our God. It would be very difficult to draw a line between holy wonder and *real worship*, for when the soul is overwhelmed with the majesty of God's glory, though it may not express itself in song or even utter its voice with bowed head in humble prayer, yet it silently adores. Our incarnate God is to be worshipped as "the Wonderful." That God considers fallen man, but does not sweep him away with the broom of destruction, and instead undertakes to be man's Redeemer and pay his ransom price, is indeed marvelous! But to each believer, redemption is most marvelous as he views it in relation to himself. It is indeed a miracle of grace that Jesus should forsake the thrones and royalties above to suffer without dignity below *for you*. Let your soul lose itself in wonder, because wonder in this way is a very appropriate emotion. Holy wonder will lead you to *grateful worship* and heartfelt thanksgiving. It will cause within you *godly watchfulness*; you will be afraid to sin against such a love as this. Feeling the presence of the mighty God in the gift of His dear Son, you will take your shoes off, because the place you stand is holy ground.[64] You will be moved at the same time to *glorious hope*. If Jesus has done such marvelous things on your behalf, you will feel that heaven itself is not too great for your expectation. Who can be astonished at anything, when he has once been astonished at the manger and the cross? What is there wonderful left after one has seen the Savior? Dear reader, it may be that from the quietness and solitude of your life, you are scarcely able to imitate the shepherds of Bethlehem, who told what they had seen and heard, but at least you can fill up the circle of the worshippers before the throne by wondering at what God has done.[65]

≈ January 27 ≈

*But Mary kept all these things, and pondered them
in her heart (Luke 2:19)*

There was an exercise on the part of this blessed woman: three powers of her being. First, her memory—she kept all these things. Second, her affections—she kept them in her heart. And third, her intellect—she pondered them. She applied all three powers to the things she had heard: memory, affection, and understanding. Beloved, remember what you have heard of your Lord Jesus, and what He has done for you. Make your heart the golden pot of manna to preserve the memorial of the heavenly bread whereon you have fed in days gone by. Let your memory treasure up everything about Christ, which you have either felt or known or believed, and then let your fond affections hold *Him* fast for evermore. Love the person of your Lord! Bring forth the alabaster box of your heart, even though it is broken, and let all the precious ointment of your affection come streaming on His pierced feet.[66] Let your intellect be exercised concerning the Lord Jesus. Meditate upon what you read. Do not stop at the surface; dive into the depths. Do not be as the swallow that touches the brook with her wing, but be as the fish that penetrates the lowest wave. Abide with your Lord. Do not let him be as a wayfaring man that tarries only for a night. Constrain Him, saying, "Abide with us, for the day is far spent."[67] Hold Him and do not let Him go. The word "ponder" means to weigh. Make ready the balances of judgment. Oh, but where are the scales that can weigh the Lord Christ? "He taketh up the isles as a very little thing"[68]—who shall take *Him* up? "He weigheth the mountains in scales"[69]—in what scales shall we weigh *Him*? If it must be so, if your understanding cannot comprehend, let your affections apprehend; and if your spirit cannot compass the Lord Jesus in the grasp of understanding, let it embrace Him in the arms of affection.

January 28

*And the shepherds returned, glorifying and praising God
for all the things that they had heard and seen, as it was
told unto them (Luke 2:20).*

What was the subject of their praise? They praised God for what
they had heard—for the good tidings of great joy that a Savior
was born unto them. Let us copy them; let us also raise a song
of thanksgiving that we have heard of Jesus and His salvation.
They also *praised God for what they had seen.* There is the
sweetest music—what we have experienced, what we have felt
within, what we have made our own—"the things which we
have made touching the King."[70] It is not enough to *hear* about
Jesus. Mere hearing may tune the harp, but the fingers of living
faith must create the music. If you have seen Jesus with the God-
giving sight of faith, do not allow cobwebs to linger among the
harp-strings, but loud to the praise of sovereign grace, awake
your psaltery and harp. One point for which they praised God
was the agreement between what they had heard and what
they had seen. Observe the last sentence—"As it was told unto
them." Have you not found the gospel to be in yourselves just
what the Bible said it would be? Jesus said He would give you
rest[71]—have you not enjoyed the sweetest peace in Him? He said
you should have joy, and comfort, and life through believing in
Him—have you not received all these? Are not His ways the
ways of pleasantness, and His paths the paths of peace? Surely
you can say with the queen of Sheba, "The half has not been
told me."[72] I have found Christ more sweet than His servants
ever said He was. I looked upon His likeness as they painted it,
but it was a mere daub compared with Himself; for the King in
His beauty outshines all imaginable loveliness. Surely what we
have "seen" keeps pace with, nay, far exceeds, what we have
"heard." Let us, then, glorify and praise God for a Savior so
precious, and so satisfying.

⤞ *January 29* ⤝

The dove came in to him in the evening
(Genesis 8:11).

Blessed be the Lord for another day of mercy, even though I am now weary with its toils. Unto the preserver of men I lift my song of gratitude. The dove found no rest out of the ark, and therefore returned to it; and my soul has learned yet more fully than ever, this day, that there is no satisfaction to be found in earthly things—God alone can give rest to my spirit. As to my business, my possessions, my family, my attainments, these are all well enough in their way, but they cannot fulfill the desires of my immortal nature. "Return unto your rest, O my soul, for the Lord has dealt bountifully with You."[73] It was at the still hour, when the gates of the day were closing, that with weary wing the dove came back to the master. O Lord, enable me this evening thus to return to Jesus. She could not endure to spend a night hovering over the restless waste; I cannot bear to be even for another hour away from Jesus, the rest of my heart, the home of my spirit. She did not merely alight upon the roof of the ark, she "came in to him."[74] Even so would my longing spirit look into the secret of the Lord, pierce to the interior of truth, enter into that which is within the veil, and reach to my Beloved in very deed. To Jesus must I come; my panting spirit cannot stay short of the nearest and dearest relationship with Him. Blessed Lord Jesus, be with me, reveal Yourself, and abide with me all night, so that when I awake I may be still with You. I note that the dove brought in her mouth an olive branch, at memorial of the day before and a prophecy of the future. Have I no pleasing record to bring home? No pledge and earnest of loving-kindness yet to come? Yes, my Lord, I present You my grateful acknowledgments for tender mercies, which have been new every morning[75] and fresh every evening; and now, I pray You, put forth Your hand and take Your dove into Your bosom.

*In whom also we have obtained an inheritance
(Ephesians 1:11).*

When Jesus gave Himself for us, He gave us all the rights and privileges that went with Himself;[76] so that now, although as eternal God, He has essential rights to which no creature may venture to pretend, yet as Jesus, the Mediator, the federal Head of the covenant of grace, He has no heritage apart from us.[77] All the glorious consequences of His obedience unto death are the joint riches of all who are in Him, and on whose behalf He accomplished the divine will. See, He enters into glory, but not for Himself alone. It is written, "Whither the Forerunner is *for us* entered" Hebrews 6:20. Does He stand in the presence of God? "He appears in the presence of God for us" Hebrews 9:24. Consider this, believer. You have no right to heaven in yourself. Your right lies in Christ. If you are pardoned, it is through *His* blood. If you are justified, it is through *His* righteousness. If you are sanctified, it is because *He* is made of God unto you sanctification.[78] If you shall be kept from falling, it will be because you are preserved in Christ Jesus. And if you are perfected at the last, it will be because you are complete in *Him*.[79] Thus Jesus is magnified—for all is in Him and by Him. Thus the inheritance is made certain to us—for it is obtained in Him. Thus each blessing is the sweeter, and even heaven itself the brighter, because it is Jesus, our Beloved "in whom" we have obtained all. Where is the man who shall estimate our divine portion? Weigh the riches of Christ in scales and His treasure in balances, and then think to count the treasures that belong to the saints. Reach the bottom of Christ's sea of joy, and then hope to understand the bliss that God has prepared for those who love Him. Overleap the boundaries of Christ's possessions, and then dream of a limit to the fair inheritance of the elect. "All things are yours, for ye are Christ's and Christ is God's."[80]

☙ *January 31* ☙

Then Ahimaaz ran by the way of the plain, and overran Cushi (2 Samuel 18:23).

Running is not everything. There is much in the path we select: a swift foot over hill and down dale will not keep pace with a slower traveler upon level ground. How is it with my spiritual journey, am I laboring up the hill of my own works and down into the ravines of my own humiliations and resolutions, or do I run by the plain way of "Believe and live?"[81] How blessed is it to wait upon the Lord by faith! The soul runs without weariness and walks without fainting in the way of believing.[82] Christ Jesus is the way of life, and He is a plain way, a pleasant way, a way suitable for the tottering feet and feeble knees of trembling sinners. Am I found in this way or am I hunting after another track such as priesthood or metaphysics may promise me? I read of the way of holiness, that the wayfaring man, although a fool, shall not err therein. Have I been delivered from proud reason and been brought as a little child to rest in Jesus' love and blood? If so, by God's grace I shall outrun the strongest runner who chooses any other path. This truth I may remember to my profit in my daily cares and needs. It will be my wisest course to go at once to my God, and not to wander in a roundabout manner to this friend and that. He knows my wants and can relieve them. To whom should I repair but to Himself by the direct appeal of prayer and the plain argument of the promise? "Straightforward makes the best runner." I will not parlay with the servants, but hasten to their master. In reading this passage, it strikes me that if men vie with each other in common matters, and one outruns the other, I ought to be in solemn earnestness so to run that I may obtain. Lord, help me to gird up the loins of my mind, and may I press forward toward the mark for the prize of my high calling of God in Christ Jesus.[83]

February

ᗱ *February 1* ᗧ

Your love to me was wonderful (2 Samuel 1:26).

Come, dear readers, let each one of us speak for himself of the wonderful love, not of Jonathan, but of Jesus. We will not relate what we have been told, but the things that we have tasted and handled—of the love of Christ. Your love to me, O Jesus, was wonderful when I was a stranger wandering far from You, fulfilling the desires of the flesh and of the mind. Your love restrained me from committing the sin that is unto death, and withheld me from self-destruction. Your love held back the axe when Justice said, "Cut it down! Why burden the ground with it?"[84] Your love drew me into the wilderness, stripped me there, and made me feel the guilt of my sin and the burden of my iniquity. Your love spoke thus comfortably to me when I was sorely dismayed—"Come unto Me, and I will give you rest."[85] Oh, how matchless Your love when, in a moment, You wash my sins away and make my polluted soul, crimson with the blood of my nativity and black with the grime of my transgressions, to be white as the driven snow and pure as the finest wool.[86] How You commended Your love when You whispered in my ear, "I am yours and you are Mine."[87] Kind were those accents when You said, "The Father Himself loveth you."[88] And sweet the moments, passing sweet, when You declared to me "the love of the Spirit." Never shall my soul forget those chambers of fellowship where You have unveiled Yourself to me. Had Moses his cleft in the rock where he saw the train, the back parts of his God?[89] We, too, have had our clefts in the rock, where we have seen the full splendors of the Godhead in the person of Christ. Did David remember the tracks of the wild goat, the land of Jordan and the Hermonites? We, too, can remember spots to memory dear, equal to these in blessedness. Precious Lord Jesus, give us a fresh draught of Your wondrous love to begin the month with. Amen.

February 2

And these are ancient things (1 Chronicles 4:22).

Yet not so ancient as those precious things, which are the delights of our souls. Let us for a moment recount them, telling them over as misers count their gold. *The sovereign choice* of the Father, by which He elected us unto eternal life, or ever the earth was, is a matter of vast antiquity, since no date can be conceived for it by the mind of man. We were chosen from before the foundations of the world.[90] *Everlasting love* went with the choice, for it was not a bare act of divine will by which we were set apart, but the divine affections were concerned. The Father loved us in and from the beginning. Here is a theme for daily contemplation. *The eternal purpose* to redeem us from our foreseen ruin, to cleanse and sanctify us, and at last to glorify us, was of infinite antiquity, and runs side by side with immutable love and absolute sovereignty. The covenant is always described as being everlasting, and Jesus, the second party in it, had His goings forth of old; He struck hands in sacred suretyship long before the first of the stars began to shine, and it was in Him that the elect were ordained unto eternal life. Thus in the divine purpose a most blessed covenant union was established between the Son of God and His elect people, which will remain as the foundation of their safety when time shall be no more.[91] Is it not well to be conversant with these ancient things? Is it not shameful that they should be so much neglected and even rejected by the bulk of professors? If they knew more of their own sin, would they not be more ready to adore distinguishing grace? Let us both admire and adore tonight, as we sing—

"A monument of grace, A sinner saved by blood;
The streams of love I trace, Up to the Fountain, God;
And in His sacred bosom see, Eternal thoughts of Love
to me."

☞ February 3 ☞

Tell me ... where Thou feedest, where Thou makest
Your flock to rest at noon (Song of Solomon 1:7).

These words express the desire of the believer after Christ, and his longing for present communion with Him. Where do You feed Your flock? In *Your house*? I will go, if I may find You there. In private *prayer*? Then I will pray without ceasing. In the *Word*? Then I will read it diligently. In Your *ordinances*? Then I will walk in them with all my heart. Tell me where You feed, for wherever You stand as the Shepherd, there will I lie down as a sheep; for none but You can supply my need. I cannot be satisfied to be apart from You. My soul hungers and thirsts for the refreshment of Your presence.[92] "Where do You make Your flock to rest at noon?" for whether at dawn or at noon, my only rest must be where You and Your beloved flock are. My soul's rest must be a grace-given rest, and can only be found in You. Where is the shadow of that rock? Why should I not repose beneath it? "Why should I be as one who turns aside by the flocks of your companions?" You have companions—why should I not be one? Satan tells me I am unworthy; but I always was unworthy, and yet You have long loved me; and therefore my unworthiness cannot be a barrier to my having fellowship with You now. It is true I am weak in faith, and prone to fall, but my very feebleness is the reason why I should always be where You feed Your flock, so that I may be strengthened and preserved in safety beside the still waters. Why should I turn aside? There is no reason why I should, but there are a thousand reasons why I should not, for Jesus beckons me to come. If He withdrew Himself a little, it is but to make me prize His presence more. Now that I am grieved and distressed at being away from Him, He will lead me yet again to that sheltered nook where the lambs of His fold are sheltered from the burning sun.

☙ February 4 ☞

Your refuge from the avenger of blood
(Joshua 20:3).

It is said that in the land of Canaan, cities of refuge were arranged so that any man might reach one of them within half a day at the most.[93] In like manner, the word of our salvation is near to us. Jesus is a present Savior, and the way to Him is short. It is only a simple renunciation of our own merit and a laying hold of Jesus to be our all in all. We are told that the roads to the city of refuge were strictly preserved. Every river was bridged and every obstruction removed, so that the man who fled might find an easy passage to the city. Once a year the elders went along the roads and saw to their order, so that nothing might impede the flight of anyone and cause him, through delay, to be overtaken and slain. How graciously do the promises of the gospel remove stumbling blocks from the way! Wherever there were side roads and turns, there were fixed up hand-posts with the inscription upon them—"To the city of refuge!" This is a picture of the road to Christ Jesus. It is no roundabout road of the law. It is no obeying this, that, and the other. It is a straight road: "Believe, and live." It is a road so hard that no self-righteous man can ever tread it, but so easy that every sinner, who knows himself to be a sinner, may by it finds his way to heaven. No sooner did the man-slayer reach the outskirts of the city than he was safe; it was not necessary for him to pass far within the walls, but the suburbs themselves were sufficient protection. Learn hence: If you only touch the hem of Christ's garment,[94] you shall be made whole; if you only lay hold upon Him with "faith as a grain of mustard seed," you are safe. "A little genuine grace ensures, The death of all our sins." Only waste no time, do not loiter by the way, for the avenger of blood is swift of foot; and it may be he is at your heels at this still hour of eventide.

74

❧ *February 5* ❧

At that time Jesus answered (Matthew 11:25).

This is a singular way in which to commence a verse—"At that time Jesus answered." If you will look at the context, you will not perceive that any person had asked Him a question or that He was in conversation with any human being. Yet it is written, "Jesus answered and said, I thank You, O Father."[95] When a man answers, he answers a person who has been speaking to him. Who, then, had spoken to Christ? His Father. Yet there is no record of it; and this should teach us that Jesus had constant fellowship with His Father, and that God spoke into His heart so often, so continually that it was not a circumstance singular enough to be recorded. It was the habit and life of Jesus to talk with God. Even as Jesus was, so are we in this world.[96] Let us therefore learn the lesson that this simple statement concerning Him teaches us. May we likewise have silent fellowship with the Father, so that often we may answer Him? Although the world does not know to whom we speak, may we respond to that secret voice unheard of any other ear, but our own, opened by the Spirit of God, recognizes with joy. God has spoken to us. Let us speak to God to set our seal that God is true and faithful to His promise, or to confess the sin of which the Spirit of God has convinced us, or to acknowledge the mercy which God's providence has given, or to express assent to the great truths which God the Holy Ghost has opened to our understanding. What a privilege is intimate communion of our spirits with the Father! It is a secret hidden from the world,[97] a joy with which even the nearest friend cannot interfere. If we would hear the whispers of God's love, our ear must be purged and fitted to listen to His voice. This very evening may our hearts be in such a state, that when God speaks to us, we, like Jesus, may be prepared at once to answer Him.

Pray one for another (James 5:16).

As an encouragement cheerfully to offer intercessory prayer, remember that *such prayer is the sweetest God ever hears,* for the prayer of Christ is of this character. In all the incense, which our Great High Priest now puts into the golden container, there is not a single grain for Himself. His intercession must be the most acceptable of all supplications—and the more our prayer is as Christ's, the sweeter it will be. Thus while petitions for ourselves will be accepted, our pleadings for others, having in them more of the fruits of the Spirit,[98] more love, more faith, more brotherly kindness will be the sweetest oblation that we can offer to God, the very fat of our sacrifice through the precious merits of Jesus. Remember, again, that *intercessory prayer is exceedingly prevalent.*[99] What wonders it has wrought! The Word of God teems with its marvelous deeds. Believer, you have a mighty engine in your hand. Use it well. Use it constantly. Use it with faith, and you will surely be a benefactor to your brethren. When you have the King's ear, speak to Him for the suffering members of His body. When you are favored to draw very near to His throne, and the King says to you, "Ask, and I will give you what thou wilt," let your petitions be not for yourself alone, but for the many who need His aid. If you have grace at all, and are not an intercessor, that grace must be small as a grain of mustard seed. You have just enough grace to float your soul clear from the quicksand, but you have no deep floods of grace, or else you would carry in your joyous bark a weighty cargo of the wants of others, and you would bring back from your Lord rich blessings for them, which, they might not have obtained had it not been for you.

> "Oh, let my hands forget their skill,
> My tongue be silent, cold, and still,
> This bounding heart forget to beat,
> If I forget the mercy-seat!"

ᛞ *February 7* ᛦ

And they heard a great voice from heaven saying unto them, Come up hither (Revelation 11:12).

Without considering these words in their prophetical connection, let us regard them as the invitation of our great Forerunner to His sanctified people. In due time there shall be heard "a great voice from heaven"[100] to every believer, saying, "Come up hither." This should be to the saints the subject of joyful anticipation. Instead of dreading the time when we shall leave this world to go unto the Father, we should be panting for the hour of our emancipation. Our song should be: "My heart is with Him on His throne, And ill can brook delay; Each moment listening for the voice, 'Rise up and come away.'" We are not called down to the grave, but up to the skies. Our heaven-born spirits should long for their native air. Yet should the celestial summons be the object of patient waiting. Our God knows best when to bid us, "Come up thither." We must not wish to anticipate the period of our departure early. I know that strong love will make us cry, "O Lord of Hosts, the waves divide, And land us all in heaven;" but patience must have her perfect work.[101] God ordains with accurate wisdom the most fitting time for the redeemed to abide below. Surely, if there could be regrets in heaven, the saints might mourn that they did not live longer here to do more good. Oh, for more sheaves for my Lord's granary! More jewels for His crown! But how, unless there be more work? True, there is the other side of it: that, living so briefly, our sins are the fewer. But oh! when we are fully serving God, and He is giving us to scatter precious seed and reap a hundredfold, we would even say it is well for us to abide where we are. Whether our Master shall say "go," or "stay," let us be equally well pleased so long as He indulges us with His presence.

☞ February 8 ☜

He shall save His people from their sins
(Matthew 1:21).

If asked what they consider salvation to be, many people will reply, "Being saved from hell and taken to heaven." This is one result of salvation, but it is not one tithe of what is contained in that boon. It is true our Lord Jesus Christ does redeem all His people from the wrath to come; He saves them from the fearful condemnation that their sins had brought upon them,[102] but His triumph is far more complete than this. He saves His people "from their sins."[103] Oh! sweet deliverance from our worst foes. Where Christ works a saving work,[104] He casts Satan from his throne, and will not let him be master any longer. No man is a true Christian if sin reigns in his mortal body. Sin will be in us—it will never be utterly expelled till the spirit enters glory, but it will never have *dominion*. There will be a striving for dominion—a lusting against the new law and the new spirit which God has implanted—but sin will never get the upper hand so as to be absolute monarch of our nature.[105] Christ will be Master of the heart and sin must be mortified.[106] The Lion of the tribe of Judah shall prevail, and the dragon shall be cast out. Professor! Is sin subdued in you? If your *life* is unholy, your *heart* is unchanged. If your heart is unchanged, you are an unsaved person. If the Savior has not sanctified you, renewed you, given you a hatred of sin and a love of holiness, He has done nothing in you of a saving character. Grace that does not make a man better than others is a worthless counterfeit. Christ saves His people not *in* their sins, but *from* them. "Without holiness no man shall see the Lord."[107] "Let every one that nameth the name of Christ depart from iniquity."[108] If not saved from sin, how shall we hope to be counted among His people? Lord, save me now from all evil, and enable me to honor my Savior.

Lead us not into temptation; but deliver us from evil [or, the evil one] (Luke 11:4).

What we are taught to seek or shun in prayer, we should equally pursue or avoid in action. Very earnestly, therefore, should we avoid temptation, seeking to walk so guardedly in the path of obedience that we may never tempt the devil to tempt us.[109] We are not to enter the thicket in search of the lion. We might pay dearly for such presumption. This lion may cross our path or leap upon us from the thicket, but we have nothing to do with hunting him. He, who meets with him, even though he wins the day, will find it a stern struggle. Let the Christian pray that he may be spared the encounter. Our Savior, who had experience of what temptation meant, thus earnestly admonished His disciples, "Pray that ye enter not into temptation."[110] But let us do as we will, we shall be tempted; hence the prayer: "deliver us from evil."[111] God had one Son without sin; but He has no son without temptation. The natural man is born to trouble as the sparks fly upward, and the Christian man is born to temptation just as certainly. We must be always on our watch against Satan, because, like a thief, he gives no intimation of his approach.[112] Believers who have experienced the ways of Satan know that there are certain seasons when he will most probably make an attack, just as at certain seasons bleak winds may be expected. Thus the Christian is put on a double guard by fear of danger, and the danger is averted by preparing to meet it. Prevention is better than cure. It is better to be so well armed that the devil will not attack you than to endure the perils of the fight, even though you come off a conqueror.[113] Pray this evening first that you may not be tempted, and next that if temptation is permitted, you may be delivered from the evil one.[114]

⇜ *February 10* ⇝

I have blotted out, as a thick cloud, your transgressions, and, as a cloud, your sins: return unto Me; for I have redeemed you (Isaiah 44:22).

Attentively observe THE INSTRUCTIVE SIMILITUDE: Our sins are like a *cloud*. As clouds are of many shapes and shades, so are our transgressions. As clouds obscure the light of the sun and darken the landscape beneath, so do our sins hide from us the light of Jehovah's face and cause us to sit in the shadow of death. They are earth-born things, and rise from the miry places of our nature; and when so collected that their measure is full, they threaten us with storm and tempest. Alas! that, unlike clouds, our sins yield us no genial showers, but rather threaten to deluge us with a fiery flood of destruction. O black clouds of sin, how can it be fair weather with our souls while ye remain? Let our joyful eye dwell upon THE NOTABLE ACT of divine mercy: "blotting out." God Himself appears upon the scene, and instead of manifesting His anger, reveals His grace in divine benignity. He at once and forever effectually removes the mischief, not by blowing away the cloud, but by blotting it out from existence once and for all. Against the justified man no sin remains. The great transaction of the cross has eternally removed His transgressions from him. On Calvary's summit the great deed, by which the sin of all the chosen was forever put away, was completely and effectually performed. Practically let us obey THE GRACIOUS COMMAND: "... return unto Me." Why should pardoned sinners live at a distance from their God? If we have been forgiven all our sins, let no legal fear withhold us from the boldest access to our Lord. Let backslidings be bemoaned, but let us not persevere in them. To the greatest possible nearness of communion with the Lord, let us, in the power of the Holy Spirit, strive mightily to return.[115] O Lord, this night restore us!

⊰ *February 11* ⊱

Thou hast left your first love (Revelation 2:4).

Ever to be remembered is that best and brightest of hours, when first we saw the Lord, lost our burden, received the roll of promise, rejoiced in full salvation, and went on our way in peace. It was springtime in the soul; the winter was past; the mutterings of Sinai's thunders were hushed; the flashings of its lightning were no more perceived; God was beheld as reconciled; the law threatened no vengeance; justice demanded no punishment. Then the flowers appeared in our heart. Hope, love, peace, and patience sprung from the sod. The hyacinth of repentance, the snowdrop of pure holiness, the crocus of golden faith, and the daffodil of early love all decked the garden of the soul. The time of the singing of birds had come, and we rejoiced with thanksgiving. We magnified the holy name of our forgiving God, and our resolve was, "Lord, I am Yours, wholly Yours. All I am and all I have, I devote to You. You have bought me with Your blood[116]—let me spend myself and be spent in Your service. In life and in death let me be consecrated to You." How have we kept this resolve? Our espousal love burned with a holy flame of devotion to Jesus—is it the same *now*? Might not Jesus well say to us, "I am somewhat against you, because you have left thy first love"?[117] Alas! it is but little we have done for our Master's glory. Our winter has lasted all too long. We are as cold as ice when we should feel a summer's glow and bloom with sacred flowers. We give to God pence when He deserves pounds, nay, deserves our heart's blood to be coined in the service of His church and of His truth. But shall we continue thus? O Lord, after you have so richly blessed us, shall we be ungrateful and become indifferent to Your good cause and work? O quicken us that we may return to our first love, and do our first works! Send us a genial spring, O Sun of Righteousness.

He shall give you another Comforter, that He may abide with you for ever (John 14:16).

Great Father revealed Himself to believers of old before the coming of His Son, and was known to Abraham, Isaac, and Jacob as the God Almighty. Then Jesus came, and the ever-blessed Son was the delight of His people's eyes in His own proper person. At the time of the Redeemer's ascension, the Holy Spirit became the head of the present dispensation, and His power was gloriously manifested in and after Pentecost.[118] He remains at this hour the present Immanuel—God with us, dwelling in and with His people, quickening, guiding, and ruling in their midst. Is His presence recognized, as it ought to be? We cannot control His working; He is most sovereign in all His operations, but are we sufficiently anxious to obtain His help, or sufficiently watchful lest we provoke Him to withdraw His aid? Without Him we can do nothing, but by His almighty energy the most extraordinary results can be produced. Everything depends upon his manifesting or concealing His power. Do we always look up to Him both for our inner life and our outward service with the respectful dependence, which is fitting? Do we not too often run before His call and act independently of His aid? Let us humble ourselves this evening for past neglects, and now entreat the heavenly dew to rest upon us, the sacred oil to anoint us, the celestial flame to burn within us. The Holy Ghost is no temporary gift. He abides with the saints. All we have to do is seek Him properly and well, and we will find Him. He is jealous, but He is compassionate; if He leaves in anger, He returns in mercy. Condescending and tender, He does not weary of us, but awaits to be gracious still.

> "Sin has been hammering my heart,
> Unto a hardness, void of love,
> Let supplying grace to cross his art,
> Drop from above."

There is therefore now no condemnation (Romans 8:1).

Come, my soul, think of this. Believing in Jesus, you are actually and effectually cleared from guilt; thou are led out of your prison. You are no more in shackles as a bond-slave; you are delivered *now* from the bondage of the law; you are freed from sin, and canst walk at large as a freeman, your Savior's blood has procured your full discharge.[119] You have a right now to approach your Father's throne. No flames of vengeance are there to scare you now, no fiery sword; justice cannot strike down the innocent. Your disabilities are taken away: you were once unable to see your Father's face; you can see it now. You could not speak with Him: but now you have access with boldness.[120] Once there was a fear of hell upon you; but you have no fear of it now, for how can there be punishment for the guiltless? He who believes is not condemned, and cannot be punished.[121] And more than all, the privileges you might have enjoyed, if you had never sinned, are yours now that you are justified. All of the blessing that you would have had if you had kept the law, and more, are yours, because Christ has kept it for you. All the love and the acceptance that perfect obedience could have obtained of God belong to you, because Christ was perfectly obedient on your behalf, and has imputed all His merits to your account, so that you might be exceeding rich through Him, who for your sake became exceeding poor.[122] Oh! how great the debt of love and gratitude you owe to your Savior!

"A debtor to mercy alone, Of covenant mercy I sing;
Nor fear with Your righteousness on,
My person and offerings to bring
The terrors of law and of God,
With me can have nothing to do;
My Savior's obedience and blood
Hide all my transgressions from view."

✎ *February 14* ✐

She was healed immediately (Luke 8:47).

One of the most touching and teaching of the Savior's miracles is before us tonight. The woman was very ignorant. She imagined that virtue came out of Christ by a law of necessity, without His knowledge or direct will. Moreover, she was a stranger to the generosity of Jesus' character, or she would not have gone behind to steal the cure that He was so ready to bestow. Misery should always place itself right in the face of mercy. Had she known the love of Jesus' heart, she would have said, "I have but to put myself where He can see me—His omniscience will teach Him my case, and His love at once will work my cure." We admire her faith, but we marvel at her ignorance. After she had obtained the cure, she rejoiced with trembling: glad was she that the divine virtue had wrought a marvel in her, but she feared Christ might retract the blessing and put a negative upon the grant of His grace. Little did she comprehend the fullness of His love! We have not so clear a view of Him as we could wish. We know not the heights and depths of His love, but we know of a surety that He is too good to withdraw from a trembling soul the gift that it has been able to obtain. But here is the marvel of it: little was her knowledge, but her faith, because it was real faith, saved her and saved her at once. There was no tedious delay—faith's miracle was instantaneous. If we have faith as a grain of mustard seed, salvation is our present and eternal possession. If in the list of the Lord's children we are written as the feeblest of the family, yet, being heirs through faith, no power, human or devilish, can eject us from salvation. If we dare not lean our heads upon His bosom with John, yet if we can venture in the press behind Him and touch the hem of His garment, we are made whole. Courage, timid one! Your faith has saved you; go in peace. "Being justified by faith, we *have* peace with God."[123]

⊰ *February 15* ⊱

Whereby they have made you glad (Psalm 45:8).

And who are thus privileged to make the Savior glad? His church—His people. But is it possible? He makes *us* glad, but how can *we make Him glad*? By our love. Ah! we think it so cold, so faint; and so, indeed, we must sorrowfully confess it to be, but it is very sweet to Christ. Hear His own eulogy of that love in the golden Canticle: "How fair is your love, my sister, my spouse! How much better is your love than wine!"[124] See, loving heart, how He delights in you. When you lean your head on His bosom, you not only receive, but you give Him joy. When you gaze with love upon His all-glorious face, you not only obtain comfort, but impart delight. Our *praise*, too, gives Him joy—not the song of the lips alone, but the melody of the heart's deep gratitude. Our *gifts*, too, are very pleasant to Him; He loves to see us lay our time, our talents, and our substance upon the altar, not for the value of what we give, but for the sake of the motive from which the gift springs. To Him the lowly offerings of His saints are more acceptable than the thousands of gold and silver. *Holiness* is like frankincense and myrrh to Him. Forgive your enemy, and you make Christ glad. Distribute your substance to the poor, and He rejoices. Be the means of saving souls, and you give Him to see of the travail of His soul. Proclaim His gospel, and you are a sweet savor unto Him. Go among the ignorant and lift up the cross, and you have given Him honor. It is in your power even now to break the alabaster box, and pour the precious oil of joy upon His head, as did the woman of old, whose memorial is to this day set forth wherever the gospel is preached.[125] Will you be backward then? Will you not perfume your beloved Lord with the myrrh and aloes and cassis of your heart's praise? Yes, ye ivory palaces, ye shall hear the songs of the saints!

85

Your good Spirit (Nehemiah 9:20).

Common, too common is the sin of forgetting the Holy Spirit. This is folly and ingratitude. He deserves well at our hands, for He is good, supremely good. As God, He is *good essentially*. He shares in the threefold ascription of Holy, holy, holy, which ascends to the Triune Jehovah. He is unmixed purity and truth and grace. He is *good benevolently*, tenderly bearing with our waywardness, striving with our rebellious wills, quickening us from our death in sin, and then training us for the skies as a loving nurse fosters her child. How generous, forgiving, and tender is this patient Spirit of God. He is *good operatively*. All His works are good in the most eminent degree: He suggests good thoughts, prompts good actions, reveals good truths, applies good promises, assists in good attainments, and leads to good results. There is no spiritual good in all the world of which He is not the author and sustainer, and heaven itself will owe the perfect character of its redeemed inhabitants to His work. He is *good officially*. Whether as Comforter, Instructor, Guide, Sanctifier, Quickener, or Intercessor, He fulfils His office well, and each work is fraught with the highest good to the church of God.[126] They who yield to His influences become good. They who obey His impulses do good. They who live under His power receive good. Let us then act toward so good a person according to the dictates of gratitude. Let us revere His person, and adore Him as God over all, blessed forever. Let us own His power, and our need of Him by waiting upon Him in all our holy enterprises. Let us hourly seek His aid, and never grieve Him. And let us speak to His praise whenever occasion occurs. The church will never prosper until it believes in the Holy Ghost more reverently. He is so good and kind, that it is sad indeed that He should be grieved by slights and negligence.

⇥ *February 17* ⇤

Whereas the Lord was there (Ezekiel 35:10).

Edom's princes saw the whole country left desolate and counted upon its easy conquest, but there was one great difficulty in their way—quite unknown to them—"The Lord was there." In His presence lay the special security of the chosen land. Whatever may be the machinations and devices of the enemies of God's people, there is still the same effectual barrier to thwart their plans. The saints are God's heritage, and He is in the midst of them and will protect His own. What comfort this assurance yields us in our troubles and spiritual conflicts! We are constantly opposed, and yet perpetually preserved! How often Satan shoots his arrows against our *faith*, but our faith defies the power of hell's fiery darts. They are not only turned aside, but they are quenched upon its shield, for "the Lord is there."[127] *Our good works* are the subjects of Satan's attacks. Never has a saint had a virtue or a grace which was not the target for hellish bullets: whether it was hope bright and sparkling, or love warm and fervent, or patience all-enduring, or zeal flaming like coals of fire, the old enemy of everything that is good has tried to destroy it. The only reason that anything virtuous or lovely survives in us is this: "The Lord is there." If the Lord is with us through life, we need not fear for our dying confidence; for *when we come to die*, we shall find that "the Lord is *there*." Where the billows are most tempestuous and the water is most chilled, we shall feel the bottom and know that it is good. Our feet shall stand upon the Rock of Ages when time is passing away. Beloved, from the first of a Christian's life to the last, the only reason that he does not perish is that "the Lord is there." When the God of everlasting love shall change and leave His elect to perish, then may the Church of God be destroyed, but not till then, because it is written, JEHOVAH SHAMMAH. "The Lord is there."

ᗏ *February 18* ᗒ

Father, I have sinned (Luke 15:18).

It is quite certain that those whom Christ has washed in His precious blood need not make a confession of sin, as culprits or criminals before God the Judge, for Christ has forever taken away all their sins in a legal sense, so that they no longer stand where they can be condemned. Instead, they are once and for all accepted in the Beloved, but having become children and offending as children, ought they not every day to go before their heavenly Father and confess their sin, and acknowledge their iniquity in that character?[128] Nature teaches that it is the duty of erring children to make a confession to their earthly father. The grace of God in the heart teaches us that we, as Christians, owe the same duty to our heavenly Father. We daily offend, and ought not to rest without daily pardon. For, supposing that my trespasses against my Father are not at once taken to Him to be washed away by the cleansing power of the Lord Jesus. What will be the consequence? If I have not sought forgiveness and been washed from these offences against my Father, I shall feel at a distance from Him. I shall doubt His love to me. I shall tremble at Him. I shall be afraid to pray to Him. I shall grow like the prodigal, who, although still a child, was far off from his father.[129] But if, with a child's sorrow at offending so gracious and loving a Parent, I go to Him and tell Him all, and rest not till I realize that I am forgiven, then I shall feel a holy love for my Father, and shall go through my Christian career, not only as saved, but enjoying present peace in God through Jesus Christ, my Lord. There is a wide distinction between confessing sin *as a culprit*, and confessing sin *as a child*. The Father's bosom is the place for penitent confessions. We have been cleansed once and for all, but our feet still need to be washed from the defilement of our daily walk as children of God.

February 19

He first findeth his own brother Simon (John 1:41).

This case is an excellent pattern of all cases where spiritual life is vigorous. As soon as a man has found Christ, he begins to find others. I will not believe that you have tasted of the honey of the gospel if thou can eat it all yourself. True grace puts an end to all spiritual monopoly. Andrew *first* found his own brother Simon, and then others. Relationship has a very strong demand upon our first individual efforts. Andrew, you did well to begin with Simon. I doubt whether there are not some Christians giving away tracts at other people's houses who would do well to give away a tract at their own—whether there are not some engaged in works of usefulness abroad who are neglecting their special sphere of usefulness at home. You may or you may not be called to evangelize the people in any particular locality, but certainly you are called to see after your own servants, your own kinsfolk and acquaintance. Let your religion begin at home. Many tradesmen export their best commodities—the Christian should not. He should have all his conversation everywhere of the best savor, but let him be careful to put forth the sweetest fruit of spiritual life and testimony in his own family. When Andrew went to find his brother, he little imagined how eminent Simon would become. *Simon Peter was worth ten Andrews* so far as we can gather from sacred history, and yet Andrew was instrumental in bringing him to Jesus. You may be very deficient in talent yourself, and yet you may be the means of drawing to Christ one who shall become eminent in grace and service. Ah! dear friend, you little know the possibilities in you. You may but speak a word to a child, and in that child there may be slumbering a noble heart, which shall stir the Christian church in years to come. Andrew has only two talents, but he finds Peter. Go thou and do likewise.

Then was Jesus led up of the Spirit into the wilderness to be tempted of the devil (Matthew 4:1).

A Holy character does not avert temptation—Jesus was tempted. When Satan tempts us, his sparks fall upon tinder, but in Christ's case, it was like striking sparks on water, and yet the enemy continued his evil work. Now, if the devil goes on striking when there is no result, how much more will he do it when he knows what inflammable stuff our hearts are made of. Though you become greatly sanctified by the Holy Ghost, expect that the great dog of hell will bark at you still. In the haunts of men we expect to be tempted, but even seclusion will not guard us from the same trial. Jesus Christ was led away from human society into the wilderness, and was tempted by the devil. Solitude has its charms and its benefits, and may be useful in checking the lust of the eye and the pride of life,[130] but the devil will follow us into the loveliest retreats. Do not suppose that it is only the worldly-minded who have dreadful thoughts and blasphemous temptations, for even spiritually minded persons endure the same; and in the holiest position, we may suffer the darkest temptation. The utmost consecration of spirit will not insure you against satanic temptation. Christ was consecrated through and through. It was His meat and drink to do the will of Him who sent Him;[131] and yet He was tempted![132] Your hearts may glow with a seraphic flame of love to Jesus, and yet the devil will try to bring you down to Laodicean lukewarmness. If you will tell me when God permits a Christian to lay aside his armor, I will tell you when Satan has left off temptation. Like the old knights in wartime, we must sleep with helmet and breastplate buckled on, for the arch-deceiver will seize our first unguarded hour to make us his prey. The Lord keep us watchful in all seasons, and give us a final escape from the jaw of the lion and the paw of the bear.

February 21

Understandest thou what thou readest? (Acts 8:30)

We would be better teachers and less liable to be carried about by every wind of doctrine, if we sought to have a more intelligent understanding of the Word of God. Because the Holy Ghost, the Author of the Scriptures, is the only One who can enlighten us rightly to understand them, we should constantly ask His teaching and guidance into all truth. When the prophet Daniel had to interpret Nebuchadnezzar's dream, what did he do?[133] He set himself to earnest prayer that God would open up the vision. The apostle John, in his vision at Patmos, saw a book sealed with seven seals that none was found worthy to open or even so much as to look upon.[134] The Lion of the tribe of Judah, who had prevailed to open it, later opened the book but it is written first—"I wept much." The tears of John, his liquid prayers, were, so far as he was concerned, the sacred keys by which the folded book was opened. Therefore, if, for your own and others' profiting, you desire to be "filled with the knowledge of God's will in all wisdom and spiritual understanding,"[135] remember that prayer is your best means of study. Like Daniel, you shall understand the dream and the interpretation thereof when you have sought unto God. And like John, you shall see the seven seals of precious truth unloosed after you have wept much. Stones are not broken except by an earnest use of the hammer; and the stonebreaker must go down on his knees. Use the hammer of diligence, and let the knee of prayer be exercised, and there is not a stony doctrine in revelation, which is useful for you to understand, that will not fly into shivers under the exercise of prayer and faith. You may force your way through anything with the leverage of prayer. Thoughts and reasoning are like the steel wedges that give a hold upon truth; but prayer is the lever, which forces open the iron chest of sacred mystery, that we may get the treasure hidden within.

❧ *February 22* ❧

The Lord is slow to anger, and great in power
(Nahum 1:3).

Jehovah "is slow to anger." When mercy comes into the world she drives winged horses; the axles of her chariot-wheels are red hot with speed. But when wrath goes forth, it toils on with tardy footsteps, for God takes no pleasure in the sinner's death. God's rod of mercy is ever in His hands outstretched; His sword of justice is in its scabbard, held down by that pierced hand of love that bled for the sins of men. "The Lord is slow to anger," because He is GREAT IN POWER. He is truly great in power who has power over himself. When God's power restrains Him, then it is power indeed; the power that binds omnipotence is omnipotence surpassed. A man who has a strong mind can bear to be insulted long, and only resents the wrong when a sense of right demands his action. The weak mind is irritated at a little. The strong mind bears it like a rock that does not move, even though a thousand waves break upon it and cast their pitiful malice in spray upon its summit. God marks His enemies, and yet does not stir Himself. He holds in His anger. If He were less divine than He is, He would long before this have sent forth the whole of His thunder, and emptied the magazines of heaven. He would long before this have blasted the earth with the wondrous fires of its lower regions, and man would have been utterly destroyed; but the greatness of His power brings us mercy.[136] Dear reader, what is your state this evening? Can you by humble faith look to Jesus and say, "My substitute, Thou art my rock, my trust?" Then, beloved, be not afraid of God's power, for by faith you have fled to Christ for refuge.[137] The power of God need no more terrify you than the shield and sword of the warrior need terrify those whom he loves. Rather rejoice that He who is "great in power" is your Father and Friend.

February 23

""Take up the cross, and follow Me"
(Mark 10:21).

You have not the making of your own cross, although unbelief is a master carpenter at cross-making. Neither are you permitted to choose your own cross, although self-will would eagerly be lord and master, but your cross is prepared and appointed for you by divine love, and you are cheerfully to accept it. You are to take up the cross as your chosen badge and burden willingly. This night Jesus bids you submit your shoulder to His easy yoke. Do not kick at it in petulance, or trample on it in vainglory, or fall under it in despair, or run away from it in fear, but take it up like a true follower of Jesus. Jesus was a cross-bearer; He leads the way in the path of sorrow. Surely you could not desire a better guide! And if He carried a cross, what nobler burden would you desire? The Via Crucis is the way of safety; fear not to tread its thorny paths. Beloved, the cross is not made of feathers or lined with velvet. It is heavy and galling to disobedient shoulders, but it is not an iron cross. Although your fears have painted it with iron colors, it is a wooden cross that a man can carry, for the Man of sorrows tried the load. Take up your cross, and by the power of the Spirit of God, you will soon be so in love with it that, like Moses, you would not exchange the reproach of Christ for all the treasures of Egypt. Remember that Jesus carried it, and it will smell sweetly. Remember that the crown will soon follow it, and the thought of the coming weight of glory will greatly lighten the present heaviness of trouble. The Lord help you to bow your spirit in submission to the divine will before you fall asleep this night, that waking with tomorrow's sun, you may go forth to the day's cross with the holy and submissive spirit that becomes a follower of the Crucified.

⌁ *February 24* ⌁

O Lord of hosts, how long wilt thou not have mercy upon Jerusalem? ... And the Lord answered the angel ... with good words and comfortable words (Zechariah 1:12-13).

What a sweet answer to an anxious inquiry! This night let us rejoice in it. O Zion, there are good things in store for you; your time of travail shall soon be over; your children shall be brought forth; your captivity shall end. Bear patiently the rod for a season, and under the darkness still trust in God, for His love burns toward you. God loves the church with a love too deep for human imagination. He loves her with all His infinite heart. Therefore let her sons be of good courage; she cannot be far from prosperity to whom God speaks "good words and comfortable words." The prophet goes on to tell us what these comfortable words are: "I am jealous for Jerusalem and for Zion with a great jealousy."[138] The Lord loves His church so much that He cannot bear that she should go astray to others; and when she has done so, He cannot endure that she should suffer too much or too heavily. He will not have his enemies afflict her. He is displeased with them, because they increase her misery. When God seems most to leave His church, His heart is warm toward her. History shows that whenever God uses a rod to chasten His servants, He always breaks it afterwards, as if He loathed the rod that gave His children pain. "Like as a father pities his children, so the Lord pities those who fear Him."[139] God has not forgotten us because He smites. His blows are not evidence of lack of love. If this is true of His church *collectively*, it is of necessity true also of *each individual member*. You may fear that the Lord has passed you by, but it is not so. He, who counts the stars and calls them by their names, is in no danger of forgetting His own children. He knows your case as thoroughly as if you were the only creature He ever made or the only saint He ever loved. Approach Him and be at peace.[140]

⚞ *February 25* ⚟

But Jonah rose up to flee unto Tarshish from the presence of the Lord, and went down to Joppa (Jonah 1:3).

Instead of going to Nineveh to preach the Word, as God bade him, Jonah disliked the work, and went down to Joppa to escape from it. There are occasions when God's servants shrink from duty. But what is the consequence? What did Jonah lose by his conduct? He lost the presence and comfortable enjoyment of God's love. When we serve our Lord Jesus, as believers should do, our God is with us. Although we have the whole world against us, if we have God with us, what does it matter?[141] But the moment we start back and seek our own inventions, we are at sea without a pilot. Then may we bitterly lament and groan out, "O my God, where hast Thou gone? How could I have been so foolish as to shun Your service, and in this way to lose all the bright shining of Your face? This is a price too high. Let me return to my allegiance, that I may rejoice in Your presence." In the next place, Jonah *lost all peace of mind*. Sin soon destroys a believer's comfort. It is the poisonous upas tree, from whose leaves distil deadly drops that destroy the life of joy and peace. Jonah lost everything upon which he might have drawn for comfort in any other case. He could not plead the promise of divine protection, for he was not in God's ways. He could not say, "Lord, I meet with these difficulties in the discharge of my duty, therefore help me through them." He was reaping his own deeds; he was filled with his own ways. Christian, do not play the Jonah, unless you wish to have all the waves and the billows rolling over your head. You will find in the long run that it is far harder to shun the work and will of God than to at once yield yourself to it. *Jonah lost his time*, for he had to go to Tarshish after all. It is hard to contend with God; let us yield ourselves at once.

Behold, if the leprosy have covered all his flesh, he shall pronounce him clean that has the plague (Leviticus 13:13).

Strange enough this regulation appears, yet there was wisdom in it, for the throwing out of the disease proved that the constitution was sound. This evening it may be well for us to see the typical teaching of so singular a rule. We, too, are lepers, and may read the law of the leper as applicable to ourselves. When a man sees himself to be altogether lost and ruined, covered all over with the defilement of sin and in no part free from pollution; when he disclaims all righteousness of his own and pleads guilty before the Lord, then he is clean through the blood of Jesus and the grace of God. Hidden, unfelt, unconfessed iniquity is the true leprosy. But when sin is seen and felt, it has received its deathblow, and the Lord looks with eyes of mercy upon the soul afflicted with it. Nothing is more deadly than self-righteousness, or more hopeful than contrition. We must confess that we are "nothing else but sin," for no confession short of this will be the whole truth. If the Holy Spirit is at work with us, convincing us of sin,[142] there will be no difficulty in making such an acknowledgment. It will spring spontaneously from our lips. What comfort does the text afford to truly awakened sinners: the very circumstance that so grievously discouraged them is here turned into a sign and symptom of a hopeful state! Stripping comes before clothing; digging out the foundation is the first thing in building—and a thorough sense of sin is one of the earliest works of grace in the heart. O thou poor leprous sinner, utterly destitute of a sound spot, take heart from the text, and come as you are to Jesus—"For let our debts be what they may, however great or small, As soon as we have naught to pay, our Lord forgives us all. 'Tis perfect poverty alone that sets the soul at large: While we can call one mite our own, we have no full discharge."

⊰ *February 27* ⊱

Whose goings forth have been from of old, from everlasting (Micah 5:2).

The Lord Jesus had goings forth for His people as their representative before the throne, long before they appeared upon the stage of time. It was "from everlasting" that He signed the pact with His Father: that He would pay blood for blood, suffering for suffering, agony for agony, and death for death on behalf of His people. It was "from everlasting" that He gave Himself up without a murmuring word. That from the crown of His head to the sole of His foot He might sweat great drops of blood,[143] that He might be spit upon, pierced, mocked, rent asunder, and crushed beneath the pains of death. His goings forth as our Surety were from everlasting. Pause, my soul, and wonder! You have goings forth in the person of Jesus "from everlasting." Not only did Christ love you when you were born into the world, but His delights were with the sons of men before there were any sons of men. Often did He think of them. From everlasting to everlasting, He had set His affection upon them. What! my soul, has He been so long about your salvation, and will not He accomplish it? Has He from everlasting been going forth to save me, and will He lose me now? What! has He carried me in His hand as His precious jewel, and will He now let me slip from between His fingers? Did he choose me before the mountains were brought forth or the channels of the deep were dug, and will He reject me now? Impossible! I am sure He would not have loved me so long if He had not been a changeless Lover. If He could grow weary of me, He would have been tired of me long before now. If He had not loved me with a love as deep as hell and as strong as death, He would have turned from me long ago. Oh, joy above all joys, to know that I am His everlasting and inalienable inheritance, given to Him by His Father or ever the earth was! Everlasting love shall be the pillow for my head this night.

February 28

The barrel of meal wasted not, neither did the cruse of oil fail, according to the word of the Lord, which He spake by Elijah (1 Kings 17:16).

See the faithfulness of divine love. You observe that this woman had daily necessities. She had herself and her son to feed in a time of famine; and now, in addition, the prophet Elijah was to be fed, too. But though the need was threefold, yet the supply of meal wasted not, for she had a *constant supply*. Each day she made calls upon the barrel, but yet each day it remained the same. You, dear reader, have daily necessities, and because they come so frequently, you are apt to fear that the barrel of meal will one day be empty and the cruse of oil will fail you. Rest assured that according to the Word of God, this shall not be the case. Each day, though it bring its trouble, shall bring its help; and though you should live to outnumber the years of Methuselah, and though your needs should be as many as the sands of the seashore, yet shall God's grace and mercy last through all your necessities, and you shall never know a real lack. For three long years, in this widow's days, the heavens never saw a cloud and the stars never wept a holy tear of dew upon the wicked earth. Famine and desolation and death made the land a howling wilderness, but this woman never was hungry, but always was joyful in abundance. So shall it be with you. You shall see the sinner's hope perish, for he trusts his native strength; you shall see the proud Pharisee's confidence totter, for he builds his hope upon the sand; you shall see even your own schemes blasted and withered, but you yourself shall find that your place of defense shall be the munition of rocks: "Your bread shall be given you, and your water shall be sure."[144] Better have God for your guardian than the Bank of England for your possession. You might spend the wealth of the Indies, but you can never exhaust the infinite riches of God.

February 29

Now we have received ... the spirit which is of God;
that we might know the things that are freely given to us
of God (1 Corinthians 2:12).

Dear reader, have you received the spirit, which is of God, wrought by the Holy Ghost in your soul? The necessity of the work of the Holy Spirit in the heart may be clearly seen from this fact: Everything that has been done by God the Father and God the Son must be ineffectual to us unless the Spirit shall reveal these things to our souls. What effect does the doctrine of election have upon any man until the Spirit of God enters into him? Election is a dead letter in my consciousness until the Spirit of God calls me out of darkness into marvelous light.[145] *Then*, through my calling, I see my election. And knowing myself to be called of God, I know myself to have been chosen in the eternal purpose. His Father made a covenant with the Lord Jesus Christ, but what avails that covenant to us until the Holy Spirit brings us its blessings and opens our hearts to receive them?[146] There hang the blessings on the nail—Christ Jesus, but being short of stature, we cannot reach them. The Spirit of God takes them down and hands them to us, and thus they become actually ours. Covenant blessings in themselves are like the manna in the skies, far out of mortal reach, but the Spirit of God opens the windows of heaven and scatters the living bread around the camp of the spiritual Israel. Christ's finished work is like wine stored in the wine-vat; through unbelief we can neither draw nor drink. The Holy Spirit dips our vessel into this precious wine, and then we drink. But without the Spirit, we are as truly dead in sin as though the Father never had elected, and the Son had never bought us with His blood.[147] The Holy Spirit is absolutely necessary to our wellbeing. Let us walk lovingly toward Him and tremble at the thought of grieving Him.

March

≈ *March 1* ≈

He is precious (1 Peter 2:7).

As all the rivers run into the sea, so all delights center in our Beloved. The glances of His eyes outshine the sun. The beauties of His face are fairer than the choicest flowers. No fragrance is like the breath of His mouth. Gems of the mine and pearls from the sea are worthless things when measured by His preciousness. Peter tells us that Jesus is precious, but he did not and could not tell us *how* precious, nor could any of us compute the value of God's unspeakable gift.[148] Words cannot set forth the preciousness of the Lord Jesus to His people, nor fully tell how essential He is to their satisfaction and happiness. Believer, have you not found in the midst of plenty a sore famine if your Lord has been absent? The sun was shining, but Christ had hidden Himself, and all the world was black to you; or it was night, and since the bright and morning star was gone, no other star could yield you so much as a ray of light. What a howling wilderness is this world without our Lord! If once He hides Himself from us, withered are the flowers of our garden; our pleasant fruits decay; the birds suspend their songs; and a tempest overturns our hopes. All earth's candles cannot make daylight if the Sun of Righteousness is eclipsed. He is the soul of our soul, the light of our light, and the life of our life. Dear reader, what would you do in the world without Him, when you wake up and look forward to the day's battle? What would you do at night, when you come home jaded and weary, if there were no door of fellowship between you and Christ? Blessed be His name; He will not suffer us to try our lot without Him, for Jesus never forsakes His own.[149] Yet, let the thought of *what life would be without Him* enhance His preciousness.

⇥ *March 2* ⇤

Unto me, who am less than the least of all saints, is this grace given, that I should preach among the Gentiles the unsearchable riches of Christ (Ephesians 3:8).

The apostle Paul felt it a great privilege to be allowed to preach the gospel. He did not look upon his calling as drudgery, but he entered upon it with intense delight. Yet while Paul was thus thankful for his office, his success in it greatly humbled him. The fuller a vessel becomes, the deeper it sinks in the water. Idlers may indulge a fond conceit of their abilities, because they are untried; but the earnest worker soon learns his own weakness. If you seek humility, *try hard work*; if you would know your nothingness, attempt some great thing for Jesus. If you would feel how utterly powerless you are apart from the living God, attempt especially the great work of proclaiming the unsearchable riches of Christ, and you will know, as you never knew before, what a weak unworthy thing you are. Although the apostle thus knew and confessed his weakness, he was never perplexed as to the *subject* of his ministry. From his first sermon to his last, Paul preached Christ, and nothing but Christ.[150] He lifted up the cross, and extolled the Son of God who bled thereon. Follow his example in all your personal efforts to spread the glad tidings of salvation, and let "Christ and Him crucified" be your ever-recurring theme. The Christian should be like those lovely spring flowers that, when the sun is shining, open their golden cups, as if saying, "Fill us with your beams!" but when the sun is hidden behind a cloud, they close their cups and droop their heads. So should the Christian feel the sweet influence of Jesus; Jesus must be his sun, and he must be the flower that yields itself to the Sun of Righteousness. Oh! to speak of Christ alone, this is the subject that is both "seed for the sower, and bread for the eater."[151] This is the live coal for the lip of the speaker, and the master key to the heart of the hearer.

⚹ *March 3* ⚹

*He saw the Spirit of God descending like a dove
(Matthew 3:16).*

As the Spirit of God descended upon the Lord Jesus, the head, so
He also, in measure, descends upon the members of the mystical
body. His descent is to us after the same fashion as that in which
it fell upon our Lord. There is often a singular *rapidity* about
it, because if ever we are aware, we are impelled onward and
heavenward beyond all expectation. Yet is there none of the hurry
of earthly haste, for the wings of the dove are as soft as they are
swift. *Quietness* seems essential to many spiritual operations;
the Lord is in the still small voice, and like the dew, His grace is
distilled in silence. The dove has always been the chosen type of
purity, and the Holy Spirit is holiness itself. Where He comes,
everything that is pure and lovely and of good report is made to
abound; and sin and uncleanness depart. *Peace* reigns also where
the Holy Dove comes with power. He bears the olive branch,
which shows that the waters of divine wrath are assuaged.
Gentleness is a sure result of the Sacred Dove's transforming
power; hearts touched by His benign influence are meek and
lowly henceforth and forever. *Harmlessness* follows, as a matter
of course. Eagles and ravens may hunt their prey—the turtledove
can endure wrong, but cannot inflict it. We must be harmless
as doves.[152] The dove is an apt picture of *love*, the voice of the
turtle is full of affection; and so, the soul visited by the blessed
Spirit abounds in love to God, in love to the brethren, in love
to sinners, and above all, in love to Jesus. The brooding of the
Spirit of God upon the face of the deep[153] first produced order
and life. In our hearts, He causes and fosters new life and light.
Blessed Spirit, as Thou didst rest upon our dear Redeemer,[154]
even so rest upon us from this time forward and forever.

They shall be abundantly satisfied with the fatness of
Your house (Psalm 36:8).

Sheba's queen was amazed at the sumptuousness of Solomon's table. She lost all heart when she saw the provision of a single day; and she marveled equally at the company of servants who were feasted at the royal board. But what is this to the hospitalities of the God of grace? Ten thousand thousand of His people are daily fed. Hungry and thirsty, they bring large appetites with them to the banquet, but not one of them returns unsatisfied. There is enough for each, enough for all, enough for evermore. Though the host that feed at Jehovah's table is as countless as the stars of heaven, yet each one has his portion of meat. Think how much grace one saint requires, so much that nothing but the Infinite could supply him for one day; and yet the Lord spreads His table, not for one, but many saints; not for one day, but for many years; not for many years only, but for generation after generation. Observe the full feasting to which the text refers: the guests at mercy's banquet are satisfied, nay, more "abundantly satisfied," not with ordinary fare, but with fatness, the peculiar fatness of God's own house; and such feasting is guaranteed by a faithful promise to all those children of men who put their trust under the shadow of Jehovah's wings.[155] I once thought that if I might but get the broken meat at God's back door of grace I should be satisfied like the woman who said, "The dogs eat of the crumbs that fall from the master's table."[156] But no child of God is ever served with scraps and leavings. Like Mephibosheth, they all eat from the King's own table.[157] In matters of grace, we all have Benjamin's mess—we all have ten times more than we could have expected, and though our necessities are great, yet are we often amazed at the marvelous plenty of grace which God gives us experimentally to enjoy.

*Say unto my soul, I am your salvation
(Psalm 35:3).*

What does this sweet prayer teach me? It shall be my evening's petition, but first let it yield me an instructive meditation. The text informs me first of all that David had his doubts, for why should he pray, "Say unto my soul, I am your salvation," if he were not sometimes exercised with doubts and fears? Let me, then, be of good cheer, for I am not the only saint who has to complain of weakness of faith. If David doubted, I need not conclude that I am no Christian because I have doubts. The text reminds me that David was not content while he had doubts and fears, but he repaired at once to the mercy-seat to pray for assurance, for he valued it as much fine gold. I, too, must labor after an abiding sense of my acceptance in the Beloved,[158] and must have no joy when His love is not shed abroad in my soul. When my Bridegroom is gone from me, my soul must and will fast. I learn also that David knew where to obtain full assurance. He went to his God in prayer, crying, "Say unto my soul, I am your salvation." I must be much alone with God if I would have a clear sense of Jesus' love. If my prayers should cease, then my eye of faith will grow dim. Much in prayer, much in heaven. Slow in prayer, slow in progress. I notice that David would not be satisfied unless his assurance had a divine source. "Say unto my soul." Lord, do *Thou* say it! Nothing short of a divine testimony in the soul will ever content the true Christian. Moreover, David could not rest unless his assurance had *a vivid personality* about it. "Say unto *my* soul, I am *your* salvation." Lord, if You say this to all the saints, it is nothing unless You say it to me. Lord, I have sinned. I deserve not Your smile. I scarcely dare to ask it, but oh! say to *my* soul, even to *my* soul, "I am *your* salvation." Let me have a present, personal, infallible, indisputable sense that I am Yours, and that Thou art mine.

ᗘ *March 6* ᗘ

Before destruction the heart of man is haughty
(Proverbs 18:12).

It is an old and common saying, that "coming events cast their shadows before them." The wise man teaches us that a haughty heart is the prophetic prelude of evil. Pride is as safely the sign of destruction as the change of mercury in the barometer is the sign of rain, and far more infallibly so than that. When men have ridden the high horse, destruction has always overtaken them. Let David's aching heart show that there is an eclipse of a man's glory when he dotes upon his own greatness. 2 Samuel 24:10. See Nebuchadnezzar, the mighty builder of Babylon, creeping on the earth, devouring grass like oxen until his nails had grown like bird's claws and his hair like eagle's feathers. Daniel 4:33. Pride made the boaster a beast, as once before it made an angel a devil. God hates high looks, and never fails to bring them down. All the arrows of God are aimed at proud hearts. O Christian, is your heart haughty this evening? Pride can get into the Christian's heart as well as into the sinner's. It can delude him into dreaming that he is "rich and increased in goods, and has need of nothing."[159] Are you glorying in your graces or your talents? Are you proud of yourself, that you have had holy frames and sweet experiences? Mark you, reader, there is a destruction coming to you, also. Your flaunting poppies of self-conceit will be pulled up by the roots. Your mushroom graces will wither in the burning heat, and your self-sufficiency shall become as straw for the dunghill. If we forget to live at the foot of the cross in deepest lowliness of spirit, God will not forget to make us smart under His rod. Destruction will come to you, O unduly exalted believer, the destruction of your joys and of your comforts, though there can be no destruction of your soul. Wherefore, "He that glorieth, let him glory *in the Lord*."[160]

☜ *March 7* ☞

It is better to trust in the Lord, than to put confidence in man (Psalm 118:8).

Doubtless the reader has been tried with the temptation to rely upon the things that are seen, instead of resting alone upon the invisible God. Christians often look to man for help and counsel, and mar the noble simplicity of their reliance upon their God. If this evening's portion meets the eye of a child of God anxious about worldly things, then would we reason with him awhile. You trust in Jesus, and only in Jesus, for your salvation, then why are you troubled? "Because of my great care." Is it not written, "Cast your burden upon the Lord?"[161] "Be careful for nothing, but in everything by prayer and supplication make known your wants unto God."[162] Can you not trust God for worldly things? "Ah! I wish I could." If you cannot trust God for worldly things, how dare you trust Him for spiritual things? Can you trust Him for your soul's redemption, and not rely upon Him for a few lesser mercies? Is not God enough for your need, or is His all-sufficiency too narrow for your wants? Do you want another eye besides His, who sees every secret thing? Is His heart faint? Is His arm weary? If so, seek another god, but if He is infinite, omnipotent, faithful, true, and all-wise, why do you gad about to seek another confidence? Why do you rake the earth to find another foundation when this is strong enough to bear all the weight that you could ever build thereon? Christian, mix not your wine with water; do not alloy your gold of faith with the dross of human confidence. Wait only upon God, and let your expectation be from Him. Do not covet Jonah's gourd, but rest in Jonah's God. Let the sandy foundations of terrestrial trust be the choice of fools. As one who sees the storm coming, build for yourself an abiding place upon the Rock of Ages.[163]

⊰ *March 8* ⊱

She called his name Ben-oni (son of sorrow), but his father called him Benjamin (son of my right hand) (Genesis 35:18).

To every matter there is a bright, as well as a dark, side. Rachel was overwhelmed with the sorrow of her own travail and death; Jacob, though weeping the mother's loss, could see the mercy of the child's birth. It is well for us if, while the flesh mourns over trials, our faith triumphs in divine faithfulness. Samson's lion yielded honey, and so will our adversities, if rightly considered.[164] The stormy sea feeds multitudes with its fishes; the wild wood blooms with beauteous flowerets; the stormy wind sweeps away the pestilence; and the biting frost loosens the soil. Dark clouds distil bright drops, and black earth grows gay flowers. A vein of good is to be found in every mine of evil. Sad hearts have peculiar skill in discovering the most disadvantageous point of view from which to gaze upon a trial; if there were only one slough in the world, they would soon be up to their necks in it, and if there were only one lion in the desert they would hear it roar. About us all there is a tinge of this wretched folly, and we are apt, at times, like Jacob, to cry, "All these things are against me." Faith's way of walking is to cast all care upon the Lord,[165] and then to anticipate good results from the worst calamities. Like Gideon's men, she does not fret over the broken pitcher, but rejoices that the lamp blazes forth the more. Out of the rough oyster-shell of difficulty, she extracts the rare pearl of honor, and from the deep ocean-caves of distress, she uplifts the priceless coral of experience. When her flood of prosperity ebbs, she finds treasures hid in the sands. When her sun of delight goes down, she turns her telescope of hope to the starry promises of heaven. When death itself appears, faith points to the light of resurrection beyond the grave, thus making our dying Benoni to be our living Benjamin.

✄ *March 9* ✄

Abide in Me (John 15:4).

Communion with Christ is a certain cure for every ill. Whether it is the wormwood of woe or the cloying excess of earthly delight, close fellowship with the Lord Jesus will take bitterness from the one and satiety from the other. Live near to Jesus, Christian, and it is matter of secondary importance whether you live on the mountain of honor or in the valley of humiliation. Living near to Jesus, you are covered with the wings of God, and underneath you are the everlasting arms.[166] Let nothing keep you from that hallowed relationship, which is the choice privilege of a soul wedded to THE WELL-BELOVED. Do not be content with an interview now and then, but seek always to retain His company, for only in His presence do you have either comfort or safety. Jesus should not be a friend who calls upon us now and then, but one with whom we walk evermore. You have a difficult road before you: see, O traveler to heaven, do not go without your guide. You have to pass through the fiery furnace. Do not enter unless, like Shadrach, Meshach, and Abednego, you have the Son of God to be your companion.[167] You have to storm the Jericho of your own corruptions. Attempt not the warfare until, like Joshua, you have seen the Captain of the Lord's host, with His sword drawn in His hand. Meet the Esau of your many temptations; do not meet him until you have laid hold upon the angel at Jabbok's brook, and prevailed.[168] In every case, in every condition, you will need Jesus. You will need Him most of all when the iron gates of death open to you. Stay close to your soul's Husband; lean your head upon His bosom; ask to be refreshed with the spiced wine of His pomegranate; and you will be found of Him at the last without spot or wrinkle or any such thing.[169] Seeing you have lived with Him and lived in Him here, you will abide with Him forever.

⇻ *March 10* ⇺

Man ... is of few days, and full of trouble
(Job 14:1).

It may be of great service to us, before we fall asleep, to remember this mournful fact, for it may lead us let go of earthly things. There is nothing very pleasant in the recollection that we are not above the shafts of adversity, but it may humble us and prevent our boasting like the psalmist: "My mountain standeth firm: I shall never be moved."[170] It may stay us from taking too deep root in this soil from which we are so soon to be transplanted into the heavenly garden. Let us recollect the frail tenure upon which we hold our *temporal mercies*. If we would remember that all the trees of earth are marked for the woodman's axe, we should not be so ready to build our nests in them. We should love, but we should love with the love which expects death, and which reckons upon separations. Our dear relations are but loaned to us, and the hour when we must return them to the lender's hand may be even at the door. The like is certainly true of our worldly goods. Do not riches take to themselves wings and fly away? Our *health* is equally precarious. Frail flowers of the field, we must not reckon upon blooming forever. There is a time appointed for weakness and sickness, when we shall have to glorify God by suffering, and not by earnest activity. There is no single point in which we can hope to escape from the sharp arrows of affliction; out of our few days there is not one secure from sorrow.[171] Man's life is a cask full of bitter wine; he who looks for joy in it would do better to seek for honey in an ocean of brine. Beloved reader, set not your affections upon things of earth. Seek those things that are above,[172] for *here* the moth devoured and the thief broke through, but *there* all joys are perpetual and eternal. The path of trouble is the way home. Lord, make this thought a pillow for many a weary head!

Thou shalt be called, Sought out
(Isaiah 62:12).

The surpassing grace of God is seen very clearly in that we were not only sought, but sought *out*. Men *seek* for a thing, which is lost upon the floor of the house, but in such a case there is only seeking, not seeking out. The loss is more perplexing and the search more persevering when a thing is sought *out*. We were mingled with the mire: we were as when some precious piece of gold falls into the sewer, and men gather out and carefully inspect a mass of abominable filth, and continue to stir and rake, and search among the heap until the treasure is found.[173] Or, to use another example, we were lost in a labyrinth; we wandered hither and thither, and when mercy came after us with the gospel, it did not find us at the first coming, it had to search for us and seek us out. We as lost sheep were so desperately lost, and had wandered into such a strange country that it did not seem possible that even the Good Shepherd should track our devious roaming.[174] Glory be to unconquerable grace, we were sought *out*! No gloom could hide us, no filthiness could conceal us, and we were found and brought home. Glory be to infinite love, God the Holy Spirit restored us! The lives of some of God's people, if they could be written, would fill us with holy astonishment. Strange and marvelous are the ways that God used in their cases to find His own. Blessed be His name, He never relinquishes the search until the chosen are sought out effectually. They are not a people sought today and cast away tomorrow. Almightiness and wisdom combined will make no failures; they shall be called, "Sought out!" That any should be sought out is matchless grace, but that *we* should be sought out is grace beyond degree! We can find no reason for it except God's own sovereign love, and can only lift up our hearts in wonder, and praise the Lord that this night we wear the name of "Sought out."

☞ *March 12* ☜

To whom belongest thou?
(1 Samuel 30:13).

No neutralities can exist in religion. We are either ranked under the banner of Prince Immanuel, to serve and fight His battles, or we are vassals of the black prince, Satan. "To whom belongest thou?" Reader, let me assist you in your response. Have you been "born again?" If you have, you belong to Christ, but without the new birth you cannot be His. *In whom do you trust?* Those who believe in Jesus are the sons of God.[175] *Whose work are you doing?* You are sure to serve your master, for he whom you serve is thereby owned to be your lord.[176] *What company do you keep?* If you belong to Jesus, you will fraternize with those who wear the livery of the cross. "Birds of a feather flock together." *What is your conversation?* Is it heavenly or is it earthly? *What have you learned of your Master?* Servants learn much from their masters to whom they are apprenticed. If you have served your time with Jesus, it will be said of you, as it was of Peter and John, "They took knowledge of them, that they had been with Jesus." We press the question, "To whom belongest thou?" Answer honestly before you give sleep to your eyes. If you are not Christ's you are in a hard service—Run away from your cruel master! Enter into the service of the Lord of Love, and you shall enjoy a life of blessedness. If you *are* Christ's, let me advise you to do four things. You belong to Jesus—obey him; let His word be your law; let His wish be your will. You belong to the Beloved, then *love Him*; let your heart embrace Him; let your whole soul be filled with Him. You belong to the Son of God, then *trust Him*; rest nowhere but on Him. You belong to the King of kings; then *be decided for Him*. Thus, without your being branded upon the brow, all will know to whom you belong.

Then he put forth his hand, and took her, and pulled her in unto him into the ark (Genesis 8:9).

Wearied out with her wanderings, the dove returns at length to the ark as her only resting place. How heavily she flies—she will drop—she will never reach the ark! But she struggles on. Noah has been looking out for his dove all day long, and is ready to receive her. She has just strength to reach the edge of the ark. She can hardly alight upon it and is ready to drop when Noah puts forth his hand and pulls her in unto him. Mark that: "pulled her in unto him." She did not fly right in herself, but was too fearful or too weary. She flew as far as she could, and then he put forth his hand and pulled her in unto him. This act of mercy was shown to the wandering dove, and she was not chided for her wanderings. Just as she was, she was pulled into the ark. So you, seeking sinner, with all your sin, will be received. "Only return"—those are God's two gracious words—"only return." What! nothing else? No, "only return." She had no olive branch in her mouth this time, nothing at all but just herself and her wanderings; but it is "only return," and she does return, and Noah pulls her in. Fly, wanderer. Fly, fainting one. Dove, as you are, though you think yourself to be black as the raven with the mire of sin, back, back to the Savior. Every moment you wait only increases your misery; your attempts to plume yourself and make yourself fit for Jesus are all vanity. Come to Him just as you are. "Return, thou backsliding Israel." He does not say, "Return, thou *repenting* Israel" (there is such an invitation doubtless), but "thou *backsliding* one," as a backslider with all your backslidings about you, Return, return, return! Jesus is waiting for you! He will stretch forth His hand and "pull you in"—in to Himself, your heart's true home.[177]

⭐ *March 14* ⭐

I will take heed to my ways
(Psalm 39:1).

Fellow pilgrim, say not in your heart, "I will go hither and thither, and I shall not sin," for you are never so out of danger of sinning as to boast of security. The road is very miry; it will be hard to pick your path so as not to soil your garments. This is a world of pitch; you will need to watch often, if in handling it you are to keep your hands clean. There is a robber at every turn of the road to rob you of your jewels; there is a temptation in every mercy; there is a snare in every joy; and if you ever reach heaven, it will be a miracle of divine grace to be ascribed entirely to your Father's power. Be on your guard. When a man carries a bombshell in his hand, he should mind that he does not go near a candle; and you too must take care that you enter not into temptation. Even your common actions are sharply edged tools; you must mind how you handle them. There is nothing in this world to foster a Christian's piety, but everything to destroy it. How anxious should you be to look up to God, that *He* might keep you! Your prayer should be, "Hold thou me up, and I shall be safe." Having prayed, you must also watch, guarding every thought, word, and action with holy jealousy. Do not expose yourselves unnecessarily, but if called to exposure, if you are bidden to go where the darts are flying, never venture forth without your shield. If once the devil finds you without your shield, he will rejoice that his hour of triumph is come, and will soon make you fall down wounded by his arrows. Though slain you cannot be, wounded you may be. "Be sober; be vigilant, danger may be in an hour when all seems securest to you."[178] Therefore, take heed to your ways, and watch unto prayer. No man ever fell into error through being too watchful. May the Holy Spirit guide us in all our ways, so shall they always please the Lord.

He did it with all his heart and prospered
(2 Chronicles 31:21).

This is no unusual occurrence; it is the general rule of the moral universe that those men prosper who do their work with all their hearts, while those are almost certain to fail who go to their labor leaving half their hearts behind them. God does not give harvests to idle men except harvests of thistles, nor is He pleased to send wealth to those who will not dig in the field to find its hidden treasure. It is universally confessed that if a man would prosper, he must be diligent in business.[179] It is the same in religion as it is in other things. If you would prosper in your work for Jesus, let it be *heart* work, and let it be done with all your heart. Put as much force, energy, heartiness, and earnestness into religion as you ever do into business, for it deserves far more. The Holy Spirit helps our infirmities, but He does not encourage our idleness. He loves active believers. Who are the most useful people in the Christian church? The people who do what they undertake for God *with all their hearts*. Who are the most successful Sabbath-school teachers? The most talented? No; the most zealous; the men and women whose hearts are on fire, those are the people who see their Lord riding forth prosperously in the majesty of His salvation. Whole-heartedness shows itself in *perseverance*; there may be failure at first, but the earnest worker will say, "It is the Lord's work, and it must be done; my Lord has bidden me do it, and in His strength I will accomplish it." Christian, are you thus "with all your heart" serving your Master? Remember the earnestness of Jesus! Think what heart-work was His! He could say, "The zeal of your house has eaten Me up."[180] When He sweated great drops of blood, it was no light burden He had to carry upon those blessed shoulders; and when He poured out His heart, it was no weak effort He was making for the salvation of His people. Was Jesus in earnest, and are we lukewarm?

Keep back Your servant also from presumptuous sins
(Psalm 19:13).

Such was the prayer of the "man after God's own heart." Did holy David need to pray thus? How needful, then, must such a prayer be for us babes in grace! It is as if he said, "Keep me back, or I shall rush headlong over the precipice of sin." Our evil nature, like an ill-tempered horse, is apt to run away. May the grace of God put the bridle upon it and hold it in, so that it will not rush into mischief. What might not the best of us do if it were not for the checks that the Lord sets upon us both in providence and in grace! The psalmist's prayer is directed against the worst form of sin—that which is done with deliberation and willfulness. Even the holiest need to be "kept back" from the vilest transgressions. It is a solemn thing to find the apostle Paul warning saints against the most loathsome sins. "Mortify therefore your members which are upon the earth; fornication, uncleanness, inordinate affection, evil concupiscence, and covetousness, which is idolatry."[181] What! do saints want warning against such sins as these? Yes, they do. The whitest robes, unless their purity is preserved by divine grace, will be defiled by the blackest spots. Experienced Christian, do not boast in your experience. You will trip yet if you look away from Him who is able to keep you from falling.[182] When your love is fervent, your faith is constant, and your hopes are bright, do not say, "We shall never sin." Rather cry, "Lead us not into temptation." There is enough tinder in the heart of the best of people to light a fire that shall burn to the lowest hell unless God quenches the sparks as they fall. Who would have dreamed that righteous Lot could be found drunken and committing uncleanness? Hazael said, "Is your servant a dog, that he should do this thing?" We are very apt to use the same self-righteous question. May infinite wisdom cure us of the madness of self-confidence.

Blessed are the peacemakers: for they shall be called the children of God (Matthew 5:9).

This is the seventh of the beatitudes: and seven was the number of perfection among the Hebrews. It may be that the Savior placed the peacemaker the seventh on the list because he most nearly approaches the perfect man in Christ Jesus. He, who would have perfect blessedness, so far as it can be enjoyed on earth, must attain to this seventh benediction, and become a peacemaker. There is significance also in the position of the text. The verse which precedes it speaks of the blessedness of "the pure in heart: for they shall see God." It is well to understand that we are to be "first pure, then peaceable." Our peaceableness is never to be a compact with sin or toleration of evil. We must set our faces like flints against everything contrary to God and His holiness. Purity being a settled matter in our souls, we can go on to peaceableness. Not less does the verse that follows seem to have been put there on purpose. However peaceable we may be in this world, yet we shall be misrepresented and misunderstood. This is not surprising, for even the Prince of Peace, by His very peacefulness, brought fire upon the earth. He, Himself, although He loved mankind and did no ill, was "despised and rejected of men, a man of sorrows and acquainted with grief."[183] Lest, therefore, the peaceable in heart should be surprised when they meet with enemies, it is added in the following verse, "Blessed are they which are persecuted for righteousness' sake: for theirs is the kingdom of heaven." Thus, the peacemakers are not only pronounced to be blessed, but they are compassed about with blessings. Lord, give us grace to climb to this seventh beatitude! Purify our minds that we may be "first pure, then peaceable," and fortify our souls, that our peaceableness may not lead us into cowardice and despair, when for Your sake we are persecuted.

*As the Father has loved Me, so have I loved you
(John 15:9).*

As the Father loves the Son, in the same manner Jesus loves His people. What is that divine method? He loved Him without beginning, and thus Jesus loves His members. "I have loved you with an everlasting love."[184] You can trace the beginning of human affection; you can easily find the beginning of your love for Christ, but His love for us is a stream whose source is hidden in eternity. God the Father loves Jesus *without any change.* Christian, take this for your comfort: there is no change in Jesus Christ's love to those who rest in Him. Yesterday you were on Tabor's top, and you said, "He loves me." Today you are in the valley of humiliation, but He loves you still the same. On the hill Mizar and among the Hermons, you heard His voice, which spoke so sweetly with the turtle-notes of love. Now on the sea, or even in the sea, when all His waves and billows go over you, His heart is faithful to His ancient choice. The Father loves the Son *without any end*, and thus does the Son love His people. Saint, you need not fear the loosing of the silver cord, for His love for you will never cease. Rest confident that Christ will go with you even down to the grave, and that up again from it He will be your guide to the celestial hills. Moreover, the Father loves the Son *without any measure*. It is the same immeasurable love that the Son bestows upon His chosen ones. The whole heart of Christ is dedicated to His people. He "loved us and gave Himself for us."[185] His is a love which passeth knowledge.[186] Ah! we have indeed an immutable Savior, a precious Savior, one who loves without measure, without change, without beginning, and without end, even as the Father loves Him! There is much food here for those who know how to digest it. May the Holy Ghost lead us into its marrow and fatness!

And she did eat, and was sufficed, and left
(Ruth 2:14).

Whenever we are privileged to eat of the bread that Jesus gives, we are, like Ruth, satisfied with the full and sweet repast. When Jesus is the host, no guest goes empty from the table. Our *head* is satisfied with the precious truth that Christ reveals. Our *heart* is content with Jesus, as the altogether lovely object of affection. Our *hope* is satisfied, for whom have we in heaven but Jesus? And our desire is satiated, for what can we wish for more than "to know Christ and to be found in Him?"[187] Jesus fills our *conscience* till it is at perfect peace, our *judgment* with persuasion of the certainty of His teachings, our *memory* with recollections of what He has done, and our *imagination* with the prospects of what He is yet to do. As Ruth was "sufficed, *and left,*" so is it with us. We have had deep draughts; we have thought that we could take in all of Christ, but when we have done our best, we have had to leave a vast remainder. We have sat at the table of the Lord's love, and said, "Nothing but the infinite can ever satisfy me; I am such a great sinner that I must have infinite merit to wash my sin away." We have had our sin removed, and found that there was merit to spare. We have had our hunger relieved at the feast of sacred love, and found that there was a redundancy of spiritual meat remaining. There are certain sweet things in the Word of God that we have not enjoyed yet, and that we are obliged to leave for a while. We are like the disciples to whom Jesus said, "I have yet many things to say unto you, but ye cannot bear them now."[188] Yes, there are graces to which we have not attained, places of fellowship nearer to Christ that we have not reached, and heights of communion that our feet have not climbed. At every banquet of love there are many baskets of fragments left. Let us magnify the liberality of our glorious Boaz.

Husbands, love your wives, even as Christ also loved the church (Ephesians 5:25).

What a golden example Christ gives to His disciples! Few masters could venture to say, "If you would practice my teaching, imitate my life," but as the life of Jesus is the exact transcript of perfect virtue, He can point to Himself as the paragon of holiness, as well as the teacher of it. The Christian should take nothing short of Christ for his model. Under no circumstances ought we to be content unless we reflect the grace, which was in Him. As a husband, the Christian is to look upon the portrait of Christ Jesus, and he is to paint according to that copy. The true Christian is to be such a husband as Christ was to His church. The love of a husband is *special*. The Lord Jesus cherishes for the church a peculiar affection, which is set upon her above the rest of mankind: "I pray for them, I pray not for the world."[189] The elect church is the favorite of heaven, the treasure of Christ, the crown of His head, the bracelet of His arm, the breastplate of His heart, the very center and core of His love. A husband should love his wife with a *constant* love, for thus Jesus loves His church. He does not vary in His affection. He may change in His display of affection, but the affection itself is still the same. A husband should love his wife with an *enduring* love, for nothing "shall be able to separate us from the love of God, which is in Christ Jesus our Lord."[190] A true husband loves his wife with a *hearty* love—fervent and intense. It is not mere lip service. Ah! beloved, what more could Christ have done in proof of His love than He has done? Jesus has a *delighted love* toward His spouse. He prizes her affection, and delights in her with sweet complacence. Believer, you wonder at Jesus' love. You admire it. Are you imitating it? In your domestic relationships is the rule and measure of your love, "even as Christ loved the Church?"

✒ *March 21* ✒

*Canst thou bind the sweet influences of Pleiades, or
loose the bands of Orion? (Job 38:31)*

If inclined to boast of our abilities, the grandeur of nature may
soon show us how puny we are. We cannot move the least of
all the twinkling stars, or quench so much as one of the beams
of the morning. We speak of power, but the heavens laugh us to
scorn. When the Pleiades shine forth in spring with vernal joy,
we cannot restrain their influences, and when Orion reigns aloft,
and the year is bound in winter's fetters, we cannot relax the icy
bands. The seasons revolve according to the divine appointment;
the whole race of men cannot effect a change therein. Lord, what
is man?[191] In the spiritual world, as in the natural, man's power
is limited on all hands. When the Holy Spirit sheds abroad His
delights in the soul, none can disturb. All the cunning and malice
of men are ineffectual to stay the genial quickening power of the
Comforter. When He deigns to visit a church and revive it, the
most inveterate enemies cannot resist the good work. They may
ridicule it, but they can no more restrain it than they can push
back the spring when the Pleiades rule the hour. God wills it,
and so it must be. On the other hand, if the Lord, in sovereignty
or in justice, binds up a man so that he is in soul bondage, who
can give him liberty? He alone can remove the winter of spiritual
death from an individual or a people. He looses the bands of
Orion, and none but He. What a blessing it is that He can do
it. O that He would perform the wonder tonight. Lord, end my
winter and let my spring begin. I cannot, with all my longings,
raise my soul out of her death and dullness, but all things are
possible with You. I need celestial influences, the clear shining
of Your love, the beams of Your grace, and the light of Your
countenance. These are the Pleiades to me. I suffer much from sin
and temptation. These are my wintry signs, my terrible Orion.
Lord, work wonders in me and for me. Amen.

"Father, I will that they also, whom Thou hast given
Me, be with Me where I am" (John 17:24).

O death! why do you touch the tree beneath whose spreading branches weariness has rest? Why do you snatch away the excellent of the earth, in whom is all our delight? If you must use your axe, use it upon the trees that yield no fruit. You might be thanked then. But why do you fell the goodly cedars of Lebanon? O put down your axe, and spare the righteous. But no, it must not be; death smites the best of our friends. The most generous, the most prayerful, the most holy, and the most devoted must die. And why? It is through Jesus' prevailing prayer—"Father, I will that they also, whom Thou hast given Me, be with Me where I am." It is *that* which bears them on eagle's wings to heaven. Every time a believer mounts from this earth to paradise, it is an answer to Christ's prayer. A good old divine remarks, "Many times Jesus and His people pull against one another in prayer. You bend your knee in prayer and say 'Father, I ask that Your saints be with me where *I* am.' Christ says, 'Father, I ask that they also, whom Thou hast given Me, be with Me where I am.'" Thus the disciple is at cross-purposes with his Lord. The soul cannot be in both places. The beloved one cannot be with Christ and with you, too. Now, which pleader shall win the day? If you had your choice, if the King should step from His throne, and say, "Here are two supplicants praying in opposition to one another. Which shall be answered?" Oh! I am sure, though it is agony, you would leap to your feet, and say, "Jesus, not my will, but Yours be done." You would give up your prayer for your loved one's life, if you realized that Christ is praying in the opposite direction—"Father, I will that they also, whom Thou hast given Me, be with Me where I am." Lord, Thou shalt have them. By faith we let them go.

*"I tell you that, if these should hold their peace, the
stones would immediately cry out" (Luke 19:40).*

But could the stones cry out? Assuredly they could if He who
opens the mouth of those who cannot speak should bid them lift
up their voice. Certainly if they were to speak, they would have
much to testify in praise of Him who created them by the Word
of His power; they could extol the wisdom and power of their
Maker, who called them into being. Shall not *we* speak well of
Him who made us anew, and out of stones raised up children
unto Abraham? The old rocks could tell of chaos and order, and
the handiwork of God in successive stages of creation's drama.
Can *we* not talk of God's decrees, of God's great work in ancient
times, in all that He did for His church in the days of old? If the
stones were to speak, they could tell of their *breaker*, how he took
them from the quarry, and made them fit for the temple. Can *we*
not tell of our glorious Breaker, who broke our hearts with the
hammer of His Word, that He might build us into His temple?
If the stones should cry out, they would magnify their *builder*,
who polished them and fashioned them after the similitude of a
palace. Shall we not speak of our Architect and Builder, who has
put us in our place in the temple of the living God? If the stones
could cry out, they might have a long, long story to tell by way
of memorial, for many a time has a great stone been rolled as
a memorial before the Lord. We, too, can testify of Ebenezers,
stones of help, and pillars of remembrance. The broken stones
of the law cry out against us, but Christ Himself, who has rolled
away the stone from the door of the sepulcher,[192] speaks for us.
Stones might well cry out, but we will not let them. We will hush
their noise with ours; we will break forth into sacred song and
bless the majesty of the Most High, all our days glorifying Him
who is called by Jacob, the Shepherd and Stone of Israel.

ᘍ *March 24* ᘘ

In that hour Jesus rejoiced in spirit (Luke 10:21).

The Savior was "a man of sorrows,"[193] but every thoughtful mind has discovered the fact that down deep in His innermost soul, He carried an inexhaustible treasury of refined and heavenly joy. Of all the human race, there was never a man who had a deeper, purer, or more abiding peace than our Lord Jesus Christ. "He was anointed with the oil of gladness above His fellows."[194] His vast benevolence must, from the very nature of things, have afforded Him the deepest possible delight, for benevolence is joy. There were a few remarkable seasons when this joy manifested itself. "At that hour Jesus rejoiced in spirit, and said, I thank You, O Father, Lord of heaven and earth."[195] Christ had His songs, though it was night with Him. Though His face was marred, and His countenance had lost the luster of earthly happiness, yet sometimes it was lit up with a matchless splendor of unparalleled satisfaction, as He thought upon the recompense of the reward and, in the midst of the congregation, sang His praise unto God. In this, the Lord Jesus is a blessed picture of His Church on earth. At this hour, the church expects to walk in sympathy with her Lord along a thorny road. She is forcing her way to the crown through much tribulation. Her office is to bear the cross. Her lot is to be scorned and counted an alien by her mother's children. And yet the Church has a deep well of joy, of which none can drink but her own children. There are stores of wine and oil and corn hidden in the midst of our Jerusalem, upon which the saints of God are evermore sustained and nurtured. Sometimes, as in our Savior's case, we have our seasons of intense delight, for "There is a river, the streams whereof shall make glad the city of our God."[196] Exiles though we are, we rejoice in our King; yea, in Him we exceedingly rejoice, while in His name we set up our banners.

⤝ *March 25* ⤞

The Son of man (John 3:13).

How constantly our Master used the title, "The Son of man!" If He had chosen, He might always have spoken of Himself as the Son of God, the Everlasting Father, the Wonderful, the Counselor, the Prince of Peace;[197] but behold the lowliness of Jesus! He prefers to call Himself the Son of man. Let us learn a lesson of humility from our Savior; let us never court great titles or proud degrees. There is here, however, a far sweeter thought. Jesus loved manhood so much that He delighted to honor it. Since it is a high honor, and indeed, the greatest dignity of manhood that Jesus is the Son of man, He is wont to display this name, that He may hang royal stars upon the breast of manhood, and show forth the love of God to Abraham's seed. Son of man—whenever He said that word, He shed a halo round the head of Adam's children. Yet there is perhaps a more precious thought still. Jesus Christ called Himself the Son of man to express His oneness and sympathy with His people. He thus reminds us that He is the one whom we may approach without fear. As a man, we may take to Him all our grief and trouble, for He knows them by experience; He Himself has suffered as the "Son of man," He is able to succor and comfort us. All hail, Thou blessed Jesus! inasmuch as Thou art evermore using the sweet name, which acknowledges that Thou art a brother and a near kinsman, it is to us a dear token of Your grace, Your humility, and Your love.

"Oh see how Jesus trusts Himself,
Unto our childish love,
As though by His free ways with us,
Our earnestness to prove!
His sacred name a common word,
On earth He loves to hear;
There is no majesty in Him,
Which love may not come near."

～ *March 26* ～

When He cometh in the glory of His Father with the holy angels (Mark 8:38).

If we have been partakers with Jesus in His shame,[198] we shall be sharers with Him in the luster that shall surround Him when He appears again in glory. Are you, beloved one, with Christ Jesus? Does a vital union knit you to Him? Then you are today with Him in His shame; you have taken up His cross, and gone with Him without the camp bearing His reproach. You will doubtlessly be with Him when the cross is exchanged for the crown. But judge yourself this evening, for if you are not with Him in the regeneration, neither will you be with Him when He will come in His glory. If you start back from the black side of communion, you will not understand its bright, its happy period, when the King shall come, and all His holy angels with Him.[199] What! are *angels with Him*? And yet He did not take up angels—He took up the seed of Abraham. Are the holy angels *with Him*? Come, my soul, if you are indeed His own beloved, you cannot be far from Him. If His friends and His neighbors are called together to see His glory, what do you think if you are married to Him? Shall you be distant? Though it is a day of judgment, yet you cannot be far from that heart, which, having admitted angels into intimacy, has admitted you into union. Has He not said to you, O my soul, "I will betroth you unto Me in righteousness, and in judgment, and in loving kindness?"[200] Have not His own lips said it, "I am married unto you, and My delight is in you?" If the angels, who are but friends and neighbors, shall be with Him, it is abundantly certain that His own beloved Hephzibah, in whom is all His delight, shall be near to Him, and sit at His right hand. Here is a morning star of hope for you, of such exceeding brilliance, that it may well light up the darkest and most desolate experience.

⌁ *March 27* ⌁

And she said, "Truth, Lord: yet the dogs eat of the
crumbs which fall from their master's table"
(Matthew 15:27).

This woman gained comfort in her misery by thinking GREAT THOUGHTS OF CHRIST. The Master had talked about the children's bread. "Now," argued she, "since Thou art the Master of the table of grace, I know that Thou art a generous housekeeper, and there is sure to be abundance of bread on Your table; there will be such an abundance for the children that there will be crumbs to throw on the floor for the dogs, and the children will fare none the worse because the dogs are fed." She thought Him one who kept so good a table that all that she needed would only be a crumb in comparison. Yet remember, what she wanted was to have the devil cast out of her daughter. It was a very great thing to her, but she had such a high esteem of Christ that she said, "It is nothing to Him; it is but a crumb for Christ to give." This is the royal road to comfort. Great thoughts of your sin alone will drive you to despair, but great thoughts of Christ will pilot you into the haven of peace. "My sins are many, but oh! it is nothing to Jesus to take them all away. The weight of my guilt presses me down as a giant's foot would crush a worm, but it is no more than a grain of dust to Him, because He has already borne its curse in His own body on the tree. It will be but a small thing for Him to give me full remission, although it will be an infinite blessing for me to receive it." The woman opens her soul's mouth very wide, expecting great things of Jesus, and He fills it with His love. Dear reader, do the same. She confessed what Christ laid at her door, but she laid fast hold upon Him, and drew arguments even out of His hard words; she believed great things of Him, and she thus overcame Him. SHE WON THE VICTORY BY BELIEVING IN HIM. Her case is an instance of prevailing faith; and if we would conquer like her, we must imitate her tactics.

✄ *March 28* ☞

I will accept you with your sweet savor
(Ezekiel 20:41).

The merits of our great Redeemer are as sweet savor to the Most High. Whether we speak of the active or passive righteousness of Christ, there is an equal fragrance. There was a sweet savor in His active life by which He honored the law of God, and made every precept to glitter like a precious jewel in the pure setting of His own person. Such, too, was His passive obedience, when He endured with unmurmuring submission, hunger and thirst, cold and nakedness, and at length sweat great drops of blood in Gethsemane,[201] gave His back to the smiters, and His cheeks to them that plucked out the hair,[202] and was fastened to the cruel wood, that He might suffer the wrath of God in our behalf. These two things are sweet before the Most High. And for the sake of His doing and His dying, His substitutionary sufferings and His vicarious obedience, the Lord our God accepts us. What preciousness must there be in Him to overcome our want of preciousness! What a sweet savor to put away our ill savor! What a cleansing power in His blood to take away sin such as ours! And what glory in His righteousness to make such unacceptable creatures to be accepted in the Beloved![203] Mark, believer, how sure and unchanging must be our acceptance, since it is *in Him*! Take care that you never doubt your acceptance in Jesus. You cannot be accepted without Christ; but, when you have received His merit, you cannot be unaccepted. Notwithstanding all your doubts, and fears, and sins, Jehovah's gracious eye never looks upon you in anger; though He sees sin in you, in yourself, yet when He looks at you through Christ, He sees no sin. You are always accepted in Christ, are always blessed and dear to the Father's heart. Therefore lift up a song, and as you see the smoking incense of the merit of the Savior coming up, this evening, before the sapphire throne, also let the incense of your praise go up.

I called Him, but He gave me no answer
(Song of Solomon 5:6).

Prayer sometimes tarries, like a petitioner at the gate, until the King comes forth to fill her bosom with the blessings that she seeks. The Lord, when He has given great faith, has been known to try it by long delays. He has suffered His servants' voices to echo in their ears as from a brazen sky. They have knocked at the golden gate, but it has remained immovable, as though it were rusted upon its hinges. Like Jeremiah, they have cried, "Thou hast covered Yourself with a cloud, that our prayer should not pass through." Thus have true saints continued long in patient waiting without reply, not because their prayers were not vehement, nor because they were unaccepted, but because it so pleased Him, who is a Sovereign and who gives according to His own pleasure. If it pleases Him to bid our patience exercise itself, shall He not do as He wills with His own! Beggars must not be choosers either as to time, place, or form. But we must be careful not to take delays in prayer for denials. God's long-dated bills will be punctually honored; we must not suffer Satan to shake our confidence in the God of truth by pointing to our unanswered prayers. Unanswered petitions are not unheard. God keeps a file for our prayers—they are not blown away by the wind; they are treasured in the King's archives. This is a registry in the court of heaven, wherein every prayer is recorded. Tried believer, your Lord has a tear-bottle in which the costly drops of sacred grief are put away, and a book in which your holy groanings are numbered. By-and-by, your suit shall prevail. Can you not be content to wait a little? Will not your Lord's time be better than your time? By-and-by He will comfortably appear, to your soul's joy, and make you put away the sackcloth and ashes of long waiting, and put on the scarlet and fine linen of full fruition.

✒ *March 30* ✒

Let us search and try our ways, and turn again to the Lord (Lamentations 3:40).

The spouse who fondly loves her absent husband longs for his return; a long protracted separation from her lord is a semi-death to her spirit. So it is with souls who love the Savior much. They must see His face; they cannot bear that He should be away upon the mountains of Bether, and no more hold communion with them. A reproaching glance, an uplifted finger will be grievous to loving children, who fear to offend their tender father, and are only happy in his smile. Beloved, it was so once with you. A text of Scripture, a threatening, a touch of the rod of affliction, and you went to your Father's feet, crying, "Show me wherefore Thou contendest with me?"[204] Is it so now? Are you content to follow Jesus afar off? Can you contemplate suspended communion with Christ without alarm? Can you bear to have your Beloved walking contrary to you, because you walk contrary to Him? Have your sins separated you from your God. Is your heart at rest? O let me affectionately warn you, for it is a grievous thing when we can live contentedly without the present enjoyment of the Savior's face. Let us labor to feel what an evil thing this is—little love to our own dying Savior, little joy in our precious Jesus, little fellowship with the Beloved! Hold a true Lent in your souls, while you sorrow over your hardness of heart. Do not stop at sorrow! Remember where you first received salvation. Go at once to the cross. There, and there only, can you get your spirit quickened. No matter how hard, how insensible, how dead we may have become, let us go again in all the rags and poverty and defilement of our natural condition. Let us clasp that cross. Let us look into those languid eyes. Let us bathe in that fountain filled with blood—this will bring back to us our first love. This will restore the simplicity of our faith and the tenderness of our heart.

⇚ *March 31* ⇛

*And Rizpah the daughter of Aiah took sackcloth, and
spread it for her upon the rock, from the beginning of
harvest until water dropped upon them out of heaven,
and suffered neither the birds of the air to rest on them
by day, nor the beasts of the field by night
(2 Samuel 21:10).*

If the love of a woman to her slain sons could make her prolong her
mournful vigil for so long a period, shall we weary of considering
the sufferings of our blessed Lord? She drove away the birds of
prey. Shall we not chase from our meditations those worldly and
sinful thoughts that defile both our minds and the sacred themes
upon which we are occupied? Away, ye birds of evil wing! Leave
the sacrifice alone! She bore the heats of summer, the night dews
and the rains, unsheltered and alone. Sleep was chased from her
weeping eyes. Her heart was too full for slumber. Behold how she
loved her children! Shall Rizpah thus endure, and shall we start
at the first little inconvenience or trial? Are we such cowards that
we cannot bear to suffer with our Lord? She chased away even
the wild beasts with courage unusual in her gender. Will we not
be ready to encounter every foe for Jesus' sake? Her children were
slain by other hands than hers, and yet she wept and watched.
What ought we to do who have by our sins crucified our Lord?
Our obligations are boundless; our love should be fervent and
our repentance thorough. To watch with Jesus should be our
business, to protect His honor our occupation, to abide by His
cross our solace. Those ghastly corpses might well have affrighted
Rizpah, especially by night, but in our Lord, at whose cross-foot
we are sitting, there is nothing revolting, but everything attractive.
Never was living beauty so enchanting as a dying Savior. Jesus,
we will watch with you yet awhile, and do Thou graciously unveil
Yourself to us. Then shall we not sit beneath sackcloth, but in a
royal pavilion.

April

⪢ April 1 ⪡

It is time to seek the Lord. (Hosea 10:12).

This month of April is said to derive its name from the Latin verb *aperio*, which means *to open*, because all the buds and blossoms are now opening, and we have arrived at the gates of the flowery year. Reader, if you are yet unsaved, may your heart, in accord with the universal awakening of nature, be opened to receive the Lord. Every blossoming flower warns you that *it is time to seek the Lord*. Do not be out of tune with nature, but let your heart bud and bloom with holy desires. Do you tell me that the warm blood of youth leaps in your veins? Then, I entreat you, give your vigor to the Lord. It was my unspeakable happiness to be called in early youth, and I could eagerly and gladly praise the Lord every day for it. Salvation is priceless. Let it come when it may, but oh! an early salvation has a double value in it. Young men and maidens, since you may perish before you reach your prime, "It is time to seek the Lord." You, who feel the first signs of decay, quicken your pace. That hollow cough, that hectic flush are warnings that you must not trifle with. For you it is indeed time to seek the Lord. Did I observe a little grey mingled with your once luxurious tresses? Years are stealing on apace, and death is drawing nearer by hasty marches. Let each return of spring arouse you to set your house in order. Dear reader, if you are now advanced in life, let me entreat and implore you to delay no longer. There is a day of grace for you now—be thankful for that, but it is a limited season and grows shorter every time that clock ticks. Here in this silent chamber, on this first night of another month, I speak to you as best I can by paper and ink, and from my inmost soul, as God's servant, I lay before you this warning, "It is time to seek the Lord." Slight not that work; it may be your last call from destruction, the final syllable from the lip of grace.

April 2

He shall see His seed; He shall prolong His days, and the pleasure of the Lord shall prosper in His hand (Isaiah 53:10).

Plead for the speedy fulfillment of this promise, all you who love the Lord. It is easy work to pray when we are grounded and bottomed as to our desires, upon God's own promise. How can He, who gave the Word, refuse to keep it? Unchanging truth cannot demean itself by a lie, and eternal faithfulness cannot degrade itself by neglect. God must bless His Son. His covenant binds Him to it.[205] That which the Spirit prompts us to ask for Jesus is that which God decrees to give Him. Whenever you are praying for the kingdom of Christ, let your eyes behold the dawning of the blessed day which draws near, when the Crucified shall receive His coronation in the place where men rejected Him. Courage to you, who prayerfully work and toil for Christ with success of the very smallest kind. It shall not be so always. Better times are before you. Your eyes cannot see the blissful future. Borrow the telescope of faith. Wipe the misty breath of your doubts from the glass. Look through it and behold the coming glory. Reader, let us ask, *do you* make this your constant prayer? Remember that the same Christ who tells us to say, "Give us this day our daily bread,"[206] had first given us this petition, "Hallowed be Your name; Your kingdom come; Your will be done in earth as it is in heaven." Let not your prayers be all concerning your own sins, your own wants, your own imperfections, your own trials. Rather, let them climb the starry ladder and get up to Christ Himself. Then, as you draw nigh to the blood-sprinkled mercy-seat, offer this prayer continually, "Lord, extend the kingdom of Your dear Son." Such a petition, fervently presented, will elevate the spirit of all your devotions. Mind that you prove the sincerity of your prayer by laboring to promote the Lord's glory.

～ *April 3* ～

All we like sheep have gone astray; we have turned every one to his own way; and the Lord has laid on Him the iniquity of us all (Isaiah 53:6).

Here a confession of sin *common* to all the elect people of God. They have all fallen, and therefore, in common chorus, they all say, from the first who entered heaven to the last who shall enter there, "All we like sheep have gone astray." The confession, while thus unanimous, is also *special* and particular: "We have turned every one to his own way." There is a peculiar sinfulness about every one of the individuals: All are sinful, but each one with some special aggravation not found in his fellow. It is the mark of genuine repentance that while it naturally associates itself with other penitents, also takes up a position of loneliness. "We have turned every one to his own way," is a confession that each man had sinned against light peculiar to himself, or sinned with an aggravation that he could not perceive in others. This confession is *unreserved*; there is neither a word to detract from its force nor a syllable by way of excuse. The confession is a giving up of all pleas of self-righteousness. It is the declaration of men who are consciously guilty—guilty with aggravations, guilty without excuse. They stand with their weapons of rebellion broken into pieces, and cry, "All we like sheep have gone astray; we have turned every one to his own way." Yet we hear no sorrowful wailings attending this confession of sin, for the next sentence makes it almost a song. "The Lord has laid on Him the iniquity of us all." It is the most grievous sentence of the three, but it overflows with comfort. Strange is it that where misery was concentrated, mercy reigned; where sorrow reached her climax, weary souls find rest. The Savior bruised is the healing of bruised hearts. See how the lowliest penitence gives place to assured confidence through simply gazing at Christ on the cross!

☞ *April 4* ☜

*Come ye, and let us go up to the mountain of the Lord
(Isaiah 2:3).*

It is exceedingly beneficial to our souls to mount above this present evil world to something nobler and better. The cares of this world and the deceitfulness of riches are apt to choke everything good within us, and we grow fretful, desponding, perhaps proud and carnal.[207] It is well for us to cut down these thorns and briers, for heavenly seed sown among them is not likely to yield a harvest. Where shall we find a better sickle with which to cut them down than communion with God and the things of the kingdom?[208] In the valleys of Switzerland many of the inhabitants are deformed, and all wear a sickly appearance, for the atmosphere is charged with miasma, and is close and stagnant. But farther up on the mountain, you find a hardy race, who breathes the clear, fresh air as it blows from the virgin snows of the Alpine summits. It would be well if the dwellers in the valley could frequently leave their abodes among the marshes and the fever mists, and inhale the bracing element upon the hills. It is to such an exploit of climbing that I invite you this evening. May the Spirit of God assist us to leave the mists of fear and the fevers of anxiety, and all the ills that gather in this valley of earth, and to ascend the mountains of anticipated joy and blessedness. May God the Holy Spirit cut the cords that keep us here below, and assist us to mount! We sit too often like chained eagles fastened to the rock, but unlike the eagle, we begin to love our chain, and would, perhaps, if it came really to the test, be loath to have it snapped. May God now grant us grace, if we cannot escape from the chain as to our flesh, yet to do so as to our spirits; and leaving the body, like a servant, at the foot of the hill, may our soul, like Abraham, attain the top of the mountain, there to indulge in communion with the Most High.

◄ *April 5* ►

Before honor is humility (Proverbs 15:33).

Humiliation of soul always brings a positive blessing with it. If we empty our hearts of self God will fill them with His love. He who desires close communion with Christ should remember the Word of the Lord, "To this man will I look, even to him that is poor and of a contrite spirit, and trembleth at My word."[209] Stoop if you would climb to heaven. Do we not say of Jesus, "He descended that He might ascend?"[210] So must you. You must grow downward, that you may grow upward; for the sweetest fellowship with heaven is to be had by humble souls, and by them alone. God will deny no blessing to a thoroughly humbled spirit. "Blessed are the poor in spirit: for theirs is the kingdom of heaven,"[211] with all its riches and treasures. The whole exchequer of God shall be made over by deed of gift to the soul that is humble enough to be able to receive it without growing proud because of it. God blesses us all up to the full measure and extremity of what it is safe for Him to do. If you do not get a blessing, it is because it is not safe for you to have one. If our heavenly Father were to let your unhumbled spirit win a victory in His holy war, you would pilfer the crown for yourself. Meeting with a fresh enemy you would fall a victim. So you are kept low for your own safety. When a man is sincerely humble, and never ventures to touch so much as a grain of the praise, there is scarcely any limit to what God will do for him. Humility makes us ready to be blessed by the God of all grace, and fits us to deal efficiently with our fellow men. True humility is a flower, which will adorn any garden. This is a sauce with which you may season every dish of life, and you will find an improvement in every case. Whether it be prayer or praise, whether it be work or suffering, the genuine salt of humility cannot be used in excess.

In the name of the Lord I will destroy them
(Psalm 118:12).

Our Lord Jesus, by His death, did not purchase a right to a part of us only, but to the entire man. He contemplated in His passion the sanctification of us wholly: spirit, soul, and body,[212] that in this triple kingdom He Himself might reign supreme without a rival. It is the business of the newborn nature, which God has given to the regenerate to assert the rights of the Lord Jesus Christ. My soul, so far as you are a child of God, you must conquer all the rest of yourself, which yet remains unblessed. You must subdue all your powers and passions to the silver scepter of Jesus' gracious reign. And you must never be satisfied till He who is King by purchase becomes also King by gracious coronation, and reigns in you supremely. Seeing, then, that sin has no right to any part of us, we go about a good and lawful warfare when we seek, in the name of God, to drive it out. O my body, you are a member of Christ. Shall I tolerate your subjection to the prince of darkness? O my soul, Christ has suffered for your sins, and redeemed you with His most precious blood. Shall I suffer your memory to become a storehouse of evil, or your passions to be firebrands of iniquity? Shall I surrender my judgment to be perverted by error, or my will to be led in fetters of iniquity? No, my soul, you are Christ's, and sin has no right to you.[213] Be courageous concerning this, O Christian! be not dispirited, as though your spiritual enemies could never be destroyed. You are able to overcome them—not in your own strength—the weakest of them would be too much for you in that. But you can and shall overcome them through the blood of the Lamb.[214] Do not ask, "How shall I dispossess them, for they are greater and mightier than I?" but go to the strong for strength. Wait humbly upon God, and the mighty God of Jacob will surely come to the rescue, and you shall sing of victory through His grace.

⋙ *April 7* ⋘

Deliver me from bloodguiltiness, O God, Thou God of my salvation; and my tongue shall sing aloud of Your righteousness (Psalm 51:14).

In this SOLEMN CONFESSION, it is pleasing to observe that David plainly names his sin. He does not call it manslaughter, nor speak of it as an imprudence by which an unfortunate accident occurred to a worthy man, but he calls it by its true name: bloodguiltiness. He did not actually kill the husband of Bathsheba, but still it was planned in David's heart that Uriah should be slain, and he was, before the Lord, his murderer.[215] Learn in confession to be honest with God. Do not give fair names to foul sins; call them what you will, they will smell no sweeter. What God sees them to be, that do you labor to feel them to be and with all openness of heart, acknowledge their real character. Observe that David was evidently oppressed with the heinousness of his sin. It is easy to use words, but it is difficult to feel their meaning. The fifty-first Psalm is the photograph of a contrite spirit. Let us seek after the like brokenness of heart; for however excellent our words may be, if our heart is not conscious of the hell-deservingness of sin, we cannot expect to find forgiveness. Our text has in it AN EARNEST PRAYER—it is addressed to the God of *salvation*. It is His prerogative to forgive; it is His very name and office to save those who seek His face. Better still, the text calls Him the God of *my* salvation. Yes, blessed be His name, while I am yet going to Him through Jesus' blood, I can rejoice in the God of *my* salvation. The psalmist ends with A COMMENDABLE VOW: If God will deliver him, he will sing—nay, more, he will "sing aloud." Who can sing in any other style of such a mercy as this! But note the subject of the song—"YOUR RIGHTEOUSNESS." We must sing of the finished work of a precious Savior; and he who knows most of forgiving love will sing the loudest.

ᗔ *April 8* ᗗ

I will fear no evil: for Thou art with me (Psalm 23:4).

Behold, how independent of outward circumstances the Holy Ghost can make the Christian! What a bright light may shine within us when it is all dark without! How firm, how happy, how calm, how peaceful we may be when the world shakes to and fro, and the pillars of the earth are removed! Even death itself, with all its terrible influences, has no power to suspend the music of a Christian's heart, but rather makes that music become more sweet, more clear, more heavenly, till the last kind act that death can do is to let the earthly strain melt into the heavenly chorus, the temporal joy into the eternal bliss! Let us have confidence, then, in the blessed Spirit's power to comfort us. Dear reader, are you looking forward to poverty? Fear not; the divine Spirit can give you, in your want, a greater plenty than the rich have in their abundance. You know not what joys may be stored up for you in the cottage around which grace will plant the roses of content. Are you conscious of a growing failure of your bodily powers? Do you expect to suffer long nights of languishing and days of pain? O be not sad! That bed may become a throne to you. You little know how every pang that shoots through your body may be a refining fire to consume your worthlessness—a beam of glory to light up the secret parts of your soul. Are the eyes growing dim? Jesus will be your light. Do the ears fail you? Jesus' name will be your soul's best music, and His person your dear delight. Socrates used to say, "Philosophers can be happy without music;" and Christians can be happier than philosophers when all outward causes of rejoicing are withdrawn. In You, my God, my heart shall triumph, come what may of ills without! By your power, O blessed Spirit, my heart shall be exceeding glad, though all things should fail me here below.[216]

Your gentleness has made me great (Psalm 18:35).

The words are capable of being translated, "Your *goodness* has made me great." David gratefully ascribed all his greatness not to his own goodness, but the goodness of God. "Your *providence*," is another reading; and providence is nothing more than goodness in action. Goodness is the bud of which providence is the flower, or goodness is the seed of which providence is the harvest. Some render it, "Your *help*," which is but another word for providence; providence being the firm ally of the saints, aiding them in the service of their Lord. Or again, "Your *humility* has made me great." "Your *condescension*" may, perhaps, serve as a comprehensive reading, combining the ideas mentioned, including that of *humility*. It is God's making Himself little that is the cause of our being made great. We are so little that if God should manifest His greatness without condescension, we should be trampled under His feet; but God, who must stoop to view the skies, and bow to see what angels do, turns His eye yet lower and looks to the lowly and contrite, and makes them great. There are yet other readings, as for instance, the Septuagint, which reads, "Your discipline"—Your fatherly correction—"has made me great;" while the Chaldee paraphrase reads, "Your word has increased me." Still the idea is the same. David ascribes all his own greatness to the condescending goodness of his Father in heaven. May this sentiment be echoed in our hearts this evening while we cast our crowns at Jesus' feet, and cry, "Your gentleness has made me great." How marvelous has been our experience of God's gentleness! How gentle have been His corrections! How gentle His forbearance! How gentle His teachings! How gentle His drawings! Meditate upon this theme, O believer. Let gratitude be awakened; let humility be deepened; let love be quickened before you fall asleep tonight.

For there stood by me this night the angel of God
(Acts 27:23).

Tempest and long darkness, coupled with imminent risk of shipwreck, had brought the crew of the vessel into a sad case. One man alone among them remained perfectly calm, and by his word, the rest were reassured. Paul was the only man who had heart enough to say, "Sirs, be of good cheer." There were veteran Roman legionaries on board, and brave old mariners, and yet their poor Jewish prisoner had more spirit than they all. He had a secret Friend who kept his courage up. The Lord Jesus dispatched a heavenly messenger to whisper words of consolation in the ear of His faithful servant. Therefore he wore a shining countenance and spoke like a man at ease. If we fear the Lord, we may look for timely interpositions when our case is at its worst. Angels are not kept from us by storms, or hindered by darkness. Seraphs think it no humiliation to visit the poorest of the heavenly family. If angels' visits are few and far between at ordinary times, they shall be frequent in our nights of tempest and tossing. Friends may drop from us when we are under pressure, but our relationships with the inhabitants of the angelic world shall be more abundant; and in the strength of love-words, brought to us from the throne by the way of Jacob's ladder, we shall be strong to do exploits.[217] Dear reader, is this an hour of distress with you? Then ask for peculiar help. Jesus is the angel of the covenant, and if His presence is now earnestly sought, it will not be denied. What that presence brings in heart-cheer those remember who, like Paul, have had the angel of God standing by them in a night of storm, when anchors would no longer hold, and rocks were nigh.

"O angel of my God, be near,
Amid the darkness hush my fear;
Loud roars the wild tempestuous sea,
Your presence, Lord, shall comfort me."

⊸ *April 11* ⊱

Look upon mine affliction and my pain; and forgive all my sins (Psalm 25:18).

It is well for us when prayers about our sorrows are linked with pleas concerning our sins—when, being under God's hand, we are not wholly taken up with our pain, but remember our offenses against God. It is well, also, to take both sorrow and sin to the same place. It was to God that David carried his sorrow. It was to God that David confessed his sin. Observe, then, we must take our sorrows to God. Even your little sorrows you may roll upon God, for He counteth the hairs of your head.[218] Your great sorrows you may commit to Him, for He holdeth the ocean in the hollow of His hand. Go to Him, whatever your present trouble may be, and you shall find Him able and willing to relieve you. But we must take our sins to God, too. We must carry them to the cross, that the blood may fall upon them, to purge away their guilt, and to destroy their defiling power. The special lesson of the text is this: that we are to go to the Lord with sorrows and with sins in the right spirit. Note that all David asks concerning his sorrow is, "Look upon mine affliction and my pain," but the next petition is vastly more express, definite, decided, and plain—"Forgive all my sins." Many sufferers would have put it, "Remove my affliction and my pain, and look at my sins." But David does not say so; he cries, "Lord, as for my affliction and my pain, I will not dictate to Your wisdom. Lord, look at them, I will leave them to You, I should be glad to have my pain removed, but do as Thou wilt. But as for my sins, Lord, I know what I want with them; I must have them forgiven. I cannot endure to lie under their curse for a moment." A Christian counts sorrow lighter in the scale than sin; he can bear that his troubles should continue, but he cannot support the burden of his transgressions.[219]

147

❧ *April 12* ❧

The king's garden (Nehemiah 3:15).

Mention of the king's garden by Nehemiah brings to mind the *paradise*, which the King of kings prepared for Adam. Sin has utterly ruined that fair abode of all delights, and driven forth the children of men to till the ground, which yields thorns and briers unto them.[220] My soul, remember the fall, for it was *your* fall. Weep much because the Lord of love was so shamefully ill treated by the head of the human race, of which you are a member, as undeserving as any. Behold how dragons and demons dwell on this fair earth, which once was a garden of delights. See yonder another King's garden, which the King waters with His bloody sweat—Gethsemane, whose bitter herbs are sweeter far to renewed souls than even Eden's luscious fruits. There the mischief of the serpent in the first garden was undone.[221] There the curse was lifted from earth, and borne by the woman's promised seed.[222] My soul, bethink you much of the agony and the passion, resort to the garden of the olive-press, and view your great Redeemer rescuing you from your lost estate. This is the garden of gardens indeed, wherein the soul may see the guilt of sin and the power of love, two sights which surpass all others. Is there no other King's garden? Yes, *my heart*, you are, or should be, such. How do the flowers flourish? Do any choice fruits appear? Does the King walk within and rest in the bowers of my spirit? Let me see that the plants are trimmed and watered, and the mischievous foxes hunted out. Come, Lord, and let the heavenly wind blow at Your coming, that the spices of Your garden may flow abroad. Nor must I forget the King's garden of *the Church*. O Lord, send prosperity unto it. Rebuild her walls, nourish her plants, ripen her fruits, and from the huge wilderness, reclaim the barren waste, and make thereof "a King's garden."

⇜ *April 13* ⇝

And he shall put his hand upon the head of the burnt-offering; and it shall be accepted for him to make atonement for him (Leviticus 1:4).

Our Lord's being made "sin for us"[223] is set forth here by the very significant transfer of sin to the bull, which was made by the elders of the people.[224] The laying of the hand was not a mere touch of contact, for in some other places of Scripture the original word means "leaning heavily," as in the expression, "Your wrath lieth hard upon me" (Psalm 88:7). Surely this is the very essence and nature of faith, which doth not only bring us into contact with the great Substitute, but teaches us to lean upon Him with all the burden of our guilt. Jehovah made to meet upon the head of the Substitute all the offenses of His covenant people, but each one of the chosen is brought personally to ratify this solemn covenant act, when by grace he is enabled by faith to lay his hand upon the head of the "Lamb slain from before the foundation of the world."[225] Believer, do you remember that rapturous day when you first realized pardon through Jesus the sin-bearer? Can you not make glad confession, and join with the writer in saying, "My soul recalls her day of deliverance with delight. Laden with guilt and full of fears, I saw my Savior as my Substitute, and I laid my hand upon Him. Oh! how timidly at first, but courage grew and confidence was confirmed until I leaned my soul entirely upon Him; and now it is my unceasing joy to know that my sins are no longer imputed to me,[226] but laid on Him, and like the debts of the wounded traveler, Jesus, like the good Samaritan, has said of all my future sinfulness, 'Set that to My account.'"[227] Blessed discovery! Eternal solace of a grateful heart!

> "My numerous sins transferr'd to Him,
> Shall never more be found,
> Lost in His blood's atoning stream,
> Where every crime is drown'd!"

Say ye to the righteous, that it shall be well with him
(Isaiah 3:10).

It *is well with the righteous* ALWAYS. If it had said, "Say ye to the righteous, that it is well with him in his prosperity," we must have been thankful for so great a boon, for prosperity is an hour of peril, and it is a gift from heaven to be secured from its snares. Or if it had been written, "It is well with him when under persecution,"[228] we must have been thankful for so sustaining an assurance, for persecution is hard to bear. But when no time is mentioned, all time is included. God's "shalls" must be understood always in their largest sense. From the beginning of the year to the end of the year, from the first gathering of evening shadows until the daystar shines, in all conditions and under all circumstances, it shall be well with the righteous.[229] It is so well with him that we could not imagine it to be better. He is *well fed*, for he feeds upon the flesh and blood of Jesus. He is *well clothed*, for he wears the imputed righteousness of Christ. He is *well housed*, for he dwells in God. He is *well married*, for his soul is knit in bonds of marriage union to Christ. He is *well provided for*, for the Lord is his Shepherd. He is well endowed, for heaven is his inheritance. It is well with the righteous—well upon divine authority; the mouth of God speaks the comforting assurance. O beloved, if God declares that all is well, ten thousand devils may declare it to be ill, but we laugh them all to scorn. Blessed be God for a faith, which enables us to believe God when the creatures contradict Him. It is, says the Word, at all times well with you, you righteous one. Then, beloved, if you cannot see it, let God's word stand you in stead of sight;[230] yea, believe it on divine authority more confidently than if your eyes and your feelings told it to you. Whom God blesses is blessed indeed, and what His lip declares is truth most sure and steadfast.

ᚼ April 15 ᚾ

Lift them up for ever (Psalm 28:9).

God's people need lifting up. They are very heavy by nature. They have no wings, or, if they have, they are like the dove of old, which lay among the pots; and they need divine grace to make them mount on wings covered with silver and feathers of yellow gold. By nature sparks fly upward, but the sinful souls of men fall downward. O Lord, "lift them up forever!" David himself said, "Unto You, O God, do I lift up my soul,"[231] and he here feels the necessity that other men's souls should be lifted up as well as his own. When you ask this blessing for yourself, forget not to seek it for others, also. There are three ways in which God's people require to be lifted up. *They require being elevated in character.* Lift them up, O Lord; do not suffer Your people to be like the world's people! The world lieth in the wicked one; lift them out of it![232] The world's people are looking after silver and gold, seeking their own pleasures and the gratification of their lusts. Lord, lift Your people up above all this; keep them from being "muck-rakers," as John Bunyan calls the man who was always scraping after gold! Set their hearts upon their risen Lord and the heavenly heritage! Moreover, believers need to be prospered in conflict. In the battle, if they seem to fall, O Lord, be pleased to give them the victory. If the foot of the foe is upon their necks for a moment, help them to grasp the sword of the Spirit, and eventually to win the battle. Lord, lift up Your children's spirits in the day of conflict; let them not sit in the dust, mourning forever. Suffer not the adversary to vex them sore and make them fret, but if they have been like Hannah, persecuted, let them sing of the mercy of a delivering God. We may also ask our Lord to lift them up at the last! Lift them up by taking them home. Lift their bodies from the tomb, and raise their souls to Your eternal kingdom in glory.

～ April 16 ～

And his hands were steady until the going down
of the sun (Exodus 17:12).

So mighty was the prayer of Moses that all depended upon it. The petitions of Moses discomfited the enemy more than the fighting of Joshua. Yet both were needed. No, in the soul's conflict, force and fervor, decision and devotion, and valor and vehemence must join their forces, and all will be well. You must wrestle with your sin, but the major part of the wrestling must be done alone in private with God. Prayer, like Moses', holds up the token of the covenant before the Lord. The rod was the emblem of God's working with Moses, the symbol of God's government in Israel. Learn, O pleading saint, to hold up the promise and the oath of God before Him. The Lord cannot deny His own declarations. Hold up the rod of promise, and have what you will.[233] Moses grew weary, and then his friends assisted him. When at any time your prayer flags, let faith support one hand, and let holy hope uplift the other. Do this, and prayer, seating itself upon the stone of Israel, the rock of our salvation, will persevere and prevail. Beware of faintness in devotion;[234] if Moses felt it, who can escape? It is far easier to fight with sin in public than to pray against it in private. It is remarked that Joshua never grew weary in the fighting, but Moses grew weary in the praying. The more spiritual an exercise, the more difficult it is for flesh and blood to maintain it. Let us cry, then, for special strength, and may the Spirit of God, who helps our infirmities,[235] as He allowed help to Moses, enable us like him to continue with our hands steady "until the going down of the sun," till the evening of life is over, till we shall come to the rising of a better sun in the land where prayer is swallowed up in praise.

⊸ *April 17* ⊱

We would see Jesus (John 12:21).

Evermore the worldling's cry is, "Who will show us any good?" He seeks satisfaction in earthly comforts, enjoyments, and riches. But the quickened sinner knows of only one good. "O that I knew where I might find HIM!" When he is truly awakened to feel his guilt, if you could pour the gold of India at his feet, he would say, "Take it away. I want to find HIM." It is a blessed thing for a man, that he has brought his desires into a focus, so that they all center in one object. When he has fifty different desires, his heart resembles a lake of stagnant water, spread out into a marsh, breeding miasma and pestilence. But when all his desires are brought into one channel, his heart becomes like a river of pure water, running swiftly to fertilize the fields. Happy is he who has one desire, if that one desire is set on Christ, though it may not yet have been realized. If Jesus is a soul's desire, it is a blessed sign of divine work within. Such a man will never be content with mere ordinances. He will say, "I want Christ. I *must* have Him—mere ordinances are of no use to me. I want *Himself*. Do not offer me these. You offer me the empty pitcher while I am dying of thirst; give me water, or I die. Jesus is my soul's desire. I would see Jesus!"[236] Is this your condition, my reader, at this moment? Have you only one desire, and is that after Christ? Then you are not far from the kingdom of heaven. Have you only one wish in your heart—that you may be washed from all your sins in Jesus' blood? Can you really say, "I would give all I have to be a Christian; I would give up everything I have and hope for, if I might only feel that I have an interest in Christ"? Then, despite all your fears, be of good cheer, the Lord loves you, and you shall come out into daylight soon, and rejoice in the liberty with which Christ makes men free.

☞ *April 18* ☜

And thou saidst, I will surely do you good
(Genesis 32:12).

When Jacob was on the other side of the brook Jabbok, and Esau was coming with armed men, he earnestly sought God's protection. He pleaded for this reason: "And Thou saidst, I will surely do you good." Oh, the force of that plea! He was holding God to His word—"Thou saidst." The attribute of God's faithfulness is a splendid horn of the altar to lay hold upon, but the promise, which has in it the attribute and something more, is a yet mightier holdfast—"Thou saidst, I will surely do you good." And has *He* said, and shall He not do it?[237] "Let God be true, and every man a liar." Shall not *He* be true? Shall *He* not keep His word? Shall not every word that cometh out of His lips stand fast and be fulfilled? Solomon, at the opening of the temple, used this same mighty plea. He pleaded with God to remember the word, which He had spoken to his father David, and to bless that place. When a man gives a promissory note, his honor is engaged; he signs his hand, and he must discharge it when the due time comes, or else he loses credit. It shall never be said that God dishonors His bills. The credit of the Most High never was impeached, and never shall be. He is punctual to the moment. He never is before His time, but He never is behind it. Search God's word through, and compare it with the experience of God's people, and you shall find the two tally from the first to the last. Many a gray-bearded patriarch has said with Joshua, "Not one thing has failed of all the good things which the Lord your God spake concerning you; all are come to pass."[238] If you have a divine promise, you need not plead it with an "if." You may urge it with certainty. The Lord meant to fulfill the promise, or He would not have given it. God does not give His words merely to quiet us and to keep us hopeful for a while with the intention of putting us off at last. When He speaks, it is because He means to do as He has said.

ᘒ *April 19* ᘒ

The Amen (Revelation 3:14).

The word AMEN solemnly confirms that which went before; and Jesus is the great Confirmer; immutable, forever is "the Amen" in all *His promises*. *Sinner*, I would comfort you with this reflection. Jesus Christ said, "Come unto me all ye that labor and are heavy laden, and I will give you rest."[239] If you come to Him, He will say "Amen" in your soul. His promise shall be true *to you*. He said in the days of His flesh, "The bruised reed I will not break."[240] O you poor, broken, bruised heart, if you comest to Him, He will say "Amen" to you, and that shall be true in your soul as in hundreds of cases in bygone years. *Christian*, is not this very comforting to you also, that there is not a word that has gone out of the Savior's lips that He has ever retracted? The words of Jesus shall stand when heaven and earth shall pass away.[241] If you get a hold of only half a promise, you shall find it true. Beware of him who is called "Clip-promise," who will destroy much of the comfort of God's word. Jesus is Yea and Amen in all *His offices*. He was a Priest to pardon and cleanse once, He is Amen as Priest still. He was a King to rule and reign for His people, and to defend them with His mighty arm. He is an Amen King, the same still. He was a Prophet of old, to foretell good things to come. His lips are most sweet and drop with honey still—He is an Amen Prophet. He is Amen as to the merit of His blood. He is Amen as to His righteousness. That sacred robe shall remain most fair and glorious when nature shall decay. He is Amen in every single title which He bears; your Husband, never seeking a divorce; your Friend, sticking closer than a brother;[242] your Shepherd, with you in death's dark vale; your Help and your Deliverer; your Castle and your High Tower; the Horn of your Strength, your Confidence, your Joy, your All in All, and your Yea and Amen in all.

ᴀ April 20 ᴀ

Fight the Lord's battles (1 Samuel 18:17).

The sacramental host of God's elect is warring still on earth, Jesus Christ being the Captain of their salvation. He has said, "Lo! I am with you always, even unto the end of the world."[243] Hark to the shouts of war! Now let the people of God stand fast in their ranks, and let no man's heart fail him. It is true that just now in England the battle is turned against us, and unless the Lord Jesus shall lift His sword, we know not what may become of the church of God in this land; but let us be of good courage and play the man. There never was a day when Protestantism seemed to tremble more in the scales than now that a fierce effort is making to restore the Romish antichrist to his ancient seat. We greatly want a bold voice and a strong hand to preach and publish the old gospel for which martyrs bled and confessors died. The Savior is, by His Spirit, still on earth; let this cheer us. He is ever in the midst of the fight, and therefore the battle is not doubtful. And as the conflict rages, what a sweet satisfaction it is to know that the Lord Jesus, in His office as our great Intercessor, is prevalently pleading for His people! O anxious gazer, look not so much at the battle below, for there you shalt be enshrouded in smoke and amazed with garments rolled in blood; but lift your eyes yonder where the Savior lives and pleads, for while He intercedes, the cause of God is safe. Let us fight as if it all depended upon us, but let us look up and know that all depends upon Him. Now, by the lilies of Christian purity and by the roses of the Savior's atonement, by the roes and by the hinds of the field, we charge you who are lovers of Jesus, to do valiantly in the Holy War, for truth and righteousness, for the kingdom and crown jewels of your Master. Onward! "For the battle is not yours but God's."[244]

April 21

Who is even at the right hand of God (Romans 8:34).

He, who was once despised and rejected of men,[245] now occupies the honorable position of a beloved and honored Son. The right hand of God is *the place of majesty and favor*.[246] Our Lord Jesus is His people's representative. When He died for them, they had rest. He rose again for them; they had liberty. When He sat down at His Father's right hand, they had favor and honor, and dignity. The raising and elevation of Christ is the elevation, the acceptance, and enshrinement, the glorifying of all His people, for He is their head and representative. This sitting at the right hand of God, then, is to be viewed as the acceptance of the person of the Surety, the reception of the Representative, and therefore, the acceptance of *our* souls. O saint, see in this your sure freedom from condemnation. "Who is he that condemneth?"[247] Who shall condemn the men who are in Jesus at the right hand of God? The right hand is *the place of power*. Christ at the right hand of God has all power in heaven and in earth.[248] Who shall fight against the people who have such power vested in their Captain? O my soul, what can destroy you if Omnipotence is your helper? If the shield of the Almighty covers you, what sword can smite you? Rest you secure. If Jesus is your all-prevailing King, and has trodden your enemies beneath His feet; if sin, death, and hell are all vanquished by Him, and you are represented in Him, by no possibility can you be destroyed.[249]

"Jesus' tremendous name, Puts all our foes to flight:
Jesus, the meek, the angry Lamb, A Lion is in fight.
By all hell's host withstood; We all hell's host overthrow;
And conquering them, through Jesus' blood,
We still to conquer go."

April 22

Thou shalt not be afraid for the terror by night
(Psalm 91:5).

What is this terror? It may be the cry of fire, or the noise of thieves, or fancied appearances, or the shriek of sudden sickness or death. We live in the world of death and sorrow; we may therefore look for ills as well in the night-watches as beneath the glare of the broiling sun. Nor should this alarm us, for no matter what the terror may be, the promise is that the believer shall not be afraid. Why should he? Let us put it more closely: Why should we? God our Father is here, and will be here all through the lonely hours. He is an almighty Watcher, a sleepless Guardian, and a faithful Friend.[250] Nothing can happen without His direction, for even hell itself is under His control. Darkness is not dark to Him. He has promised to be a wall of fire around His people—and who can break through such a barrier? Worldlings may well be afraid, for they have an angry God above them, a guilty conscience within them, and a yawning hell beneath them; but we who rest in Jesus are saved from all these through rich mercy. If we give way to foolish fear, we dishonor our profession and lead others to doubt the reality of godliness.[251] We ought to be afraid of being afraid, lest we should vex the Holy Spirit by foolish distrust.[252] Down, then, ye dismal forebodings and groundless apprehensions. God has not forgotten to be gracious or shut up His tender mercies. It may be night in the soul, but there need be no terror, for the God of love changes not. Children of light may walk in darkness, but they are not therefore cast away, nay, they are now enabled to prove their adoption by trusting in their heavenly Father as hypocrites cannot do.

"Though the night be dark and dreary, Darkness cannot hide
from You; Thou art He, who, never weary,
Watchest where Your people be."

Lo, in the midst of the throne … stood a Lamb as it had been slain (Revelation 5:6).

Why should our exalted Lord appear in His wounds in glory? The wounds of Jesus are His glories, His jewels, and His sacred ornaments. To the eye of the believer, Jesus is passing fair because He is "white and ruddy"—white with innocence and ruddy with His own blood. We see Him as the lily of matchless purity, and as the rose crimsoned with His own gore. Christ is lovely upon Olivet and Tabor, and by the sea, but oh! there never was such a matchless Christ as He that did hang upon the cross. There we beheld all His beauties in perfection, all His attributes developed, all His love drawn out, all His character expressed. Beloved, the wounds of Jesus are far more fair in our eyes than all the splendor and pomp of kings. The thorny crown is more than an imperial diadem. It is true that He bears not now the scepter of reed, but there was a glory in it that never flashed from scepter of gold. Jesus wears the appearance of a slain Lamb as His court dress in which He wooed our souls, and redeemed them by His complete atonement. Nor are these only the ornaments of Christ. They are the *trophies* of His love and of His victory. He has divided the spoil with the strong. He has redeemed for Himself a great multitude that no man can number, and these scars are the memorials of the fight. Ah! if Christ thus loves to retain the thought of His sufferings for His people, *how precious should his wounds be to us*!

"Behold how every wound of His, A precious balm distils, Which heals the scars that sin had made, And cures all mortal ills. Those wounds are mouths that preach His grace; The ensigns of His love; The seals of our expected bliss, In paradise above."

The flowers appear on the earth; the time of the singing of birds is come, and the voice of the turtle is heard in our land (Song of Solomon 2:12).

Sweet is the season of spring. The long and dreary winter helps us to appreciate its genial warmth, and promise of summer enhances its present delights. After periods of depression of spirit, it is delightful to behold again the light of the Sun of Righteousness; then our slumbering graces rise from their lethargy like the crocus and the daffodil from their beds of earth. Then is our heart made merry with delicious notes of gratitude far more melodious than the warbling of birds, and the comforting assurance of peace, infinitely more delightful than the turtle's note, is heard within the soul. Now is the time for the soul to seek communion with her Beloved; now must she rise from her native sordidness, and come away from her old associations. If we do not hoist the sail when the breeze is favorable, we shall be blameworthy. Times of refreshing ought not to pass over us unimproved. When Jesus Himself visits us in tenderness and entreats us to arise, can we be so base as to refuse His request? He has Himself risen that He may draw us after Him. He now by His Holy Spirit has revived us, that we may, in newness of life, ascend into the heavenlies, and hold communion with Him. Let our wintry state suffice us for coldness and indifference. When the Lord creates a spring within, let our sap flow with vigor, and our branch blossom with high resolve. O Lord, if it is not springtime in my chilly heart, I pray You make it so, for I am heartily weary of living at a distance from You. Oh! the long and dreary winter, when wilt Thou bring it to an end? Come, Holy Spirit, and renew my soul! Quicken Thou me! Restore me and have mercy on me! This very night I would earnestly implore the Lord to take pity upon His servant, and send me a happy revival of spiritual life!

☞ *April 25* ☞

If any man hear My voice, and open the door, I will come in to him (Revelation 3:20).

What is your desire this evening? Is it set upon heavenly things? Do you long to enjoy the high doctrine of eternal love? Do you desire liberty in very close communion with God? Do you aspire to know the heights, depths, lengths, and breadths?[253] Then you must draw near to Jesus; you must get a clear sight of Him in His preciousness and completeness; you must view Him in His work, in His offices, in His person. He, who understands Christ, receives an anointing from the Holy One, by which He knows all things. Christ is the great master key of all the chambers of God. There is no treasure house of God that will not open and yield up all its wealth to the soul that lives near to Jesus. Are you saying, "O that He would dwell in my bosom?" "Would that He would make my heart His dwelling-place forever?" Open the door, beloved, and He will come into your souls. He has long been knocking, and all with this object: that He may dine with you, and you with Him. *He dines with you* because you provide the house or the heart. *You dine with Him* because He brings the provision. He could not dine with you if it were not in your heart (you finding the house). Nor could you dine with Him, for you would have a bare cupboard if He did not bring provision with Him. Fling wide, then, the portals of your soul. He will come with that love which you long to feel; He will come with that joy into which you cannot work your poor depressed spirit; He will bring the peace which now you have not; He will come with His flagons of wine and sweet apples of love, and cheer you till you have no other sickness but that of "love o'erpowering, love divine."[254] Only open the door to Him, drive out His enemies, give Him the keys of your heart, and He will dwell there forever. Oh, wondrous love, that brings such a guest to dwell in such a heart!

⋙ *April 26* ⋘

Blessed is he that watcheth (Revelation 16:15).

"We die daily," said the apostle.[255] This was the life of the early Christians; they went everywhere with their lives in their hands. We are not in this day called to pass through the same fearful persecutions. If we were, the Lord would give us grace to bear the test, but the tests of Christian life, though presently and outwardly not so terrible, are yet more likely to overcome us than even those of the fiery age. We have to bear the sneer of the world—that is little. Its blandishments, its soft words, its oily speeches, its fawning, and its hypocrisy are far worse. Our danger is that we grow rich and become proud, that we give ourselves up to the fashions of this present evil world and lose our faith. Or if wealth is not the trial, worldly care is quite as mischievous. If we cannot be torn in pieces by the roaring lion,[256] we may be hugged to death by the bear. The devil little cares which it is, so long as he destroys our love for Christ and our confidence in Him. I fear that the Christian church is far more likely to lose her integrity in these soft and silken days than in those rougher times. We must be awake now, for we traverse the enchanted ground, and are most likely to fall asleep at our own peril, unless our faith in Jesus is a reality, and our love for Jesus a vehement flame. Many in these days of easy profession are likely to prove tares and not wheat: hypocrites with fair masks on their faces, but not the trueborn children of the living God. Christian, do not think that these are times in which you can dispense with watchfulness or with holy ardor; you need these things more than ever. And may God the eternal Spirit display His omnipotence in you, that you may be able to say, in all these softer things, as well as in the rougher, "We are more than conquerors through Him that loved us."[257]

✒ April 27 ✒

The Lord is King for ever and ever (Psalm 10:16).

Jesus Christ is no despotic claimant of *divine right*, but He is really and truly the Lord's anointed! "It has pleased the Father that in Him should all fullness dwell."[258] God has given to Him all power and all authority.[259] As the Son of man, He is now head over all things to His church, and He reigns over heaven, and earth, and hell, with the keys of life and death at His girdle. Certain princes have delighted to call themselves kings by the *popular will*, and certainly our Lord Jesus Christ is such in His church. If it could be put to the vote whether He should be King in the church, every believing heart would crown Him. O that we could crown Him more gloriously than we do! We would count no expense to be wasted that could glorify Christ. Suffering would be pleasure, and loss would be gain, if thereby we could surround His brow with brighter crowns and make Him more glorious in the eyes of men and angels. Yes, He shall reign. Long live the King! All hail to You, King Jesus! Go forth, you virgin souls who love your Lord. Bow at His feet. Strew His way with the lilies of your love and the roses of your gratitude. "Bring forth the royal diadem, and crown Him Lord of all." Moreover, our Lord Jesus is King in Zion by right of conquest: He has taken and carried by storm the hearts of His people, and has slain their enemies who held them in cruel bondage. In the Red Sea of His own blood, our Redeemer has drowned the Pharaoh of our sins. Shall He not be King in Jeshurun? He has delivered us from the iron yoke and heavy curse of the law.[260] Shall not the Liberator be crowned? We are His portion, whom He has taken out of the hand of the Amorite with His sword and with His bow. Who shall snatch His conquest from His hand? All hail, King Jesus! We gladly own Your gentle sway! Rule in our hearts forever, Thou lovely Prince of Peace.

⇜ April 28 ⇝

All the house of Israel are impudent and hardhearted
(Ezekiel 3:7).

Are there no exceptions? No, not one. Even the favored race is thus described. Are the best so bad? Then what must the worst be? Come, my heart, consider how far you have a share in this universal accusation, and while considering, be ready to take shame unto yourself herein you may have been guilty. The first charge is *impudence*, or being hardheaded, a want of holy shame, an unhallowed boldness in evil. Before my conversion, I could sin and feel no compunction, hear of my guilt and yet remain unhumbled, and even confess my iniquity and manifest no inward humiliation on account of it. For a sinner to go to God's house and pretend to pray to Him and praise Him argues a brazen nature of the worst kind! Alas! since the day of my new birth I have doubted my Lord to His face, murmured unblushingly in His presence, worshipped before Him in a slovenly manner, and sinned without bewailing myself concerning it. If my head were not harder than flint, I should have far more holy fear, and a far deeper contrition of spirit. Woe is me. I am one of the impudent house of Israel. The second charge is *hardheartedness*, and I must not venture to plead innocent here. Once I had nothing but a heart of stone,[261] and although through grace I now have a new and fleshy heart, much of my former stubbornness remains. I am not affected by the death of Jesus as I ought to be; neither am I moved by the ruin of my fellow men, the wickedness of the times, the chastisement of my heavenly Father, and my own failures, as I should be. O that my heart would melt at the recital of my Savior's sufferings and death. Would to God I were rid of this millstone deep within me, this hateful body of death. Blessed be the name of the Lord, the disease is not incurable. The Savior's precious blood is the universal solvent, and me, even me, it will effectually soften till my heart melts as wax before the fire.[262]

✒ *April 29* ✒

The Lord taketh pleasure in His people (Psalm 149:4).

How comprehensive is the love of Jesus! There is no part of His people's interests that He does not consider, and there is nothing that concerns their welfare that is not important to Him. Not merely does He think of you, believer, as an immortal being, but as a mortal being, too. Do not deny it or doubt it. "The very hairs of your head are all numbered."[263] "The steps of a good man are ordered by the Lord: and he delighteth in His way."[264] It would be a sad thing for us if this mantle of love did not cover all our concerns, for what mischief might be wrought to us in that part of our business which did not come under our gracious Lord's inspection! Believer, rest assured that the heart of Jesus cares about your meaner affairs. The breadth of His tender love is such that you may resort to Him in all matters. In all your afflictions, He is afflicted, and like as a father pities his children, so He pities you. The meanest interests of all His saints are all borne upon the broad bosom of the Son of God. Oh, what a heart is His, that does not merely comprehend the persons of His people, but comprehends also the diverse and innumerable concerns of them all! Do you think, O Christian, that you can measure the love of Christ? Think of what His love has brought you—justification, adoption, sanctification, and eternal life! The riches of His goodness are unsearchable;[265] you will never be able to tell them out or even conceive them. Oh, the breadth of the love of Christ! Shall such a love as this have half our hearts? Shall it have a cold love in return? Shall Jesus' marvelous, loving kindness and tender care meet with but faint response and tardy acknowledgment? O my soul, tune your harp to a glad song of thanksgiving! Go to your rest rejoicing, for you are no desolate wanderer, but a beloved child, watched over, cared for, supplied, and defended by your Lord.

⫷ *April 30* ⫸

How precious also are Your thoughts unto me, O God
(Psalm 139:17).

Divine omniscience affords no comfort to the ungodly mind, but to the child of God it overflows with consolation. God is always thinking upon us, never turns aside His mind from us, has us always before His eyes; and this is precisely as we would have it, for it would be dreadful to exist for a moment beyond the observation of our heavenly Father. His thoughts are always tender, loving, wise, prudent, far-reaching, and bring to us countless benefits. Hence it is a choice delight to remember them. The Lord always thought upon His people: hence their election and the covenant of grace by which their salvation is secured. He always will think upon them: hence their final perseverance by which they shall be brought safely to their final rest. In all our wanderings, the watchful glance of the Eternal Watcher is evermore fixed upon us—we never roam beyond the Shepherd's eye. In our sorrows, He observes us incessantly. Not a pang escapes Him. In our toils, He marks all our weariness and writes in His book all the struggles of His faithful ones. These thoughts of the Lord encompass us in all our paths, and penetrate the innermost region of our being. Not a nerve or tissue, valve or vessel of our bodily organization is uncared for. All the littles of our little world are thought upon by the great God. Dear reader, is this precious to you? Then hold to it. Never be led astray by those philosophic fools who preach up an impersonal God, and talk of self-existent, self-governing matters. The Lord lives and thinks upon us. This is a truth far too precious for us to be lightly robbed of it. The notice of a nobleman is valued so highly that he who has it counts his fortune made, but what is it to be thought of by the King of kings! If the Lord thinks upon us, all is well, and we may rejoice evermore.

May

⚛ *May 1* ⚛

I am the rose of Sharon (Song of Solomon 2:1).

Whatever there may be of beauty in the material world, Jesus Christ possesses all that in the spiritual world in a tenfold degree. Among flowers, the rose is deemed the sweetest, but Jesus is infinitely more beautiful in the garden of the soul than the rose can in the gardens of earth. He takes the first place as the fairest among ten thousand. He is the sun, and all others are the stars. The heavens and the day are dark in comparison with Him, for the King in His beauty transcends all. "I am the rose of *Sharon*." This was the best and rarest of roses. Jesus is not "the rose" alone, He is "the rose of Sharon," just as He calls His righteousness "gold," and then adds, "the gold of Ophir"—the best of the best. He is positively lovely, and superlatively the loveliest. There is variety in His charms. The rose is delightful to the eye, and its scent is pleasant and refreshing; so each of the senses of the soul—whether taste, feeling, hearing, sight, or spiritual smell—finds appropriate gratification in Jesus. *Even the recollection of His love is sweet.* Take the rose of Sharon, and pull it leaf from leaf, and collect the leaves in the jar of memory, and you shall find each leaf fragrant long afterwards, filling the house with perfume. Christ *satisfies the highest taste* of the most educated spirit to the very full. The greatest amateur in perfumes is quite satisfied with the rose. And when the soul has arrived at her highest pitch of true taste, she shall still be content with Christ, nay, she shall be the better able to appreciate Him. Heaven itself possesses nothing that excels the rose of Sharon. What emblem can fully set forth His beauty? Human speech and earth-born things fail to tell of Him. All of Earth's choicest charms, put together, feebly picture His abounding preciousness. Blessed rose, bloom in my heart forever!

These all died in faith (Hebrews 11:13).

Behold the epitaph of all those blessed saints who fell asleep before the coming of our Lord! It does not matters how they died, whether of old age or by violent means. This one point, in which they all agree, is the most worthy of record: "These all died in faith." In faith they lived—it was their comfort, their guide, their motive and their support; and in the same spiritual grace they died, ending their life-song in the sweet strain in which they had so long continued. They did not die resting in the flesh or upon their own attainments; they made no advance from their first way of acceptance with God, but held to the way of faith to the end. To die by faith is a precious as to live by it. Dying in faith has distinct reference to *the past*. They believed the promises, which had gone before, and were assured that their sins were blotted out through the mercy of God. Dying in faith has to do with *the present*. These saints were confident of their acceptance with God. They enjoyed the beams of His love and rested in His faithfulness. Dying in faith looks into *the future*. They fell asleep, affirming that the Messiah would surely come, and that when He would in the last days appear upon the earth, they would rise from their graves to behold Him.[266] To them the pains of death were nothing more than birth pangs of a better state. Take courage, my soul, as you read this epitaph. Your course, through grace, is one of faith, and sight seldom cheers you; this has also been the pathway of the brightest and the best. Faith was the orbit in which these stars of the first magnitude moved all the time of their shining here; and happy are you that it is yours. Look anew tonight to Jesus, the author and finisher of your faith,[267] and thank Him for giving you like precious faith with souls now in glory.

A very present help (Psalm 46:1).

Covenant blessings are not meant to be looked at only, but to be appropriated. Even our Lord Jesus is given to us for our present use. Believer, you dost not make use of Christ, as you ought to do? When you are in trouble, why do you not tell Him all your grief? Has He not a sympathizing heart, and can He not comfort and relieve you? No, you are going about to all your friends, save your best Friend, and telling your tale everywhere except into the bosom of your Lord. Art you burdened with this day's sins? Here is a fountain filled with blood: use it, saint, use it. Has a sense of guilt returned upon you? The pardoning grace of Jesus may be proved again and again. Come to Him at once for cleansing. Dost you deplore your weakness? He is your strength: why not lean upon Him? Dost you feel naked? Come hither, soul; put on the robe of Jesus' righteousness. Stand not looking at it, but wear it. Strip off your own righteousness, and your own fears too: put on the fair white linen, for it was meant to *wear*. Dost you feel yourself sick? Pull the night-bell of prayer, and call up the Beloved Physician! He will give the cordial that will revive you. Thou art poor, but then you have "a kinsman, a mighty man of wealth." What! wilt you not go to Him, and ask Him to give you of His abundance, when He has given you this promise, that you shalt be joint heir with Him,[268] and has made over all that He is and all that He has to be your? There is nothing Christ dislikes more than for His people to make a show-thing of Him, and not to use Him. He loves to be employed by us. The more burdens we put on His shoulders, the more precious will He be to us.

> "Let us be simple with Him, then,
> Not backward, stiff, or cold,
> As though our Bethlehem could be,
> What Sinai was of old."

☙ *May 4* ☚

Being born again, not of corruptible seed, but of incorruptible (1 Peter 1:23).

Peter most earnestly exhorted the scattered saints to love each other "with a pure heart fervently"[269] and he wisely fetched his argument, not from the law or nature or philosophy, but from that high and divine nature which God has implanted in His people. Just as some judicious tutor of princes might labor to beget and foster in them a kingly spirit and dignified behavior, finding arguments in their position and descent, so, looking upon God's people as heirs of glory, princes of the blood royal, descendants of the King of kings, earth's truest and oldest aristocracy, Peter said to them, "See that ye love one another, because of your noble birth, being born of incorruptible seed; because of your pedigree, being descended from God, the Creator of all things; and because of your immortal destiny, for you shall never pass away, though the glory of the flesh shall fade, and even its existence shall cease." It would be well if, in the spirit of humility, we recognized the true dignity of our regenerated nature, and lived up to it. What is a Christian? If you compare him with a king, he adds priestly sanctity to royal dignity. The king's royalty often lies only in his crown, but with a Christian, it is infused into his inmost nature. He is as much above his fellows, through his new birth, as a man is above the beast that perishes. Surely he ought to carry himself, in all his dealings, as one who is not of the multitude, but chosen out of the world, distinguished by sovereign grace, written among "the peculiar people"[270] and who therefore cannot grovel in the dust as others,[271] nor live after the manner of the world's citizens. Let the dignity of your nature and the brightness of your prospects, O believers in Christ, constrain you to cleave unto holiness and to avoid the very appearance of evil.

✐ May 5 ✐

He that handleth a matter wisely shall find good: and
whoso trusteth in the Lord, happy is he
(Proverbs 16:20).

Wisdom is man's true strength; and, under its guidance, he best accomplishes the ends of his being. Wisely handling the matter of life gives to man the richest enjoyment, and presents the noblest occupation for his powers; hence by it he finds good in the fullest sense. Without wisdom, man is as the wild ass's colt, running hither and thither, wasting strength, which might be profitably employed. Wisdom is the compass by which man is to steer across the trackless waste of life; without it he is a derelict vessel, the sport of winds and waves. A man must be prudent in such a world as this, or he will find no good, but be betrayed into unnumbered ills. The pilgrim will sorely wound his feet among the briers of the wood of life if he does not pick his steps with the utmost caution. He who is in a wilderness infested with robber bands must handle matters wisely if he would journey safely. If, trained by the Great Teacher, we follow where He leads, we shall find good, even while in this dark abode. There are celestial fruits to be gathered this side of Eden's bowers, and songs of paradise to be sung amid the groves of earth. But where shall this wisdom be found? Many have dreamed of it, but have not possessed it. Where shall we learn it? Let us listen to the voice of the Lord, for He has declared the secret; He has revealed to the sons of men wherein true wisdom lieth, and we have it in the text, "Whoso trusteth in the Lord, happy is he."[272] The true way to handle a matter wisely is to trust in the Lord. This is the sure clue to the most intricate labyrinths of life, follow it and find eternal bliss. He who trusts in the Lord has a diploma for wisdom granted by inspiration: happy is he now, and happier shall he be above. Lord, in this sweet eventide walk with me in the garden, and teach me the wisdom of faith.

⇜ *May 6* ⇝

*All the days of my appointed time will I wait
(Job 14:14).*

A little stay on earth will make heaven more heavenly. Nothing
makes rest so sweet as toil; nothing renders security so pleasant
as exposure to alarms. The bitter quassia [wood] cups of earth
will give a relish to the new wine, which sparkles in the golden
bowls of glory. Our battered armor and scarred countenances
will render more illustrious our victory above, when we are
welcomed to the seats of those who have overcome the world.
We should not have full *fellowship with Christ* if we did not for
a while sojourn below, for He was baptized with a baptism of
suffering among men, and we must be baptized with the same
if we would share his kingdom. Fellowship with Christ is so
honorable that the sorest sorrow is a light price by which to
procure it. Another reason for our lingering here is for the good
of others. We would not wish to enter heaven till our work is
done, and it may be that we are yet ordained to minister light
to souls benighted in the wilderness of sin. Our prolonged stay
here is doubtless *for God's glory.* A tried saint, like a well-cut
diamond, glitters much in the King's crown. Nothing reflects so
much honor on a workman as a protracted and severe trial of
his work, and its triumphant endurance of the ordeal without
giving way in any part. We are God's workmanship, in whom
He will be glorified by our afflictions. It is for the honor of Jesus
that we endure the trial of our faith with sacred joy. Let each
man surrender his own longings to the glory of Jesus, and feel,
"If my lying in the dust would elevate my Lord by so much as an
inch, let me still lie among the pots of earth. If to live on earth
forever would make my Lord more glorious, it should be my
heaven to be shut out of heaven." Our time is fixed and settled
by eternal decree. Let us not be anxious about it, but wait with
patience till the gates of pearl shall open.

ᗡ *May 7* ᗡ

*Jesus saith unto him, Rise, take up your bed, and walk
(John 5:8).*

Like many others, the impotent man had been waiting for a
wonder to be wrought and a sign to be given. Wearily did he
watch the pool, but no angel came, or came not for him. Yet,
thinking it to be his only chance, he waited still, and did not know
that there was One near him whose word could heal him in a
moment. Many are in the same plight: they are waiting for some
singular emotion, remarkable impression, or celestial vision; they
wait in vain and watch in vain. Even supposing that, in a few
cases, remarkable signs are seen, these are rare, and no man has
a right to look for them in his own case—especially one who
feels his impotency to avail himself of the moving of the water
even if it came. It is a very sad reflection that tens of thousands
are now waiting in the use of means, and ordinances, and vows,
and resolutions, and have so waited time out of mind, in vain,
utterly in vain. Meanwhile these poor souls forget the present
Savior, who bids them look unto Him and be saved. He could
heal them at once, but they prefer to wait for an angel and a
wonder. To trust Him is the sure way to every blessing, and He
is worthy of the most implicit confidence; but unbelief makes
them prefer the cold porches of Bethesda to the warm bosom of
His love. O that the Lord may turn His eye upon the multitudes
who are in this case tonight; may He forgive the slights which
they put upon His divine power, and call them by that sweet,
constraining voice to rise from the bed of despair, and in the
energy of faith take up their bed and walk. O Lord, hear our
prayer for all such at this calm hour of sunset, and before the
day breaketh may they look and live. Courteous reader, is there
anything in this portion for you?

Acquaint now yourself with Him (Job 22:21).

If we would rightly "acquaint ourselves with God, and be at peace,"[273] we must know Him as He has revealed Himself, not only in *the unity of His essence and subsistence*, but also in the plurality of His persons. God said, "Let us make man in our own image"[274]—let not man be content until he knows something of the "us" from whom his being was derived. Endeavour to know the Father. Bury your head in His bosom in deep repentance, and confess that you are not worthy to be called His son. Receive the kiss of His love. Let the ring, the token of His eternal faithfulness, be on your finger.[275] Sit at His table and let your heart make merry in His grace. Then press forward and seek to know much of *the Son of God* who is the brightness of His Father's glory,[276] and yet in unspeakable condescension of grace became man for our sakes. Know Him in the singular complexity of His nature: eternal God, and yet suffering, finite man. Follow Him as He walks the waters with the tread of deity, and as He sits upon the well in the weariness of humanity. Be not satisfied unless you know much of Jesus Christ as your Friend, your Brother, your Husband, your all. Forget not the Holy Spirit. Endeavour to obtain a clear view of His nature and character, His attributes, and His works. Behold that Spirit of the Lord, who first of all moved upon chaos, and brought forth order, who now visits the chaos of your soul, and creates the order of holiness. Behold Him as the Lord and giver of spiritual life, the Illuminator, the Instructor, the Comforter, and the Sanctifier. Behold Him as, like holy unction, He descends upon the head of Jesus, and then afterwards rests upon *you* who are as the skirts of His garments. Such an intelligent, scriptural, and experimental belief in the Trinity in Unity is yours if you truly know God; and such knowledge *brings peace indeed*.

☜ *May 9* ☞

Come, my beloved, let us go forth into the field ... let us see if the vine flourish (Song of Solomon 7:11,12).

The church was about to engage in earnest labor, and desired her Lord's company in it. She does not say, "I will go," but "let us go." It is blessed working when Jesus is at our side! It is the business of God's people to be trimmers of God's vines. Like our first parents, we are put into the garden of the Lord for usefulness; let us therefore go forth into the field. Observe that the church, when she is in her right mind, in all her many labors desires to enjoy communion with Christ. Some imagine that they cannot serve Christ actively, and yet have fellowship with Him: they are mistaken. Doubtless it is very easy to fritter away our inward life in outward exercises, and come to complain with the spouse, "They made me keeper of the vineyards; but mine own vineyard have I not kept:" but there is no reason why this should be the case except our own folly and neglect. It is certain that a professor may do nothing, and yet grow as lifeless in spiritual things as those who are most busy. Mary was not praised for sitting still, but for her *sitting at Jesus' feet.*[277] Even so, Christians are not to be praised for neglecting duties under the pretence of having secret fellowship with Jesus. It is not sitting, but sitting at Jesus' feet that is commendable. Do not think that activity is in itself an evil; it is a great blessing and a means of grace to us. Paul called it a grace given to him to be allowed to preach; and every form of Christian service may become a personal blessing to those engaged in it. Those who have most fellowship with Christ are not recluses or hermits, who have much time to spare, but indefatigable laborers who are toiling for Jesus, and who, in their toil, have Him side by side with them, so that they are workers together with God. Let us remember then, in anything we have to do for Jesus, that we can do it and should do it in close communion with Him.

⤋ *May 10* ⤌

The only begotten of the Father, full of grace and truth
(John 1:14).

Believer, YOU can bear your testimony that Christ is the only
begotten of the Father, as well as the first begotten from the
dead. You can say, "He is divine to me, if He be human to all
the world beside. He has done for me that which none but a
God could do. He has subdued my stubborn will, melted a heart
of stubbornness, opened gates of brass, and snapped bars of
iron. He has turned my mourning into laughter for me, and my
desolation into joy.[278] He has led my captivity captive,[279] and
made my heart rejoice with joy unspeakable and full of glory.[280]
Let others think as they will of Him. To me He must be the only
begotten of the Father: blessed be His name. And He is *full of
grace*. Ah! had He not been I should never have been saved. He
drew me when I struggled to escape from His grace; and when at
last I came all trembling like a condemned culprit to His mercy-
seat, He said, 'Your sins which are many are all forgiven you: be
of good cheer.' And He is *full of truth*. True have His promises
been; not one has failed. I bear witness that never has a servant
had such a master as I have; never brother such a kinsman as He
has been to me; never spouse such a husband as Christ has been
to my soul; never sinner a better Savior; never mourner a better
comforter than Christ has been to my spirit. I want none beside
Him. In life He is my life, and in death He shall be the death of
death. In poverty Christ is my riches; in sickness He makes my
bed; in darkness He is my star; and in brightness He is my sun.
He is the manna of the camp in the wilderness, and He shall be
the new corn of the host when they come to Canaan. Jesus is to
me all grace and no wrath, all truth and no falsehood. Of truth
and grace He is *full*, infinitely full. My soul, this night, bless with
all your might 'the only Begotten.'"

ᵂᴬ *May 11* ᴿ

Only be you strong and very courageous (Joshua 1:7).

Our God's tender love for His servants makes Him concerned for the state of their inward feelings. He desires them to be of good courage. Some esteem it a small thing for a believer to be vexed with doubts and fears, but God thinks not so. From this text it is plain that our Master would not have us entangled with fears. He would have us without carefulness,[281] without doubt, without cowardice. Our Master does not think so lightly of our unbelief as we do. When we are desponding, we are subject to a grievous malady, not to be trifled with, but to be carried at once to the beloved Physician. Our Lord loveth not to see our countenance sad. It was a law of Ahasuerus that no one should come into the king's court dressed in mourning. This is not the law of the King of kings, for we may come mourning as we are. But still He would have us put off the spirit of heaviness[282] and put on the garment of praise, for there is much reason to rejoice. The Christian man ought to be of a courageous spirit, in order that he may glorify the Lord by enduring trials in an heroic manner. If he is fearful and fainthearted, it will dishonor his God. Besides, *what a bad example it is.* This disease of doubtfulness and discouragement is an epidemic that soon spreads among the Lord's flock. One downcast believer makes twenty souls sad. Moreover, unless your courage is kept up, *Satan will be too much for you.* Let your spirit be joyful in God your Savior, the joy of the Lord shall be your strength,[283] and no fiend of hell shall make headway against you. But cowardice throws down the banner. Moreover, *labor is light* to a man of cheerful spirit, and *success waits upon cheerfulness.* The man who toils, rejoicing in his God and believing with all his heart, has success guaranteed. He who sows in hope shall reap in joy;[284] therefore, dear reader, "be thou strong, and very courageous."[285]

*Fear not to go down into Egypt; for I will there make of
you a great nation: I will go down with you into Egypt;
and I will also surely bring you up again
(Genesis 46:3-4).*

Jacob must have shuddered at the thought of leaving the land of
his father's sojourning, and dwelling among heathen strangers. It
was *a new scene and likely to be a trying one.* Who shall venture
among couriers of a foreign monarch without anxiety? Yet the
way was *evidently appointed* for him, and therefore he resolved
to go. This is frequently the position of believers now—they are
called to perils and temptations altogether untried.[286] At such
seasons let them imitate Jacob's example by offering sacrifices
of prayer unto God, and seeking His direction; let them not take
a step until they have waited upon the Lord for His blessing.
Then they will have Jacob's companion to be their friend and
helper. How blessed to feel assured that the Lord is with us in all
our ways,[287] and condescends to go down into our humiliations
and banishments with us! Even beyond the ocean our Father's
love beams like the sun in its strength. We cannot hesitate to
go where Jehovah promises His presence. Even the valley of
deathshade grows bright with the radiance of this assurance.[288]
Marching onward with faith in their God, believers *shall have
Jacob's promise.* They shall be brought up again, whether it is
from the troubles of life or the chambers of death. Jacob's seed
came out of Egypt in due time, and so shall all the faithful pass
unscathed through the tribulation of life and the terror of death.
Let us *exercise Jacob's confidence.* "*Fear not,*"[289] is the Lord's
command and His divine encouragement to those who at His
bidding are launching upon new seas. The divine presence and
preservation forbid so much as one unbelieving fear. Without our
God, we should fear to move, but when He bids us to, it would
be dangerous to tarry.[290] Reader, go forward, and fear not.

Thou art my portion, O Lord (Psalm 119:57).

Look at your possessions, O believer, and compare your portion with the lot of your fellowmen. Some of them have their portion in the field. They are rich, and their harvests yield them a golden increase, but what are harvests compared with your God, who is the God of harvests? What are bursting granaries compared with Him, who is the Husbandman, and feeds you with the bread of heaven?[291] Some have their portion in the city. Their wealth is abundant and flows to them in constant streams until they become a very reservoir of gold, but what is gold compared with your God? You could not live on it; your spiritual life could not be sustained by it. Put it on a troubled conscience, and could it allay its pangs? Apply it to a desponding heart, and see if it could stop a solitary groan, or give one grief the less? But you have God, and in Him you have more than gold or riches than ever you could buy. Some have their portion in that which most men love—applause and fame, but ask yourself, is not your God more to you than that? What if trumpets should be loud in your ovation, would this prepare you to pass the Jordan, or cheer you in prospect of judgment?[292] No, there are griefs in life which wealth cannot alleviate; and there is the deep need of a dying hour, for which no riches can provide. But when you have *God* for your portion, you have more than all else put together. In Him every want is met, whether in life or in death. With God for your portion, you are rich indeed, for He will supply your need,[293] comfort your heart, assuage your grief, guide your steps, be with you in the dark valley, and then take you home to enjoy Him as your portion forever. "I have enough," said Esau; this is the best thing a worldly man can say, but Jacob replies, "I have all things," which is a note too high for carnal minds.

He shall gather the lambs with His arm, and carry them in His bosom (Isaiah 40:11).

Who is He of whom such gracious words are spoken? He is THE GOOD SHEPHERD. Why does He carry the lambs in His bosom? Because He has a tender heart, and any weakness at once melts His heart. The sighs, the ignorance, the feebleness of the little ones of His flock draw forth His compassion. *It is His office*, as a faithful High Priest, to consider the weak. Besides, He purchased them with blood; they are His property.[294] He must and will care for that which cost Him so dearly. Then He is *responsible for each lamb*, bound by covenant engagements not to lose one. Moreover, they are all a part of His glory and reward.[295] But how may we understand the expression, "He will *carry* them?" Sometimes He carries them by not permitting them to endure much trial. Providence deals tenderly with them. Often they are "carried" by being filled with an unusual degree of love, so that they bear up and stand fast. Though their knowledge may not be deep, they have great sweetness in what they do know. Frequently He "carries" them by giving them a very simple faith, which takes the promise just as it stands, and believingly runs with every trouble straight to Jesus. The simplicity of their faith gives them an unusual degree of confidence, which carries them above the world. "He carries the lambs *in His bosom*." Here is boundless affection. Would He put them in His bosom if He did not love them much? Here is *tender nearness*: so near are they, that they could not possibly be nearer. Here is hallowed familiarity: there are precious love-passages between Christ and His weak ones. Here is *perfect safety*: in His bosom who can hurt them? They must hurt the Shepherd first. Here is *perfect rest and sweetest comfort*. Surely we are not sufficiently sensible of the infinite tenderness of Jesus![296]

May 15

Made perfect (Hebrews 12:23).

Remember that there are two kinds of perfection which the Christian needs—the perfection of justification in the person of Jesus, and the perfection of sanctification wrought in him by the Holy Spirit. At present, corruption yet remains even in the breasts of the regenerate—experience soon teaches us this. Within us are still lusts and evil imaginations. But I rejoice to know that the day is coming when God shall finish the work which He has begun; and He shall present my soul, not only perfect in Christ, but perfect through the Spirit, without spot or blemish or any such thing.[297] Can it be true that this poor sinful heart of mine is to become holy even as God is holy? Can it be that this spirit, which often cries, "O wretched man that I am! Who shall deliver me from the body of this sin and death?" shall get rid of sin and death[298]—that I shall have no evil things to vex my ears, and no unholy thoughts to disturb my peace? Oh, happy hour! May it be hastened! When I cross the Jordan, the work of sanctification will be finished; but not till that moment shall I even claim perfection in myself. Then my spirit shall have its last baptism in the Holy Spirit's fire. I think I long to die to receive that last and final purification, which shall usher me into heaven. Not an angel more pure than I shall be, for I shall be able to say, in a double sense, "I am clean," through Jesus' blood and through the Spirit's work. Oh, how should we extol the power of the Holy Ghost in thus making us fit to stand before our Father in heaven! Yet let not the hope of perfection; hereafter make us content with imperfection now. If it does this, our hope cannot be genuine; for a good hope is a purifying thing, even now. The work of grace must be abiding in us now or it cannot be *perfected then*. Let us pray to "be filled with the Spirit," that we may bring forth *increasingly* the fruits of righteousness.[299]

✒ *May 16* ✒

And he said, "Thus saith the Lord, Make this valley
full of ditches. For thus saith the Lord, Ye shall not see
wind, neither shall ye see rain; yet that valley shall be
filled with water, that ye may drink, both ye and your
cattle, and your beasts" (2 Kings 3:16-17).

The armies of the three kings were famishing for want of water. God was about to send it, and in these words, the prophet announced the coming blessing. Here was a case of human helplessness: not a drop of water could all the valiant men procure from the skies or find in the wells of earth. Thus often the people of the Lord are at their wits' end; they see the vanity of the creature, and learn experimentally where their help is to be found. Still the people were to make a believing preparation for the divine blessing; they were to dig the trenches in which the precious liquid would be held. The church must, by her varied agencies, efforts, and prayers, make herself ready to be blessed. She must make the pools and the Lord will fill them. This must be done in faith, in the full assurance that the blessing is about to descend. By-and-by there was a singular bestowal of the needed boon. Not as in Elijah's case did the shower pour from the clouds,[300] but in a silent and mysterious manner, the pools were filled. The Lord has His own sovereign modes of action. He is not tied to manner and time as we are, but does as He pleases among the sons of men. It is ours thankfully to receive from Him and not to dictate to Him. We must also notice the remarkable abundance of the supply. There was enough for the need of all. And so it is in the gospel blessing: all the wants of the congregation and of the entire church shall be met by the divine power in answer to prayer;[301] and above all this, victory shall be speedily given to the armies of the Lord. What am I doing for Jesus? What trenches am I digging? O Lord, make me ready to receive the blessing, which Thou art so willing to bestow.

Thou art My servant; I have chosen you (Isaiah 41:9).

If we have received the grace of God in our hearts, its practical effect has been to make us God's *servants*. We may be unfaithful servants; we certainly are unprofitable ones, and yet, blessed be His name—we are His servants, wearing His livery, feeding at His table, and obeying His commands. We were once the servants of sin, but He who made us free has now taken us into His family and taught us obedience to His will. We do not serve our Master perfectly, but we would if we could. As we hear God's voice saying unto us, "Thou art My servant," we can answer with David, "I am your servant; Thou hast loosed my bonds." But the Lord calls us not only His *servants*, but His *chosen* ones—"I have chosen you." We have not chosen Him first, but He has chosen us.[302] If now we are God's servants, we were not always so; to sovereign grace the change must be ascribed. The eye of sovereignty singled us out, and the voice of unchanging grace declared, "I have loved you with an everlasting love."[303] Long before time began or space was created, God had written upon His heart the names of His elect people, had predestinated them to be conformed unto the image of His Son, and ordained them heirs of all the fullness of His love, His grace, and His glory.[304] What comfort is here! Has the Lord loved us so long, and will He yet cast us away? He knew how stiff-necked we should be. He understood that our hearts were evil. And yet He made the choice. Ah! Our Savior is no fickle lover. He does not feel enchanted for a while with some gleams of beauty from His church's eye, and then afterwards cast her off because of her unfaithfulness. Nay, He married her in old eternity; and it is written of Jehovah, "He hateth putting away."[305] The eternal choice is a bond upon *our* gratitude and upon *His* faithfulness, which neither can disown.

✈ *May 18* ✈

Afterward (Hebrews 12:11).

How happy are tried Christians, *afterward*. No calm more deep than that which succeeds a storm. Who has not rejoiced in clear shinings after rain? Victorious banquets are for well-exercised soldiers. After killing the lion we eat the honey; after climbing the Hill Difficulty, we sit down in the arbor to rest; after traversing the Valley of Humiliation, after fighting with Apollyon, *[reference to John Bunyan's Pilgrim's Progress]* the shining one appears with the healing branch from the tree of life. Our sorrows, like the passing keels of the vessels upon the sea, leave a silver line of holy light behind them "afterward." It is peace, sweet, deep peace, which follows the horrible turmoil that once reigned in our tormented, guilty souls. See, then, the happy estate of a Christian! He has his best things last, and he therefore in this world receives his worst things first. But even his worst things are "afterward" good things, harsh ploughings yielding joyful harvests. Even now he grows rich by his losses, rises by his falls, lives by dying, and becomes full by being emptied. If then, his grievous afflictions yield him so much peaceable fruit[306] in this life, what shall be the full vintage of joy "afterward" in heaven? If his dark nights are as bright as the world's days, what shall his days be? If even his starlight is more splendid than the sun, what must his sunlight be? If he can sing in a dungeon, how sweetly will he sing in heaven! If he can praise the Lord in the fires,[307] how will he extol Him before the eternal throne! If evil is good to him *now*, what will the overflowing goodness of God be to him *then*? Oh, blessed "afterward!" Who would not be a Christian? Who would not bear the present cross for the crown which cometh afterwards? But herein is work for patience, for the rest is not for today, or the triumph for the present, but "afterward." Wait, O soul, and let patience have her perfect work.

⚞ *May 19* ⚟

And he requested for himself that he might die
(1 Kings 19:4).

It was a remarkable thing that the man who was never to die, for whom God had ordained an infinitely better lot, the man who should be carried to heaven in a chariot of fire,[308] and be translated, that he should not see death—should thus pray, "Let me die, I am no better than my fathers." We have here memorable proof that God does not always answer prayer in kind, though He always does in effect. He gave Elias something better than that which he asked for, and thus really heard and answered him. It was strange that the lion-hearted Elijah should be so depressed by Jezebel's threat that he would ask to die, and blessedly kind was it on the part of our heavenly Father that He did not take His desponding servant at his word. There is a limit to the doctrine of the prayer of faith. We are not to expect that God will give us everything we choose to ask for. We know that we sometimes ask and do not receive, because we ask amiss.[309] If we ask for that which is not promised—if we run counter to the spirit which the Lord would have us cultivate—if we ask contrary to His will or the decrees of His providence—if we ask merely for the gratification of our own ease, and without an eye to His glory, we must not expect that we shall receive. Yet, when we ask in faith, nothing doubting, if we receive not the precise thing asked for, we shall receive an equivalent and more than an equivalent for it. As one remarks, "If the Lord does not pay in silver, He will in gold; and if He does not pay in gold, He will in diamonds." If He does not give you precisely what you ask for, He will give you that which is tantamount to it, and that which you will greatly rejoice to receive in lieu thereof. Be then, dear reader, much in prayer, and make this evening a season of earnest intercession, but take heed what you ask.

May 20

I drew them with cords of a man, with bands of love (Hosea 11:4).

Our heavenly Father often draws us with the cords of love, but ah! how backward we are to run toward Him! How slowly do we respond to His gentle impulses! He draws us to exercise a more simple faith in Him, but we have not yet attained to Abraham's confidence.[310] We do not leave our worldly cares with God, but, like Martha, we cumber ourselves with much serving.[311] Our meager faith brings leanness into our souls. We do not open our mouths wide, though God has promised to fill them.[312] Does He not this evening draw us to trust Him? Can we not hear Him say, "Come, My child, and trust Me. The veil is rent; enter into My presence, and approach boldly to the throne of My grace.[313] I am worthy of your fullest confidence. Cast your cares on Me.[314] Shake yourself from the dust of your cares, and put on your beautiful garments of joy." But, alas! though called with tones of love to the blessed exercise of this comforting grace, we will not come. At another time *He draws us to closer communion with Himself.* We been sitting on the doorstep of God's house, and He bids us advance into the banqueting hall and dine with Him, but we decline the honor. There are secret rooms not yet opened to us; Jesus invites us to enter them, but we hold back. Shame on our cold hearts! We are but poor lovers of our sweet Lord Jesus, not fit to be His servants, much less to be His brides, and yet He has exalted us to be bone of His bone and flesh of His flesh, married to Him by a glorious marriage-covenant.[315] Herein is love! But it is love that *takes no denial.* If we do not obey the gentle drawings of His love, He will send affliction to drive us into closer intimacy with Himself. Have us nearer He will. What foolish children we are to refuse those bands of love, and so bring upon our backs that scourge of small cords, which Jesus knows how to use!

❧ *May 21* ❧

There is corn in Egypt (Genesis 42:2).

Famine pinched all the nations, and it seemed inevitable that Jacob and his family should suffer great want, but the God of providence, who never forgets the objects of electing love, had stored a granary for His people by giving the Egyptians warning of the scarcity, and leading them to treasure up the grain of the years of plenty.[316] Little did Jacob expect deliverance from Egypt, but there was the corn in store for him. Believer, though all things are apparently against you, rest assured that God has made a reservation on your behalf. In the roll of your griefs there is a saving clause. Somehow He will deliver you, and somewhere He will provide for you. The quarter from which your rescue shall arise may be a very unexpected one, but help will assuredly come in your extremity, and you shalt magnify the name of the Lord. If men do not feed you, ravens shall;[317] and if earth does not yield wheat, heaven shall drop with manna.[318] Therefore be of good courage, and rest quietly in the Lord. God can make the sun rise in the west if He pleases, and make the source of distress the channel of delight. The corn in Egypt was all in the hands of the beloved Joseph; he opened or closed the granaries at will. And so the riches of providence are all in the absolute power of our Lord Jesus, who will dispense them liberally to His people. Joseph was abundantly ready to provide for his own family; and Jesus is unceasing in His faithful care for His brethren. Our business is to go after the help, which is provided for us. We must not sit still in despondency, but bestir ourselves. Prayer will bear us soon into the presence of our royal Brother. Once before His throne, we have only to ask and have. His stores are not exhausted. There is corn still. His heart is not hard; He will give the corn to us. Lord, forgive our unbelief, and this evening, constrain us to draw largely from Your fullness and receive grace for grace.

⇢ *May 22* ⇠

Behold, Thou art fair, my Beloved
(Song of Solomon 1:16).

From every point, our Well-beloved is most fair. Our various experiences are meant by our heavenly Father to furnish fresh standpoints from which we may view the loveliness of Jesus. How amiable are our trials when they carry us aloft where we may gain clearer views of Jesus than ordinary life could afford us! We have seen Him from the top of Amana, from the top of Shenir and Hermon,[319] and He has shone upon us like the sun. But we have seen Him also "from the lions' dens, from the mountains of the leopards," and He has lost none of His loveliness. From the languishing of a sick bed, from the borders of the grave, have we turned our eyes to our soul's spouse, and He has never been otherwise than "all fair." Many of His saints have looked upon Him from the gloom of dungeons and from the red flames of the stake, yet have they never uttered an ill word of Him, but have died extolling His surpassing charms.[320] Oh, noble and pleasant employment to be forever gazing at our sweet Lord Jesus! Is it not unspeakably delightful to view the Savior in all His offices, to perceive Him matchless in each, to shift the kaleidoscope, as it were, and to find fresh combinations of peerless graces? In the manger and in eternity, on the cross and on His throne, in the garden and in His kingdom, among thieves or in the midst of cherubim, He is everywhere "altogether lovely." Examine carefully every little act of His life, and every trait of His character, and He is as lovely in the minute as in the majestic. Judge Him as you will, you cannot find fault; weigh Him as you please, and He will not be found wanting. Eternity shall not discover the shadow of a spot in our Beloved, but rather, as ages revolve, His hidden glories shall shine forth with yet more inconceivable splendor, and His unutterable loveliness shall more and more ravish all celestial minds.

Thou hast bought me no sweet cane with money
(Isaiah 43:24).

Worshippers at the temple were accustomed to bringing presents of sweet perfumes to be burned upon the altar of God, but Israel, in the time of her backsliding, became ungenerous and made but few votive offerings to her Lord. This was evidence of coldness of heart toward God and His house. Reader, does this never occur with you? Might not the complaint of the text be occasionally, if not frequently, brought against you? Those who are poor in pocket, if rich in faith, will be accepted none the less because their gifts are small. But, poor reader, do you give in fair proportion to the Lord, or is the widow's mite kept back from the sacred treasury?[321] The rich believer should be thankful for the talent entrusted to him, but should not forget his large responsibility, for where much is given, much will be required.[322] But, rich reader, are you mindful of your obligations, and rendering to the Lord according to the benefit you receive? Jesus gave His blood for us; what shall we give to Him? We are His, and all that we have, for He has purchased us unto Himself. Can we act as if we were our own?[323] O for more consecration! and to this end, O for more love! Blessed Jesus, how good it is of You to accept our sweet cane bought with money! Nothing is too costly as a tribute to Your unrivalled love, and yet Thou dost receive with favor the smallest sincere token of affection! Thou dost receive our poor forget-me-nots and love-tokens as though they were intrinsically precious, though indeed they are but as the bunch of wild flowers which the child brings to its mother. Never may we grow miserly toward You, and from this hour never may we hear You complain of us again for withholding the gifts of our love. We will give You the first fruits of our increase, and pay You tithes of all, and then we will confess, "Of Your own have we given You."

Only let your conversation be as it becometh the gospel of Christ (Philippians 1:27).

The word "conversation" does not merely mean our talk with one another, but the whole course of our life and behavior in the world. The Greek word signifies the actions and the privileges of citizenship, and thus we are commanded to let our actions, as citizens of the New Jerusalem, be such as becomes the gospel of Christ. What sort of conversation is this? In the first place, *the gospel is very simple*. So Christians should be simple and plain in their habits. There should be about our manner, our speech, our dress, and our whole behavior that simplicity, which is the very soul of beauty. The gospel is *preeminently true*, it is gold without dross; and the Christian's life will be lusterless and valueless without the jewel of truth. The gospel is a very *fearless gospel*. It boldly proclaims the truth, whether men like it or not. We must be equally faithful and unflinching. But the gospel is also *very gentle*. Mark this spirit in its Founder: "A bruised reed He will not break."[324] Some professors are sharper than a thorn-hedge; such men are not like Jesus. Let us seek to win others by the gentleness of our words and acts. The gospel is *very loving*. It is the message of the God of love to a lost and fallen race. Christ's last command to His disciples was, "Love one another."[325] O for more real, hearty union and love to all the saints; for more tender compassion toward the souls of the worst and vilest of men! We must not forget that the gospel of Christ is *holy*. It never excuses sin; it pardons it, but only through atonement. If our life is to resemble the gospel, we must shun, not merely the grosser vices, but everything that would hinder our perfect conformity to Christ. For His sake, for our own sakes and for the sakes of others, we must strive day by day to let our conversation be more in accordance with His gospel.

❧ *May 25* ☙

*And they rose up the same hour, and returned Jerusalem
... and they told what things were done in the way, and
how He was known of them (Luke 24:33, 35).*

When the two disciples had reached Emmaus, and were refreshing
themselves at the evening meal, the mysterious stranger who had
so enchanted them upon the road took bread and broke it, made
Himself known to them, and then vanished out of their sight. They
had constrained Him to abide with them, because the day was far
spent; but now, although it was much later, their love was a lamp
to their feet, yea, and wings also. They forgot the darkness; their
weariness was all gone; and forthwith they journeyed back the
threescore *[sixty]* furlongs *[220 yards or 201 meters per furlong]*
to tell the gladsome news of a risen Lord, who had appeared to
them by the way. They reached the Christians in Jerusalem, and
were received by a burst of joyful news before they could tell
their own tale. These early Christians were all on fire to speak
of Christ's resurrection, and to proclaim what they knew of the
Lord. They made common property of their experiences. This
evening let their example impress us deeply. We, too, must bear
our witness concerning Jesus. John's account of the sepulcher
needed to be supplemented by Peter,[326] and Mary could speak
of something further still;[327] combined, we have a full testimony
from which nothing can be spared. We have each of us peculiar
gifts and special manifestations, but the one object God has in
view is the perfecting of the whole body of Christ. We must,
therefore, bring our spiritual possessions and lay them at the
apostle's feet and make distribution unto all of what God has
given to us.[328] Keep back no part of the precious truth, but speak
what you know and testify what you have seen. Let not the toil or
darkness or possible unbelief of your friends weigh one moment
in the scale. Up, and be marching to the place of duty, and there
tell what great things God has shown to your soul.

Continue in the faith (Acts 14:22).

Perseverance is the badge of true saints. The Christian life is not a *beginning* only in the ways of God, but also a *continuance* in the same as long as life lasts. It is with a Christian as it was with the great Napoleon. He said, "Conquest has made me what I am, and conquest must maintain me." So, under God, dear brother in the Lord, conquest has made you what you are, and conquest must sustain you. Your motto must be, "Excelsior." He only is a true conqueror, and shall be crowned at the last, who continues till war's trumpet is blown no more. Perseverance is, therefore, the target of all our spiritual enemies. The *world* does not object to your being a Christian for a time, if she can but tempt you to cease your pilgrimage, and settle down to buy and sell with her in Vanity Fair. The *flesh* will seek to ensnare you and prevent your pressing on to glory. "It is weary work being a pilgrim; come, give it up. Am I always to be mortified? Am I never to be indulged? Give me at least a break from this constant warfare." *Satan* will make many a fierce attack on your perseverance; it will be the mark for all his arrows. He will strive to hinder you in service. He will insinuate that you are doing no good and that you want rest. He will endeavor to make you weary of *suffering*. He will whisper, "Curse God, and die."[329] Or he will attack your *steadfastness*: "What is the good of being so zealous? Be quiet like the rest; sleep as do others, and let your lamp go out as the other virgins do."[330] Or he will assail your *doctrinal sentiments*: "Why do you hold to these denominational creeds? Sensible men are getting more liberal; they are removing the old landmarks. Fall in with the times." Wear your shield, Christian, therefore, close upon your armor,[331] and cry mightily unto God, that by His Spirit you may endure to the end.

≈ *May 27* ≈

What is your servant, that thou shouldest look upon
such a dead dog as I am? (2 Samuel 9:8)

If Mephibosheth was thus humbled by David's kindness, what shall we be in the presence of our gracious Lord? The more grace we have, the less we shall think of ourselves, for grace, like light, reveals our impurity. Eminent saints have scarcely known to what to compare themselves, their sense of unworthiness has been so clear and keen. "I am," says holy Rutherford, "a dry and withered branch, a piece of dead carcass, dry bones, and not able to step over a straw." In another place he writes, "Except as to open outbreakings, I want nothing of what Judas and Cain had." The meanest objects in nature appear to the humbled mind to have a preference above itself, because they have never contracted sin. A dog may be greedy, fierce, or filthy, but it has no conscience to violate, no Holy Spirit to resist. A dog may be a worthless animal, and yet by a little kindness it is soon won to love its master, and is faithful unto death; but we forget the goodness of the Lord, and do not follow at His call. The term "dead dog" is the most expressive of all terms of contempt, but it is none too strong to express the self-abhorrence of instructed believers. They do not affect mock modesty. They mean what they say. They have weighed themselves in the balances of the sanctuary, and found out the vanity of their nature. At best, we are but clay, animated dust, and mere walking mounds; but viewed as sinners, we are monsters indeed. Let it be published in heaven as a wonder that the Lord Jesus should set His heart's love upon such as we are. Dust and ashes though we be, we must and will "magnify the exceeding greatness of His grace." Could not His heart find rest in heaven? Must He come to these tents of Kedar[332] for a spouse, and choose a bride upon whom the sun had looked? O heavens and earth, break forth into a song, and give all glory to our sweet Lord Jesus.

✒ *May 28* ✒

This I recall to my mind, therefore have I hope
(Lamentations 3:21).

Memory is frequently the bondslave of despondency. Despairing minds call to remembrance every dark foreboding in the past, and dilate upon every gloomy feature in the present; thus memory, clothed in sackcloth, presents to the mind a cup of mingled gall and wormwood. There is, however, no necessity for this. Wisdom can readily transform memory into an angel of comfort. That same recollection, which in its left hand brings so many gloomy omens, may be trained to bear in its right a wealth of hopeful signs. She need not wear a crown of iron; she may encircle her brow with a fillet of gold, all spangled with stars. Thus it was in Jeremiah's experience: in the previous verse memory had brought him to deep humiliation of soul: "My soul has them still in remembrance, and is humbled in me"; and now this same memory restored him to life and comfort. "This I recall to my mind, therefore have I hope." Like a two-edged sword, his memory first killed his pride with one edge, and then slew his despair with the other. As a general principle, if we would exercise our memories more wisely, we might, in our very darkest distress, strike a match that would instantaneously kindle the lamp of comfort. There is no need for God to create a new thing upon the earth in order to restore believers to joy; if they would prayerfully rake the ashes of the past, they would find light for the present; and if they would turn to the book of truth and the throne of grace, their candle would soon shine as before. Be it ours to remember the loving-kindness of the Lord, and to rehearse His deeds of grace. Let us open the volume of recollection that is so richly illuminated with memorials of mercy, and we shall soon be happy. Thus memory may be, as Coleridge calls it, "the bosom-spring of joy," and when the Divine Comforter bends it to His service, it may be chief among earthly comforters.

✒ *May 29* ✒

Cursed be the man before the Lord, that riseth up and buildeth this city Jericho (Joshua 6:26).

Since he was cursed who rebuilt Jericho, much more the man who labors to restore Popery among us. In our fathers' days the gigantic walls of Popery fell by the power of their faith, the perseverance of their efforts, and the blast of their gospel trumpets; and now there are some who would rebuild that accursed system upon its old foundation. O Lord, be pleased to thwart their unrighteous endeavors, and pull down every stone that they build. It should be a serious business with us to be thoroughly purged of every error that may have a tendency to foster the spirit of Popery, and when we have made a clean sweep at home, we should seek in every way to oppose its all too rapid spread abroad in the church and in the world. This last can be done in secret by fervent prayer, and in public by decided testimony. We must warn with judicious boldness those who are inclined toward the errors of Rome;[333] we must instruct the young in gospel truth, and tell them of the black doings of Popery in the olden times. We must aid in spreading the light more thoroughly through the land, for priests, like owls, hate daylight. Are we doing all we can for Jesus and the gospel? If not, our negligence plays into the hands of the priesthood. What are we doing to spread the Bible, which is the Pope's bane and poison? Are we casting abroad good, sound gospel writings? Luther once said, "The devil hates goose quills" and, doubtless, he has good reason, for ready writers, by the Holy Spirit's blessing, have done his kingdom much damage. If the thousands who will read this short word this night will do all they can to hinder the rebuilding of this accursed Jericho, the Lord's glory shall speed among the sons of men. Reader, what can you do? What will you do?

ᴥ *May 30* ᴥ

That henceforth we should not serve sin (Romans 6:6).

Christian, what have you to do with sin? Has it not cost you enough already? Burnt child, will you play with the fire? What! when you have already been between the jaws of the lion, will you step a second time into his den? Have you not had enough of the old serpent? Did he not poison all your veins once, and will you play upon the hole of the asp, and put your hand upon the cockatrice's den a second time? *[Cockatrice is a mythological serpent able to kill with its stare.]* Oh, do not be so mad! So foolish! Did sin ever yield you real pleasure? Did you find solid satisfaction in it? If so, go back to your old drudgery, and wear the chain again if it delights you. But inasmuch as sin never did give you what it promised to bestow, but deluded you with lies, be not a second time snared by the old fowler— be free, and let the remembrance of your ancient bondage forbid you to enter the net again! It is contrary to the designs of eternal love, which all have an eye to your purity and holiness; therefore do not run counter to the purposes of your Lord. Another thought should restrain you from sin: Christians can never sin cheaply; they pay a heavy price for iniquity. Transgression destroys peace of mind, obscures fellowship with Jesus, hinders prayer, and brings darkness over the soul. Therefore do not be the serf and bondman of sin. There is yet a higher argument: Each time you "serve sin," you have "Crucified the Lord afresh, and put Him to an open shame."[334] Can you bear that thought? Oh! if you have fallen into any special sin during this day, it may be my Master has sent this admonition this evening to bring you back before you have backslidden very far. Turn you to Jesus anew. He has not forgotten His love to you; His grace is still the same. With weeping and repentance, come to His footstool, and be once more received into His heart; you shall be set upon a rock again, and your goings shall be established.[335]

☙ *May 31* ❧

Who healeth all your diseases (Psalm 103:3).

As humbling as is the statement, yet the fact is certain, that we are all more or less suffering under the disease of sin. What a comfort to know that we have a great Physician who is both able and willing to heal us! Let us think of Him awhile tonight. His cures are very speedy—there is life in a look at Him. His cures are radical—He strikes at the center of the disease; and hence, His cures are sure and certain. He never fails, and *the disease never returns*. There is no relapse where Christ heals; no fear that His patients should be merely patched up for a season. He makes new men of them.[336] A new heart also does He give them, and a right spirit does He put with them. He is well skilled in *all* diseases. Physicians generally have some *specialty*. Although they may know a little about almost all our pains and ills, there is usually one disease which they have studied above all others, but Jesus Christ is thoroughly acquainted with the whole of human nature. He is as much at home with one sinner as with another, and never yet did He meet with an out-of-the-way case that was difficult to Him. He has had extraordinary complications of strange diseases to deal with, but He has known exactly with one glance of His eye how to treat the patient. He is the only universal doctor; and the medicine He gives is the only true cure-all, healing in every instance. Whatever our spiritual malady may be, we should apply at once to this Divine Physician. There is no brokenness of heart that Jesus cannot bind up. "His blood cleanseth from all sin."[337] We have but to think of the myriads who have been delivered from all sorts of diseases through the power and virtue of His touch, and we shall joyfully put ourselves in His hands. We trust Him, and sin dies; we love Him, and grace lives; we wait for Him and grace is strengthened; we see Him as He is, and grace is perfected forever.

June

⚜ June 1 ⚜

He will make her wilderness like Eden (Isaiah 51:3).

I think I see in vision a howling wilderness, a great and terrible desert like the Sahara. I perceive nothing in it to relieve the eye; all around I am wearied with a vision of hot and arid sand, strewn with ten thousand bleaching skeletons of wretched men who have expired in anguish, having lost their way in the pitiless waste. What an appalling sight! How horrible! a sea of sand without a bound and without an oasis, a cheerless graveyard for a race forlorn! But behold and wonder! Upon a sudden, springing up from the scorching sand I see a plant of renown; and as it grows, it buds. The bud expands—it is a rose, and at its side a lily bows its modest head; and, miracle of miracles! as the fragrance of those flowers is diffused the wilderness is transformed into a fruitful field, and all around it blossoms exceedingly. The glory of Lebanon is given unto it, the excellency of Carmel and Sharon.[338] Call it not Sahara; call it Paradise. Speak not of it any longer as the valley of deathshade, for where the skeletons lay bleaching in the sun, behold a resurrection is proclaimed, and up spring the dead, a mighty army, full of life immortal. Jesus is that plant of renown, and His presence makes all things new. Nor is the wonder less in each individual's salvation. Yonder I behold you, dear reader, cast out an infant—unswathed, unwashed, defiled with your own blood, left to be food for beasts of prey. But lo, a jewel has been thrown into your bosom by a divine hand, and for its sake you have been pitied and tended by divine providence; you are washed and cleansed from your defilement; you are adopted into heaven's family;[339] the fair seal of love is upon your forehead; and the ring of faithfulness is on your hand. You are now a prince unto God, though once an orphan cast away. O prize exceedingly the matchless power and grace that changes deserts into gardens,[340] and makes the barren heart to sing for joy.

ᐊ *June 2* ᐅ

Good Master (Matthew 19:16).

If the young man in the gospel used this title in speaking to our Lord, how much more fitly may I thus address Him! He is indeed my Master in both senses, a ruling Master and a teaching Master. I delight to run upon His errands and to sit at His feet. I am both His servant and His disciple, and count it my highest honor to own the double character. If He should ask me why I call Him "good," I should have a ready answer. It is true that "there is none good but one, that is, God," but then He is God, and all the goodness of Deity shines forth in Him.[341] In my experience, I have found Him good, so good, indeed, that all the good I have has come to me through Him. He was good to me when I was dead in sin, for He raised me by His Spirit's power. He has been good to me in all my needs, trials, struggles, and sorrows. Never could there be a better Master, for His service is freedom; His rule is love. I wish I were one-thousandth part as good a servant. When He teaches me as my Rabbi, He is unspeakably good. His doctrine is divine. His manner is condescending, and His spirit is gentleness itself. No error mingles with His instruction—pure is the golden truth that He brings forth, and all His teachings lead to goodness, sanctifying as well as edifying the disciple. Angels find Him a good Master and delight to pay their homage at His footstool. The ancient saints proved Him to be a good Master, and each of them rejoiced to sing, "I am Your servant, O Lord!" My own humble testimony must certainly be to the same effect. I will bear this witness before my friends and neighbors, for possibly they may be led by my testimony to seek my Lord Jesus as their Master. O that they would do so! They would never repent so wise a deed. If they would but take His easy yoke, they would find themselves in so royal a service that they would enlist in it forever.[342]

June 3

He humbled Himself (Philippians 2:8).

Jesus is the great teacher of lowliness of heart. We need daily to learn of Him. See the Master taking a towel and washing His disciples' feet![343] Follower of Christ, will you not humble yourself? See Him as the Servant of servants, and surely you cannot be proud! Is not this sentence the compendium of His biography, *He humbled Himself*? Was He not on earth always stripping off first one robe of honor and then another, till naked, He was fastened to the cross, and there did He not empty out His inmost self, pouring out His life-blood, giving up for all of us, till they laid Him penniless in a borrowed grave? How low was our dear Redeemer brought! How then can we be proud? Stand at the foot of the cross, and count the purple drops by which you have been cleansed; see the thorn-crown; mark His scourged shoulders, still gushing with crimson rills; see hands and feet given up to the rough iron, and His whole self to mockery and scorn; see the bitterness and the pangs and the throes of inward grief, showing themselves in His outward frame; hear the thrilling shriek, "My God, my God, why hast Thou forsaken Me?"[344] And if you do not lie prostrate on the ground before that cross, you have never seen it. If you are not humbled in the presence of Jesus, you do not know Him. You were so lost that nothing could save you but the sacrifice of God's only begotten son. Think of that, and as Jesus stooped for you, bow yourself in lowliness at His feet. A sense of Christ's amazing love for us has a greater tendency to humble us than even a consciousness of our own guilt. May the Lord bring us in contemplation to Calvary; then our position will no longer be that of the pompous man of pride, but we shall take the humble place of one who loves much because much has been forgiven him.[345] Pride cannot live beneath the cross. Let us sit there and learn our lesson, and then rise and carry it into practice.

⊰ *June 4* ⊱

Received up into glory (1 Timothy 3:16).

We have seen our well-beloved Lord in the days of His flesh, humiliated and sore vexed, for He was "despised and rejected of men, a man of sorrows, and acquainted with grief."[346] He, whose brightness is as the morning, wore the sackcloth of sorrow as His daily dress: shame was His mantle, and reproach was His vesture. Yet now, inasmuch as He has triumphed over all the powers of darkness[347] upon the bloody tree, our faith beholds our King returning with dyed garments from Edom, robed in the splendor of victory. How glorious must He have been in the eyes of seraphs, when a cloud received Him out of mortal sight, and He ascended up to heaven![348] Now He wears the glory, which He had with God or ever the earth was, and yet another glory above all—that which He has well earned in the fight against sin, death, and hell. As victor He wears the illustrious crown.[349] Hark how the song swells high! It is a new and sweeter song: "Worthy is the Lamb that was slain, for He has redeemed us unto God by His blood!"[350] He wears the glory of an Intercessor who can never fail, of a Prince who can never be defeated, of a Conqueror who has vanquished every foe, of a Lord who has the heart's allegiance of every subject. Jesus wears all the glory, which the pomp of heaven can bestow upon Him, which ten thousand times ten thousand angels can minister to Him. You cannot with your utmost stretch of imagination conceive His exceeding greatness; yet there will be a further revelation of it when He shall descend from heaven in great power, with all the holy angels—"Then shall He sit upon the throne of His glory."[351] Oh, the splendor of that glory! It will ravish His people's hearts. Nor is this the close, for eternity shall sound His praise, "Your throne, O God, is for ever and ever!" Reader, if you would joy in Christ's glory hereafter, He must be glorious in your sight now. *Is He so?*

⫸ June 5 ⫷

He that loveth not knoweth not God (1 John 4:8).

The distinguishing mark of a Christian is his confidence in the love of Christ, and the yielding of his affections to Christ in return. First, faith sets her seal upon the man by enabling the soul to say with the apostle, "Christ loved me and gave Himself for me." Then love gives the countersign, and stamps upon the heart gratitude and love to Jesus in return. "We love Him because He first loved us."[352] In those grand old ages, which are the heroic period of the Christian religion, this double mark was clearly to be seen in all believers in Jesus; they were men who knew the love of Christ, and rested upon it as a man leans upon a staff whose trustiness he has tried. The love they felt toward the Lord was not a quiet emotion, which they hid within themselves in the secret chamber of their souls, and which they only spoke of in their private assemblies when they met on the first day of the week, and sang hymns in honor of Christ Jesus, the crucified. Instead, it was a passion with them of such a vehement and all-consuming energy, that it was visible in all their actions, spoke in their common talk, and looked out of their eyes even in their commonest glances. Love to Jesus was a flame that fed upon the core and heart of their being; and, therefore, from its own force burned its way into the outer man, and shone there. Zeal for the glory of King Jesus was the seal and mark of all genuine Christians. Because of their dependence upon Christ's love they *dared* much, and because of their love to Christ they *did* much, and it is the same now. The children of God are ruled in their inmost powers by love—the love of Christ constrains them;[353] they rejoice that divine love is set upon them, they feel it shed abroad in their hearts by the Holy Ghost,[354] which is given unto them, and then by force of gratitude they love the Savior with a pure heart, fervently. My reader, do *you* love Him? Before you sleep give an honest answer to a weighty question!

ᗘ *June 6* ᗢ

Are they Israelites? So am I (2 Corinthians 11:22).

We have here A PERSONAL CLAIM, and one that *needs proof*. The apostle knew that *His* claim was indisputable, but there are many people who have no right to the title who yet claim to belong to the Israel of God. If we are with confidence declaring, "So am I also an Israelite," let us only say it after having searched our heart as in the presence of God. But if we can give proof that we are following Jesus, if we can from the heart say, "I trust Him wholly, trust Him only, trust Him simply, trust Him now, and trust Him ever," then the position which the saints of God hold belongs to us—all their enjoyments are our possessions; we may be the very least in Israel, "less than the least of all saints."[355] Yet since the mercies of God belong to the saints AS SAINTS, and not as advanced saints or well-taught saints, we may put in our plea and say, "Are they Israelites? So am I; therefore the promises are mine, grace is mine, glory will be mine." The claim, rightfully made, is one that will yield untold comfort. When God's people are rejoicing that they are His, what happiness if they can say, "So AM I!" When they speak of being pardoned and justified and accepted in the Beloved, how joyful to respond, "Through the grace of God, SO AM I." But this claim not only has its enjoyments and privileges, but also its conditions and duties. We must share with God's people in cloud as well as in sunshine. When we hear them spoken of with contempt and ridicule for being Christians, we must come boldly forward and say, "So am I." When we see them working for Christ, giving their time, their talent, and their whole heart to Jesus, we must be able to say, "So do I." O let us prove our gratitude by our devotion, and live as those who, having claimed a privilege, are willing to take the responsibility connected with it.

⇥ *June 7* ⇤

Be zealous (Revelation 3:19).

If you would see souls converted, if you would hear the cry that "the kingdoms of this world have become the kingdoms of our Lord,"[356] if you would place crowns upon the head of the Savior, and His throne lifted high, then be filled with zeal. For, under God, the way of the world's conversion must be by the zeal of the church. Every grace shall do exploits,[357] but this shall be first; prudence, knowledge, patience, and courage will follow in their places, but zeal must lead the van. It is not the extent of your knowledge, though that is useful; it is not the extent of your talent, though that is not to be despised; it is your zeal that shall do great exploits. This zeal is the fruit of the Holy Spirit; it draws its vital force from the continued operations of the Holy Ghost in the soul. If our inner life dwindles, if our heart beats slowly before God, we shall not know zeal; but if all be strong and vigorous within, then we cannot but feel a loving anxiety to see the kingdom of Christ come, and His will done on earth, even as it is in heaven. A deep *sense of gratitude* will nourish Christian zeal. Looking to the hole of the pit from which we were dug, we find abundant reason why we should spend and be spent for God. And zeal is also stimulated by *the thought of the eternal future*. It looks with tearful eyes down to the flames of hell, and it cannot slumber. It looks up with anxious gaze to the glories of heaven, and it cannot but bestir itself. It feels that time is short compared with the work to be done, and therefore it devotes all that it has to the cause of its Lord. And it is ever strengthened by *the remembrance of Christ's example*. He was clothed with zeal as with a cloak.[358] How swift the chariot-wheels of duty went with Him! He knew no loitering by the way. Let us prove that we are His disciples by manifesting the same spirit of zeal.

⇝ *June 8* ⇝

*Thou shalt see now whether My word shall come to pass
unto you or not (Numbers 11:23).*

God had made a positive promise to Moses that for the space
of a whole month He would feed the vast host in the wilderness
with flesh.[359] Moses, being overtaken by a fit of unbelief, looks
to the outward means, and is at a loss to know how the promise
can be fulfilled. He looked to the creature instead of the Creator.
But doth the Creator expect the creature to fulfill His promise
for Him? No. He who makes the promise always fulfils it by
His own unaided omnipotence. If He speaks, it is done—done
by Himself. His promises do not depend for their fulfillment
upon the co-operation of the puny strength of man. We can at
once perceive the mistake, which Moses made. And yet how
commonly we do the same! God has promised to supply our
needs, and we look to the creature to do what God has promised
to do; and then, because we perceive the creature to be weak and
feeble, we indulge in unbelief. Why do we look to that quarter
at all? Will you look to the North Pole to gather fruits ripened
in the sun? Verily, you would act no more foolishly if you did
this than when you look to the weak for strength, and to the
creature to do the Creator's work. Let us, then, put the question
on the right footing. The ground of faith is not the sufficiency
of the visible means for the performance of the promise, but
the all-sufficiency of the invisible God, who will most surely do
as He has said. If after clearly seeing that the responsibility lies
with the Lord and not with the creature. We dare to indulge in
mistrust, the question of God comes home mightily to us: "Has
the Lord's hand waxed short?"[360] May it happen, too, in His
mercy, that with the question there may flash upon our souls
that blessed declaration, "Thou shalt see now whether My word
shall come to pass unto you or not."

☙ June 9 ❧

Search the Scriptures (John 5:39).

The Greek word here rendered *search* signifies a strict, close, diligent, curious search, such as men make when they are seeking gold, or hunters when they are in earnest after game. We must not rest content with having given a superficial reading to a chapter or two, but with the candle of the Spirit, we must deliberately seek out the hidden meaning of the Word. Holy Scripture requires searching—much of it can only be learned by careful study. There is milk for babes, but also meat for strong men. The rabbis wisely say that a mountain of matter hangs upon every word, yea, upon every title of Scripture. Tertullian exclaims, "I adore the fullness of the Scriptures." No man who merely skims the book of God can profit thereby; we must dig and mine until we obtain the hidden treasure. The door of the Word only opens to the key of diligence. The Scriptures claim searching. They are the writings of God, bearing the divine stamp and authorization—who shall dare to treat them with levity? He who despises them despises the God who wrote them. God forbid that any of us should leave our Bibles to become swift witnesses against us in the great day of account. The word of God will repay searching. God does not bid us sift a mountain of chaff with here and there a grain of wheat in it, but the Bible is winnowed corn—we have but to open the granary door and find it. Scripture grows upon the student. It is full of surprises. Under the teaching of the Holy Spirit, to the searching eye it glows with splendor of revelation, like a vast temple paved with wrought gold, and roofed with rubies, emeralds, and all manner of gems. No merchandise is like the merchandise of Scripture truth. Last, *the Scriptures reveal Jesus*: "They are they which testify of Me."[361] No more powerful motive can be urged upon Bible readers than this: He who finds Jesus finds life, heaven, and all things. Happy is he who, searching his Bible, discovers his Savior.

ᗡ June 10 ᗡ

They are they which testify of Me (John 5:39).

Jesus Christ is the Alpha and Omega of the Bible.[362] He is the constant theme of its sacred pages; from first to last, they testify of Him. At the creation we at once discern Him as one of the sacred Trinity. We catch a glimpse of Him in the promise of the woman's seed.[363] We see Him typified in the ark of Noah. We walk with Abraham, as He sees Messiah's day. We dwell in the tents of Isaac and Jacob, feeding upon the gracious promise. We hear the venerable Israel talking of Shiloh. And in the numerous types of the law, we find the Redeemer abundantly foreshadowed. Prophets and kings, priests and preachers all look one way—they all stand as the cherubs did over the ark, desiring to look within and to read the mystery of God's great propitiation.[364] Still more manifestly in the New Testament, we find our Lord the one pervading subject. It is not an ingot here and there, or dust of gold thinly scattered, but here you stand upon a solid floor of gold; for the whole substance of the New Testament is Jesus crucified, and even its closing sentence is bejeweled with the Redeemer's name.[365] We should always read Scripture in this light; we should consider the word to be as a mirror into which Christ looks down from heaven; and then we, looking into it, see His face reflected as in a glass—darkly, it is true, but still in such a way as to be a blessed preparation for seeing Him as we shall see Him face to face.[366] This volume contains Jesus Christ's letters to us, perfumed by His love. These pages are the garments of our King, and they all smell of myrrh, and aloes, and cassia. *[fragrant, aromatic plants]* Scripture is the royal chariot in which Jesus rides, and its path is paved with love for the daughters of Jerusalem. The Scriptures are the swaddling bands of the holy child Jesus. Unroll them and you find your Savior. The quintessence of the word of God is Christ.

⇜ *June 11* ⇝

There brake He the arrows of the bow, the shield, and the sword, and the battle (Psalm 76:3).

Our Redeemer's glorious cry, "It is finished,"[367] was the death-knell of all the adversaries of His people, the breaking of "the and the battle." Behold the hero of Golgotha using His cross as an anvil, and His woes as a hammer, dashing to shivers bundle after bundle of our sins, those poisoned "arrows of the bow;" trampling on every indictment and destroying every accusation. What glorious blows the mighty Breaker gives with a hammer far more ponderous than the fabled weapon of Thor! How the diabolical darts fly to fragments, and the infernal shields are broken like potters' vessels! Behold, He draws from its sheath of hellish workmanship the dread sword of satanic power! He snaps it across His knee, as a man breaks the dry wood of kindling, and casts it into the fire. Beloved, no sin of a believer can now be an arrow mortally to wound him, no condemnation can now be a sword to kill him, for the punishment of our sin was borne by Christ.[368] Our blessed Substitute and Surety made full atonement for all our iniquities. Who now accuses? Who now condemns? Christ has died, yea rather, has risen again.[369] Jesus has emptied the quivers of hell, has quenched every fiery dart, and broken off the head of every arrow of wrath. The ground is strewn with the splinters and relics of the weapons of hell's warfare, which are only visible to us to remind us of our former danger, and of our great deliverance.[370] Sin has no more dominion over us.[371] Jesus has made an end of it, and put it away forever. O you enemy, destructions are come to a perpetual end. Talk of all the wondrous works of the Lord. You, who make mention of His name, keep not silence, neither by day nor when the sun goes to his rest. Bless the Lord, O my soul.

⇜ *June 12* ⇝

*Who has saved us, and called us with an holy calling
(2 Timothy 1:9).*

The apostle uses the perfect tense and says, "Who has saved
us." Believers in Christ Jesus *are* saved. They are not looked
upon as persons who are in a hopeful state, and may ultimately
be saved, but they *are* already saved. Salvation is not a blessing
to be enjoyed upon the deathbed, and to be sung of in a future
state above, but a matter to be obtained, received, promised,
and enjoyed now. The Christian is perfectly saved *in God's
purpose*; God has ordained him unto salvation, and that purpose
is complete. He is saved also as to the price, which has been paid
for him. "It is finished" was the cry of the Savior before He died.
The believer is also perfectly saved *in His covenant head*, for as
he fell in Adam, so he lives in Christ.[372] This complete salvation
is accompanied by a holy calling. Those whom the Savior saved
upon the cross are in due time effectually called by the power
of God the Holy Spirit unto holiness. They leave their sins; they
endeavor to be like Christ. They choose holiness, not out of
any compulsion, but from the stress of a new nature,[373] which
leads them to rejoice in holiness just as naturally as aforetime
they delighted in sin. God neither chose them nor called them
because they were holy, but He called them that they might be
holy—holiness is the beauty produced by His workmanship in
them. The excellencies that we see in a believer are as much
the work of God as the atonement itself. Thus is brought out
very sweetly the fullness of the grace of God. Salvation must be
of race, because the Lord is the author of it; and what motive
except grace could move Him to save the guilty? Salvation
must be of grace, because the Lord works in such a manner
that our righteousness is forever excluded. Such is the believer's
privilege—a present salvation. Such is the evidence that he is
called to it—a holy life.

❧ June 13 ❧

Remove far from me vanity and lies (Proverbs 30:8).

"O my God, be not far from me" Psalm 38:21. Here we have two great lessons—what to deprecate and what to supplicate. The happiest state of a Christian is the holiest state. As there is the most heat nearest to the sun, so there is the most happiness nearest to Christ. No Christian enjoys comfort when his eyes are fixed on vanity—he finds no satisfaction unless his soul is quickened in the ways of God. The world may win happiness elsewhere, but he cannot. I do not blame ungodly men for rushing to their pleasures. Why should I? Let them have their fill. That is all they have to enjoy. A converted wife who despaired of her husband was always very kind to him, for she said, "I fear that this is the only world in which he will be happy, and therefore I have made up my mind to make him as happy as I can in it." Christians must seek their delights in a higher sphere than the insipid frivolities or sinful enjoyments of the world.[374] Vain pursuits are dangerous to renewed souls. We have heard of a philosopher who, while he looked *up* to the stars, fell into a pit; but how deeply do they fall who look *down*. Their fall is fatal. No Christian is safe when his soul is slothful, and his God is far from him. Every Christian is always safe as to the great matter of his standing in Christ, but he is not safe as regards his experience in holiness and communion with Jesus in this life. Satan does not often attack a Christian who is living near to God. It is when the Christian departs from his God, becomes spiritually starved, and endeavors to feed on vanities, that the devil discovers his vantage hour. He may sometimes stand foot to foot with the child of God, who is active in his Master's service, but the battle is generally short; he, who slips as he goes down into the Valley of Humiliation, every time he takes a false step, invites Apollyon to assail him. O for grace to walk humbly with our God!

215

⇥ *June 14* ⇤

O Lord, to us belongeth confusion of face ... because we have sinned against You (Daniel 9:8).

A deep sense and clear sight of sin, its heinousness and the punishment, which it deserves, should make us lie low before the throne. We have sinned as Christians. Alas! that it should be so. Favored as we have been, we have yet been ungrateful: Privileged beyond most, we have not brought forth fruit in proportion. Who is there, although he may long have been engaged in the Christian warfare, that will not blush when he looks back upon the past? As for our days before we were regenerated, may they be forgiven and forgotten; but since then, though we have not sinned as before, yet we have sinned against light and against love—light which has really penetrated our minds, and love in which we have rejoiced. Oh, the atrocity of the sin of a pardoned soul! An unpardoned sinner sins cheaply compared with the sin of one of God's own elect ones, who has had communion with Christ and leaned his head upon Jesus' bosom. Look at David![375] Many will talk of his sin, but I pray you look at his repentance, and hear his broken bones, as each one of them moans out its sorrowful confession! Mark his tears, as they fall upon the ground, and the deep sighs with which he accompanies the softened music of his harp! We have erred. Let us, therefore, seek the spirit of penitence. Look again at Peter! We speak much of Peter's denying his Master.[376] Remember, it is written, "He wept bitterly." Have *we* no denials of our Lord to be lamented with tears? Alas! these sins of ours, before and after conversion, would consign us to the place of inextinguishable fire if it were not for the sovereign mercy, which has made us to differ, snatching us like brands from the burning. My soul, bow down under a sense of your natural sinfulness, and worship your God. Admire the grace, which saves you—the mercy, which spares you—the love, which pardons you!

ᗢ *June 15* ᗧ

He openeth, and no man shutteth (Revelation 3:7).

Jesus is the keeper of the gates of paradise and before every believing soul He sets an open door, which no man or devil shall be able to close against it.[377] What joy it will be to find that faith in Him is the golden key to the everlasting doors. My soul, do you carry this key in your bosom, or are you trusting to some deceitful picklock, which will fail you at last? Hear this parable of the preacher, and remember it. The great King has made a banquet, and He has proclaimed to all the world that none shall enter but those who bring with them the fairest flower that blooms. The spirits of men advance to the gate by thousands, and they bring each one the flower, which he esteems the queen of the garden; but in crowds they are driven from the royal presence, and enter not into the festive halls. Some bear in their hand the deadly nightshade of superstition, or the flaunting poppies of Rome, or the hemlock of self-righteousness, but these are not dear to the King. The bearers are shut out of the pearly gates. My soul, have you gathered the rose of Sharon? Dost you wear the lily of the valley in your bosom constantly?[378] If so, when you comes up to the gates of heaven you will know its value, for you have only to show this choicest of flowers, and the Porter will open. Not for a moment will He deny you admission, for to that rose the Porter opens always. You shall find your way with the rose of Sharon in your hand up to the throne of God Himself, for heaven itself possesses nothing that excels its radiant beauty, and of all the flowers that bloom in paradise there is none that can rival the lily of the valley. My soul, get Calvary's blood red rose into your hand by faith. By love, wear it. By communion, preserve it. By daily watchfulness, make it your all in all, and you shall be blessed beyond all bliss, happy beyond a dream. Jesus, be mine forever—my God, my heaven, my all.

⪻ *June 16* ⪼

The Lord is my light and my salvation; whom shall I fear? The Lord is the strength of my life; of whom shall I be afraid? (Psalm 27:1)

"The Lord is my light and my salvation." Here is personal interest: "my light," "my salvation." The soul is assured of it, and therefore declares it boldly. Into the soul at the new birth divine light is poured as the precursor of salvation; where there is not enough light to reveal our own darkness and to make us long for the Lord Jesus, there is no evidence of salvation. After conversion, our God is our joy, comfort, guide, teacher, and in every sense our light. He is light within, light around, light reflected from us, and light to be revealed to us. Note, it is not said merely that the Lord gives light, but that He is light;[379] nor that He gives salvation, but that He is salvation.[380] He, then, who by faith has laid hold upon God, has all covenant blessings in his possession. This being made sure as a fact, the argument drawn from it is put in the form of a question, "Whom shall I fear?" It is a question, which is its own answer. The powers of darkness are not to be feared, for the Lord, our light, destroys them; and the damnation of hell is not to be dreaded by us, for the Lord is our salvation. This is a very different challenge from that of boastful Goliath,[381] for it rests not upon the conceited vigor of an arm of flesh, but upon the real power of the omnipotent I AM. "The Lord is the strength of my life." Here is a third glowing epithet: to show that the writer's hope was fastened with a threefold cord, which could not be broken. We may well accumulate terms of praise where the Lord lavishes deeds of grace. Our life derives all its strength from God; and if He deigns to make us strong, we cannot be weakened by all the machinations of the adversary. "Of whom shall I be afraid?" The bold question looks into the future as well as the present. "If God be for us," who can be against us, either now or in time to come?[382]

Help, LORD (Psalm 12:1).
Then Israel sang this song, Spring up, O well;
sing ye unto it (Numbers 21:17).

Famous was the well of Beer in the wilderness,[383] because it was *the subject of a promise*: "That is the well whereof the Lord spake unto Moses, Gather the people together, and I will give them water." The people needed water, and their gracious God promised it. We need fresh supplies of heavenly grace, and in the covenant, the Lord has pledged Himself to give all we require. The well next became *the cause of a song*. Before the water gushed forth, cheerful faith prompted the people to sing; and as they saw the crystal fount bubbling up, the music grew yet more joyous. In like manner, we who believe the promise of God should rejoice in the prospect of divine revivals in our souls, and as we experience them, our holy joy should overflow. Are we thirsting? Let us not murmur, but sing. Spiritual thirst is bitter to bear, but we need not bear it—the promise indicates a well. Let us be of good heart and look for it. Moreover, the well was *the center of prayer*. "Spring up, O well." What God has engaged to give, we must enquire after, or we manifest that we have neither desire nor faith. This evening let us ask that the Scripture we have read and our devotional exercises may not be an empty formality, but a channel of grace to our souls. O that God the Holy Spirit would work in us with all His mighty power, filling us with all the fullness of God. Lastly, the well was *the object of effort*. "The nobles of the people dug it with their staves." The Lord would have us active in obtaining grace. Our staves are ill adapted for digging in the sand, but we must use them to the utmost of our ability. Prayer must not be neglected; the assembling of ourselves together must not be forsaken;[384] ordinances must not be slighted. The Lord will give us His peace most plenteously, but not in a way of idleness. Let us, then, bestir ourselves to seek Him in whom are all our fresh springs.

*I am come into my garden, my sister, my spouse
(Song of Solomon 5:1).*

The heart of the believer is Christ's garden. He bought it with His precious blood, and He enters it and claims it as His own. A garden *implies separation*. It is not the open common; it is not a wilderness; it is walled around or hedged in. Would that we could see the wall of separation between the church and the world made broader and stronger. It makes one sad to hear Christians saying, "Well, there is no harm in this; there is no harm in that," thus getting as near to the world as possible. Grace is at low ebb in that soul that can even raise the question of how far it may go in worldly conformity. A garden is *a place of beauty*; it far surpasses the wild uncultivated lands. The genuine Christian must seek to be more excellent in his life than the best moralist, because Christ's garden ought to produce the best flowers in all the world. Even the best is poor compared with that which Christ deserves; let us not put Him off with withering and dwarf plants. The rarest, richest, choicest lilies and roses ought to bloom in the place which Jesus calls His own. The garden is *a place of growth*. The saints are not to remain undeveloped, always mere buds and blossoms. We should grow in grace and in the knowledge of our Lord and Savior Jesus Christ.[385] Growth should be rapid where Jesus is the Husbandman, and the Holy Spirit the dew from above. A garden is *a place of retirement*. So the Lord Jesus Christ would have us reserve our souls as a place in which He can manifest Himself, as He does not unto the world. O that Christians were more retired, that they kept their hearts more closely shut up for Christ! We often worry and trouble ourselves like Martha, with much serving, so that we have not the room for Christ that Mary had,[386] and do not sit at His feet as we should. The Lord grant the sweet showers of His grace to water His garden this day.

*My Beloved is mine, and I am His: He feedeth among
the lilies. Until the day break, and the shadows flee
away, turn, my Beloved, and be Thou like a roe or a
young hart upon the mountains of Bether
(Song of Solomon 2:16-17).*

Surely if there is a happy verse in the Bible, it is this—"My
Beloved is mine, and I am His." So peaceful, so full of assurance,
so overrunning with happiness and contentment is it that it
might well have been written by the same hand that penned the
twenty-third Psalm. Yet though the prospect is exceeding fair
and lovely—earth cannot show its superior—it is not entirely a
sunlit landscape. There is a cloud in the sky, which casts a shadow
over the scene. Listen, "Until the day break, and the shadows flee
away." There is a word, too, about the "mountains of Bether,"
or, "the mountains of division;" and to our love, anything like
division is bitterness. Beloved, this may be your present state of
mind. You do not doubt your salvation. You know that Christ is
yours, but you are not feasting with Him. You understand your
vital interest in Him, so that you have no shadow of a doubt of
your being His and of His being yours, but still His left hand is
not under your head nor does His right hand embrace you.[387] A
shade of sadness is cast over your heart, perhaps by affliction,
certainly by the temporary absence of your Lord, so even while
exclaiming, "I am His," you are forced to take to your knees
and pray, "Until the day break, and the shadows flee away, turn,
my Beloved." "Where is He?" asks the soul. And the answer
comes, "He feedeth among the lilies." If we would find Christ,
we must get into communion with His people. We must come
to the ordinances with His saints. Oh, for an evening glimpse
of Him! Oh, to dine with Him tonight!

✒ June 20 ✒

Straightway they forsook their nets, and followed Him
(Mark 1:18).

When they heard the call of Jesus, Simon and Andrew obeyed at once without demur. If we would always, punctually and with resolute zeal, put in practice what we hear upon the spot, or at the first fit occasion, our attendance at the means of grace, and our reading of good books could not fail to enrich us spiritually. He will not lose his loaf, who has taken care at once to eat it. Neither can he be deprived of the benefit of the doctrine, who has already acted upon it. Most readers and hearers become moved so far as to purpose to amend, But, alas! the proposal is a blossom, which has not been knit, and therefore no fruit comes of it. They wait, they waver, and then they forget till, like the ponds in nights of frost, when the sun shines by day, they are only thawed in time to be frozen again. That fatal *tomorrow* is blood red with the murder of fair resolutions; it is the slaughterhouse of the innocents. We are very concerned that our little book of "Evening Readings" should not be fruitless, and therefore we pray that readers may not be readers only, but doers, of the word.[388] The practice of truth is the most profitable reading of it. Should the reader be impressed with any duty while perusing these pages, let him hasten to fulfill it before the holy glow has departed from his soul, and let him leave his nets and all that he has sooner than be found rebellious to the Master's call. Do not give place to the devil by delay! Haste while opportunity and quickening are in happy conjunction. Do not be caught in your own nets, but break the meshes of worldliness, and away where glory calls you. Happy is the writer who shall meet with readers resolved to carry out his teachings: His harvest shall be a hundredfold, and his Master shall have great honor. Would to God that such might be our reward upon these brief meditations and hurried hints. Grant it, O Lord, unto your servant!

⤳ June 21 ⤝

The foundation of God standeth sure (2 Timothy 2:19).

The foundation upon which our faith rests is this: that "God was in Christ reconciling the world unto himself, not imputing their trespasses unto them."[389] The great fact on which genuine faith relies is that "the Word was made flesh and dwelt among us,"[390] and that "Christ also has suffered for sin, the just for the unjust, that He might bring us to God."[391] "Who Himself bare our sins in His own body on the tree."[392] "For the chastisement of our peace was upon Him, and by His stripes we are healed."[393] In one word, the great pillar of the Christian's hope is *substitution*. The vicarious sacrifice of Christ for the guilty, Christ being made sin for us that we might be made the righteousness of God in Him,[394] Christ offering up a true and proper expiatory and substitutionary sacrifice in the room, place, and stead of as many as the Father gave Him, who are known to God by name, and are recognized in their own hearts by their trusting in Jesus. This is the cardinal fact of the gospel. If this foundation were removed, what could we do? But it standeth firm as the throne of God. We know it; we rest on it; we rejoice in it. Our delight is to hold it, to meditate upon it, and to proclaim it while we desire to be actuated and moved by gratitude for it in every part of our life and conversation. In these days, a direct attack is made upon the doctrine of the atonement. Men cannot bear substitution. They gnash their teeth at the thought of the Lamb of God bearing the sin of man.[395] But we, who know by experience the preciousness of this truth, will proclaim it in defiance of them confidently and unceasingly. We will neither dilute it nor change it, nor fritter it away in any shape or fashion. It shall still be Christ, a *positive substitute*, bearing human guilt and suffering in the stead of men. We cannot, dare not give it up, for it is our life, and despite every controversy we feel that "Nevertheless the foundation of God standeth sure."[396]

That those things which cannot be shaken may remain
(Hebrews 12:27).

We have many things in our possession at the present moment which can be shaken, and it ill becomes a Christian man to set much store by them, for there is nothing stable beneath these rolling skies; change is written upon all things. Yet, we have certain "things which *cannot* be shaken," and I invite you this evening to think of them, that if the things which can be shaken should all be taken away, you may derive real comfort from the things that cannot be shaken, which will remain. Whatever your losses have been or may be, you enjoy present salvation. You are standing at the foot of His cross, trusting alone in the merit of Jesus' precious blood, and no rise or fall of the markets can interfere with your salvation in Him—no breaking of banks, no failures and bankruptcies can touch that. Then you are *a child of God* this evening. God is your Father. No change of circumstances can ever rob you of that. Although by losses brought to poverty and stripped bare, you can say, "He is my Father still. In my Father's house are many mansions;[397] therefore will I not be troubled." You have another permanent blessing: namely, *the love of Jesus Christ*. He who is God and Man loves you with all the strength of His affectionate nature—nothing can affect that. The fig tree may not blossom, and the flocks may cease from the field,[398] but it matters not to the man who can sing, "My Beloved is mine, and I am His." Our best portion and richest heritage we cannot lose. Whatever troubles come, let us play the man; let us show that we are not such little children as to be cast down by what may happen in this poor fleeting state of time. Our country is Immanuel's land; our hope is above the sky; and therefore, calm as the summer's ocean, we will see the wreck of everything earthborn, and yet rejoice in the God of our salvation.

✒ *June 23* ✒

Waiting for the adoption (Romans 8:23).

Even in this world saints are God's children, but men cannot discover them to be so, except by certain moral characteristics. The adoption is not manifested; the children are not yet openly declared. Among the Romans a man might adopt a child and keep it private for a long time, but there was a second adoption in public. When the child was brought before the constituted authorities, its former garments were taken off, and the father who took it to be his child gave it raiment suitable to its new condition of life. "Beloved, now are we the sons of God, and it doth not yet appear what we shall be."[399] We are not yet arrayed in the apparel, which befits the royal family of heaven; we are wearing in this flesh and blood just what we wore as the sons of Adam; but we know that "when *He* shall appear," who is the "first-born among many brethren," we shall be like Him and see Him as He is.[400] Cannot you imagine that a child taken from the lowest ranks of society, and adopted by a Roman senator, would say to himself, "I long for the day when I shall be publicly adopted. Then I shall leave off these plebeian garments, and be robed as becomes my senatorial rank?" Happy in what he has received, for that very reason, he groans to get the fullness of what is promised him. So it is with us today. We are waiting till we shall put on our proper garments, and shall be manifested as the children of God. We are young nobles and have not yet worn our coronets. We are young brides and the marriage day is not yet come, and by the love our Spouse bears us, we are led to long and sigh for the bridal morning. Our very happiness makes us groan after more. Our joy, like a swollen spring, longs to well up like an Iceland geyser, leaping to the skies; and it heaves and groans within our spirit for want of space and room by which to manifest itself to men.

ᚦ *June 24* ᚦ

Shadrach, Meshach, and Abednego, answered and said,
"Be it known unto you, O king, that we will not serve
your gods" (Daniel 3:16, 18).

The narrative of the manly courage and marvelous deliverance of the three holy children, or rather champions, is well calculated to excite in the minds of believers firmness and steadfastness in upholding the truth in the teeth of tyranny and in the very jaws of death. Let young Christians especially learn from their example, both in matters of faith in religion and matters of uprightness in business, never to sacrifice their consciences. Lose all rather than lose your integrity, and when all else is gone, still hold fast a clear conscience as the rarest jewel which can adorn the bosom of a mortal. Be not guided by the will-o'-the-wisp of policy, but by the pole star of divine authority. Follow the right at all hazards. When you see no present advantage, walk by faith and not by sight. Do God the honor to trust Him when it comes to matters of loss for the sake of principle. See whether He will be your debtor! See if He does not even in this life prove His word that "Godliness, with contentment, is great gain,"[401] and that they who "seek first the kingdom of God and His righteousness, shall have all these things added unto them."[402] Should it happen that, in the providence of God, you are a loser by conscience, you shall find that if the Lord pays you not back in the silver of earthly prosperity, He will discharge His promise in the gold of spiritual joy. Remember that a man's life consists not in the abundance of that which he possesses.[403] To wear a guileless spirit, to have a heart void of offense, and to have the favor and smile of God are greater riches than the mines of Ophir could yield or the traffic of Tyre could win. "Better is a dinner of herbs where love is, than a stalled ox and inward contention therewith."[404] An ounce of heart's-ease is worth a ton of gold.

☜ *June 25* ☞

The dove found no rest for the sole of her foot
(Genesis 8:9).

Reader, can you find rest apart from the ark, Christ Jesus? Then be assured that your religion is vain. Are you satisfied with anything short of a conscious knowledge of your union and interest in Christ? Then woe unto you. If you profess to be a Christian, yet find full satisfaction in worldly pleasures and pursuits, your profession is false. If your soul can stretch herself at rest, and find the bed long enough and the coverlet broad enough to cover her in the chambers of sin, then you are a hypocrite and far enough from any right thoughts of Christ or perception of His preciousness. But if, on the other hand, you feel that if you could indulge in sin without punishment, yet it would be a punishment of itself, and that if you could have the whole world and abide in it forever, it would be quite enough misery not to be parted from it, for your God—your God—is what your soul craves after, then be of good courage. You are a child of God. With all your sins and imperfections, take this to your comfort: If your soul has no rest in sin, you are not as the sinner is! If you are still crying after and craving after something better, Christ has not forgotten you, for you have not quite forgotten Him. The believer cannot do without his Lord; words are inadequate to express his thoughts of Him. We cannot live on the sands of the wilderness; we want the manna, which drops from on high. Our skin bottles of creature confidence cannot yield us a drop of moisture, but we drink of the rock, which follows us, and that rock is Christ.[405] When you feed on Him, your soul can sing, "He has satisfied my mouth with good things, so that my youth is renewed like the eagle's,"[406] but if you have Him not, your bursting wine vat and well-filled barn can give you no sort of satisfaction. Rather lament over them in the words of wisdom, "Vanity of vanities, all is vanity!"[407]

ᗐ *June 26* ᗌ

Having escaped the corruption that is in the world through lust (2 Peter 1:4).

Vanish forever all thought of indulging the flesh if you would live in the power of your risen Lord. It is wrong that a man who is alive in Christ should dwell in the corruption of sin. "Why seek ye the living among the dead?" said the angel to Magdalene.[408] Should the living dwell in the sepulcher? Should divine life be immured in the charnel house of fleshly lust? How can we partake of the cup of the Lord and yet drink the cup of Belial?[409] Surely, believer, from open lusts and sins you are delivered. Have you also escaped from the more secret and delusive lime-twigs of the satanic fowler? Have you come forth from the lust of pride? Have you escaped from slothfulness? Have you clean escaped from carnal security? Are you seeking day by day to live above worldliness, the pride of life, and the ensnaring vice of avarice? Remember, it is for this that you have been enriched with the treasures of God. If you are indeed the chosen of God and beloved by Him, do not suffer all the lavish treasure of grace to be wasted upon you. Follow after holiness; it is the Christian's crown and glory. An unholy church! it is useless to the world, and of no esteem among men. It is an abomination, hell's laughter, and heaven's abhorrence. An unholy church has brought the worst evils, which have ever come upon the world, upon her. O Christian, the vows of God are upon you. You are God's priest.[410] Act as such. You are God's king. Reign over your lusts. You are God's chosen.[411] Do not associate with Belial. Heaven is your portion. Live like a heavenly spirit, so shall you prove that you have true faith in Jesus, for there cannot be faith in the heart unless there be holiness in the life.

"Lord, I desire to live as one
Who bears a blood-bought name,
As one who fears but grieving You,
And knows no other shame."

ᔦ June 27 ᔧ

"Let every man abide in the same calling wherein he was called (1 Corinthians 7:20).

Some people have the foolish notion that the only way in which they can live for God is by becoming ministers, missionaries, or Bible women. Alas! how many would be shut out from any opportunity of magnifying the Most High if this were the case. Beloved, it is not office; it is earnestness. It is not position; it is grace, which will enable us to glorify God. God is most surely glorified in that cobbler's stall where the godly worker, as he plies the awl, sings of the Savior's love, ay, glorified far more than in many a church-funded stall where official religiousness performs its scanty duties. The name of Jesus is glorified by the poor unlearned carter as he drives his horse and blesses his God or speaks to his fellow laborer by the roadside, as much as by the popular divine who, throughout the country, like Boanerges, is thundering out the gospel. God is glorified by our serving Him in our proper vocations. Take care, dear reader, that you do not forsake the path of duty by leaving your occupation. Take care you do not dishonor your profession while in it. Think little of yourselves, but do not think too little of your callings. Every lawful trade may be sanctified by the gospel to noblest ends. Turn to the Bible, and you will find the most menial forms of labor connected either with most daring deeds of faith or with persons whose lives have been illustrious for holiness. Therefore be not discontented with your calling. Whatever God has made your position or your work, abide in that, unless you are quite sure that He calls you to something else. Let your first care be to glorify God to the utmost of your power where you are.[412] Fill your present sphere to His praise, and if He needs you in another, He will show it you. This evening lay aside vexatious ambition and embrace peaceful content.

But Aaron's rod swallowed up their rods (Exodus 7:12).

This incident is an instructive emblem of the sure victory of the divine handiwork over all opposition. Whenever a divine principle is cast into the heart, though the devil may fashion a counterfeit and produce swarms of opponents, as sure as ever God is in the work, it will swallow up all its foes. If God's grace takes possession of a man, the world's magicians may throw down all their rods; and every rod may be as cunning and poisonous as a serpent, but Aaron's rod will swallow up their rods. The sweet attractions of the cross will woo and win the man's heart, and he who lived only for this deceitful earth will now have an eye for the upper spheres, and a wing to mount into celestial heights. When grace has won the day, the worldling seeks the world to come. The same fact is to be observed in the life of the believer. What multitudes of foes has our faith had to meet! Our old sins—the devil threw them down before us, and they turned to serpents. What hosts of them! Ah, but the cross of Jesus destroys them all.[413] Faith in Christ makes short work of all our sins. Then the devil has launched forth another host of serpents in the form of worldly trials, temptations, unbelief; but faith in Jesus is more than a match for them, and overcomes them all.[414] The same absorbing principle shines in the faithful service of God! With an enthusiastic love for Jesus difficulties are surmounted, sacrifices become pleasures, and sufferings are honors. But if religion is thus a consuming passion in the heart, then it follows that there are many persons who profess religion, but have it not; for what they have will not bear this test. Examine yourself, my reader, on this point. Aaron's rod *proved* its heaven-given power. Is your religion doing so? If Christ is anything, He must be everything. O rest not till love and faith in Jesus are the master passions of your soul!

≈ *June 29* ≈

Howbeit, in the business of the ambassadors of the
princes of Babylon, who sent unto him to enquire of the
wonder that was done in the land, God left him, to try
him, that He might know all that was in his heart
(2 Chronicles 32:31).

Hezekiah was growing so inwardly great, and priding himself so much upon the favor of God, that self-righteousness crept in, and through his carnal security, the grace of God was for a time, in its more active operations, withdrawn. Here is quite enough to account with the Babylonians; for if the grace of God should leave the best Christian, there is enough of sin in his heart to make him the worst of transgressors. If left to yourselves, you who are warmest for Christ would cool down like Laodicea[415] into sickening lukewarmness. You who are sound in the faith would be white with the leprosy of false doctrine. You who now walk before the Lord in excellency and integrity would reel to and fro, and stagger with a drunkenness of evil passion. Like the moon, we borrow our light. Bright as we are when grace shines on us, we are darkness itself when the Sun of Righteousness withdraws Himself. Therefore let us cry to God never to leave us. "Lord, take not your Holy Spirit from us! Withdraw not from us Your indwelling grace! Hast Thou not said, 'I, the Lord do keep it; I will water it every moment. Lest any hurt it, I will keep it night and day?'[416] Lord, keep us everywhere. Keep us when in the valley, that we murmur not against Your humbling hand. Keep us when on the mountain, that we wax not giddy through being lifted up. Keep us in youth, when our passions are strong. Keep us in old age, when becoming conceited of our wisdom, we may therefore prove greater fools than the young and giddy. Keep us when we come to die, lest, at the very last, we should deny You! Keep us living, keep us dying, keep us laboring, keep us suffering, keep us fighting, keep us resting, keep us everywhere, for everywhere we need You, O our God!"

*Ah Lord God, behold, Thou hast made the heaven and
the earth by your great power and stretched out arm,
and there is nothing too hard for You (Jeremiah 32:17).*

At the very time when the Chaldeans surrounded Jerusalem,
and when the sword, famine and pestilence had desolated the
land, Jeremiah was commanded by God to purchase a field, and
have the deed of transfer legally sealed and witnessed. This was
a strange purchase for a rational man to make. Prudence could
not justify it, for it was buying with scarcely a probability that
the person purchasing could ever enjoy the possession. But it was
enough for Jeremiah that his God had bidden him, for well he
knew that God will be justified of all His children. He reasoned
thus: "Ah, Lord God! Thou canst make this plot of ground of use
to me; Thou canst rid this land of these oppressors; Thou canst
make me yet sit under my vine and my fig-tree in the heritage
which I have bought; for Thou didst make the heavens and the
earth, and there is nothing too hard for You." This gave a majesty
to the early saints, that they dared to do at God's command things
that carnal reason would condemn.[417] Whether it is a Noah who
is to build a ship on dry land,[418] an Abraham who is to offer
up his only son,[419] or a Moses who is to despise the treasures of
Egypt, or a Joshua who is to besiege Jericho seven days, using
no weapons but the blasts of rams' horns[420]—they all act upon
God's command, contrary to the dictates of carnal reason. And
the Lord gives them a rich reward as the result of their obedient
faith. Would to God we had in the religion of these modern
times a more potent infusion of this heroic faith in God. If we
would venture more upon the naked promise of God, we should
enter a world of wonders to which as yet we are strangers. Let
Jeremiah's place of confidence be ours—nothing is too hard for
the God that created the heavens and the earth.

July

✍ *July 1* ☞

The voice of the Lord God walking in the garden in the cool of the day (Genesis 3:8).

My soul, now that the cool of the day has come, retire awhile and hearken to the voice of your God. He is always ready to speak with you when you are prepared to hear. If there is any slowness to commune, it is not on His part, but altogether on your own, for He stands at the door and knocks. If His people will but open, He rejoices to enter.[421] But in what state is my heart, which is my Lord's garden? May I venture to hope that it is well trimmed and watered, and is bringing forth fruit fit for Him? If not, He will have much to reprove, but still I pray Him to come unto me, for nothing can so certainly bring my heart into a right condition as the presence of the Sun of Righteousness, who brings healing in His wings.[422] Come, therefore, O Lord, my God. My soul invites You earnestly and waits for You eagerly. Come to me, O Jesus, my well-beloved, and plant fresh flowers in my garden, such as I see blooming in such perfection in Your matchless character! Come, O my Father, who art the Husbandman, and deal with me in Your tenderness and prudence! Come, O Holy Spirit, and bedew my whole nature, as the herbs are now moistened with the evening dews. O that God would speak to me. Speak, Lord, for Your servant heareth! O that He would walk with me. I am ready to give up my whole heart and mind to Him, and every other thought is hushed. I am only asking what He delights to give. I am sure that He will condescend to have fellowship with me, for He has given me His Holy Spirit to abide with me forever. Sweet is the cool twilight, when every star seems like the eye of heaven, and the cool wind is as the breath of celestial love. My Father, my elder Brother, my sweet Comforter, speak now in loving kindness, for Thou hast opened mine ear and I am not rebellious.

July 2

Unto You will I cry, O Lord my rock; be not silent to me: lest, if Thou be silent to me, I become like them that go down into the pit (Psalm 28:1).

A cry is the natural expression of sorrow and a suitable utterance when all other modes of appeal fail us; but the cry must be alone directed to the Lord, for to cry to man is to waste our entreaties upon the air. When we consider the readiness of the Lord to hear and His ability to aid, we shall see good reason for directing all our appeals at once to the God of our salvation. It will be in vain to call to the rocks in the Day of Judgment,[423] but our Rock attends to our cries. "Be not silent to me." Mere formalists may be content without answers to their prayers, but genuine suppliants cannot; they are not satisfied with the results of prayer itself in calming the mind and subduing the will—they must go further and obtain actual replies from heaven, or they cannot rest. And because of those replies they long to receive at once, they dread even a little of God's silence. God's voice is often so terrible that it shakes the wilderness; but His silence is equally full of awe to an eager suppliant. When God seems to close His ear, we must not therefore close our mouths, but rather cry with more earnestness; for when our note grows shrill with eagerness and grief, He will not long deny us a hearing. What a dreadful case should we be in if the Lord should become forever silent to our prayers? "Lest, if Thou be silent to me, I become like them that go down into the pit." Deprived of the God who answers prayer, we should be in a more pitiable plight than the dead in the grave, and should soon sink to the same level as the lost in hell. We *must* have answers to prayer. Ours is an urgent case of dire necessity. Surely the Lord will speak peace to our agitated minds, for He never can find it in His heart to permit His own elect to perish.

236

❧ *July 3* ☙

If we suffer, we shall also reign with Him
(2 Timothy 2:12).

We must not imagine that we are suffering for Christ and with Christ, if we are not in Christ. Beloved friend, are you trusting to Jesus only? If not, whatever you may have to mourn over on earth, you are not "suffering with Christ," and have no hope of reigning with Him in heaven. Neither are we to conclude that all a Christian's sufferings are sufferings with Christ, for *it is essential that he be called by God to suffer*. If we are rash and imprudent and run into positions for which neither providence nor grace has fitted us, we ought to question whether we are not rather sinning than communing with Jesus. If we let passion take the place of judgment, and self-will reign instead of Scriptural authority, we shall fight the Lord's battles with the devil's weapons. If we cut our own fingers, we must not be surprised. Again, in troubles, which come upon us as the result of sin, we must not dream that we are suffering with Christ. When Miriam spoke evil of Moses, and the leprosy polluted her,[424] she was not suffering for God. Moreover, suffering, which God accepts, *must have God's glory as its end*. If I suffer that I may earn a name or win applause, I shall get no other reward than that of the Pharisee. It is requisite also that love to Jesus and love to His elect, is always the mainspring of all our patience. We must manifest the Spirit of Christ in meekness, gentleness, and forgiveness. Let us search and see if we truly *suffer with Jesus*. And if we do thus suffer, what is our "light affliction" compared with reigning with Him?[425] Oh, it is so blessed to be in the furnace with Christ, and such an honor to stand in the pillory with Him, that if there were no future reward, we might count ourselves happy in present honor; but when the recompense is so eternal, so infinitely more than we had any right to expect, shall we not take up the cross eagerly, and go on our way rejoicing?

⌁ *July 4* ⌁

He that has clean hands, and a pure heart; who has not lifted up his soul unto vanity, nor sworn deceitfully (Psalm 24:4).

Outward practical holiness is a very precious mark of grace. It is to be feared that many professors have perverted the doctrine of justification by faith in such a way as to treat good works with contempt; if so, they will receive everlasting contempt at the last great day. If our hands are not clean, let us wash them in Jesus' precious blood, and so let us lift up pure hands unto God. But "clean hands" will not suffice, unless they are connected with "a pure heart." True religion is heart-work. We may wash the outside of the cup and the platter as long as we please, but if the inward parts are filthy, we are filthy altogether in the sight of God, for our hearts are more truly ourselves than our hands are. The very life of our being lies in the inner nature, and hence the imperative need of purity within. The pure in heart shall see God.[426] All others are but blind bats. The man who is born for heaven "has not lifted up his soul unto vanity." All men have their joys by which their souls are lifted up; the worldling lifts up his soul in carnal delights, which are mere empty vanities. But the saint loves more substantial things. Like Jehoshaphat,[427] he is lifted up in the ways of the Lord. He, who is content with husks, will be reckoned with the swine. Does the world satisfy you? Then you have your reward and portion in this life; make much of it, for you shalt know no other joy. "Nor sworn deceitfully." The saints are men of honor still. The Christian man's word is his only oath; but that is as good as twenty oaths of other men.[428] False speaking will shut any man out of heaven, for a liar shall not enter into God's house,[429] whatever may be his professions or doings. Reader, does the text before us condemn you, or do you hope to ascend into the hill of the Lord?

⇜ *July 5* ⇝

Trust ye in the Lord forever: for in the Lord Jehovah is everlasting strength (Isaiah 26:4).

Seeing that we have such a God to trust, let us rest upon Him with all our weight. Let us resolutely drive out all unbelief, and endeavor to get rid of doubts and fears, which so much mar our comfort, since there is no excuse for fear where God is the foundation of our trust. A loving parent would be sorely grieved if his child could not trust him; and how ungenerous, how unkind is our conduct when we put so little confidence in our heavenly Father, who has never failed us and never will. It would do well to banish doubt from the household of God; but it is to be feared that old Unbelief is as nimble nowadays as when the psalmist asked, "Is His mercy clean gone for ever? Will He be favorable no more?"[430] David had not made any very lengthy trial of the mighty sword of the giant Goliath, and yet he said, "There is none like it."[431] He had tried it once in the hour of his youthful victory, and it had proved itself to be of the right metal, and therefore he praised it ever afterwards. Even so should we speak well of our God: there is none like unto Him in the heaven above or the earth beneath. "To whom then will ye liken Me, or shall I be equal? saith the Holy One."[432] There is no rock like unto the rock of Jacob, our enemies themselves being judges. So far from suffering doubts to live in our hearts, we will take the whole detestable crew, as Elijah did the prophets of Baal, and slay them over the brook;[433] and for a stream to kill them at, we will select the sacred torrent that wells forth from our Savior's wounded side. We have been in many trials, but we have never yet been cast where we could not find in our God all that we needed. Let us then be encouraged to trust in the Lord forever, assured that His everlasting strength will be, as it has been, our help, and stay.

July 6

How many are mine iniquities and sins? (Job 13:23)

Have you ever really weighed and considered how great is the sin of God's people? Think how heinous is your own transgression, and you will find that not only does a sin here and there tower up like an alp, but that your iniquities are heaped upon each other, as in the old fable of the giants who piled Pelian upon Ossa, mountain upon mountain. What an aggregate of sin there is in the life of one of the most sanctified of God's children! Attempt to multiply this, the sin of one only, by the multitude of the redeemed, "a number which no man can number," and you will have some conception of the great mass of the guilt of the people for whom Jesus shed His blood. But we arrive at a more adequate idea of the magnitude of sin by the greatness of the remedy provided. It is the blood of Jesus Christ, God's only and well-beloved Son.[434] God's Son! Angels cast their crowns before Him! All the choral symphonies of heaven surround His glorious throne. "God over all, blessed forever. Amen." And yet He takes upon Himself the form of a servant,[435] and is scourged and pierced, bruised and torn, and at last slain, since nothing but the blood of the incarnate Son of God could make atonement for our offenses. No human mind can adequately estimate the infinite value of the divine sacrifice, for as great as is the sin of God's people, the atonement that takes it away is immeasurably greater. Therefore, the believer, even when sin rolls like a black flood, and the remembrance of the past is bitter, can yet stand before the blazing throne of the great and holy God, and cry, "Who is he that condemneth?[436] It is Christ that died; yea rather, that has risen again."[437] While the recollection of his sin fills him with shame and sorrow, he at the same time makes it a foil to show the brightness of mercy—guilt is the dark night in which the fair star of divine love shines with serene splendor.

⤜ *July 7* ⤛

When I passed by you, I said unto you, "Live"
(Ezekiel 16:6).

Saved one, consider gratefully this mandate of mercy. Note that this command of God is *majestic*. In our text, we perceive a sinner with nothing in him but sin, expecting nothing but wrath, but the eternal Lord passes by in His glory. He looks, He pauses, and He pronounces the solitary, but royal word, "Live." There speaks God. Who but He could venture thus to deal with life and dispense it with a single syllable? Again, this command is *manifold*. When He says, "Live," it includes many things. Here is judicial life. The sinner is ready to be condemned, but the mighty One says, "Live," and he rises pardoned and absolved. It is spiritual life. We knew not Jesus—our eyes could not see Christ, our ears could not hear His voice—Jehovah said "Live," and we were quickened who were dead in trespasses and sins.[438] Moreover, it includes glory-life, which is the perfection of spiritual life. "I said unto you, Live," and that word rolls on through all the years of time till death comes, and in the midst of the shadows of death, the Lord's voice is still heard, "Live!" In the morning of the resurrection it is that self-same voice, which is echoed by the archangel, "Live." And as holy spirits rise to heaven to be blessed forever in the glory of their God, it is in the power of this same word, "Live." Note again, that it is an *irresistible* mandate. Saul of Tarsus is on the road to Damascus to arrest the saints of the living God. A voice is heard from heaven and a light is seen above the brightness of the sun, and Saul is crying out, "Lord, what wilt you have me to do?"[439] This mandate is a mandate of *free grace*. When sinners are saved, it is only and solely because God *will* do it to magnify His free, unpurchased, unsought grace. Christians, see your position: debtors to grace. Show your gratitude by earnest, Christlike lives, and as God has bidden you live, see to it that you live in earnest.

*Lead me in Your truth, and teach me: for Thou art
the God of my salvation; on You do I wait all the day
(Psalm 25:5).*

When the believer has begun with trembling feet to walk in the
way of the Lord, he asks to be still led onward like a little child
upheld by his parent's helping hand, and he craves to be further
instructed in the alphabet of truth. Experimental teaching is the
burden of this prayer. David knew much, but he felt his ignorance,
and desired to be still in the Lord's school. Four times over in
two verses he applies for a scholarship in the college of grace. It
would do well for many professors, if instead of following their
own devices and cutting out new paths of thought for themselves,
they would enquire for the good old ways of God's own truth and
beseech the Holy Ghost to give them sanctified understandings and
teachable spirits. "For you are the God of my salvation."[440] The
Three-One Jehovah is the Author and Perfecter of salvation to
His people.[441] Reader, is He the God of *your* salvation? Do you
find all the grounds of your eternal hopes in the Father's election,
in the Son's atonement, and in the Spirit's quickening? If so, you
may use this as an argument for obtaining further blessings. If
the Lord has ordained to save you, surely He will not refuse to
instruct you in His ways. It is a happy thing when we can address
the Lord with the confidence that David here manifests. It gives
us great power in prayer and comfort in trial. "On You do I wait
all the day." Patience is the fair handmaid and daughter of faith;
we cheerfully wait when we are certain that we shall not wait
in vain. It is our duty and our privilege to wait upon the Lord
in service, in worship, in expectancy, and in trust all the days of
our life. Our faith will be tried faith, and if it is of the true kind,
it will bear continued trial without yielding. We shall not grow
weary of waiting upon God if we remember how long and how
graciously He once waited for us.[442]

⇜ *July 9* ⇝

And God divided the light from the darkness
(Genesis 1:4).

A believer has two principles at work within him. In his natural estate he was subject to one principle only, which was darkness. Now light has entered, and the two principles disagree. Mark the apostle Paul's words in the seventh chapter of Romans: "I find then a law, that, when I would do good, evil is present with me. For I delight in the law of God after the inward man: but I see another law in my members, warring against the law of my mind, and bringing me into captivity to the law of sin, which is in my members."[443] How is this state of things occasioned? "The Lord divided the light from the darkness." Darkness, by itself, is quiet and undisturbed, but when the Lord sends in light, there is a conflict, for the one is in opposition to the other: a conflict which will never cease till the believer is altogether light in the Lord. If there be a division *within* the individual Christian, there is certain to be *a division without*. So soon as the Lord gives to any man light, he proceeds to separate himself from the darkness around; he secedes from a merely worldly religion of outward ceremonial, for nothing short of the gospel of Christ will now satisfy him, and he withdraws himself from worldly society and frivolous amusements, and seeks the company of the saints. "We know we have passed from death unto life, because we love the brethren."[444] The light gathers to itself, and the darkness to itself. What God has divided, let us never try to unite, but as Christ went without the camp, bearing His reproach, so let us come out from the ungodly and be a peculiar people.[445] He was holy, harmless, undefiled, and separate from sinners. As He was, so we are to be nonconformists to the world,[446] dissenting from all sin, and distinguished from the rest of mankind by our likeness to our Master.

July 10

And the evening and the morning were the first day
(Genesis 1:5).

The evening was "darkness" and the morning was "light," and yet the two together are called by the name that is given to the light alone! This is somewhat remarkable, but it has an exact analogy in spiritual experience. In every believer there is darkness and light, and yet he is not to be named a sinner because there is sin in him, but he is to be named a saint because he possesses some degree of holiness. This will be a most comforting thought to those who are mourning their infirmities, and who ask, "Can I be a child of God while there is so much darkness in me?" Yes; for you, like the day, take not your name from the evening, but from the morning; and you are spoken of in the word of God as if you were even now perfectly holy as you will be soon.[447] You are called the child of light, though there is darkness in you still. You are named after what is the predominating quality in the sight of God, which will one day be the only principle remaining. Observe that the evening comes first. Naturally we are darkness first in order of time, and the gloom is often first in our mournful apprehension, driving us to cry out in deep humiliation, "God be merciful to me, a sinner."[448] The place of the morning is second; it dawns when grace overcomes nature. It is a blessed aphorism of John Bunyan, "That which is last, lasts forever." That which is first yields in due season to the last; but nothing comes after the last. So that though you are naturally darkness, when once you become light in the Lord, there is no evening to follow. "Your sun shall no more go down." The first day in this life is an evening and a morning; but the second day, when we shall be with God, forever, shall be a day with no evening, but one, sacred, high, eternal noon.

≈ July 11 ≈

Tell ye your children of it, and let your children tell their
children, and their children another generation
(Joel 1:3).

In this simple way, by God's grace, a living testimony for truth
is always to be kept alive in the land—the beloved of the Lord
are to hand down their witness for the gospel, and the covenant
to their heirs, and these again to their next descendants. This is
our *first* duty: we are to begin at the family hearth. He is a bad
preacher who does not commence his ministry at home. The
heathen are to be sought by all means, and the highways and
hedges are to be searched, but home has a prior claim, and woe
unto those who reverse the order of the Lord's arrangements. To
teach our children is a *personal* duty; we cannot delegate it to
Sunday School Teachers, or other friendly aids. These can assist
us, but cannot deliver us from the sacred obligation. Proxies and
sponsors are wicked devices in this case. Mothers and fathers
must, like Abraham, command their households in the fear of
God, and talk with their offspring concerning the wondrous
works of the Most High. Parental teaching is a *natural* duty—
who is more fit to look to the child's wellbeing as those who are
the authors of his actual being? To neglect the instruction of our
offspring is worse than brutish.[449] Family religion is *necessary*
for the nation, for the family itself, and for the church of God.
By a thousand plots Popery is covertly advancing in our land,
and one of the most effectual means for resisting its inroads
is left almost neglected: namely, the instruction of children in
the faith. Would that parents would awaken to a sense of the
importance of this matter. It is a pleasant duty to talk of Jesus
to our sons and daughters, and the more so because it has often
proved to be an *accepted* work, for God has saved the children
through the parents' prayers and admonitions.[450] May every
house into which this volume shall come honor the Lord and
receive His smile.

ᗺ *July 12* ᗡ

His heavenly kingdom (2 Timothy 4:18).

Yonder city of the great King is a place of *active service.* Ransomed spirits serve Him day and night in His temple. They never cease to fulfill the good pleasure of their King. They always "rest," so far as ease and freedom from care is concerned; and never "rest," in the sense of indolence or inactivity. Jerusalem the golden is the place of *communion* with all the people of God. We shall sit with Abraham, Isaac, and Jacob in eternal fellowship. We shall hold high converse with the noble host of the elect, all reigning with Him,[451] who by His love and His potent arm has brought them safely home. We shall not sing solos, but in chorus shall we praise our King. Heaven is a place of *victory realized.* Whenever, Christian, you have achieved a victory over your lusts—whenever after hard struggling, you have laid a temptation dead at your feet—you have in that hour a foretaste of the joy that awaits you when the Lord shall shortly tread Satan under your feet,[452] and you shall find yourself more than conqueror through Him who has loved you.[453] Paradise is a place of *security.* When you enjoy the full assurance of faith, you have the pledge of that glorious security, which shall be yours when you are a perfect citizen of the heavenly Jerusalem. O my sweet home, Jerusalem, you happy harbor of my soul! Thanks, even now, to Him whose love has taught me to long for You; but louder thanks in eternity, when I shall possess You.

> "My soul has tasted of the grapes,
> And now it longs to go
> Where my dear Lord His vineyard keeps,
> And all the clusters grow.
> Upon the true and living vine,[454]
> My famish'd soul would feast,
> And banquet on the fruit divine,
> An everlasting guest."

When I cry unto You, then shall mine enemies turn back: this I know; for God is for me (Psalm 56:9).

It is impossible for any human speech to express the full meaning of this delightful phrase, "God is for me." He was "for us" before the worlds were made. He was "for us," or He would not have given His well-beloved son. He was "for us" when He smote the Only begotten, and laid the full weight of His wrath upon Him—He was "for *us*," though He was against *Him*. He was "for us" when we were ruined in the fall—He loved us notwithstanding all. He was "for us" when we were rebels against Him, and with a high hand were bidding Him defiance.[455] He was "for us," or He would not have brought us humbly to seek His face. He has been "for us" in many struggles. We have been summoned to encounter hosts of dangers. We have been assailed by temptations from without and within. How could we have remained unharmed to this hour if He had not been "for us?" He is "for us" with all the infinity of His being, with all the omnipotence of His love, with all the infallibility of His wisdom. Arrayed in all His divine attributes, He is "for us,"—eternally and immutably "for us." He is "for us" when yon blue skies shall be rolled up like a worn out vesture—"for us" throughout eternity. And because He is "for us," the voice of prayer will always ensure His help. "When I cry unto You, then shall mine enemies be turned back." This is no uncertain hope, but a well-grounded assurance: " … this I know." I will direct my prayer unto You, and will look up for the answer, assured that it will come, and that mine enemies shall be defeated, "for God is for me." O believer, how happy are you with the King of kings on your side! How safe with such a Protector! How sure your cause pleaded by such an Advocate! If God is for you, who can be against you?[456]

*As it began to dawn, came Magdalene, to see the
sepulcher (Matthew 28:1).*

Let us learn from Mary Magdalene how to obtain fellowship with
the Lord Jesus. Notice how she sought. She sought the Savior *very
early* in the morning. If you can wait for Christ, and be patient in
the hope of having fellowship with Him at some distant season,
you will never have fellowship at all; for the heart that is fitted
for communion is a hungering and a thirsting heart. She sought
Him also with *very great boldness*. Other disciples fled from the
sepulcher, for they trembled and were amazed; but Mary, it is
said, "stood" at the sepulcher. If you would have Christ with
you, seek Him boldly. Let nothing hold you back. Defy the world.
Press on where others flee. She sought Christ faithfully—she
stood *at the sepulcher*.[457] Some find it hard to stand by a living
Savior, but she stood by a dead one. Let us seek Christ after this
mode, cleaving to the very least thing that has to do with Him,
remaining faithful though all others should forsake Him. Note
further, she sought Jesus earnestly—she stood "weeping." Those
tear-droppings were as spells that led the Savior captive, and
made Him come forth and show Himself to her. If you desire
Jesus' presence, weep after it! If you cannot be happy unless He
comes and says to you, "Thou art My beloved,"[458] you will soon
hear His voice. Lastly, she sought the Savior *only*. What cared she
for angels? She turned herself back from them; her search was
only for her Lord. If Christ is your one and only love, and your
heart has cast out all rivals, you will not long lack the comfort
of His presence. Mary Magdalene sought thus because she loved
much. Let us arouse ourselves to the same intensity of affection.
Let our hearts, like Mary's, be full of Christ; and our love, like
hers, will be satisfied with nothing short of Himself. O Lord,
reveal Yourself to us this evening!

⇥ *July 15* ⇤

He appeared first to Mary Magdalene (Mark 16:9).

Jesus "appeared first to Mary Magdalene," probably not only on account of her great love and persevering seeking, but because, as the context intimates, she had been a special trophy of Christ's delivering power. Learn from this: that the greatness of our sin before conversion should not make us imagine that we may not be specially favored with the very highest grade of fellowship. She was one who had left all to become *a constant attendant on the Savior*. He was her first, chief object. Many who were on Christ's side did not take up Christ's cross; *she* did. She spent her substance in relieving His wants. If we would see much of Christ, let us *serve* Him. Tell me who they are that sit most often under the banner of His love, and drink deepest draughts from the cup of communion, and I am sure they will be those who give most, who serve best, and who abide closest to the bleeding heart of their dear Lord. But notice *how* Christ revealed Himself to this sorrowing one—by a *word*, "Mary."[459] It needed but one word *in His voice*, and at once she knew Him. Her heart owned allegiance by another word; her heart was too full to say more. That one word would naturally be the most fitting for the occasion. It implies obedience. She said, "Master." There is no state of mind in which this confession of allegiance will be too cold. No, when your spirit glows most with the heavenly fire, then you will say, "I am Your servant, Thou hast loosed my bonds." If you can say, "Master," if you feel that His will is your will, then you stand in a happy, holy place. He must have said, "Mary," or else you could not have said, "Rabboni." See, then, from all this, how Christ honors those who honor Him, how love draws our Beloved, how it needs but one word of His to turn our weeping to rejoicing, how His presence makes the heart's sunshine.

⤞ *July 16* ⤝

Thou shalt arise, and have mercy upon Zion: for the time to favor her, yea, the set time is come. For Your servants take pleasure in her stones, and favor the dust thereof (Psalm 102:13-14).

A selfish man in trouble is exceedingly hard to comfort, because the springs of his comfort are entirely within himself, and when he is sad, all his springs are dry. But a large-hearted man, full of Christian philanthropy, has other springs from which to supply himself with comfort beside those which lie within. He can go to his God first of all, and there find abundant help; and he can discover arguments for consolation in things relating to the world at large, to his country, and, above all, to the church. David in this Psalm was exceedingly sorrowful; he wrote, "I am like an owl of the desert, I watch, and am as a sparrow alone upon the house top."[460] The only way in which he could comfort himself, was in the reflection that God would arise and have mercy upon Zion. Though *he* was sad, yet Zion should prosper. However low his own estate, yet Zion should arise. Christian man! learn to comfort yourself in God's gracious dealing toward the church. That which is so dear to your Master, should it not be dear above all else to you? Though your way is dark, can you not gladden your heart with the triumphs of His cross and the spread of His truth? Our own personal troubles are forgotten while we look not only upon what God *has* done and is doing for Zion, but on the glorious things He *will yet do* for His Church. Try this, O believer, whenever you are sad of heart and in heaviness of spirit: forget yourself and your little concerns, and seek the welfare and prosperity of Zion. When you bend your knee in prayer to God, limit not your petition to the narrow circle of your own life, tried though it be, but send out your longing prayers for the church's prosperity, "Pray for the peace of Jerusalem,"[461] and your own soul shall be refreshed.

☞ *July 17* ☜

Let not one of them escape (1 Kings 18:40).

When the prophet Elijah had received the answer to his prayer, and the fire from heaven had consumed the sacrifice in the presence of all the people, he called upon the assembled Israelites to take the priests of Baal, and sternly cried, "Let not one of them escape." He took them all down to the brook Kishon, and slew them there.[462] So must it be with our sins—they are all doomed; not one must be preserved. Our darling sin must die. Spare it not for its much crying. Strike, though it is as dear as an Isaac. Strike, for God struck at sin when it was laid upon His own Son. With stern unflinching purpose must you condemn to death that sin which was once the idol of your heart. Do you ask how you are to accomplish this? Jesus will be your power. You have grace to overcome sin given you in the covenant of grace; you have strength to win the victory in the crusade against inward lusts, because Christ Jesus has promised to be with you even unto the end.[463] If you would triumph over darkness, set yourself in the presence of the Sun of Righteousness. There is no place so well adapted for the discovery of sin and recovery from its power and guilt as the immediate presence of God. Job never knew how to get rid of sin half so well as he did when his eye of faith rested upon God, and then he abhorred himself, and repented in dust and ashes. The fine gold of the Christian is oft becoming dim. We need the sacred fire to consume the dross. Let us fly to our God, He is a consuming fire;[464] He will not consume our spirit, but our sins. Let the goodness of God excite us to a sacred jealousy, and to a holy revenge against those iniquities, which are hateful in His sight. Go forth to battle with Amalek in His strength, and utterly destroy the accursed crew. Let not one of them escape.

≪ *July 18* ≫

Neither shall one thrust another; they shall walk every one in his path (Joel 2:8).

Locusts always keep their rank, and although their number is legion, they do not crowd upon each other, so as to throw their columns into confusion. This remarkable fact in natural history shows how thoroughly the Lord has infused the spirit of order into His universe, since the smallest animate creatures are as much controlled by it as are the rolling spheres or the seraphic messengers. It would be wise for believers to be ruled by the same influence in all their spiritual life. In their Christian graces no one virtue should usurp the sphere of another, or eat out the vitals of the rest for its own support. Affection must not smother honesty. Courage must not elbow weakness out of the field. Modesty must not jostle energy. Patience must not slaughter resolution. So also with *our duties*, one must not interfere with another; public usefulness must not injure private piety; church work must not push family worship into a corner. It is ill to offer God one duty stained with the blood of another. Each thing is beautiful in its season, but not otherwise. It was to the Pharisee that Jesus said, "This ought ye to have done, and not to have left the other undone."[465] The same rule applies to *our personal position*, we must take care to know our place, take it, and keep to it. We must minister as the Spirit has given us ability,[466] and not intrude upon our fellow servant's domain. Our Lord Jesus taught us not to covet the high places, but to be willing to be the least among the brethren.[467] Far from us be an envious, ambitious spirit, let us feel the force of the Master's command, and do as He bids us, keeping rank with the rest of the host. Tonight let us see whether we are keeping the unity of the Spirit in the bonds of peace,[468] and let our prayer be that, in all the churches of the Lord Jesus, peace and order may prevail.

*A bruised reed shall He not break, and smoking flax
shall He not quench (Matthew 12:20).*

What is weaker than the bruised reed or the smoking flax? A reed
that grows in the fen or marsh, let but the wild duck light upon
it and it snaps; let but the foot of man brush against it and it is
bruised and broken; every wind that flits across the river moves
it to and fro. You can conceive of nothing more frail or brittle or
whose existence is more in jeopardy than a bruised reed. Then
look at the smoking flax— what is it? It has a spark within it,
it is true, but it is almost smothered; an infant's breath might
blow it out. Nothing has a more precarious existence than its
flame. *Weak things* are here described, yet Jesus says of them,
"The smoking flax I will not quench; the bruised reed I will not
break." Some of God's children are made strong to do mighty
works for Him; God has His Samsons here and there who can
pull up Gaza's gates and carry them to the top of the hill.[469] He
has a few mighties who are lion-like men, but the majority of
His people are a timid, trembling race. They are like starlings,
frightened at every passer by: a little fearful flock. If temptation
comes, they are taken like birds in a snare; if trial threatens,
they are ready to faint. Their frail skiff is tossed up and down
by every wave. They are drifted along like a sea bird on the
crest of the billows—weak things, without strength, wisdom,
or foresight. Yet, weak as they are, and *because* they are so
weak, they have this promise made especially to them. Herein
is grace and graciousness! Herein is love and loving kindness!
How it opens to us the compassion of Jesus—so gentle, tender,
and considerate! We need never shrink back from *His* touch.
We need never fear a harsh word from *Him*. Though He might
well chide us for our weakness, He does not rebuke. Bruised
reeds shall have no blows from Him, and the smoking flax no
damping frowns.

⇜ *July 20* ⇝

And now what hast thou to do in the way of Egypt, to drink the waters of Sihor? (Jeremiah 2:18)

By sundry miracles, by diverse mercies, by strange deliverances Jehovah had proved Himself to be worthy of Israel's trust. Yet they broke down the hedges with which God had enclosed them as a sacred garden; they forsook their own true and living God, and followed after false gods. Constantly did the Lord reprove them for this infatuation, and our text contains one instance of God's reproaching them, "What hast thou to do in the way of Egypt, to drink the waters of the muddy river?"—for so it may be translated, "Why do you wander afar and leave your own cool stream from Lebanon? Why do you forsake Jerusalem to turn aside to Noph and to Tahapanes? Why are you so strangely set on mischief, that you canst not be content with the good and healthful, but wouldst follow after that which is evil and deceitful?" Is there not here a word of disapproval and warning to the Christian? O true believer, called by grace and washed in the precious blood of Jesus, you have tasted of better drink than the muddy river of this world's pleasure can give you; you have had fellowship with Christ; you have obtained the joy of seeing Jesus and leaning your head upon His bosom. Do the trifles, songs, honors, and the merriment of this earth content you after that? Have you eaten the bread of angels, and can you live on husks? Good Rutherford once said, "I have tasted of Christ's own manna, and it has put my mouth out of taste for the brown bread of this world's joys." I think it should be so with you. If you are wandering after the waters of Egypt, O return quickly to the one living fountain. The waters of Sihor may be sweet to the Egyptians, but they will prove only bitterness to you. What have you to do with them? Jesus asks you this question this evening—what will you answer Him?

☞ July 21 ☜

Why go I mourning? (Psalm 42:9)

Can you answer this, believer? Can you find any reason why you are so often mourning instead of rejoicing? Why yield to gloomy anticipations? Who told you that the night would never end in day? Who told you that the sea of circumstances would ebb out till there should be nothing left but long leagues of the mud of horrible poverty? Who told you that the winter of your discontent would proceed from frost to frost, from snow, and ice, and hail, to deeper snow, and yet more heavy tempest of despair? Do you not know that day follows night, that flood comes after ebb, and that spring and summer succeed winter? Have hope then! Always have hope! For God fails you not. Do you not know that your God loves you in the midst of all this? Mountains, when in darkness hidden, are as real as in day, and God's love is as true to you now as it was in your brightest moments. No father chastens always. Your Lord hates the rod as much as you do. He only cares to use it for that reason which should make you willing to receive it, namely, that it works your lasting good. You shall yet climb Jacob's ladder with the angels, and behold Him who sits at the top of it—your covenant God. You shall yet, amidst the splendors of eternity, forget the trials of time, or only remember them to bless the God who led you through them and wrought your lasting good by them. Come; sing in the midst of tribulation. Rejoice even while passing through the furnace. Make the wilderness to blossom like the rose! Cause the desert to ring with your exulting joys, for these light afflictions will soon be over, and then "forever with the Lord," your bliss shall never wane.[470]

"Faint not nor fear, His arms are near,
He changeth not, and thou art dear;
Only believe and thou shalt see,
That Christ is all in all to you."

255

ᖙ *July 22* ᖚ

Behold the Man! (John 19:5)

If there is one place where our Lord Jesus most fully becomes the joy and comfort of His people, it is where He plunged deepest into the depths of woe. Come hither, gracious souls, and behold the Man in the garden of Gethsemane. Behold His heart so brimming with love that He cannot hold it in—so full of sorrow that it must find a vent. Behold the bloody sweat as it distils from every pore of His body and falls upon the ground.[471] Behold the Man as they drive the nails into His hands and feet. Look up, repenting sinners, and see the sorrowful image of your suffering Lord. Mark Him, as the ruby drops stand on the thorn-crown, and adorn with priceless gems the diadem of the King of Misery. Behold the Man when all His bones are out of joint, and He is poured out like water and brought into the dust of death.[472] God has forsaken Him, and hell compasses Him about. Behold and see; was there ever sorrow like His sorrow that is done unto Him? All you who pass by, draw near and look upon this spectacle of grief—unique, unparalleled, a wonder to men and angels, a prodigy unmatched. Behold the Emperor of Woe who had no equal or rival in His agonies! Gaze upon Him, mourners, for if there is not consolation in a crucified Christ, there is no joy in earth or heaven. If in the ransom price of His blood there is not hope, you harps of heaven, there is no joy in you, and the right hand of God shall know no pleasures forevermore. We have only to sit more continually at the cross foot to be less troubled with our doubts and woes. We have but to see *His* sorrows, and *our* sorrows we shall be ashamed to mention. We have but to gaze into His wounds and heal our own. If we would live aright, it must be by the contemplation of His death. If we would rise to dignity, it must be by considering His humiliation and His sorrow.

July 23

The blood of Jesus Christ His Son cleanseth us from all sin (1 John 1:7).

"Cleanseth," says the text—not "shall cleanse." There are multitudes that think that as a dying hope, they may look forward to pardon. Oh! how infinitely better to have cleansing now than to depend on the bare possibility of forgiveness when I come to die. Some imagine that a sense of pardon is an attainment only obtainable after many years of Christian experience. But forgiveness of sin is a *present* thing—a privilege for this day, a joy for this very hour. The moment a sinner trusts Jesus, he is fully forgiven. The text, being written in the present tense, also indicates *continuance*; it was "cleanseth" yesterday, it is "cleanseth" today, it will be "cleanseth" tomorrow. It will be always so with you, Christian, until you cross the river. Every hour you may come to this fountain, for it cleanseth still. Notice, likewise, the *completeness* of the cleansing: "The blood of Jesus Christ His Son cleanseth us from *all* sin"—not only from sin, but "from all sin."[473] Reader, I cannot tell you the exceeding sweetness of this word, but I pray God the Holy Ghost to give you a taste of it. Manifold are our sins against God. Whether the bill is little or great, the same receipt can discharge one as the other. The blood of Jesus Christ is as blessed and divine a payment for the transgressions of blaspheming Peter as for the shortcomings of loving John. Our iniquity is gone, all gone at once and all gone forever. Blessed completeness! What a sweet theme to dwell upon as one gives himself to sleep.

"Sins against a holy God;
Sins against His righteous laws;
Sins against His love, His blood;
Sins against His name and cause;
Sins immense as is the sea—
From them all He cleanseth me."

☙ July 24 ☙

His camp is very great (Joel 2:11).

Consider, my soul, the mightiness of the Lord who is your glory and defense. He is a man of war. Jehovah is His name. All *the forces of heaven* are at His beck. Legions wait at His door: Cherubim and seraphim, watchers and holy ones, principalities and powers are all attentive to His will. If our eyes were not blinded by the ophthalmia of the flesh, we should see horses and chariots of fire round about the Lord's beloved. *The powers of nature* are all subject to the absolute control of the Creator: stormy wind and tempest, lightning and rain, and snow, and hail, and the soft dews and cheering sunshine come and go at His decree. He loosens the bands of Orion, and tightens the sweet influences of the Pleiades. Earth, sea, and air, and the places under the earth are the barracks for Jehovah's great armies. Space is His camping ground, light is His banner, and flame is His sword. When He goes forth to war, famine ravages the land, pestilence smites the nations, hurricane sweeps the sea, tornado shakes the mountains, and earthquake makes the solid world to tremble. As for *animate creatures*: they all own His dominion. From the great fish, which swallowed the prophet, down to "all manner of flies,"[474] which plagued the field of Zoan, all are His servants. The palmerworm, the caterpillar, and the cankerworm are squadrons of His great army, for His camp is very great.[475] My soul, see to it that you are at peace with this mighty King, yea, more, be sure to enlist under His banner, for to war against Him is madness, and to serve Him is glory. Jesus, Immanuel, God with us, is ready to receive recruits for the army of the Lord. If I am not already enlisted, let me go to Him before I sleep, and beg to be accepted through His merits; and if I be already, as I hope I am, a soldier of the cross, let me be of good courage, for the enemy is powerless compared with my Lord, whose camp is very great.

☞ July 25 ☜

In their affliction they will seek Me early (Hosea 5:15).

Losses and adversities are frequently the means that the great Shepherd uses to fetch home His wandering sheep. Like fierce dogs, they worry the wanderers back to the fold. There is no making lions tame if they are too well fed; they must be brought down from their great strength and their stomachs must be lowered, and then they will submit to the tamer's hand. Often have we seen the Christian rendered obedient to the Lord's will by lack of bread and hard labor. When rich and increased in goods, many professors carry their heads much too loftily and speak exceeding boastfully. Like David, they flatter themselves, "My mountain standeth fast; I shall never be moved."[476] When the Christian grows wealthy, is in good repute, has good health, and a happy family, he too often admits Mr. Carnal Security to feast at his table. And then if he is a true child of God, there is a rod preparing for him. Wait awhile, and it may be you will see his substance melt away as a dream. There goes a portion of his estate—how soon the acres change hands. That debt, that dishonored bill—how fast his losses roll in. Where will they end? It is a blessed sign of divine life if, when these embarrassments occur one after another, he begins to be distressed about his backslidings and betakes himself to his God. Blessed are the waves that wash the mariner upon the rock of salvation! Losses in business are often sanctified to our soul's enriching. If the chosen soul will not come to the Lord full-handed, it shall come empty. If God, in His grace, finds no other means of making us honor Him among men, He will cast us into the deep. If we fail to honor Him on the pinnacle of riches, He will bring us into the valley of poverty. Yet faint not, heir of sorrow, when you are thus rebuked, rather recognize the loving hand which chastens, and say, "I will arise, and go unto my Father."[477]

That He may set him with princes (Psalm 113:8).

Our spiritual privileges are of the highest order. "Among princes" *is the place of select society.* "Truly our fellowship is with the Father, and with His Son Jesus Christ."[478] Speak of select society; there is none like this! "We are a chosen generation, a peculiar people, a royal priesthood."[479] "We are come unto the general assembly and church of the first-born, whose names are written in heaven."[480] The saints have courtly audience; princes have admittance to royalty when common people must stand afar off. The child of God has free access to the inner courts of heaven. "For through Him we both have access by one Spirit unto the Father."[481] "Let us come boldly," says the apostle, "to the throne of the heavenly grace."[482] Among princes there is *abundant wealth,* but what is the abundance of princes compared with the riches of believers? "All things are yours, and ye are Christ's, and Christ is God's."[483] "He that spared not His own Son, but delivered Him up for us all, how shall He not with Him also freely give us all things?"[484] Princes have *peculiar power.* A prince of heaven's empire has great influence. He wields a scepter in his own domain; he sits upon Jesus' throne, for "He has made us kings and priests unto God,[485] and we shall reign forever and ever." We reign over the united kingdom of time and eternity. Princes, again, have special honor. We may look down upon all earth-born dignity from the eminence upon, which grace has placed us. For what is human grandeur to this? "He has raised us up together, and made us sit together in heavenly places in Christ Jesus."[486] We share the honor of Christ, and compared with this, earthly splendors are not worth a thought. Communion with Jesus is a richer gem than ever glittered in imperial diadem. Union with the Lord is a coronet of beauty outshining all the blaze of imperial pomp.

Who shall lay anything to the charge of God's elect?
(Romans 8:33)

Most blessed challenge! How unanswerable it is! Every sin of the elect was laid upon the great Champion of our salvation, and by the atonement, carried away. There is no sin against His people in God's book. He sees no sin in Jacob, neither iniquity in Israel; they are justified in Christ forever. When the guilt of sin was taken away, the punishment of sin was removed. For the Christian, there is no stroke from God's angry hand—nay, not so much as a single frown of punitive justice. The believer may be chastised by his Father, but God the Judge has nothing to say to the Christian, except "I have absolved you: you are acquitted." For the Christian, there is no penal death in this world, much less any second death. He is completely freed from all the punishment, as well as the guilt of sin. The power of sin is removed, too. It may stand in our way and agitate us with perpetual warfare, but sin is a conquered foe to every soul in union with Jesus. There is no sin, which a Christian cannot overcome if he will only rely upon his God to do it. They who wear the white robe in heaven overcame through the blood of the Lamb, and we may do the same.[487] No lust is too mighty, no besetting sin too strongly entrenched. We can overcome through the power of Christ. Do believe it, Christian, that your sin is a condemned thing. It may kick and struggle, but it is doomed to die. God has written condemnation across its brow. Christ has crucified it, "nailing it to His cross."[488] Go now and mortify it, and the Lord help you to live to His praise, for sin with all its guilt, shame, and fear, is gone.

> "Here's pardon for transgressions past,
> It matters not how black their cast;
> And, O my soul, with wonder view,
> For sins to come here's pardon, too."

Who went about doing good (Acts 10:38).

Few words, but yet an exquisite miniature of the Lord Jesus Christ. There are not many touches, but they are the strokes of a master's pencil. Of the Savior and only of the Savior is it true in the fullest, broadest, and most unqualified sense. "He went about doing good." From this description, it is evident that He did good *personally*. The evangelists constantly tell us that He touched the leper with His own finger, that He anointed the eyes of the blind, and that in cases where He was asked to speak the word only at a distance, He did not usually comply, but went Himself to the sickbed, and there personally wrought the cure. A lesson to us, if we would do good, to do it ourselves. Give alms with your own hand; a kind look or word will enhance the value of the gift. Speak to a friend about his soul; your loving appeal will have more influence than a whole library of tracts. Our Lord's mode of doing good sets forth His *incessant activity*! He did not only the good, which came close to hand, but He "went about" on His errands of mercy. Throughout the whole land of Judea, there was scarcely a village or a hamlet that was not gladdened by the sight of Him. How this reproves the creeping, loitering manner in which many professors serve the Lord. Let us gird up the loins of our minds,[489] and be not weary in well doing.[490] Does not the text imply that Jesus Christ went out of His way to do good? "He went *about* doing good." He was never deterred by danger or difficulty. He sought out the objects of His gracious intentions. So must we. If old plans will not answer, we must try new ones, for fresh experiments sometimes achieve more than regular methods. Christ's *perseverance* and the *unity* of His purpose are also suggested. The practical application of the subject may be summed up in the words, "He has left us an example that we should follow in His steps."

☙ July 29 ❧

All that the Father giveth Me shall come to Me
(John 6:37).

This declaration involves *the doctrine of election*: there are some whom the Father gave to Christ. It involves the doctrine of effectual calling: these who are given must and shall come; however stoutly they may set themselves against it, yet they shall be brought out of darkness into God's marvelous light. It teaches us *the indispensable necessity of faith*; for even those who are given to Christ are not saved except they come to Jesus.[491] Even *they* must come, for there is no other way to heaven but by the door, Christ Jesus. All that the Father gives to our Redeemer *must come to Him*, therefore none can come to heaven except they come to Christ. Oh! the power and majesty, which rest in the words "shall come." He does not say they have power to come, or they may come if they will, but they "shall come." The Lord Jesus doth by His messengers, His word, and His Spirit, sweetly and graciously compel men to come in that they may eat of His marriage supper. This He does, not by any violation of the free agency of man, but by the power of His grace. I may exercise power over another man's will, and yet that other man's will may be perfectly free, because the constraint is exercised in a manner accordant with the laws of the human mind. Jehovah Jesus knows how, by irresistible arguments addressed to the understanding, by mighty reasons appealing to the affections and the mysterious influence of His Holy Spirit operating upon all the powers and passions of the soul, how to subdue the whole man, that whereas he was once rebellious, he yields cheerfully to His government, subdued by sovereign love. But how shall those be known whom God has chosen? By this result: that they do willingly and joyfully accept Christ, and come to Him with simple and unfeigned faith,[492] resting upon Him as all their salvation and all their desire. Reader, have you thus come to Jesus?

263

⇜ *July 30* ⇝

Him that cometh to Me I will in no wise cast out
(John 6:37).

No limit is set to *the duration* of this promise. It does not merely say, "I will not cast out a sinner at his first coming," but "I will in no wise cast out." The original reads, "I will not, not cast out," or "I will never, never cast out." The text means that Christ will not at *first* reject a believer; and that as He will not do it at first, so He will not to the last. But suppose the believer sins after coming? "If any man sin we have an advocate with the Father, Jesus Christ the righteous."[493] But suppose that believers backslide? "I will heal their backsliding, I will love them freely: for Mine anger is turned away from him."[494] But believers may fall under temptation! "God is faithful, who will not suffer you to be tempted above that ye are able;[495] but will with the temptation also make a way to escape, that ye may be able to bear it." But the believer may fall into sin as David did! Yes, but He will "Purge them with hyssop, and they shall be clean; He will wash them and they shall be whiter than snow."[496] "From all their iniquities will I cleanse them."

"Once in Christ, in Christ forever,
Nothing from His love can sever."

"I give unto My sheep," saith He, "eternal life; and they shall never perish, neither shall any man pluck them out of My hand."[497] What do you say to this, O trembling, feeble mind? Is not this a precious mercy, that coming to Christ, you do not come to One who will treat you well for a little while, and then send you about your business, but He will receive you and make you His bride, and you shall be His forever? Receive no longer the spirit of bondage again to fear, but the spirit of adoption whereby you shall cry, Abba, Father![498] Oh! the grace of these words: "I will in no wise cast out."

≈⊰ *July 31* ⊱≈

And these are the singers ... they were employed in that work day and night (1 Chronicles 9:33).

Well was it so ordered in the temple that the sacred chant never ceased: forevermore did the singers praise the Lord, whose mercy endures forever.[499] As mercy did not cease to rule either by day or by night, so neither did music hush its holy ministry. My heart, there is a lesson sweetly taught to you in the ceaseless song of Zion's temple: You, too, are a constant debtor, and see you to it that your gratitude, like charity, never fails. God's praise is constant in heaven, which is to be your final dwelling-place. Learn to practice the eternal hallelujah. Around the earth as the sun scatters his light, his beams awaken grateful believers to tune their morning hymn, so that the priesthood of the saints keeps up perpetual praise up at all hours. They swathe our globe in a mantle of thanksgiving, and girdle it with a golden belt of song. The Lord always deserves to be praised for what He is in Himself, His works of creation and providence, His goodness toward His creatures, and especially the transcendent act of redemption and all the marvelous blessing flowing therefrom. It is always beneficial to praise the Lord; it cheers the day and brightens the night; it lightens toil and softens sorrow; and over earthly gladness it sheds a sanctifying radiance, which makes it less liable to blind us with its glare. Have we not something to sing about at this moment? Can we not weave a song out of our present joys or our past deliverances or our future hopes? Earth yields her summer fruits: the hay is housed, the golden grain invites the sickle, and the sun, tarrying long to shine upon a fruitful earth, shortens the interval of shade, that we may lengthen the hours of devout worship. By the love of Jesus, let us be stirred up to close the day with a psalm of sanctified gladness.

August

≈ August 1 ≈

Thou crownest the year with Your goodness
(Psalm 65:11).

All the year round, every hour of every day, God is richly blessing us. Both when we sleep and when we wake, His mercy waits upon us. The sun may leave us a legacy of darkness, but our God never ceases to shine upon His children with beams of love. Like a river, His loving kindness is always flowing with fullness as inexhaustible as His own nature. Like the atmosphere, which constantly surrounds the earth and is always ready to support the life of man, the benevolence of God surrounds all His creatures. In it, as in their element, they live and move and have their being.[500] Yet as the sun on summer days gladdens us with beams more warm and bright than at other times, and as rivers are at certain seasons swollen by the rain, and as the atmosphere itself is sometimes fraught with more fresh, more bracing, or more balmy influences than heretofore, so is it with the mercy of God. It has its golden hours, its days of overflow when the Lord magnifies His grace before the sons of men. Amongst the blessings of the nether springs, the joyous days of harvest are a special season of excessive favor. It is the glory of autumn that the ripe gifts of providence are then abundantly bestowed; it is the mellow season of realization, whereas all before was but hope and expectation. Great is the joy of harvest. Happy are the reapers who fill their arms with the liberality of heaven. The psalmist tells us that the harvest is the crowning of the year. Surely these crowning mercies call for crowning thanksgiving! Let us render it by the inward emotions of gratitude. Let our hearts be warmed; let our spirits remember, meditate, and think upon this goodness of the Lord. Then let us *praise Him with our lips*, and laud and magnify His name from whose bounty all this goodness flows. Let us glorify God by yielding *our gifts* to His cause. A practical proof of our gratitude is a special offering of thanks to the Lord of the harvest.

≈ August 2 ≈

So she gleaned in the field until even (Ruth 2:17).

Let me learn from Ruth, the gleaner. As she went out to gather the ears of corn, so must I go forth into the fields of prayer, meditation, the ordinances, and hearing the word to gather spiritual food. The gleaner gathers her portion ear by ear; her gains are little by little. So must I be content to search for single truths, if there be no greater plenty of them. Every ear helps to make a bundle, and every gospel lesson assists in making us wise unto salvation. The gleaner keeps her eyes open. If she stumbled among the stubble in a dream, she would have no load to carry home rejoicingly at eventide. I must be watchful in religious exercises lest they become unprofitable to me; I fear I have lost much already—O that I may rightly estimate my opportunities, and glean with greater diligence. *The gleaner stoops for all she finds*, and so must I. High spirits criticize and object, but lowly minds glean and receive benefit. A humble heart is a great help toward profitably hearing the gospel. The engrafted soul-saving word is not received except with meekness. A stiff back makes a bad gleaner. Down, master pride; you are a vile robber, not to be endured for a moment. *What the gleaner gathers she holds.* If she dropped one ear to find another, the result of her day's work would be scant. She is as careful to retain as to obtain, and so at last her gains are great. How often do I forget all that I hear. The second truth pushes the first out of my head, and so my reading and hearing end in much ado about nothing! Do I feel duly the importance of storing up the truth? A hungry belly makes the gleaner wise. If there is no corn in her hand, there will be no bread on her table. She labors under the sense of necessity, and hence her tread is nimble and her grasp is firm. I have even a greater necessity. Lord, help me to feel it, that it may urge me onward to glean in fields, which yield so plentiful a reward to diligence.

❧ August 3 ☙

But as He went (Luke 8:42).

Jesus is passing through the throng to the house of Jairus[501] to raise the ruler's dead daughter, but He is so profuse in goodness that He works another miracle while upon the road. While yet this rod of Aaron bears the blossom of an unaccomplished wonder, it yields the ripe almonds of a perfect work of mercy. It is enough for us, if we have some one purpose, straightway to go and accomplish it. It is imprudent to expend our energies by the way. Hastening to the rescue of a drowning friend, we cannot afford to exhaust our strength upon another in like danger. It is enough for a tree to yield one sort of fruit, and for a man to fulfill his own peculiar calling. But our Master knows no limit of power or boundary of mission. He is so prolific of grace, that like the sun, which shines as it rolls onward in its orbit, His path is radiant with loving-kindness. He is a swift arrow of love, which not only reaches its ordained target, but also perfumes the air through which it flies. Virtue is evermore going out of Jesus, as sweet fragrances exhale from flowers. It always will be emanating from Him, as water from a sparkling fountain. What delightful encouragement this truth affords us! If our Lord is so ready to heal the sick and bless the needy, then, my soul, do not be slow to put yourself in His way, that He may smile on you. Do not slack in asking, if He is so abundant in bestowing. Give earnest heed to His word now, and at all times, that Jesus may speak through it to your heart. Where He is to be found there make your resort, that you may obtain His blessing. When He is present to heal, may He not heal you? But surely He is present even now, for He always comes to hearts that need Him. And do you not need Him? Ah, *He* knows how much! Thou Son of David, turn Your eye and look upon the distress, which is now before You, and make Your suppliant whole.

271

☙ *August 4* ☞

I smote you with blasting and with mildew and with hail in all the labors of your hands (Haggai 2:17).

How destructive is hail to the standing crops, beating out the precious grain upon the ground! How grateful ought we to be when the corn is spared so terrible a ruin! Let us offer unto the Lord thanksgiving. Even more to be dreaded are those mysterious destroyers—smut, bunt, rust, and mildew. These turn the ear into a mass of soot or render it putrid, or dry up the grain, and all in a manner so beyond all human control that the farmer is compelled to cry, "This is the finger of God." Innumerable minute fungi cause the mischief, and were it not for the goodness of God, the rider on the black horse would soon scatter famine over the land. Infinite mercy spares the food of men, but in view of the active agents, which are ready to destroy the harvest, right wisely are we taught to pray, "Give us this day our daily bread."[502] The curse is abroad; we have constant need of the blessing. When blight and mildew come, they are chastisements from heaven. Men must learn to hear the rod and Him that has appointed it. Spiritually, mildew is no uncommon evil. When our work is most promising, this blight appears. We hoped for many conversions, and lo! a general apathy, an abounding worldliness, or a cruel hardness of heart! There may be no open sin in those for whom we are laboring, but there is a deficiency of sincerity and decision sadly disappointing our desires. We learn from this our dependence upon the Lord, and the need of prayer that no blight may fall upon our work. Spiritual pride or sloth will soon bring upon us the dreadful evil, and only the Lord of the harvest can remove it. Mildew may even attack our own hearts, and shrivel our prayers and religious exercises. May it please the great Husbandman to avert so serious a calamity. Shine, blessed Sun of Righteousness, and drive the blights away.

⌇ *August 5* ⌇

Shall your brethren go to war, and shall ye sit here?
(Numbers 32:6)

Being kindred has its obligations. The Reubenites and Gadites would have been unbrotherly if they had claimed the land, which had been conquered, and had left the rest of the people to fight for their portions alone. We have received much by means of the efforts and sufferings of the saints in years gone by, and if we do not make some return to the church of Christ by giving her our best energies, we are unworthy to be enrolled in her ranks. Others are combating the errors of the age manfully, or excavating perishing ones from amid the ruins of the fall. If we fold our hands in idleness, we had need be warned, lest the curse of Meroz fall upon us. The Master of the vineyard said, "Why stand ye here all the day idle?"[503] What is the idler's excuse? Personal service of Jesus becomes all the more the duty of all because some cheerfully and abundantly render it. The toils of devoted missionaries and fervent ministers shame us if we sit still in indolence. Shrinking from trial is the temptation of those who are at ease in Zion. They would eagerly escape the cross and yet wear the crown. To them the question for this evening's meditation is very applicable. If the most precious are tried in the fire, are we to escape the crucible? If the diamond must be vexed upon the wheel, are we to be made perfect without suffering? Who has commanded the wind to cease from blowing because our bark is on the deep? Why and wherefore should we be treated better than our Lord? The firstborn felt the rod, so why not the younger brethren? It is a cowardly pride, which would choose a downy pillow and a silken couch for a soldier of the cross. Wiser far is he who, being first resigned to the divine will, grows by the energy of grace to be pleased with it, and so learns to gather lilies at the cross foot, and, like Samson, to find honey in the lion.

⇜ *August 6* ⇝

Let the whole earth be filled with His glory;
Amen, and Amen (Psalm 72:19).

This is a large petition. To intercede for a whole city needs a stretch of faith, and there are times when a prayer for one man is enough to stagger us. But how far-reaching was the psalmist's dying intercession! How comprehensive! How sublime! "Let the whole earth be filled with His glory."[504] It does not exempt a single country, however crushed by the foot of superstition. It does not exclude a single nation, however barbarous. For the cannibal, as well as for the civilized, for all climes and races this prayer is uttered. It encompasses the whole circle of the earth and omits no son of Adam. We must be up and doing for our Master or we cannot honestly offer such a prayer. The petition is not asked with a sincere heart unless we endeavor, as God shall help us, to extend the kingdom of our Master. Are there not some who *neglect* both to plead and to labor? Reader, is it *your* prayer? Turn your eyes to Calvary. Behold the Lord of Life nailed to a cross, with the thorn-crown about His brow, with bleeding head, and hands, and feet. What! can you look upon this miracle of miracles, the death of the Son of God, without feeling within your bosom a marvelous adoration that language never can express? And when you feel the blood applied to your conscience, and know that He has blotted out your sins, *you are not a man* unless you start from your knees and cry, "Let the whole earth be filled with His glory; Amen, and Amen." Can you bow before the Crucified in loving homage, and not wish to see your Monarch master of the world? Out on you if you can pretend to love your Prince, and desire not to see Him the universal ruler. Your piety is worthless unless it leads you to wish that the same mercy, which has been extended to you, may bless the whole world. Lord, it is harvest-time, put in Your sickle and reap.

☞ *August 7* ☜

Satan hindered us (1 Thessalonians 2:18).

Since the first hour in which goodness came into conflict with evil, it has never ceased to be true in spiritual experience, that Satan hinders us. From all points of the compass, all along the line of battle, in the vanguard and in the rear, at the dawn of day and in the midnight hour, Satan hinders us. If we toil in the field, he seeks to break the ploughshare. If we build the wall, he labors to cast down the stones. If we would serve God in suffering or in conflict— everywhere Satan hinders us. He hinders us when we are first coming to Jesus Christ. Fierce conflicts we had with Satan when we first looked to the cross and lived. Now that we are saved, he endeavors to hinder the completeness of our personal character. You may be congratulating yourself, "I have hitherto walked consistently; no man can challenge my integrity." Beware of boasting, for your virtue will yet be tried. Satan will direct his engines against that very virtue for which you are the most famous. If you have been hitherto a firm believer, your faith will before long be attacked. If you have been meek as Moses, expect to be tempted to speak unadvisedly with your lips. The birds will peck at your ripest fruit, and the wild boar will dash his tusks at your choicest vines. Satan is sure to hinder us when we are earnest in prayer. He checks our importunity, and weakens our faith in order that, if possible, we may miss the blessing. Nor is Satan less vigilant in obstructing Christian effort. There was never a revival of religion without a revival of his opposition. As soon as Ezra and Nehemiah begin to labor, Sanballat and Tobiah are stirred up to hinder them.[505] What then? We are not alarmed because Satan hinders us, for it is a proof that we are on the Lord's side, and are doing the Lord's work, and in His strength, we shall win the victory and triumph over our adversary.

275

All things are possible to him that believeth
(Mark 9:23).

Many professed Christians are always doubting and fearing, and they forlornly think that this is the necessary state of believers. This is a mistake, for "all things are possible to him that believeth"; and it is possible for us to mount into a state in which a doubt or a fear shall be but as a bird of passage flitting across the soul, but never lingering there. When you read of the high and sweet communions enjoyed by favored saints, you sigh and murmur in the chamber of your heart, "Alas! these are not for me." O climber, if you have but faith, you shall yet stand upon the sunny pinnacle of the temple, for "all things are possible to him that believeth." You hear of exploits, which holy men have done for Jesus: what they have enjoyed of Him, how much they have been like Him, and how they have been able to endure great persecutions for His sake. And you say, "Ah! as for me, I am but a worm; I can never attain to this." But there is nothing, which one saint was, that you may not be. There is no elevation of grace, no attainment of spirituality, no clearness of assurance, no post of duty, which is not open to you if you have but the power to believe. Lay aside your sackcloth and ashes, and rise to the dignity of your true position; you are little in Israel because you will be so, not because there is any necessity for it. It is not required that you should grovel in the dust, O child of a King.[506] Ascend! The golden throne of assurance is waiting for you! The crown of communion with Jesus is ready to bedeck your brow. Wrap yourself in scarlet and fine linen, and fare sumptuously every day; for if you believe, you may eat the fat of kidneys of wheat, your land shall flow with milk and honey, and your soul shall be satisfied as with marrow and fatness. Gather golden sheaves of grace, for they await you in the fields of faith. "All things are possible to him that believeth."

☜ *August 9* ☞

He appeared first to Mary Magdalene, out of whom He had cast seven devils (Mark 16:9).

Mary of Magdala was *the victim of a fearful evil*. She was possessed by not one devil only, but seven. These dreadful inmates caused much pain and pollution to the poor frame in which they had found a lodging. Hers was a hopeless, horrible case. She could not help herself, neither could any human comfort avail. But Jesus passed that way, and unsought, and probably even resisted by the poor demoniac, He uttered the word of power, and Mary of Magdala became a trophy of the healing power of Jesus. All the seven demons left her, never to return, forcibly ejected by the Lord of all. What a blessed deliverance! What a happy change! From delirium to delight, from despair to peace, from hell to heaven! Straightway she became *a constant follower of Jesus*, catching His every word, following His wandering steps, sharing His toilsome life. In addition, she became *His generous helper*, first among that band of healed and grateful women who ministered unto Him of their substance.[507] When Jesus was lifted up in crucifixion, Mary remained *the sharer of His shame*. We find her first beholding from afar and then drawing near to the foot of the cross. She could not die on the cross with Jesus, but she stood as near it as she could, and when His blessed body was taken down, she watched to see how and where it was laid. She was the faithful and watchful believer, last at the sepulcher where Jesus slept, first at the grave when He arose. Her holy fidelity made her *a favored beholder of her beloved Rabboni*, who deigned to call her by her name, and to make her His messenger of good news to the trembling disciples and Peter.[508] Thus grace found her a maniac and made her a minister, cast out devils and gave her to behold angels, delivered her from Satan, and united her forever to the Lord Jesus. May I also be such a miracle of grace!

August 10

The Son of Man has power on earth to forgive sins
(Matthew 9:6).

Behold one of the great Physician's mightiest arts: He has power to forgive sin! While here, He lived below. Before the ransom had been paid, before the blood had been literally sprinkled on the mercy seat, He had power to forgive sin. Has He not power to do it now that He has died? What power must dwell in Him, who to the utmost farthing has faithfully discharged the debts of His people! He has boundless power now that He has finished transgression and made an end of sin. If you doubt it, see Him rising from the dead! Behold Him in ascending splendor raised to the right hand of God! Hear Him pleading before the eternal Father, pointing to His wounds, and urging the merit of His sacred passion! What power to forgive is here![509] "He has ascended on high, and received gifts for men."[510] "He is exalted on high to give repentance and remission of sins."[511] The most crimson sins are removed by the crimson of His blood. At this moment, dear reader, whatever your sinfulness, Christ has power to pardon, power to pardon you, and millions such as you are. A word will speak it. He has nothing more to do to win your pardon; all the atoning work is done. He can, in answer to your tears, forgive your sins today, and make you know it. He can breathe into your soul at this very moment a peace with God which passeth all understanding,[512] which shall spring from perfect remission of your manifold iniquities. Do you believe that? I trust you believe it. May you experience now the power of Jesus to forgive sin! Waste no time in applying to the Physician of souls, but hasten to Him with words like these:

"Jesus! Master! hear my cry;
Save me, heal me with a word;
Fainting at Your feet I lie,
Thou my whisper'd plaint hast heard."

August 11

Everlasting consolation (2 Thessalonians 2:16).

"Consolation." There is music in the word. Like David's harp, it charms away the evil spirit of melancholy.[513] It was a distinguished honor to Barnabas to be called "the son of consolation."[514] Nay, it is one of the illustrious names of a greater than Barnabas, for the Lord Jesus is "the consolation of Israel." "Everlasting consolation"—here is the cream of all, for the eternity of comfort is the crown and glory of it. What is this "everlasting consolation?" It includes a sense of pardoned sin. A Christian man has received in his heart the witness of the Spirit that his iniquities are put away like a cloud, and his transgressions like a thick cloud. If sin is pardoned, is not that an everlasting consolation? Next, the Lord gives His people an abiding sense of acceptance in Christ. The Christian knows that God looks upon him as standing in union with Jesus. Union to the risen Lord is a consolation of the most abiding order. It is, in fact, everlasting. Let sickness prostrate us. Have we not seen hundreds of believers as happy in the weakness of disease as they would have been in the strength of hale and blooming health? Let death's arrows pierce us to the heart, our comfort dies not, for have not our ears full often heard the songs of saints as they have rejoiced because the living love of God was shed abroad in their hearts in dying moments? Yes, a sense of acceptance in the Beloved is an everlasting consolation. Moreover, the Christian has a conviction of his security. God has promised to save those who trust in Christ. The Christian does trust in Christ, and he believes that God will be as good as His word, and will save him. He feels that he is safe by virtue of his being bound up with the person and work of Jesus.

☞ August 12 ☜

The bow shall be seen in the cloud (Genesis 9:14).

The rainbow, the symbol of the covenant with Noah, is typical of our Lord Jesus, who is the Lord's witness to the people. When may we *expect to see the token of the covenant*? The rainbow is only to be seen painted upon a *cloud*. When the sinner's conscience is dark with clouds, when he remembers his past sin, and mourns and laments before God, Jesus Christ is revealed to him as the covenant Rainbow, displaying all the glorious hues of the divine character and betokening peace. To the believer, when his trials and temptations surround him, it is sweet to behold the person of our Lord Jesus Christ—to see Him bleeding, living, rising, and pleading for us. God's rainbow is hung over the cloud of our sins, our sorrows, and our woes to prophesy deliverance. Nor does a *cloud* alone give a rainbow; there must be *the crystal drops* to reflect the light of the sun. So, our sorrows must not only threaten, but they must really fall upon us. There had been no Christ for us if the vengeance of God had been merely a threatening cloud. Punishment must fall in terrible drops upon the Surety. Until there is a *real* anguish in the sinner's conscience, there is no Christ for him; until the chastisement that he feels becomes grievous, he cannot see Jesus. But there must also be a sun, for clouds and drops of rain do not make rainbows unless the sun shines. Beloved, our God, who is as the sun to us, always shines, but we do not always see Him—clouds hide His face; but no matter what drops may be falling or what clouds may be threatening, if *He* does but shine, there will be a rainbow at once. It is said that when we see the rainbow, the shower is over. Certain it is, that when Christ comes, our troubles remove; when we behold Jesus, our sins vanish and our doubts and fears subside. When Jesus walks the waters of the sea, how profound the calm!

☙ *August 13* ☙

And I will remember My covenant (Genesis 9:15).

Mark the form of the promise. God does not say, "And when ye shall look upon the bow, and *ye* shall remember My covenant, *then* I will not destroy the earth," but it is gloriously put, not upon *our* memory, which is fickle and frail, but upon *God's* memory, which is infinite and immutable. "The bow shall be in the cloud; and I will look upon it, that I may remember the everlasting covenant."[515] Oh! it is not my remembering God; it is God's remembering *me* that is the ground of my safety. It is not my laying hold of His covenant, but His covenant's laying hold on me. Glory be to God! the whole of the bulwarks of salvation are secured by divine power, and even the minor towers, which we may imagine might have been left to man, are guarded by almighty strength. Even the *remembrance* of the covenant is not left to our memories, for *we* might forget, but our Lord cannot forget the saints whom He has graven on the palms of His hands.[516] It is with us as with Israel in Egypt; the blood was upon the lintel and the two side-posts, but the Lord did not say, "When *you* see the blood, I will pass over you," but "When *I* see the blood, I will pass over you."[517] My looking to Jesus brings me joy and peace, but it is God's looking to Jesus that secures my salvation and that of all His elect, since it is impossible for our God to look at Christ, our bleeding Surety, and then to be angry with us for sins already punished in Him. No, it is not left with *us* even to be saved by remembering the covenant. There is no linsey-woolsey *[course cloth]* here—not a single thread of the creature mars the fabric. It is not *of* man, neither *by* man, but of the Lord alone. We *should* remember the covenant, and we *shall* do it through divine grace, but the hinge of our safety does not hang there—it is God's remembering *us*, not our remembering *Him*; and hence the covenant is *an everlasting covenant.*

⇛ *August 14* ⇚

I know their sorrows (Exodus 3:7).

The child is cheered as he sings, "This my father knows." Shall not we be comforted as we discern that our dear Friend and tender soul-husband knows all about us?

1. *He is the Physician*, and if He knows all, there is no need that the patient should know. Hush, thou silly, fluttering heart—prying, peeping, and suspecting! All that you do not know now, you shall know hereafter. Meanwhile Jesus, the beloved Physician, knows your soul in adversities. Why need the patient analyze all the medicine or estimate all the symptoms? This is the Physician's work, not mine. It is my business to trust, and His to prescribe. If He shall write His prescription in illegible characters that I cannot read, I will not be uneasy on that account, but rely upon His unfailing skill to make all plain in the result, however mysterious in the working.

2. *He is the Master*, and His knowledge is to serve us instead of our own; we are to obey, not to judge: "The servant knoweth not what his lord doeth."[518] Shall the architect explain his plans to every laborer on the works? If he knows his own intent, is it not enough? The vessel on the wheel cannot guess to what pattern it shall be conformed, but if the potter understands his art, what matters the ignorance of the clay? My Lord must not be cross-questioned anymore by one so ignorant as I am.

3. *He is the Head.* All understanding centers there. What judgment has the arm? What comprehension has the foot? All the power to know lies in the head. Why should the member have a brain of its own when the head fulfills for it every intellectual office? Here, then, must the believer rest his comfort in sickness, not that he himself can see the end, but that Jesus knows all. Sweet Lord, be thou for ever eye, and soul, and head for us, and let us be content to know only what Thou choosest to reveal.

And I will give you an heart of flesh (Ezekiel 36:26).

A heart of flesh is known by its *tenderness concerning sin.* To have indulged a foul imagination, or to have allowed a wild desire to tarry even for a moment, is quite enough to make a heart of flesh grieve before the Lord. The heart of stone calls a great iniquity nothing, but not so the heart of flesh.

> "If to the right or left I stray,
> That moment, Lord, reprove;
> And let me weep my life away,
> For having grieved your love"

The heart of flesh is tender of God's will. My Lord Will-be-will is a great blusterer, and it is hard to subject him to God's will; but when the heart of flesh is given, the will quivers like an aspen leaf in every breath of heaven, and bows like a willow tree in every breeze of God's Spirit. The natural will is cold, hard iron, which is not to be hammered into form, but the renewed will, like molten metal, is soon moulded by the hand of grace. In the fleshy heart there is a tenderness of the affections. The hard heart does not love the Redeemer, but the renewed heart burns with affection toward Him. The hard heart is selfish and coldly demands, "Why should I weep for sin? Why should I love the Lord?" But the heart of flesh says; "Lord, Thou knowest that I love You; help me to love You more!" Many are the privileges of this renewed heart: "'Tis here the Spirit dwells, 'tis here that Jesus rests." It is fitted to receive every spiritual blessing, and every blessing comes to it. It is prepared to yield every heavenly fruit to the honor and praise of God, and therefore the Lord delights in it. A tender heart is the best defense against sin, and the best preparation for heaven. A renewed heart stands on its watchtower looking for the coming of the Lord Jesus. Have you this heart of flesh?

*Ourselves also, which have the firstfruits of the Spirit
(Romans 8:23).*

Present possession is declared. At this present moment, we
have the firstfruits of the Spirit. We have repentance, that gem
of the first water; faith, that priceless pearl; hope, the heavenly
emerald; and love, the glorious ruby. We are already made "new
creatures in Christ Jesus"[519] by the effectual working of God the
Holy Ghost. This is called the firstfruit because it comes first. As
the wave-sheaf was the first of the harvest, so the spiritual life,
and all the graces which adorn that life, are the first operations
of the Spirit of God in our souls. The firstfruits were the pledge
of the harvest. As soon as the Israelite had plucked the first
handful of ripe ears, he looked forward with glad anticipation
to the time when the wagon should creak beneath the sheaves.
So, brethren, when God gives us things which are pure, lovely,
and of good report, as the work of the Holy Spirit, these are
to us the prognostics of the coming glory. *The firstfruits were
always holy to the Lord*, and our new nature, with all its powers,
is a consecrated thing. The new life is not ours that we should
ascribe its excellence to our own merit; it is Christ's image and
creation, and is ordained for His glory. But the firstfruits were
not the harvest, and the works of the Spirit in us at this moment
are not the consummation—the perfection is yet to come. We
must not boast that we have attained, and so reckon the wave-
sheaf to be all the produce of the year. We must hunger and thirst
after righteousness, and pant for the day of full redemption.
Dear reader, this evening, open your mouth wide and God will
fill it. Let the boon in present possession excite in you a sacred
avarice for more grace. Groan within yourself for higher degrees
of consecration, and your Lord will grant them to you, for He
is able to do exceeding abundantly above what we ask or even
think.[520]

☞ *August 17* ☜

This sickness is not unto death (John 11:4).

From our Lord's words we learn that there is a limit to sickness. Here is an "unto" within which its ultimate end is restrained, and beyond which it cannot go. Lazarus might pass through death, but death was not to be the ultimatum of his sickness. In all sickness, the Lord says to the waves of pain, "Hitherto shall ye go, but no further." His fixed purpose is not the destruction, but the instruction of His people. Wisdom hangs up the thermometer at the furnace mouth, and regulates the heat.

1. *The limit is encouragingly comprehensive.* The God of providence has limited the time, manner, intensity, repetition, and effects of all our sicknesses. Each throb is decreed. Each sleepless hour predestinated. Each relapse ordained. Each depression of spirit foreknown. And each sanctifying result eternally purposed. Nothing great or small escapes the ordaining hand of Him who numbers the hairs of our head.

2. *This limit is wisely adjusted* to our strength, to the end designed and to the grace apportioned. Affliction comes not at haphazard—the weight of every stroke of the rod is accurately measured. He, who made no mistakes in balancing the clouds and meting out the heavens, commits no errors in measuring out the ingredients that compose the medicine of souls. We cannot suffer too much nor be relieved too late.

3. *The limit is tenderly appointed.* The knife of the heavenly Surgeon never cuts deeper than is absolutely necessary. "He doth not afflict willingly, nor grieve the children of men." A mother's heart cries, "Spare my child," but no mother is more compassionate than our gracious God. When we consider how hard-mouthed we are, it is a wonder that we are not driven with a sharper bit. The thought is full of consolation, that He, who has fixed the bounds of our habitation, has also fixed the bounds of our tribulation.

⌘ *August 18* ⌖

*And they gave Him to drink wine mingled with myrrh:
but He received it not (Mark 15:23).*

A golden truth is couched in the fact that the Savior put the myrrhed wine-cup from His lips. On the heights of heaven the Son of God stood of old, and as He looked down upon our globe, He measured the long descent to the utmost depths of human misery. He cast up the sum total of all the agonies, which expiation would require, and abated not a jot. He solemnly determined that to offer a sufficient atoning sacrifice He must go the whole way, from the highest to the lowest, from the throne of highest glory to the cross of deepest woe. This myrrhed cup, with its dulling influence, would have stayed Him within a little of the utmost limit of misery. Therefore, He refused it. He would not stop short of all He had undertaken to suffer for His people. Ah, how many of us have pined after relief from our grief, which would have been injurious to us! Reader, did you never pray for a discharge from hard service or suffering with a petulant and willful eagerness? Providence has taken from you the desire of your eyes with a stroke. Say, Christian, if it had been said, "If you so desire it, that loved one of yours shall live, but God will be dishonored," could you have put away the temptation, and said, "Your will be done"? Oh, it is sweet to be able to say, "My Lord, if for other reasons I need not suffer, yet if I can honor You more by suffering, and if the loss of my earthly all will bring You glory, then so let it be. I refuse the comfort, if it comes in the way of Your honor." O that we thus walked more in the footsteps of our Lord, cheerfully enduring trial for His sake, promptly and willingly putting away the thought of self and comfort when it would interfere with our finishing the work that He has given us to do. Great grace is needed, but great grace is provided.

✎ *August 19* ✎

Pull me out of the net that they have laid privily for me:
for Thou art my strength (Psalm 31:4).

Our spiritual foes are of the serpent's brood, and seek to ensnare us by subtlety. The prayer before us supposes the possibility of the believer being caught like a bird. So deftly does the fowler do his work that the net soon surrounds simple ones. The text asks that even out of Satan's meshes, the captive one may be delivered. This is a proper petition, and one, which can be granted. From between the jaws of the lion and out of the belly of hell, eternal love can rescue the saint. It may need a sharp pull to save a soul from the net of temptations, and a mighty pull to extricate a man from the snares of malicious cunning, but the Lord is equal to every emergency. The most skillfully placed nets of the hunter shall never be able to hold His chosen ones. Woe unto those who are so clever at net laying; they who tempt others shall be destroyed themselves. "For Thou art my strength." What an inexpressible sweetness is to be found in these few words! How joyfully may we encounter toils, and how cheerfully may we endure sufferings when we can lay hold upon celestial strength. Divine power will rend asunder all the toils of our enemies, confound their politics, and frustrate their knavish tricks. He is a happy man who has such matchless might engaged upon his side. Our own strength would be of little service when embarrassed in the nets of base cunning, but the Lord's strength is ever available. We have but to invoke it, and we shall find it near at hand. If by faith we are depending alone upon the strength of the mighty God of Israel, we may use our holy reliance as a plea in supplication.

> "Lord, evermore Your face we seek:
> Tempted we are, and poor, and weak;
> Keep us with lowly hearts, and meek.
> Let us not fall. Let us not fall."

And they fortified Jerusalem unto the broad wall
(Nehemiah 3:8).

Well-fortified cities have broad walls, and so had Jerusalem in her glory. The New Jerusalem must, in like manner, be surrounded and preserved by a broad wall of nonconformity to the world, and *separation* from its customs and spirit. The tendency of these days is to break down the holy barrier, and make the distinction between the church and the world merely nominal. Professors are no longer strict and Puritanical; questionable literature is read on all hands; frivolous pastimes are currently indulged; and a general laxity threatens to deprive the Lord's peculiar people of those sacred singularities that separate them from sinners. It will be an ill day for the church and the world when the proposed amalgamation shall be complete, and the sons of God and the daughters of men shall be as one. Then shall another deluge of wrath be ushered in. Beloved reader, let it be your aim in heart, in word, in dress, and in action to maintain the broad wall, remembering that the friendship of this world is extreme ill will against God.[521] The broad wall afforded a pleasant place of *resort* for the inhabitants of Jerusalem, from which they could command prospects of the surrounding country. This reminds us of the Lord's exceeding broad commandments, in which we walk at liberty in communion with Jesus, overlooking the scenes of earth, and looking out toward the glories of heaven. Separated from the world and denying ourselves all ungodliness and fleshly lusts, we are nevertheless not in prison or restricted within narrow bounds. No, we walk at liberty, because we keep His precepts. Come, reader, this evening walk with God in His statutes. As friend met friend upon the city wall, so meet your God in the way of holy prayer and meditation. You have a right to traverse the bulwarks of salvation, for you are a freeman of the royal burgh, a citizen of the metropolis of the universe.

↤ *August 21* ↦

I said not unto the seed of Jacob, Seek ye Me in vain
(Isaiah 45:19).

We may gain much solace by considering what God has *not* said.
What He has said is inexpressibly full of comfort and delight;
what He has not said is scarcely less rich in consolation. It was
one of these "said nots," which preserved the kingdom of Israel
in the days of Jeroboam, the son of Joash, for "the Lord said not
that He would blot out the name of Israel from under heaven."
2 Kings 14:27. In our text we have an assurance that God
will answer prayer, because He has "not said unto the seed of
Israel, Seek ye Me in vain." You who write bitter things against
yourselves should remember that. Let your doubts and fears say
what they will, if *God* has not cut you off from mercy, there is no
room for despair. Even the voice of conscience is of little weight
if it is not seconded by the voice of God. What God *has* said,
tremble at! But suffer not your vain imaginings to overwhelm
you with despondency and sinful despair. Many timid persons
have been vexed by the suspicion that there may be something
in God's decree which shuts *them* out from hope, but here is a
complete refutation to that troublesome fear, for no true seeker
can be decreed to wrath. "I have not spoken in secret, in a dark
place of the earth; I have not said,"[522] even in the secret of my
unsearchable decree, "Seek ye Me in vain." God has clearly
revealed that He *will* hear the prayer of those who call upon Him,
and that declaration cannot be contravened. He has so firmly, so
truthfully, so righteously spoken that there can be no room for
doubt. He does not reveal His mind in unintelligible words, but
He speaks plainly and positively, "Ask, and ye shall receive."
Believe, O trembler, this sure truth—that prayer must and shall
be heard, and that never, even in the secrets of eternity, has the
Lord said unto any living soul, "Seek ye Me in vain."

ᖆ *August 22* ᖆ

The unsearchable riches of Christ (Ephesians 3:8).

My Master has riches beyond the count of arithmetic, the measurement of reason, the dream of imagination, or the eloquence of words. They are *unsearchable*! You may look and study and weigh, but Jesus is a greater Savior than you think Him to be when your thoughts are at the greatest. My Lord is more ready to pardon than you are to sin, more able to forgive than you are to transgress. My Master is more willing to supply your wants than you are to confess them. Never tolerate low thoughts of my Lord Jesus. When you put the crown on His head, you will only crown Him with silver when He deserves gold. My Master has riches of happiness to bestow upon you now. He can make you to lie down in green pastures, and lead you beside still waters.[523] There is no music like the music of His pipe, when He is the Shepherd and you are the sheep, and you lie down at His feet. There is no love like His; neither earth nor heaven can match it. To know Christ and to be found in Him—oh! this is life, this is joy, this is marrow and fatness, wine well refined. My Master does not treat His servants churlishly; He gives to them as a king giveth to a king; He gives them two heavens—a heaven below in serving Him here and a heaven above in delighting in Him forever. His unsearchable riches will be best known in eternity. He will give you all you need on the way to heaven; your place of defense shall be the munitions of rocks, your bread shall be given you, and your waters shall be sure; but it is there, THERE, where you shall hear the song of them that triumph, the shout of them that feast, and shall have a face-to-face view of the glorious and beloved One. The unsearchable riches of Christ! This is the tune for the minstrels of earth, and the song for the harpists of heaven. Lord, teach us more and more of Jesus, and we will tell out the good news to others.

August 23

That Christ may dwell in your hearts by faith
(Ephesians 3:17).

Beyond measure it is desirable that we, as believers, should have the person of Jesus constantly before us, to inflame our love toward Him, and to increase our knowledge of Him. I would to God that my readers were all entered as diligent scholars in Jesus' college, students of Corpus Christi, or the body of Christ, resolved to attain unto a good degree in the learning of the cross. But to have Jesus ever near, the heart must be full of Him, welling up with His love, even to overrunning. Hence the apostle prays, "That Christ may *dwell in your hearts*." See how near he would have Jesus to be! You cannot get a subject closer to you than to have it in the heart itself. "That He may dwell," not that He may call upon you sometimes, as a casual visitor enters into a house and tarries for a night, but that He may *dwell*; that Jesus may become the Lord and Tenant of your inmost being, nevermore to go out. Observe the words—that He may dwell *in your heart*, that best room of the house of manhood; not in your thoughts alone, but in your affections; not merely in the mind's meditations, but in the heart's emotions. We should pant after love to Christ of a most abiding character, not a love that flames up and then dies out into the darkness of a few embers, but a constant flame, fed by sacred fuel, like the fire upon the altar which never went out. This cannot be accomplished except by faith. Faith must be strong, or love will not be fervent; the root of the flower must be healthy or we cannot expect the bloom to be sweet. Faith is the lily's root, and love is the lily's bloom. Now, reader, Jesus cannot be in your heart's love, except you have a firm hold of Him by your heart's faith; and, therefore, pray that you may always trust Christ in order that you may always love Him. If love is cold, be sure that faith is drooping.

If fire break out, and catch in thorns, so that the stacks of corn, or the standing corn, or the field, be consumed therewith; he that kindled the fire shall surely make restitution (Exodus 22:6).

But what restitution can he make who casts abroad the fire-brands of error, or the coals of lasciviousness, and sets men's souls on a blaze with the fire of hell? The guilt is beyond estimate, and the result is irretrievable. If such an offender is forgiven, what grief it will cause him in the retrospect, since he cannot undo the mischief that he has done! An ill example may kindle a flame, which years of amended character cannot quench. To burn the food of man is bad enough, but how much worse to destroy the soul! It may be useful to us to reflect how far we may have been guilty in the past, and to enquire whether, even in the present, there may not be evil in us, which has a tendency to bring damage to the souls of our relatives, friends, or neighbors. The fire of strife is a terrible evil when it breaks out in a Christian church. Where converts were multiplied, and God was glorified, jealousy and envy do the devil's work most effectually. Where the golden grain was being housed, to reward the toil of the great Boaz, the fire of enmity comes in and leaves little else but smoke and a heap of blackness. Woe unto those by whom offenses come.[524] May they never come through us, for although we cannot make restitution, we shall certainly be the chief sufferers if we are the chief offenders. Those who feed the fire deserve just censure, but he who first kindles it is most to blame.[525] Discord usually takes first hold upon the thorns; it is nurtured among the hypocrites and base professors in the church, and away it goes among the righteous, blown by the winds of hell, and no one knows where it may end. O Thou Lord and giver of peace, make us peacemakers, and never let us aid and abet the men of strife, or even unintentionally cause the least division among Your people.

☞ *August 25* ☜

If thou believest with all thine heart, thou mayest
(Acts 8:37).

These words may answer your scruples, devout reader, concerning *the ordinances*. Perhaps you say, "I should be afraid to be baptized; it is such a solemn thing to avow myself to be dead with Christ, and buried with Him. I should not feel at liberty to come to the Master's table; I should be afraid of eating and drinking damnation unto myself, not discerning the Lord's body." Ah! poor trembler, Jesus has given you liberty; be not afraid. If a stranger came to your house, he would stand at the door or wait in the hall; he would not dream of intruding unbidden into your parlor—he is not at home. But your child makes himself very free about the house; and so is it with the child of God. A stranger may not intrude where a child may venture. When the Holy Ghost has given you to feel the spirit of adoption, you may come to Christian ordinances without fear. The same rule holds good of the *Christian's inward privileges*. You think, poor seeker, that you are not allowed to rejoice with joy unspeakable and full of glory. If you are permitted to get inside Christ's door or sit at the bottom of His table, you will be well content. Ah! but you shall not have fewer privileges than the very greatest. God makes no difference in His love to His children. A child is a child to Him. He will not make him a hired servant, but he shall feast upon the fatted calf and have the music and the dancing as much as if he had never gone astray. When Jesus comes into the heart, He issues a general license to be glad in the Lord. No chains are worn in the court of King Jesus. Our admission into full privileges may be gradual, but it is sure. Perhaps our reader is saying, "I wish I could enjoy the promises and walk at liberty in my Lord's commands." "If thou believest with all thine heart, thou mayest." Loose the chains of your neck, O captive daughter, for Jesus makes you free.

ᘓ *August 26* ᘖ

The people, when they beheld Him, were greatly amazed, and running to Him saluted Him (Mark 9:15).

How great the difference between Moses and Jesus! When the prophet of Horeb had been forty days upon the mountain, he underwent a kind of transfiguration, so that his countenance shone with exceeding brightness, and he put a veil over his face, for the people could not endure to look upon his glory. Not so our Savior. He had been transfigured with a greater glory than that of Moses, and yet, it is not written that the people were blinded by the blaze of His countenance, but rather they were amazed, and running to Him, they saluted Him.[526] The glory of the law repels, but the greater glory of Jesus attracts. Though Jesus is holy and just, yet blended with His purity there is so much of truth and grace that sinners run to Him amazed at His goodness, fascinated by His love. They salute Him, become His disciples, and take Him to be their Lord and Master. Reader, it may be that just now you are blinded by the dazzling brightness of the law of God. You feel its claims on your conscience, but you cannot keep it in your life. Not that you find fault with the law. On the contrary, it commands your profoundest esteem. Still you are in no way drawn by it to God; you are rather hardened in heart and verging toward desperation. Ah, poor heart! turn your eye from Moses, with his entire repelling splendor, and look to Jesus, resplendent with milder glories. Behold His flowing wounds and thorn-crowned head! He is the Son of God, and therein He is greater than Moses, but He is the Lord of love, and therein more tender than the lawgiver. He bore the wrath of God, and in His death, revealed more of God's justice than Sinai on a blaze. That justice is now vindicated, and henceforth, it is the guardian of believers in Jesus. Look, sinner, to the bleeding Savior, and as you feel the attraction of His love, fly to His arms, and you will be saved.

Into Your hand I commit my spirit: Thou hast redeemed
me, O Lord God of truth (Psalm 31:5).

Holy men have frequently used these words in their hour of departure. We may profitably consider them this evening. The object of the faithful man's concern in life and death is not his body or his estate, but his spirit. This is his choice treasure—if this is safe, all is well. What is this mortal state compared with the soul? The believer commits his soul to the hand of his God. It came from Him; it is His own. He has aforetime sustained it. He is able to keep it, and it is most fit that He should receive it. All things are safe in Jehovah's hands. What we entrust to the Lord will be secure, both now and in that day of days toward which we are hastening. It is peaceful living and glorious dying, to repose in the care of heaven. At all times we should commit our all to Jesus' faithful hand; then, though life may hang on a thread and adversities may multiply as the sands of the sea, our soul shall dwell at ease and delight itself in quiet resting places. "Thou hast redeemed me, O Lord God of truth." Redemption is a solid basis for confidence. David had not known Calvary as we have done, but temporal redemption cheered him. Shall not eternal redemption yet more sweetly console us? Past deliverances are strong pleas for present assistance. What the Lord has done, He will do again, for He changes not. He is faithful to His promises, and gracious to His saints; He will not turn away from His people.

"Though Thou slay me I will trust,
Praise You even from the dust,
Prove, and tell it as I prove,
Your unutterable love.
You may chasten and correct,
But Thou never canst neglect;
Since the ransom price is paid,
On Your love my hope is stay'd."

⇜ *August 28* ⇝

Sing, O barren (Isaiah 54:1).

Though we have brought forth some fruit unto Christ, and have a joyful hope that we are "plants of His own right hand planting," yet there are times when we feel very barren. Prayer is lifeless. Love is cold. Faith is weak. Each grace in the garden of our heart languishes and droops. We are like flowers in the hot sun, requiring the refreshing shower. In such a condition what are we to do? The text is addressed to us in just such a state. "Sing, O barren, break forth and cry aloud." But what can I sing about? I cannot talk about the present, and even the past looks full of barrenness. Ah! I can sing of Jesus Christ. I can talk of visits, which the Redeemer has aforetimes paid to me; or if not of these, I can magnify the great love wherewith He loved His people when He came from the heights of heaven for their redemption. I will go to the cross again. Come, my soul, you were once heavy laden, and you lost your burden there. Go to Calvary again. Perhaps that very cross, which gave you life, may give you fruitfulness. What is my barrenness? It is the platform for His fruit-creating power. What is my desolation? It is the black setting for the sapphire of His everlasting love. I will go in poverty; I will go in helplessness; I will go in all my shame and backsliding; I will tell Him that I am still His child, and in confidence in His faithful heart, even I, the barren one, will sing and cry aloud. Sing, believer, for it will cheer your own heart and the hearts of other desolate ones. Sing on, for now that you are really ashamed of being barren, you will be fruitful soon.[527] Now that God makes you *loath* to be without fruit, He will soon cover you with clusters. The experience of our barrenness is painful, but the Lord's visitations are delightful. A sense of our own poverty drives us to Christ, and that is where we need to be, for in Him is our fruit found.

All the days of his separation shall he eat nothing that is made of the vine tree, from the kernels even to the husk (Numbers 6:4).

Nazarites had taken, among other vows, one that banned them from the use of wine. In order that they might not violate the obligation, they were forbidden to drink the vinegar of wine or strong liquors. To make the rule still more clear, they were not to touch the unfermented juice of grapes, nor even to eat the fruit either fresh or dried. In order, altogether, to secure the integrity of the vow, they were not even allowed anything that had to do with the vine. They were, in fact, to avoid the appearance of evil. Surely this is a lesson to the Lord's separated ones, teaching them to come away from sin in every form, to avoid not merely its grosser shapes, but even its spirit and similitude. Strict walking is much despised in these days, but rest assured, dear reader, it is both the safest and the happiest. He who yields a point or two to the world is in fearful peril; he who eats the grapes of Sodom will soon drink the wine of Gomorrah. A little crevice in the sea-bank in Holland lets in the sea, and the gap speedily swells till a province is drowned. Worldly conformity, in any degree, is a snare to the soul, and makes it more and more liable to presumptuous sins. Moreover, just as the Nazarite who drank grape juice could not be quite sure whether it might not have endured a degree of fermentation, and consequently could not be clear in heart that his vow was intact, so the yielding, temporizing Christian cannot wear a conscience void of offense, but must feel that the inward monitor is in doubt of him. Things doubtful we need not doubt about; they are wrong to us. Things tempting we must not dally with, but flee from them with speed. Better be sneered at as a Puritan than be despised as a hypocrite. Careful walking may involve much self-denial, but it has pleasures of its own which are more than a sufficient recompense.

Heal me, O Lord, and I shall be healed
(Jeremiah 17:14).
I have seen His ways, and will heal him (Isaiah 57:18).

It is the sole prerogative of God to remove spiritual disease. Men may instrumentally heal natural disease, but even then the honor is to be given to God who gives virtue to medicine, and bestows power to the human frame to cast off disease. As for spiritual sicknesses, these remain with the great Physician alone. He claims it as His prerogative, "I kill and I make alive, I wound and I heal." One of the Lord's choice titles is Jehovah-Rophi, the Lord that healeth you. "I will heal you of your wounds," is a promise, which could not come from the lip of man, but only from the mouth of the eternal God. On this account the psalmist cried unto the Lord, "O Lord, heal me, for my bones are sore vexed,"[528] and again, "Heal my soul, for I have sinned against You." For this, also, the godly praise the name of the Lord, saying, "He healeth all our diseases."[529] He who made man can restore man; He who was at first the creator of our nature can create it anew. What a transcendent comfort it is that in the person of Jesus, "dwelleth all the fullness of the Godhead bodily!"[530] My soul, whatever your disease may be, this great Physician can heal you. If He is God, there can be no limit to His power. Come then with the blind eye of darkened understanding, come with the limping foot of wasted energy, come with the maimed hand of weak faith and the fever of an angry temper, or the fever of shivering despondency. Come just as you are, for He who is God can certainly restore you from your plague. None shall restrain the healing virtue, which proceeds from Jesus our Lord. Legions of devils have been made to own the power of the beloved Physician, and never once has He been baffled. All His patients have been cured in the past and shall be in the future, and you shall be one among them, my friend, if you will but rest yourself in Him this night.

～ *August 31* ～

If we walk in the light, as He is in the light (1 John 1:7).

As He is in the light! Can we ever attain to this? Shall we ever be able to walk as clearly in the light as He whom we call, "Our Father," of whom it is written, "God is light, and in Him is no darkness at all"?[531] Certainly, this is the model that it set before us, for the Savior Himself said, "Be ye perfect, even as your Father who is in heaven is perfect;"[532] and although we may feel that we can never rival the perfection of God, yet we are to seek after it, and never to be satisfied until we attain to it. The youthful artist, as he grasps his early pencil, can hardly hope to equal Raphael or Michelangelo, but still, if he did not have a noble *beau ideal [an idea of something beautiful or perfect]* before his mind, he would only attain to something very mean and ordinary. But what is meant by the expression that the Christian is to walk in light as God is in the light? We conceive it to import *likeness*, but not *degree*. We are as truly in the light, we are as heartily in the light, we are as sincerely in the light, as honestly in the light, though we cannot be there in the same measure. I cannot dwell in the sun; it is too bright a place for my residence, but I can *walk* in the light of the sun; and so, though I cannot attain to that perfection of purity and truth which belongs to the Lord of hosts by nature as the infinitely good, yet I can set the Lord always before me, and strive, by the help of the indwelling Spirit, after conformity to His image. That famous old commentator, John Trapp, says, "We may be in the light as God is in the light for *quality*, but not for *equality*." We are to have the same light, and are as truly to have it and walk in it as God does, though, as for equality with God in His holiness and purity, that must be left until we cross the Jordan and enter into the perfection of the Most High. Mark that the blessings of sacred fellowship and perfect cleansing are bound up with walking in the light.

September

ᘒᘓ *September 1* ᘒᘓ

Trust in Him at all times (Psalm 62:8).

Faith is as much the rule of temporal as of spiritual life; we ought to have faith in God for our earthly affairs as well as for our heavenly business. It is only as we learn to trust in God for the supply of all our daily need that we shall live above the world. We are not to be idle; *that* would show we did *not* trust in God, who works hitherto, but in the devil, which is the father of idleness. We are not to be imprudent or rash; that would be to trust chance and not the living God, who is a God of economy and order. Acting in all prudence and uprightness, we are to rely simply and entirely upon the Lord at all times. Let me commend to you a life of trust in God in temporal things. Trusting in God, you will not be compelled to mourn because you have used sinful means to grow rich. Serve God with integrity, and if you achieve no success, at least no sin will lie upon your conscience. Trusting God, you will not be guilty of self-contradiction. He, who trusts in craft, sails this way today and that way the next, like a vessel tossed about by the fickle wind; but he who trusts in the Lord is like a vessel propelled by steam. She cuts through the waves, defies the wind, and makes one bright silvery straightforward track to her destined haven. Be a person with living principles within; never bow to the varying customs of worldly wisdom. Walk in your path of integrity with steadfast steps, and show that you are invincibly strong in the strength which confidence in God alone can confer. Thus you will be delivered from carking care. You will not be troubled with evil tidings, and your heart will be fixed, trusting in the Lord.[533] How pleasant to float along the stream of providence! There is no more blessed way of living than a life of dependence upon a covenant-keeping God. We have no care, for He cares for us; we have no troubles, because we cast our burdens upon the Lord.

⇜ *September 2* ⇝

Except ye see signs and wonders, ye will not believe
(John 4:48).

A craving after marvels was a symptom of the sickly state of men's minds in our Lord's day; they refused solid nourishment and pined after mere wonder. The gospel, which they so greatly needed, they would not have; they eagerly demanded the miracles that Jesus did not always choose to give. Many nowadays must see signs and wonders, or they will not believe. Some have said in their heart, "I must feel deep horror of soul, or I never will believe in Jesus." But what if you never should feel it, as probably you never may? Will you go to hell out of spite against God, because He will not treat you like another? One has said to himself, "If I had a dream, or if I could feel a sudden shock of I know not what, then I would believe." Thus you undeserving mortals dream that my Lord is to be dictated to by you! You are beggars at His gate, asking for mercy, and you need to draw up rules and regulations as to how He shall give that mercy. Think you that He will submit to this? My Master is of a generous spirit, but He has a right royal heart, He spurns all dictation and maintains His sovereignty of action. Why, dear reader, if such is your case, do you crave for signs and wonders? Is not the gospel its own sign and wonder? Is not this a miracle of miracles, that "God so loved the world that He gave His only begotten Son, that whosoever believeth in Him might not perish"? Surely that precious word, "Whosoever will, let him come and take the water of life freely"[534] and that solemn promise, "Him that cometh unto Me, I will in no wise cast out," are better than signs and wonders! A truthful Savior ought to be believed. He is truth itself. Why will you ask proof of the veracity of One who cannot lie? The devils themselves declared Him to be the Son of God. Will you mistrust Him?

September 3

The Lord trieth the righteous (Psalm 11:5).

All events are under the control of Providence; consequently all the trials of our outward life are traceable at once to the great First Cause. Out of the golden gate of God's ordinance the armies of trial march forth in array, clad in their iron armor, and armed with weapons of war. All providences are doors to trial. Even our mercies, like roses, have their thorns.[535] Men may be drowned in seas of prosperity as well as in rivers of affliction. Our mountains are not too high and our valleys are not too low for temptations. Trials lurk on all roads.[536] Everywhere, above and beneath, we are beset and surrounded with dangers. Yet no shower falls without permission from the threatening cloud; every drop has its order before it hastens to the earth. The trials, which come from God, are sent to prove and strengthen our graces, and so at once to illustrate the power of divine grace, to test the genuineness of our virtues, and to add to their energy. Our Lord in His infinite wisdom and superabundant love, sets so high a value upon His people's faith that He will not screen them from those trials by which faith is strengthened.[537] You would never have possessed the precious faith, which now supports you, if the trial of your faith had not been like unto fire. You are a tree that never would have rooted so well if the wind had not rocked you to and fro, and made you take firm hold upon the precious truths of the covenant grace.[538] Worldly ease is a great foe to faith; it loosens the joints of holy valor, and snaps the sinews of sacred courage. The balloon never rises until the cords are cut; affliction does this sharp service for believing souls. While the wheat sleeps comfortably in the husk, it is useless to man. It must be threshed out of its resting place before its value can be known. Thus it is well that Jehovah tries the righteous, for it causes them to grow rich toward God.

ᚥ *September 4* ᚥ

Just balances, just weights, a just ephah, and a just hin,
shall ye have (Leviticus 19:36).

Weights, and scales, and measures were to be all according to the standard of justice. Surely no Christian man will need to be reminded of this in his business, for if righteousness were banished from all the world beside, it should find a shelter in believing hearts. There are, however, other balances which weigh moral and spiritual things, and these often need examining. We will call in the officer tonight. The balances in which we weigh our own and other men's characters, are they quite accurate? Do we not turn our own ounces of goodness into pounds, and other persons' bushels of excellence into pecks? See to weights and measures here, Christian. The scales in which we measure our trials and troubles, are they according to standard? Paul, who had more to suffer than we have, called his afflictions light, and yet we often consider ours to be heavy—surely something must be amiss with the weights! We must see to this matter, lest we get reported to the court above for unjust dealing. Those weights with which we measure our doctrinal belief, are they quite fair? The doctrines of grace should have the same weight with us as the precepts of the word, no more and no less; but it is to be feared that with many one scale or the other is unfairly weighted. It is a grand matter to give just measure in truth. Christian, be careful here. Those measures in which we estimate our obligations and responsibilities look rather small. When a rich man gives no more to the cause of God than the poor contribute, is that a just ephah *[approximately a bushel]* and a just hin *[approximately a gallon and a half of liquid]*. When ministers are half starved—is that honest dealing? When the poor are despised while ungodly, rich men are held in admiration, is that a just balance? Reader, we might lengthen the list, but we prefer to leave it as your evening's work to find out and destroy all unrighteous balances, weights, and measures.

ℳ *September 5* ℰ

Hast thou entered into the springs of the sea?
(Job 38:16).

Some things in nature must remain a mystery to the most intelligent and enterprising investigators. Human knowledge has bounds beyond which it cannot pass. Universal knowledge is for God alone. If this be so in the things, which are seen and temporal, I may rest assured that it is even more so in matters spiritual and eternal. Why, then, have I been torturing my brain with speculations as to destiny and will, fixed fate, and human responsibility? These deep and dark truths I am no more able to comprehend than to find out the depth, which couches beneath, from which old ocean draws her watery stores. Why am I so curious to know the reason of my Lord's providences, the motive of His actions, and the design of His visitations? Shall I ever be able to clasp the sun in my fist and hold the universe in my palm? Yet these are as a drop of a bucket compared with the Lord my God. Let me not strive to understand the infinite, but spend my strength in love. What I cannot gain by intellect, I can possess by affection, and let that suffice me. I cannot penetrate the heart of the sea, but I can enjoy the healthful breezes, which sweep over its bosom, and I can sail over its blue waves with propitious winds. If I could enter the springs of the sea, the feat would serve no useful purpose either to myself or to others. It would not save the sinking bark or give the drowned mariner back to his weeping wife and children; neither would my solving deep mysteries avail me a single whit, for the least love to God and the simplest act of obedience to Him are better than the profoundest knowledge. My Lord, I leave the infinite to You, and pray You to put far from me such a love for the tree of knowledge as might keep me from the tree of life.

September 6

If ye be led of the Spirit, ye are not under the law
(Galatians 5:18).

He, who looks at his own character and position from a legal point of view, will not only despair when he comes to the *end* of his reckoning, but if he is a wise man, he will despair at the *beginning*; for if we are to be judged on the footing of the law, there shall no flesh living be justified. How blessed to know that we dwell in the domains of grace and not of law! When thinking of my state before God, the question is not, "Am I perfect in myself before the law?" but, "Am I perfect in Christ Jesus?" That is a very different matter. We need not enquire, "Am I without sin naturally?" but, "Have I been washed in the fountain opened for sin and for uncleanness?" It is not "Am I in myself well pleasing to God?" but, "Am I accepted in the Beloved?"[539] The Christian views his evidences from the top of Sinai, and grows alarmed concerning his salvation. It would be far better if he read his title by the light of Calvary. "Why," says he, "my faith has unbelief in it; it is not able to save me." Suppose he had considered *the object* of his faith instead of his faith. Then he would have said, "There is no failure in *Him*, and therefore I am safe." He sighs over his hope, "Ah! my hope is marred and dimmed by an anxious carefulness about present things; how can I be accepted?" Had he regarded the ground of his hope, he would have seen that the promise of God standeth sure, and that whatever our doubts may be, the oath and promise never fail. Ah! believer, it is safer always for you to be led of the Spirit into gospel liberty than to wear legal fetters [shackles]. Judge yourself at what *Christ* is rather than at what *you* are.[540] Satan will try to mar your peace by reminding you of your sinfulness and imperfections; you can only meet his accusations by faithfully adhering to the gospel and refusing to wear the yoke of bondage.[541]

⇜ *September 7* ⇝

There is sorrow on the sea; it cannot be quiet
(Jeremiah 49:23).

We know little of what sorrow may be upon the sea at this moment. We are safe in our quiet chamber, but far away on the salt sea, the hurricane may be cruelly seeking for the lives of men. Hear how the death fiends howl among the cordage; how every timber starts as the waves beat like battering rams upon the vessel! God help you, poor drenched and wearied ones! My prayer goes up to the great Lord of sea and land, that He will make the storm a calm, and bring you to your desired haven! Nor ought I to offer prayer alone; I should try to benefit those hardy men who risk their lives so constantly. Have I ever done anything for them? What can I do? How often does the boisterous sea swallow up the mariner! Thousands of corpses lie where pearls lie deep. There is death—sorrow on the sea, which is echoed in the long wail of widows and orphans. The salt of the sea is in many eyes of mothers and wives. Remorseless billows, ye have devoured the love of women, and the stay of households. What a resurrection shall there be from the caverns of the deep when the sea gives up her dead! Till then there will be sorrow on the sea. As if in sympathy with the woes of earth, the sea is for ever fretting along a thousand shores, wailing with a sorrowful cry like her own birds, booming with a hollow crash of unrest, raving with uproarious discontent, chafing with hoarse wrath, or jangling with the voices of ten thousand murmuring pebbles. The roar of the sea may be joyous to a rejoicing spirit, but to the son of sorrow, the wide, wide ocean is even more forlorn than the wide, wide world. This is not our rest, and the restless billows tell us so. There is a land where there is no more sea[542]—our faces are steadfastly set toward it; we are going to the place of which the Lord has spoken. Till then, we cast our sorrows on the Lord who trod the sea of old, and who maketh a way for His people through the depths thereof.[543]

The exceeding greatness of His power to us-ward who believe according to the working of His mighty power, which He wrought in Christ, when He raised Him from the dead (Ephesians 1:19-20).

In the resurrection of Christ, as in our salvation, there was put forth nothing short of *a divine power*. What shall we say of those who think that conversion is wrought by the free will of man, and is due to his own betterment of disposition? When we shall see the dead rise from the grave by their own power, then may we expect to see ungodly sinners of their own free will turning to Christ. It is not the word preached, nor the word read in itself; all quickening power proceeds from the Holy Ghost. This power was *irresistible*. All the soldiers and the high priests could not keep the body of Christ in the tomb; Death himself could not hold Jesus in his bonds. Even thus irresistible is the power put forth in the believer when he is raised to newness of life. No sin, no corruption, no devils in hell nor sinners upon earth can stay the hand of God's grace when it intends to convert a man. If God omnipotently says, "Thou shalt," man shall not say, "I will not." Observe that the power, which raised Christ from the dead, was *glorious*. It reflected honor upon God and wrought dismay in the hosts of evil. So there is great glory to God in the conversion of every sinner. It was *everlasting power*. "Christ being raised from the dead dieth no more; death has no more dominion over Him."[544] So we, being raised from the dead, do not go back to our dead works or old corruptions, but we live unto God. "Because He lives we live also."[545] "For we are dead, and our life is hid with Christ in God." "Like as Christ was raised up from the dead by the glory of the Father, even so we also should walk in newness of life."[546] Lastly, in the text mark the union of the new life to Jesus. The same power that raised the Head works life in the members. What a blessing to be quickened together with Christ![547]

And round about the throne were four and twenty seats: and upon the seats I saw four and twenty elders sitting, clothed in white raiment (Revelation 4:4).

These representatives of the saints in heaven are said to be *around the throne*. In the passage in Canticles, where Solomon sings of the King sitting at his table, some render it "a round table." From this, some expositors, I think, without straining the text, have said, "There is an equality among the saints." That idea is conveyed by the equal nearness of the four and twenty elders. The condition of glorified spirits in heaven is that of nearness to Christ, clear vision of His glory, constant access to His court, and familiar fellowship with His person: nor is there any difference in this respect between one saint and another, but all the people of God—apostles, martyrs, ministers, or private and obscure Christians—shall all be seated *near the throne*, where they shall forever gaze upon their exalted Lord, and be satisfied with His love. They shall all be near to Christ, all ravished with His love, all eating and drinking at the same table with Him, all equally beloved as His favorites and friends, even if not all equally rewarded as servants. Let believers on earth imitate the saints in heaven in their nearness to Christ. Let us on earth be as the elders are in heaven, sitting around the throne. May Christ be the object of our thoughts, the center of our lives. How can we endure to live at such a distance from our Beloved? Lord Jesus, draw us nearer to Yourself. Say unto us, "Abide in Me, and I in you;"[548] and permit us to sing, "His left hand is under my head, and His right hand doth embrace me."

O lift me higher, nearer You,
And as I rise more pure and meet,
O let my soul's humility,
Make me lie lower at Your feet;
Less trusting self, the more I prove,
The blessed comfort of Your love.

September 10

Evening wolves (Habakkuk 1:8).

While preparing the present volume, this particular expression recurred to me so frequently, that in order to be rid of its constant importunity, I determined to give a page to it. The evening wolf, infuriated by a day of hunger, was fiercer and more ravenous than he would have been in the morning. May not the furious creature represent our doubts and fears after a day of distraction of mind, losses in business, and perhaps ungenerous taunting from our fellow men? How our thoughts howl in our ears, "Where is now your God?" How voracious and greedy they are, swallowing up all suggestions of comfort and remaining as hungry as before. Great Shepherd, slay these evening wolves, and bid Your sheep lie down in green pastures, undisturbed by insatiable unbelief. How like are the fiends of hell to evening wolves, for when the flock of Christ are in a cloudy and dark day, and their sun seems going down, they hasten to tear and to devour. They will scarcely attack the Christian in the daylight of faith, but in the gloom of soul conflict they fall upon him. O Thou who hast laid down Your life for the sheep, preserve them from the fangs of the wolf.[549] False teachers, who craftily and industriously hunt for the precious life, devouring men by their falsehoods, are as dangerous and detestable as evening wolves. Darkness is their element; deceit is their character; destruction is their end. We are most in danger from them when they wear the sheep's skin. Blessed is he who is kept from them, for thousands are made the prey of grievous wolves that enter within the fold of the church. What a wonder of grace it is when fierce persecutors are converted, for then the wolf dwells with the lamb, and men of cruel ungovernable dispositions become gentle and teachable. O Lord, convert many such: for such we will pray tonight.

Lead me, O Lord, in Your righteousness because of mine enemies (Psalms 5:8).

Very bitter is the ill will of the world against the people of Christus.[550] Men will forgive a thousand faults in others, but they will magnify the most trivial offenses in the followers of Jesus.[551] Instead of vainly regretting this, let us turn it to account, and since so many are watching for our halting, let this be a special motive for walking very carefully before God.[552] If we live carelessly, the lynx-eyed world will soon see it, and with its hundred tongues, it will spread the story, exaggerated and emblazoned by the zeal of slander. They will shout triumphantly. "Aha! So would we have it! See how these Christians act! They are hypocrites to a man." Thus will much damage be done to the cause of Christ, and much insult offered to His name. The cross of Christ is in itself an offense to the world;[553] let us take heed that we add no offense of our own. It is "to the Jews a stumbling block." Let us mind that we put no stumbling blocks where there are enough already. "To the Greeks it is foolishness." Let us not add our folly to give point to the scorn with which the worldly-wise deride the gospel. How jealous should we be of ourselves! How rigid with our consciences! In the presence of adversaries who will misrepresent our best deeds, and impugn our motives where they cannot censure our actions, how circumspect should we be! Pilgrims travel as suspected persons through Vanity Fair. Not only are we under surveillance, but also there are more spies than we are mindful of. The espionage is everywhere at home and abroad. If we fall into the enemies' hands we may sooner expect generosity from a wolf or mercy from a fiend than anything like patience with our infirmities from men who spice their infidelity toward God with scandals against His people. O Lord, lead us ever, lest our enemies trip us up!

September 12

I will sing of mercy and judgment (Psalm 101:1).

Faith triumphs in trial. When reason is thrust into the inner prison, with her feet made fast in the stocks, faith makes the dungeon walls ring with her merry notes as she I cries, "I will sing of mercy and of judgment. Unto You, O Lord, will I sing:

"Faith pulls the black mask from the face of trouble,
And discovers the angel beneath.
Faith looks up at the cloud, and sees that
'Tis big with mercy and shall break,
In blessings on her head."

There is a subject for song even in the judgments of God toward us. For, first, the trial is not so heavy as it might have been; next, the trouble is not so severe as we deserved to have borne; and our affliction is not so crushing as the burden which others have to carry.[554] Faith sees that in her worst sorrow, there is nothing punishing; there is not a drop of God's wrath in it; it is all sent in love. Faith discerns love gleaming like a jewel on the breast of an angry God. Faith says of her grief, "This is a badge of honor, for the child must feel the rod;" and then she sings of the sweet result of her sorrows, because they work her spiritual good. Nay, more, says Faith, "These light afflictions, which are but for a moment, work out for me a far more exceeding and eternal weight of glory." So Faith rides forth on the black horse, conquering and to conquer, trampling down carnal reason and fleshly sense, and chanting notes of victory amid the thickest of the fray.

"All I meet I find assists me
In my path to heavenly joy:
Where, though trials now attend me,
Trials never more annoy.
Blest there with a weight of glory,
Still the path I'll ne'er forget,
But, exulting, cry, it led me,
To my blessed Savior's seat."

⊰ *September 13* ⊱

This man receiveth sinners (Luke 15:2).

Observe *the condescension* of this fact. This Man, who towers above all other men—holy, harmless, undefiled, and separate from sinners—this Man receiveth sinners. This Man, who is no other than the eternal God, before whom angels veil their faces—this Man receiveth sinners. It needs an angel's tongue to describe such a mighty stoop of love. That any of *us* should be willing to seek after the lost is nothing wonderful— they are of our own race; but that He, the offended God, against whom the transgression has been committed, should take upon Himself the form of a servant,[555] and bear the sin of many, and should then be willing to receive the vilest of the vile, this is marvelous. "This Man receiveth sinners;" not, however, that they may remain sinners, but He receives them that He may pardon their sins, justify their persons, cleanse their hearts by His purifying word, preserve their souls by the indwelling of the Holy Ghost, and enable them to serve Him, to show forth His praise, and to have communion with Him. Into His heart's love, He receives sinners, takes them from the dunghill, and wears them as jewels in His crown, plucks them as brands from the burning, and preserves them as costly monuments of His mercy. None are so precious in Jesus' sight as the sinners for whom He died. When Jesus receives sinners, He has not some out-of-doors reception place, no casual ward where He charitably entertains them as men do passing beggars, but He opens the golden gates of His royal heart, and receives the sinner right into Himself—yea, He admits the humble penitent into personal union and makes Him a member of His body, of His flesh, and of His bones. There was never such a reception as this! This fact is still most sure this evening, He is still receiving sinners: would to God sinners would receive Him.

⤜ September 14 ⤛

I acknowledged my sin unto You, and mine iniquity have I not hid. I said, I will confess my transgressions unto the Lord; and Thou forgavest the iniquity of my sin (Psalm 32:5).

David's grief for sin was bitter. Its effects were visible upon his outward frame: "his bones waxed old;"[556] "his moisture was turned into the drought of summer." No remedy could he find, until he made a full confession before the throne of the heavenly grace. He tells us that for a time he kept silence, and his heart became more and more filled with grief: like a mountain lake whose outlet is blocked up, his soul was swollen with torrents of sorrow. He fashioned excuses; he endeavored to divert his thoughts, but it was all to no purpose; like a festering sore his anguish gathered, and as he would not use the lancet of confession, his spirit was full of torment and knew no rest. At last it came to this: that he must return unto his God in humble penitence or die outright, so he hastened to the mercy-seat, and there unrolled the volume of his iniquities before the all-seeing One, acknowledging all the evil of his ways in language such as you read in the fifty-first and other penitential Psalms. Having done this, a work so simple and yet so difficult to pride, he received at once the token of divine forgiveness; the bones which had been broken were made to rejoice, and he came forth from his closet to sing the blessedness of the man whose transgression is forgiven. See the value of a grace-wrought confession of sin! It is to be prized above all price, for in every case where there is a genuine, gracious confession, mercy is freely given, not because the repentance and confession *deserve* mercy, but for Christ's sake. Blessed be God, there is always healing for the broken heart; the fountain is ever flowing to cleanse us from our sins. Truly, O Lord, Thou art a God "ready to pardon!"[557] Therefore will we acknowledge our iniquities.

ᡃᡃᡅ *September 15* ᡃᡅ

A people near unto him (Psalm 148:14).

The dispensation of the old covenant was that of distance. When God appeared even to His servant Moses, He said, "Draw not nigh hither: put off your shoes from off your feet;"[558] and when He manifested Himself upon Mount Sinai, to His own chosen and separated people, one of the first commands was, "Thou shalt set bounds about the mount."[559] Both in the sacred worship of the tabernacle and the temple, the thought of distance was always prominent. The mass of the people did not even enter the outer court. Into the inner court none but the priests might dare to intrude; while into the innermost place, or the holy of holies, the high priest entered only once in the year. It was as if the Lord in those early ages would teach man that sin was so utterly loathsome to Him, that He must treat men as lepers put without the camp; and when He came nearest to them, He yet made them feel the width of the separation between a holy God and an impure sinner. When the gospel came, we were placed on quite another footing. The word "Go" was exchanged for "Come;" distance was made to give place to nearness, and we who aforetime were afar off, were made nigh by the blood of Jesus Christ.[560] Incarnate Deity has no wall of fire about it. "Come unto me, all ye that labor and are heavy laden, and I will give you rest,"[561] is the joyful proclamation of God as He appears in human flesh. Not now does He teach the leper his leprosy by setting him at a distance, but by Himself suffering the penalty of His defilement. What a state of safety and privilege is this nearness to God through Jesus! Do you know it by experience? If you know it, are you living in the power of it? Marvelous is this nearness, yet it is to be followed by a dispensation of greater nearness still, when it shall be said, "The tabernacle of God is with men, and He doth dwell among them."[562] Hasten it, O Lord.

⌁ *September 16* ⌁

Am I a sea, or a whale, that Thou settest a watch over me? (Job 7:12)

This was a strange question for Job to ask of the Lord. He felt himself to be too insignificant to be so strictly watched and chastened, and he hoped that he was not so unruly as to need to be so restrained. The enquiry was natural from one surrounded with such insupportable miseries, but after all, it is capable of a very humbling answer. It is true that man is not the sea, but he is even more troublesome and unruly. The sea obediently respects its boundary, and though it is only a belt of sand, it does not overleap the limit. Mighty as it is, it hears the divine *hitherto*, and when most raging with tempest, it respects the word. But self-willed man defies heaven and oppresses earth; neither is there any end to this rebellious rage. The sea, obedient to the moon, ebbs and flows with ceaseless regularity, and thus renders an active as well as a passive obedience; but man, restless beyond his sphere, sleeps within the lines of duty, indolent where he should be active. He will neither come nor go at the divine command, but sullenly prefers to do what he should not, and to leave undone that which is required of him. Every drop in the ocean, every beaded bubble, and every yeasty foam-flake, every shell and pebble feel the power of law and yield or move at once. O if only our nature were but one thousandth part as much conformed to the will of God! We call the sea fickle and false, but how constant it is! Since our fathers' days, and the old time before them, the sea is where it was, beating on the same cliffs to the same tune. We know where to find it. It forsakes not its bed and changes not in its ceaseless boom, but where is man-vain, fickle man? Can the wise man guess by what folly he will next be seduced from his obedience? We need more watching than the billowy sea, and are far more rebellious. Lord, rule us for Your own glory. Amen.

❧ *September 17* ❧

Encourage him (Deuteronomy 1:38).

God employs His people to encourage one another. He did not say to an angel, "Gabriel, my servant Joshua is about to lead my people into Canaan—go, encourage him." God never works needless miracles; if His purposes can be accomplished by ordinary means, He will not use miraculous agency. Gabriel would not have been half so well fitted for the work as Moses. A brother's sympathy is more precious than an angel's embassy. The angel, swift of wing, had better known the Master's bidding than the people's temper. An angel had never experienced the hardness of the road, nor seen the fiery serpents, nor had he led the stiff-necked multitude in the wilderness as Moses had done. We should be glad that God usually works for man by man. It forms a bond of brotherhood, and being mutually dependent on one another, we are fused more completely into one family. Brethren, take the text as God's message to you. Labor to help others, and especially strive to *encourage* them. Talk cheerily to the young and anxious enquirer; lovingly try to remove stumbling blocks out of his way. When you find a spark of grace in the heart, kneel down and blow it into a flame. Leave the young believer to discover the roughness of the road by degrees, but tell him of the strength which dwells in God, of the sureness of the promise, and of the charms of communion with Christ. Aim to comfort the sorrowful, and to animate the desponding. Speak a word in season to him that is weary, and encourage those who are fearful to go on their way with gladness.[563] God encourages you by His promises; Christ encourages you as He points to the heaven He has won for you, and the spirit encourages *you* as He works in you to will and to do of His own will and pleasure.[564] Imitate divine wisdom, and encourage others, according to the word of this evening.

ᢞ *September 18* ᢞ

And they follow me (John 10:27).

We should follow our Lord as unhesitatingly as sheep follow their shepherd, for He has a right to lead us wherever He pleases. We are not our own, we are bought with a price[565]—let us recognize the rights of the redeeming blood. The soldier follows his captain, the servant obeys his master, much more must we follow our Redeemer, to whom we are a purchased possession. We are not true to our profession of being Christians, if we question the bidding of our Leader and Commander.[566] Submission is our duty, objecting to trivial things is our folly. Often might our Lord say to us as to Peter, "What is that to you? Follow Me."[567] Wherever Jesus may lead us, *He goes before us.* If we know not where we go, we know with whom we go. With such a companion, who will dread the perils of the road? The journey may be long, but His everlasting arms will carry us to the end. The presence of Jesus is the assurance of eternal salvation: because He lives, we shall live also. We should follow Christ in simplicity and faith, because the paths in which He leads us all end in glory and immortality. It is true they may not be smooth paths—they may be covered with sharp flinty trials, but they lead to the "city which has foundations, whose builder and maker is God."[568] "All the paths of the Lord are mercy and truth unto such as keep His covenant."[569] Let us put full trust in our Leader, since we know that, come prosperity or adversity, sickness or health, popularity or contempt, His purpose shall be worked out, and that purpose shall be pure, unmingled good to every heir of mercy. We shall find it sweet to go up the bleak side of the hill with Christ; and when rain and snow blow into our faces, His dear love will make us far more blessed than those who sit at home and warm their hands at the world's fire. To the top of Amana, to the dens of lions, or to the hills of leopards, we will follow our Beloved.[570] Precious Jesus, draw us, and we will run after You.

September 19

For this child I prayed (1 Samuel 1:27).

Devout souls delight to look upon those mercies, which they have obtained in answer to supplication, for they can see God's especial love in them. When we can name our blessings Samuel, that is, "asked of God," they will be as dear to us as her child was to Hannah. Peninnah had many children, but they came as common blessings unsought in prayer. Hannah's one heaven-given child was dearer far, because he was the fruit of earnest pleadings. How sweet was that water to Samson, which he found at "the well of him that prayed!" Quassia *[bitter wood]* cups turn all waters bitter, but the cup of prayer puts sweetness into the draughts it brings. Did we pray for the conversion of our children? How doubly sweet, when they are saved, to see in them our own petitions fulfilled! Better to rejoice over them as the fruit of our pleadings than as the fruit of our bodies.[571] Have we sought of the Lord some choice spiritual gift? When it comes to us, it will be wrapped up in the gold cloth of God's faithfulness and truth, and so be doubly precious. Have we petitioned for success in the Lord's work? How joyful is the prosperity, which comes flying upon the wings of prayer! It is always best to get blessings into our house in the legitimate way, by the door of prayer; then they are blessings indeed and not temptations. Even when prayer speeds not, the blessings grow all the richer for the delay. The child Jesus was all the more lovely in the eyes of Mary when she found Him after having sought Him sorrowing.[572] That which we win by prayer we should dedicate to God, as Hannah dedicated Samuel. The gift came from heaven; let it go to heaven. Prayer brought it; gratitude sang over it; let devotion consecrate it. Here will be a special occasion for saying, "Of Your own have I given unto You." Reader, is prayer your element or your weariness? Which?

In the evening withhold not your hand
(Ecclesiastes 11:6).

In the evening of the day opportunities are plentiful; men return from their labor, and the zealous soul-winner finds time to tell abroad the love of Jesus. Have I no evening work for Jesus? If I have not, let me no longer withhold my hand from a service that requires abundant labor. Sinners are perishing for lack of knowledge;[573] he who loiters may find his skirts crimson with the blood of souls. Jesus gave both His hands to the nails. How can I keep back one of mine from His blessed work? Night and day He toiled and prayed for me. How can I give a single hour to the pampering of my flesh with luxurious ease? Up, idle heart, and stretch out your hand to work or uplift it to pray. Heaven and hell are in earnest, let me be so, and this evening sow good seed for the Lord my God. *The evening of life* has also its calls. Life is so short that a morning of manhood's vigor and an evening of decay make the whole of it. To some it seems long, but a four-pence is a great sum of money to a poor man. Life is so brief that no man can afford to lose a day. It has been well said that if a great king should bring us a great heap of gold, and bid us take as much as we could count in a day, we should make a long day of it; we should begin early in the morning, and in the evening we should not withhold our hand. But to win souls is far nobler work. How is it that we so soon withdraw from it? Some are spared to a long evening of green old age; if such be my case, let me use such talents as I still retain, and to the last hour serve my blessed and faithful Lord. By His grace I will die in harness, and lay down my charge only when I lay down my body. Age may instruct the young, cheer the faint, and encourage the desponding; if eventide has less of vigorous heat, it should have more of calm wisdom. Therefore, in the evening, I will not withhold my hand.

Gather not my soul with sinners (Psalm 26:9).

Fear made David pray thus, for something whispered, "Perhaps, after all, you mayst be gathered with the wicked." That fear, although marred by unbelief, springs mainly from holy anxiety, arising from the recollection of past sin. Even the pardoned man will enquire, "What if at the end my sins should be remembered, and I should be left out of the catalogue of the saved?"[574] He recollects his present unfruitfulness—so little grace, so little love, so little holiness. Looking forward to the future, he considers his weakness and the many temptations, which beset him, and he fears that he may fall, and become a prey to the enemy. A sense of sin and present evil and his prevailing corruptions compel him to pray in fear and trembling. "Gather not my soul with sinners."[575] Reader, if you have prayed this prayer, and if your character is rightly described in the Psalm from which it is taken, you need not be afraid that you shall be gathered with sinners. Have you the two virtues, which David had—the outward walking in integrity and the inward trusting in the Lord? Are you resting upon Christ's sacrifice, and can you compass the altar of God with humble hope? If so, rest assured, with the wicked you never shall be gathered, for that calamity is impossible. The gathering at the judgment is like to like. "Gather ye together first the tares [weeds], and bind them in bundles to burn them, but gather the wheat into my barn."[576] If, then, you are *like* God's people, you shall be *with* God's people. You cannot be gathered with the wicked, for you are too dearly bought. Redeemed by the blood of Christ, you are His forever, and where He is, there must His people be. You are loved too much to be cast away with reprobates. Shall one dear to Christ perish? Impossible! Hell cannot hold you! Heaven claims you! Trust in your Surety and fear not!

*When my heart is overwhelmed: lead me to the Rock
that is higher than I (Psalm 61:2).*

Most of us know what it is to be overwhelmed in heart; emptied as when a man wipes a dish and turns it upside down; submerged and thrown on our beam ends like a vessel mastered by the storm. Discoveries of inward corruption will do this, if the Lord permits the great deep of our depravity to become troubled and cast up mire and dirt. Disappointments and heartbreaks will do this when billow after billow rolls over us, and we are like a broken shell hurled to and fro by the surf. Blessed be God, at such seasons we are not without an all-sufficient solace, our God is the harbor of weather-beaten sails, the hospice of forlorn pilgrims. Higher than we is He: His mercy higher than our sins, His love higher than our thoughts. It is pitiful to see men putting their trust in something lower than themselves; but our confidence is fixed upon an exceeding high and glorious Lord. He is a Rock since He changes not, and a high Rock, because the tempests, which overwhelm us, roll far beneath at His feet. He is not disturbed by them, but rules them at His will. If we get under the shelter of this lofty Rock, we may defy the hurricane. All is calm under the lee of that towering cliff. Alas! such is the confusion in which the troubled mind is often cast, that we need piloting to this divine shelter. Hence the prayer of the text. O Lord, our God, by Your Holy Spirit, teach us the way of faith, lead us into Your rest. The wind blows us out to sea, the helm answers not to our puny hand; Thou, Thou alone canst steer us over the bar between yon sunken rocks, safe into the fair haven. How dependent we are upon You—we need You to bring us to You. To be wisely directed and steered into safety and peace is Your gift, and Yours alone. This night, be pleased to deal well with Your servants.[577]

Jesus said unto him, If thou canst believe (Mark 9:23).

A certain man had a demoniac son, who was afflicted with a dumb spirit. The father, having seen the futility of the endeavors of the disciples to heal his child, had little or no faith in Christ, and therefore, when he was bidden to bring his son to Him, he said to Jesus, "If Thou cast do anything, have compassion on us, and help us." Now there was an "if" in the question, but the poor trembling father had put the "if" in the wrong place: Jesus Christ, therefore, without commanding him to retract the "if," kindly puts it in its legitimate position. "Nay, verily," He seemed to say, "there should be no 'if' about My power. Concerning My willingness, the 'if' lies somewhere else." "If you canst believe, all things are possible to him that believeth."[578] The man's trust was strengthened. He offered a humble prayer for an increase of faith, and instantly Jesus spoke the word, and the devil was cast out with an injunction never to return. There is a lesson here, which we need to learn. We, like this man, often see that there is an "if" somewhere, but we are perpetually blundering by putting it in the wrong place. "If" Jesus can help me—"if" He can give me grace to overcome temptation—"if" He can give me pardon—"if" He can make me successful? Nay, "if" you can believe, He both can and will. You have misplaced your "if." If you can confidently trust, even as all things are possible to Christ, so shall all things be possible to you. Faith standeth in God's power, and is robed in God's majesty; it wears the royal apparel, and rides on the King's horse, for it is the grace, which the King delights to honor. Girding itself with the glorious might of the all-working Spirit, it becomes, in the omnipotence of God, mighty to do, to dare, and to suffer. All things, without limit, are possible to him that believeth. My soul, can you believe your Lord tonight?

I sleep, but my heart waketh (Song of Solomon 5:2).

Paradoxes abound in Christian experience, and here is one—the spouse was asleep, and yet she was awake. He only can read the believer's riddle, who has ploughed with the heifer of his experience. The two points in this evening's text are—a mournful sleepiness and a hopeful wakefulness. I *sleep*. Through sin that dwelleth in us we may become lax in holy duties, slothful in religious exercises, dull in spiritual joys, and altogether supine and careless. This is a shameful state for one in whom the quickening Spirit dwells; and it is dangerous to the highest degree. Even wise virgins sometimes slumber, but it is high time for all to shake off the bands of sloth. It is to be feared that many believers lose their strength as Samson lost his locks, while sleeping on the lap of carnal security.[579] With a perishing world around us, to sleep is cruel; with eternity so near at hand, it is madness. Yet we are none of us so much awake as we should be; a few thunderclaps would do us all good, and it may be, unless we soon bestir ourselves, we shall have them in the form of war or pestilence or personal bereavements and losses. O that we may leave forever the couch of fleshly ease, and go forth with flaming torches to meet the coming Bridegroom! *My heart waketh*. This is a happy sign. Life is not extinct, though sadly smothered. When our renewed heart struggles against our natural heaviness, we should be grateful to sovereign grace for keeping a little vitality within the body of this death. Jesus will hear our hearts, will help our hearts, will visit our hearts; for the voice of the wakeful heart is really the voice of our Beloved, saying, "Open to me." Holy zeal will surely unbar the door.

> "Oh lovely attitude! He stands,
> With melting heart and laden hands;
> My soul forsakes her every sin;
> And lets the heavenly stranger in."

Who of God is made unto us wisdom
(1 Corinthians 1:30).

Man's intellect seeks after rest, and by nature seeks it apart from the Lord Jesus Christ. Men of education are apt, even when converted, to look upon the simplicities of the cross of Christ with an eye too little reverent and loving. They are snared in the old net in which the Grecians were taken, and have a hankering to mix philosophy with revelation. The temptation with a man of refined thought and high education is to depart from the simple truth of Christ crucified, and to invent, as the term is, a more *intellectual* doctrine. This led the early Christian churches into Gnosticism, and bewitched them with all sorts of heresies. This is the root of Neology, and the other fine things, which in days gone by, were so fashionable in Germany, and are now so ensnaring to certain classes of divines. Whoever you are, good reader, and whatever your education may be, if you are the Lord's, be assured you will find no rest in philosophizing divinity. You may receive this dogma of one great thinker, or that dream of another profound reasoner, but what the chaff is to the wheat, these will be to the pure word of God. All that reason, when best guided, can find out is but the A B C of truth, and even that lacks certainty, while in Christ Jesus there is treasured up all the fullness of wisdom and knowledge. All attempts on the part of Christians to be content with systems such as Unitarian and Broad-church thinkers would approve of, must fail; true heirs of heaven must come back to the grandly simple reality which makes the ploughboy's eye flash with joy, and gladdens the pious pauper's heart—"Jesus Christ came into the world to save sinners."[580] Jesus satisfies the most elevated intellect when He is believingly received, but apart from Him the mind of the regenerate discovers no rest. "The fear of the Lord is the beginning of knowledge."[581] "A good understanding have all they that do His commandments."[582]

❧ *September 26* ☙

Howl, fir tree, for the cedar is fallen (Zechariah 11:2).

When in the forest there is heard the crash of a falling oak, it is a sign that the woodman is abroad, and every tree in the whole company may tremble lest tomorrow the sharp edge of the axe should find it out. We are all like trees marked for the axe, and the fall of one should remind us that for every one, whether great as the cedar or humble as the fir, the appointed hour is stealing on apace. I trust we do not, by often hearing of death, become callous to it. May we never be like the birds in the steeple, which build their nests when the bells are tolling, and sleep quietly when the solemn funeral peals are startling the air. May we regard death as the most weighty of all events, and be sobered by its approach. It ill behooves us to sport while our eternal destiny hangs on a thread. The sword is out of its scabbard—let us not trifle; it is furbished, and the edge is sharp—let us not play with it. He, who does not prepare for death, is more than an ordinary fool; he is a madman. When the voice of God is heard among the trees of the garden, let fig tree and sycamore and elm and cedar alike hear the sound thereof. Be ready, servant of Christ, for your Master comes on suddenly, when an ungodly world least expects Him. See to it that you are faithful in His work, for the grave shall soon be dug for you. Be ready, parents; see that your children are brought up in the fear of God, for they must soon be orphans. Be ready, men of business, take care that your affairs are correct, and that you serve God with all your hearts, for the days of your service on earth will soon be ended, and you will be called to give account for the deeds done in the body, whether good or evil. May we all prepare for the tribunal of the great King with a care, which shall be rewarded with the gracious commendation, "Well done, good and faithful servant."[583]

My Beloved put in His hand by the hole of the door, and my bowels were moved for Him (Song of Solomon 5:4).

Knocking was not enough, for my heart was too full of sleep, too cold and ungrateful to arise and open the door, but the touch of His effectual grace has made my soul bestir itself. Oh, the longsuffering of my Beloved, to tarry when He found Himself shut out, and me asleep upon the bed of sloth! Oh, the greatness of His patience, to knock and knock again, and to add His voice to His knockings, beseeching me to open to Him! How could I have refused Him! Base heart, blush and be confounded! But what greatest kindness of all is this, that He becomes His own porter and unbars the door Himself. Thrice blessed is the hand, which condescends to lift the latch and turn the key. Now I see that nothing but my Lord's own power can save such a naughty mass of wickedness as I am; ordinances fail, even the gospel has no effect upon me, till His hand is stretched out. Now, also, I perceive that His hand is good where all else is unsuccessful; He can open when nothing else will. Blessed be His name, I feel His gracious presence even now. Well may my heart stir for Him when I think of all that He has suffered for me and of my ungenerous return. I have allowed my affections to wander. I have set up rivals. I have grieved Him. Sweetest and dearest of all beloveds, I have treated You as an unfaithful wife treats her husband. Oh, my cruel sins, my cruel self. What can I do? Tears are a poor show of my repentance; my whole heart boils with indignation at myself. Wretch that I am, to treat my Lord, my All in All, my exceeding great joy as though He were a stranger. Jesus, you forgivest freely, but this is not enough, prevent my unfaithfulness in the future. Kiss away these tears, and then purge my heart and bind it with sevenfold cord to Yourself, never to wander more.

⤙ *September 28* ⤜

Go again seven times (1 Kings 18:43).

Success is certain when the Lord has promised it. Although you may have pleaded month after month without evidence of answer, it is not possible that the Lord should be deaf when His people are earnest in a matter that concerns His glory. The prophet on the top of Carmel continued to wrestle with God, and never for a moment gave way to a fear that he should be non-suited in Jehovah's courts. Six times the servant returned, but on each occasion no word was spoken but "Go again." We must not dream of unbelief, but hold to our faith even to seventy times seven. Faith sends expectant hope to look from Carmel's brow, and if nothing is beheld, she sends again and again. So far from being crushed by repeated disappointment, faith is animated to plead more fervently with her God. She is humbled, but not abashed. Her groans are deeper, and her sighings more vehement, but she never relaxes her hold or stays her hand. It would be more agreeable to flesh and blood to have a speedy answer, but believing souls have learned to be submissive, and to find it good to wait *for* as well as *upon* the Lord. Delayed answers often set the heart searching itself, and so lead to contrition and spiritual reformation: deadly blows are thus struck at our corruption, and the chambers of imagery are cleansed. The great danger is lest men should faint and miss the blessing. Reader, do not fall into that sin, but continue in prayer and watching.[584] At last the little cloud was seen, the sure forerunner of torrents of rain, and even so with you, the token for good shall surely be given, and you shall rise as a prevailing prince to enjoy the mercy you have sought. Elijah was a man of like passions with us: his power with God did not lie in his own merits. If his believing prayer availed so much, why not yours? Plead the precious blood with unceasing importunity, and it shall be with you according to your desire.

I found Him whom my soul loveth: I held Him, and would not let Him go (Song of Solomon 3:4).

Does Christ receive us when we come to Him, notwithstanding all our past sinfulness? Does He never chide us for having tried all other refuges first? And is there none on earth like Him? Is He the best of all the good, the fairest of all the fair? Oh, then let us praise Him! Daughters of Jerusalem, extol Him with timbrel *[tambourine or hand drum]* and harp! Down with your idols, up with the Lord Jesus. Now let the standards of pomp and pride be trampled under foot, but let the cross of Jesus, which the world frowns and scoffs at, be lifted on high. O for a throne of ivory for our King Solomon! let Him be set on high forever, and let my soul sit at His footstool, and kiss His feet, and wash them with my tears. Oh, how precious is Christ! How can it be that I have thought so little of Him? How is it I can go abroad for joy or comfort when He is so full, so rich, so satisfying. Fellow believer, make a covenant with your heart that you will never depart from Him, and ask your Lord to ratify it. Bid Him set you as a signet upon His finger,[585] and as a bracelet upon His arm. Ask Him to bind you about Him, as the bride decks herself with ornaments, and as the bridegroom puts on his jewels. I would live in Christ's heart; in the clefts of that rock my soul would eternally abide. The sparrow has made a house, and the swallow a nest for herself where she may lay her young, even your altars, O Lord of hosts, my King and my God; and so too would I make my nest, my home, in You, and never from You may the soul of Your turtle dove go forth again, but may I nestle close to You, O Jesus, my true and only rest.

> "When my precious Lord I find,
> All my ardent passions glow;
> Him with cords of love I bind,
> Hold and will not let Him go."

ᔍ *September 30* ☞

A living dog is better than a dead lion
(Ecclesiastes 9:4).

Life is a precious thing, and in its humblest form, it is superior to death. This truth is eminently certain in spiritual things. It is better to be the least in the kingdom of heaven than the greatest out of it. The lowest degree of grace is superior to the noblest development of unregenerate nature. Where the Holy Ghost implants divine life in the soul, there is a precious deposit that none of the refinements of education can equal. The thief on the cross excels Caesar on his throne. Lazarus among the dogs is better than Cicero among the senators. And the most unlettered Christian is superior to Plato in the sight of God. Life is the badge of nobility in the realm of spiritual things, and men without it are only coarser or finer specimens of the same lifeless material, needing to be quickened, for they are dead in trespasses and sins.[586] A living, loving, gospel sermon, however unlearned in matter and uncouth in style, is better than the finest discourse devoid of fervor and power. A living dog keeps better watch than a dead lion, and is of more service to his master; and so the poorest spiritual preacher is infinitely to be preferred to the exquisite orator who has no wisdom but that of words, no energy but that of sound. The like holds good of our prayers and other religious exercises; if we are quickened in them by the Holy Spirit, they are acceptable to God through Jesus Christ, though we may think them to be worthless things; while our grand performances in which our hearts were absent, like dead lions, are mere carrion in the sight of the living God. O for living groans, living sighs, living despondencies, rather than lifeless songs and dead calms. Better anything than death. The snarling of the dog of hell will at least keep us awake, but dead faith and dead profession, what greater curses can a man have? Quicken us, quicken us, O Lord!

October

⇜ *October 1* ⇝

He will give grace and glory (Psalm 84:11).

Bounteous is Jehovah in His nature; to give is His delight. His gifts are beyond measure precious, and are as freely given as the light of the sun. He gives grace to His elect because He wills it, to His redeemed because of His covenant, to the called because of His promise, to believers because they seek it, and to sinners because they need it. He gives grace abundantly, seasonably, constantly, readily, sovereignly—doubly enhancing the value of the boon by the manner of its bestowal. He freely renders to all His people grace in all its forms. Without ceasing, He generously pours into their souls comforting, preserving, sanctifying, directing, instructing, and assisting grace. He always will do so, whatever may occur. Sickness may befall, but the Lord will give grace; poverty may happen to us, but grace will surely be afforded; death must come, but grace will light a candle at the darkest hour. Reader, how blessed it is as years roll round, and the leaves begin again to fall, to enjoy such an unfading promise as this, "The Lord will give grace." The little conjunction "and" in this verse is a diamond rivet binding the present with the future; grace and glory always go together. God has married them, and none can divorce them. The Lord will never deny a soul glory to whom He has freely given to live upon His grace; indeed, glory is nothing more than grace in its Sabbath dress, grace in full bloom, grace like autumn fruit, mellow and perfected. How soon we may have glory none can tell! It may be before this month of October has run out we shall see the Holy City; but be the interval longer or shorter, we shall be glorified before long. Glory, the glory of heaven, the glory of eternity, the glory of Jesus, the glory of the Father, the Lord will surely give to His chosen. Oh, rare promise of a faithful God![587]

Two golden links of one celestial chain:
Who owneth grace shall surely glory gain.

335

ᗑ *October 2* ᗒ

A man greatly beloved (Daniel 10:11).

Child of God, do you hesitate to appropriate this title? Ah! has your unbelief made you forget that you are greatly beloved, too? Must you not have been greatly beloved, to have been bought with the precious blood of Christ, as of a lamb without blemish and without spot? When God smote His only begotten Son for you, what was this but being greatly beloved? You lived in sin, and rioted in it. Must you not have been greatly beloved for God to have borne so patiently with you? You were called by grace and led to a Savior, and made a child of God and an heir of heaven. All this proves, does it not, a very great and superabounding love? Since that time, whether your path has been rough with troubles or smooth with mercies, it has been full of proofs that you are "a man greatly beloved." If the Lord has chastened you, yet not in anger; if He has made you poor, yet in grace you have been rich.[588] The more unworthy you feel yourself to be, the more evidence you have that nothing but unspeakable love could have led the Lord Jesus to save such a soul as yours. The more demerit you feel, the clearer is the display of the abounding love of God in having chosen you, and called you, and made you an heir of bliss. Now, if there be such love between God and us, let us live in the influence and sweetness of it, and use the privilege of our position. Do not let us approach our Lord as though we were strangers, or as though He were unwilling to hear us—for we are greatly beloved by our loving Father. "He that spared not His own Son, but delivered Him up for us all, how shall He not with Him also freely give us all things?" Come boldly, O believer, for despite the whisperings of Satan and the doubtings of your own heart, you are greatly beloved. Meditate on the exceeding greatness and faithfulness of divine love this evening, and so go to your bed in peace.

⌁ *October 3* ⌁

He Himself has suffered being tempted
(Hebrews 2:18).

It is a commonplace thought, and yet it tastes like nectar to the weary heart—Jesus was tempted as I am. You have heard that truth many times. Have you grasped it? He was tempted to the very same sins into which we fall. Do not dissociate Jesus from our common manhood. It is a dark room, which you are going through, but Jesus went through it before. It is a sharp fight, which you are waging, but Jesus has stood foot to foot with the same enemy. Let us be of good cheer, Christ has borne the load before us, and the bloodstained footsteps of the King of glory may be seen along the road that we traverse at this hour. There is something sweeter yet—Jesus was tempted, but Jesus never sinned.[589] Then, my soul, it is not needful for you to sin, for Jesus was a man, and if one man endured these temptations and sinned not, then in His power, His members may also cease from sin. Some beginners in the divine life think that they cannot be tempted without sinning, but they mistake. There is no sin in *being tempted*, but there *is* sin in *yielding to temptation*. Herein is comfort for the sorely tempted ones. There is still more to encourage them if they reflect that the Lord Jesus, though tempted, gloriously triumphed, and as He overcame, so surely shall His followers also, for Jesus is the representative man for His people. The Head has triumphed, and the members share in the victory. Fears are needless, for Christ is with us, armed for our defense.[590] Our place of safety is the bosom of the Savior. Perhaps we are tempted just now, in order to drive us nearer to Him. Blessed be any wind that blows us into the port of our Savior's love! Happy wounds, which make us seek the beloved Physician. Tempted ones, come to your tempted Savior, for He can be touched with a feeling of your infirmities, and will succor every tried and tempted one.

✠ *October 4* ✠

If any man sin, we have an advocate with the Father,
Jesus Christ the righteous (1 John 2:1).

"If any man sin, we *have* an advocate." Yes, though we sin, we
have Him still. John does not say, "If any man sin he has forfeited
his advocate," but "we *have* an advocate," sinners though we
are. All the sin that a believer ever did or can be allowed to
commit cannot destroy his interest in the Lord Jesus Christ as
his advocate. The name here given to our Lord is suggestive.
"Jesus." Ah! then He is an advocate such as we need, for Jesus
is the name of one whose business and delight it is to save.
"They shall call His name Jesus, for He shall save His people
from their sins."[591] His sweetest name implies His success. Next,
it is "Jesus *Christ*"—*Christos*, the anointed. This shows *His*
authority to plead. The Christ has a right to plead, for He is the
Father's own appointed advocate and elected priest. If He were
of our choosing, He might fail; but if God has laid help upon
one that is mighty, we may safely lay our trouble where God
has laid His help. He is Christ, and therefore authorized; He is
Christ, and therefore *qualified*, for the anointing has fully fitted
Him for His work.[592] He can plead so as to move the heart of
God and prevail. What words of tenderness, what sentences of
persuasion will the Anointed use when He stands up to plead
for me! One more letter of His name remains, "Jesus Christ *the*
righteous." This is not only His character, BUT also His plea. It
is His character, and if the Righteous One is my advocate, then
my cause is good, or He would not have espoused it. It is His
plea, for He meets the charge of unrighteousness against me by
the plea that *He* is righteous. He declares Himself my substitute
and puts His obedience to my account. My soul, you have a
friend well fitted to be your advocate. He cannot but succeed;
leave yourself entirely in His hands.

⅀ *October 5* ⅀

He that believeth and is baptized shall be saved
(Mark 16:16).

Mr. MacDonald asked the inhabitants of the island of St. Kilda how a man must be saved. An old man replied, "We shall be saved if we repent, and forsake our sins, and turn to God." "Yes," said a middle-aged female, "and with a true heart, too." "Ay," rejoined a third, "and with prayer." Added a fourth, "It must be the prayer of the heart." "And we must be diligent, too," said a fifth, "in keeping the commandments." Thus, each having contributed his mite, feeling that a very decent creed had been made up, they all looked and listened for the preacher's approbation, but they had aroused his deepest pity. The carnal mind always maps out for itself a way in which self can work and become great, but the Lord's way is quite the reverse. Believing and being baptized are no matters of merit to be gloried in—they are so simple that boasting is excluded, and free grace bears the palm. It may be that the reader is unsaved—what is the reason? Do you think the way of salvation as laid down in the text to be dubious?[593] How can that be when God has pledged His own word for its certainty? Do you think it too easy? Why, then, do you not attend to it? Its ease leaves those without excuse who neglect it. To believe is simply to trust, to depend, and to rely upon Christ Jesus. To be baptized is to submit to the ordinance that our Lord fulfilled at Jordan, to which the converted ones submitted at Pentecost, to which the jailer yielded obedience the very night of his conversion. The outward sign saves not, but it sets forth to us our death, burial, and resurrection with Jesus, and, like the Lord's Supper, is not to be neglected. Reader, do you believe in Jesus? Then, dear friend, dismiss your fears; you shall be saved. Are you still an unbeliever, then remember there is but one door, and if you will not enter by it you will perish in your sins.[594]

∞ *October 6* ∞

He had married an Ethiopian woman (Numbers 12:1).

Strange choice of Moses, but how much more strange the choice of Him who is a prophet like unto Moses, and greater than he![595] Our Lord, who is as fair as the lily, has entered into marriage union with one who confesses herself to be black, because the sun has looked upon her. It is the wonder of angels that the love of Jesus should be set upon poor, lost, guilty men. Each believer must, when filled with a sense of Jesus' love, be also overwhelmed with astonishment that such love should be lavished on an object so utterly unworthy of it. Knowing as we do our secret guiltiness, unfaithfulness, and black-heartedness, we are dissolved in grateful admiration of the matchless freeness and sovereignty of grace. Jesus must have found the cause of His love in His own heart; He could not have found it in us, for it is not there. Even since our conversion, we have been black, though grace has made us comely. Holy Rutherford said of himself what we must each subscribe to—"His relation to me is that I am sick and He is the Physician of whom I stand in need. Alas! how often I play fast and loose with Christ! He binds, I loose; He builds, I cast down; I quarrel with Christ, and He agrees with me twenty times a day!" Most tender and faithful Husband of our souls, pursue Your gracious work of conforming us to Your image till Thou shalt present even us poor Ethiops unto Yourself, without spot or wrinkle or any such thing.[596] Moses met with opposition because of his marriage, and both himself and his spouse were the subjects of an evil eye. Can we wonder if this vain world opposes Jesus and His spouse, and especially when great sinners are converted? For this is ever the Pharisee's ground of objection, "This man receiveth sinners."[597] Still is the old cause of quarrel revived, "… because he had married an Ethiopian woman."[598]

ᗰ *October 7* ᗰ

Now on whom dost thou trust? (Isaiah 36:5).

Reader, this is an important question. Listen to the Christian's answer, and see if it is yours. "On whom dost you trust?" "I trust," says the Christian, "in a triune God. I trust *the Father*, believing that He has chosen me from before the foundations of the world; I trust Him to provide for me in providence, to teach me, to guide me, to correct me if need be, and to bring me home to His own house where the many mansions are. I trust *the Son*. Very God of very God is He—the man Christ Jesus. I trust in Him to take away all my sins by His own sacrifice, and to adorn me with His perfect righteousness. I trust Him to be my Intercessor, to present my prayers and desires before His Father's throne, and I trust Him to be my Advocate at the last great day, to plead my cause, and to justify me. I trust Him for what He is, for what He has done, and for what He has promised yet to do. And I trust the Holy Spirit—He has begun to save me from my inbred sins. I trust Him to drive them all out. I trust Him to curb my temper, to subdue my will, to enlighten my understanding, to check my passions, to comfort my despondency, to help my weakness, and to illuminate my darkness. I trust Him to dwell in me as my life, to reign in me as my King, to sanctify me wholly, spirit, soul, and body, and then to take me up to dwell with the saints in light forever." Oh, blessed trust! To trust Him whose power will never be exhausted, whose love will never wane, whose kindness will never change, whose faithfulness will never fail, whose wisdom will never be nonplussed, and whose perfect goodness can never know a diminution! Happy art you, reader, if this trust is yours! So trusting, you shalt enjoy sweet peace now, and glory hereafter, and the foundation of your trust shall never be removed.[599]

October 8

Praying in the Holy Ghost (Jude 20).

Mark the grand characteristic of true prayer—"In the Holy Ghost." The seed of acceptable devotion must come from heaven's storehouse. Only the prayer, which comes from God, can go to God. We must shoot the Lord's arrows back to Him. That desire that He writes upon our heart will move His heart and bring down a blessing, but the desires of the flesh have no power with Him.[600] Praying in the Holy Ghost is praying in *fervency*. Cold prayers ask the Lord not to hear them. Those who do not plead with fervency, plead not at all. As well speak of lukewarm fire as of lukewarm prayer—it is essential that it be red hot. It is praying *perseveringly*. The true suppliant gathers force as he proceeds, and grows more fervent when God delays to answer. The longer the gate is closed, the more vehemently does he use the knocker; and the longer the angel lingers, the more resolved is he that he will never let him go without the blessing. Beautiful in God's sight is tearful, agonizing, unconquerable importunity. It means praying *humbly*, for the Holy Spirit never puffs us up with pride. It is His office to convince of sin, and so to bow us down in contrition and brokenness of spirit. We shall never sing *Gloria in excelsis* except we pray to God *De profundis*: out of the depths must we cry or we shall never behold glory in the highest. It is *loving* prayer. Prayer should be perfumed with love, saturated with love—love to our fellow saints and love to Christ. Moreover, it must be a prayer full of *faith*. A man prevails only as he believes. The Holy Spirit is the author of faith, and strengthens it,[601] so that we pray believing God's promise. O that this blessed combination of excellent graces, priceless and sweet as the spices of the merchant, might be fragrant within us because the Holy Ghost is in our hearts! Most blessed Comforter, exert Your mighty power within us, helping our infirmities in prayer.[602]

⇜ *October 9* ⇝

But He answered her not a word (Matthew 15:23).

Genuine seekers, who as yet have not obtained the blessing, may take comfort from the story before us. The Savior did not at once bestow the blessing, even though the woman had great faith in Him. He intended to give it, but He waited awhile. "He answered her not a word." Were not her prayers good? Never better in the world. Was not her case needy? Sorrowfully needy. Did she not *feel* her need sufficiently? She felt it overwhelmingly. Was she not earnest enough? She was intensely so. Had she no faith? She had such a high degree of it that even Jesus wondered, and said, "O woman, great is your faith." See then, although it is true that faith brings peace, yet it does not always bring it instantaneously. There may be certain reasons calling for the trial of faith, rather than the reward of faith. Genuine faith may be in the soul like a hidden seed, but as yet it may not have budded and blossomed into joy and peace. A painful silence from the Savior is the grievous trial of many a seeking soul, but heavier still is the affliction of a harsh cutting reply such as this, "It is not meet to take the children's bread, and to cast it to dogs."[603] Many in waiting upon the Lord find immediate delight, but this is not the case with all. Some, like the jailer, are in a moment turned from darkness to light, but others are plants of slower growth. A deeper sense of sin may be given to you instead of a sense of pardon, and in such a case you will have need of patience to bear the heavy blow. Ah! poor heart, though Christ beat and bruise you, or even slay you, trust Him. Though He should give you an angry word, believe in the love of His heart.[604] Do not, I beseech you, give up seeking or trusting my Master, because you have not yet obtained the conscious joy which you long for. Cast yourself on Him, and perseveringly depend even where you cannot rejoicingly hope.[605]

⫷ *October 10* ⫸

And I will deliver you out of the hand of the wicked,
and I will redeem you out of the hand of the terrible
(Jeremiah 15:21).

Note the glorious personality of the promise. *I* will, *I* will. The Lord Jehovah Himself interposes to deliver and redeem His people. He pledges Himself personally to rescue them. His own arm shall do it, that He may have the glory. Here is not a word said of any effort of our own, which may be needed to assist the Lord. Neither our strength nor our weakness is taken into the account, but the lone *I*, like the sun in the heavens, shines out resplendent in all-sufficiency. Why then do we calculate our forces, and consult with flesh and blood to our grievous wounding? Jehovah has power enough without borrowing from our puny arm. Peace, ye unbelieving thoughts, be still, and know that the Lord reigns. Nor is there a hint concerning secondary means and causes. The Lord says nothing of friends and helpers. He undertakes the work alone, and feels no need of human arms to aid Him. Vain are all our lookings around to companions and relatives; they are broken reeds if we lean upon them—often unwilling when able and unable when they are willing. Since the promise comes alone from God, it would be well to wait only upon Him; and when we do so, our expectation never fails us.[606] Who are the wicked that we should fear them? The Lord will utterly consume them; they are to be pitied rather than feared. As for terrible ones, they are only terrors to those who have no God to fly to, for when the Lord is on our side, whom shall we fear? If we run into sin to please the wicked, we have cause to be alarmed, but if we hold fast our integrity, the rage of tyrants shall be overruled for our good. When the fish swallowed Jonah, he found him a morsel, which he could not digest; and when the world devours the church, it is glad to be rid of it again. In all times of fiery trial, in patience let us possess our souls.[607]

ᗧ *October 11* ᗡ

Whom He did predestinate, them He also called
(Romans 8:30).

In the second epistle to Timothy, first chapter and ninth verse, are these words—"Who has saved us, and called us with an *holy* calling." Now, here is a touchstone by which we may try our calling. It is "an holy calling, not according to our works, but according to his own purpose and grace."[608] This calling forbids all trust in our own doings, and conducts us to Christ alone for salvation, but it afterwards purges us from dead works to serve the living and true God. As He that has called you is holy, so must you be holy.[609] If you are living in sin, you are not called, but if you are truly Christ's, you can say, "Nothing pains me so much as sin; I desire to be rid of it; Lord, help me to be holy." Is this the panting of your heart? Is this the tenor of your life toward God, and His divine will? Again, in Philippians, 3:13-14, we are told of "The *high* calling of God in Christ Jesus." Is then your calling a high calling? Has it ennobled your heart, and set it upon heavenly things? Has it elevated your hopes, your tastes, and your desires? Has it upraised the constant tenor of your life, so that you spend it with God and for God? Another test we find in Hebrews 3:1—"Partakers of the *heavenly* calling."[610] Heavenly calling means a call *from* heaven. If man alone calls you, you are uncalled. Is your calling of God? Is it a call *to* heaven, as well as from heaven? Unless you are a stranger here, and heaven your home, you have not been called with a heavenly calling; for those, who have been so called, declare that they look for a city that has foundations, whose builder and maker is God, and they themselves are strangers and pilgrims upon the earth. Is your calling thus holy, high, and heavenly? Then, beloved, you have been called of God, for such is the calling wherewith God does call His people.

345

ᴪ October 12 ᴪ

The Comforter, which is the Holy Ghost
(John 14:26).

This age is peculiarly the dispensation of the Holy Spirit, in which Jesus cheers us, not by His personal presence, as He shall do by-and-by, but by the indwelling and constant abiding of the Holy Ghost, who is evermore the Comforter of the church. It is His office to console the hearts of God's people. He convinces of sin; He illuminates and instructs, but still the main part of His work lies in making glad the hearts of the renewed, in confirming the weak, and lifting up all those that are bowed down. He does this by revealing Jesus to them. The Holy Spirit consoles, but Christ *is the consolation*. If we may use the figure, the Holy Spirit is the Physician, but Jesus is the medicine. *He* heals the wound, but it is by applying the holy ointment of Christ's name and grace. He takes not of His own things, but of the things of Christ. So if we give to the Holy Spirit the Greek name of *Paraclete*, as we sometimes do, then our heart confers on our blessed Lord Jesus the title of *Paraclesis*. If the one is the Comforter, the other is the Comfort. Now, with such rich provision for his need, why should the Christian be sad and desponding? The Holy Spirit has graciously engaged to be your Comforter. Do you imagine, O you weak and trembling believer, that He will be negligent of His sacred trust? Canst you suppose that He has undertaken what He cannot or will not perform? If it is His especial work to strengthen and comfort you, do you suppose He has forgotten His business, or that He will fail in the loving office, which He sustains toward you? Nay, think not so hardly of the tender and blessed Spirit whose name is "the Comforter." He delights to give the oil of joy for mourning, and the garment of praise for the spirit of heaviness.[611] Trust you in Him, and He will surely comfort you till the house of mourning is closed forever, and the marriage feast has begun.

Love is strong as death (Song of Solomon 8:6).

Whose love can this be, which is as mighty as the conqueror of monarchs, the destroyer of the human race? Would it not sound like satire if it were applied to my poor, weak, and scarcely living love to Jesus my Lord? I do love Him, and perhaps by His grace, I could even die for Him, but as for my love in itself, it can scarcely endure a scoffing jest, much less a cruel death. Surely it is my Beloved's love, which is here spoken of—the love of Jesus, the matchless lover of souls. His love was indeed stronger than the most terrible death, for it endured the trial of the cross triumphantly. It was a lingering death, but love survived the torment; a shameful death, but love despised the shame; a punishing death, but love bore our iniquities; a forsaken, lonely death, from which the eternal Father hid His face, but love endured the curse,[612] and gloried over all. Never such love, never such death. It was a desperate duel, but love bore the palm. What then, my heart? Have you no emotions excited within you at the contemplation of such heavenly affection? Yes, my Lord, I long, I pant to feel Your love flaming like a furnace within me. Come Thou Yourself and excite the ardor of my spirit.

> "For every drop of crimson blood,
> Thus shed to make me live,
> O wherefore, wherefore have not I,
> A thousand lives to give?"

Why should I despair of loving Jesus with a love as strong as death? He deserves it. I desire it. The martyrs felt such love, and they were but flesh and blood. Then why not I? They mourned their weakness, and yet out of weakness were made strong. Grace gave them all their unflinching constancy—there is the same grace for me. Jesus, lover of my soul, shed abroad such love, even Your love in my heart, this evening.

✄ *October 14* ✄

And be not conformed to this world (Romans 12:2).

If a Christian can be saved by possibility while he conforms to this world, at any rate it must be so as by fire. Such a bare salvation is almost as much to be dreaded as desired. Reader, would you wish to leave this world in the darkness of a desponding deathbed, and enter heaven as a shipwrecked mariner climbs the rocks of his native country? Then be worldly. Be mixed up with Mammonites, and refuse to go without the camp bearing Christ's reproach. But would you have a heaven below, as well as a heaven above? Would you comprehend with all saints what are the heights and depths, and know the love of Christ which passeth knowledge? Would you receive an abundant entrance into the joy of your Lord? Then come out from among them, and be separate, and touch not the unclean thing.[613] Would you attain the full assurance of faith? You cannot gain it while you commune with sinners. Would you flame with vehement love? The drenching of godless society will damp your love. You cannot become a great Christian—you may be a babe in grace, but you never can be a perfect person in Christ Jesus while you yield yourself to the worldly maxims and modes of business of men of the world. It is ill for an heir of heaven to be a great friend with the heirs of hell.[614] It has a bad look when a courtier is too intimate with his king's enemies. Even small inconsistencies are dangerous. Little thorns make great blisters, little moths destroy fine garments, and little frivolities and little rogueries will rob religion of a thousand joys. O professor, too little separated from sinners, you know not what you lose by your conformity to the world. It cuts the tendons of your strength, and makes you creep where you ought to run. Then, for your own comfort's sake, and for the sake of your growth in grace, if you are a Christian, be a Christian, and be a marked and distinct one.

⇥ *October 15* ⇤

But the firstling of an ass thou shalt redeem with a lamb:
and if thou redeem him not, then shalt thou
break his neck (Exodus 34:20).

Every firstborn creature must be the Lord's, but since the ass was unclean, it could not be presented in sacrifice. What then? Should it be allowed to go free from the universal law? By no means. God admits of no exceptions. The ass is His due, but He will not accept it. He will not abate the claim, but yet He cannot be pleased with the victim. No way of escape remained but redemption—the creature must be saved by the substitution of a lamb in its place; or if not redeemed, it must die. My soul, here is a lesson for you. That unclean animal is yourself; you are justly the property of the Lord who made you and preserves you, but you are so sinful that God will not, cannot, accept you; and it has come to this, the Lamb of God must stand in your stead or you must die eternally. Let the entire world know of your gratitude to that spotless Lamb who has already bled for you and so redeemed you from the fatal curse of the law.[615] Must it not sometimes have been a question with the Israelite: which should die—the ass or the lamb? Would not the good man pause to estimate and compare? Assuredly there was no comparison between the value of the soul of man and the life of the Lord Jesus, and yet the Lamb dies and man the ass is spared. My soul, admire the boundless love of God to you and others of the human race. Worms are bought with the blood of the Son of the Highest! Dust and ashes redeemed with a price far above silver and gold! What a doom had been mine had not plenteous redemption been found! The breaking of the neck of the ass was but a momentary penalty, but who shall measure the wrath to come to which no limit can be imagined? Inestimably dear is the glorious Lamb who has redeemed us from such a doom.

☙ October 16 ❧

With you is the fountain of life
(Psalm 36:9).

There are times in our spiritual experience when human counsel or sympathy or religious ordinances fail to comfort or help us. Why does our gracious God permit this? Perhaps it is because we have been living too much without Him, and He therefore takes away everything upon which we have been in the habit of depending, that He may drive us to Himself. It is a blessed thing to live at the fountainhead. While our skin-bottles are full, we are content like Hagar and Ishmael, to go into the wilderness, but when those are dry, nothing will serve us but "Thou God seest me."[616] We are like the prodigal, we love the swine-troughs and forget our Father's house. Remember, we can make swine-troughs and husks even out of the forms of religion; they are blessed things, but we may put them in God's place, and then they are of no value. Anything becomes an idol when it keeps us away from God. Even the brazen serpent is to be despised as "Nehushtan," if we worship it instead of God. The prodigal was never safer than when he was driven to his father's bosom, because he could find sustenance nowhere else. Our Lord favors us with a famine in the land that it may make us seek after Him the more. The best position for a Christian is living wholly and directly on God's grace—still abiding where he stood at first—"Having nothing, and yet possessing all things."[617] Let us never for a moment think that our standing is in our sanctification, our mortification, our graces, or our feelings, but know that because Christ offered a full atonement, therefore we are saved, for we are complete in Him.[618] Having nothing of our own to trust, but resting upon the merits of Jesus—His passion and holy life furnish us with the only sure ground of confidence. Beloved, when we are brought to a thirsting condition, we are sure to turn to the fountain of life with eagerness.

☞ *October 17* ☜

He shall gather the lambs with His arm
(Isaiah 40:11).

Our good Shepherd has in His flock a variety of experiences; some are strong in the Lord and others are weak in faith, but He is impartial in His care for all His sheep. The weakest lamb is as dear to Him as the most advanced of the flock. Lambs are wont to lag behind, prone to wander, and apt to grow weary, but from all the danger of these infirmities the Shepherd protects them with His arm of power. He finds new-born souls, like young lambs, ready to perish—He nourishes them till life becomes vigorous; He finds weak minds ready to faint and die—He consoles them and renews their strength. All the little ones He gathers, for it is not the will of our heavenly Father that one of them should perish.[619] What a quick eye He must have to see them all! What a tender heart to care for them all! What a far-reaching and potent arm, to gather them all! In His lifetime on earth He was a great gatherer of the weaker sort, and now that He dwells in heaven, His loving heart yearns toward the meek and contrite, the timid and feeble, the fearful and fainting here below. How gently did He gather me to Himself, to His truth, to His blood, to His love, to His church! With what effectual grace did He compel me to come to Himself! Since my first conversion, how frequently has He restored me from my wanderings, and once again folded me within the circle of His everlasting arm! The best of all is that He does it all Himself personally, not delegating the task of love, but condescending Himself to rescue and preserve His most unworthy servant. How shall I love Him enough or serve Him worthily? I would eagerly make His name great unto the ends of the earth, but what can my feebleness do for Him? Great Shepherd, add to Your mercies this one other, a heart to love You more truly as I ought.

ᖆ *October 18* ᖅ

Behold, to obey is better than sacrifice
(1 Samuel 15:22).

Saul had been commanded to slay utterly all the Amalekites and their cattle. Instead of doing so, he preserved the king, and suffered his people to take the best of the oxen and of the sheep. When called to account for this, he declared that he did it with a view of offering sacrifice to God, but Samuel met him at once with the assurance that sacrifices were no excuse for an act of direct rebellion. The sentence before us is worthy to be printed in letters of gold, and to be hung up before the eyes of the present idolatrous generation, who are very fond of the fineries of will-worship, but utterly neglect the laws of God. Be it ever in your remembrance, that to keep strictly in the path of your Savior's command is better than any outward form of religion; and to hearken to His precept with an attentive ear is better than to bring the fat of rams, or any other precious thing to lay upon His altar. If you are failing to keep the least of Christ's commands to His disciples, I pray you be disobedient no longer. All the pretensions you make of attachment to your Master, and all the devout actions, which you may perform, are no recompense for disobedience. "To obey," even in the slightest and smallest thing, "is better than sacrifice," however pompous. Talk not of Gregorian chants, sumptuous robes, incense, and banners; the first thing which God requires of His child is obedience; and though you should give your body to be burned, and all your goods to feed the poor, yet if you do not hearken to the Lord's precepts, all your formalities shall profit you nothing.[620] It is a blessed thing to be teachable as a little child, but it is a much more blessed thing when one has been taught the lesson, to carry it out to the letter. How many adorn their temples and decorate their priests, but refuse to obey the word of the Lord! My soul, come not thou into their secret.

ᘏ *October 19* ᘔ

God, my Maker, who giveth songs in the night
(Job 35:10).

Any man can sing in the day. When the cup is full, man draws inspiration from it. When wealth rolls in abundance around him, any man can praise the God who gives a plenteous harvest or sends home a loaded argosy. It is easy enough for an Aeolian harp to whisper music when the winds blow—the difficulty is for music to swell forth when no wind is stirring. It is easy to sing when we can read the notes by daylight; but he is skillful who sings when there is not a ray of light to read by—who sings from his heart. No man can make a song in the night of himself; he may attempt it, but he will find that a song in the night must be divinely inspired. Let all things go well, I can weave songs, fashioning them wherever I go out of the flowers that grow upon my path; but put me in a desert, where no green thing grows, and wherewith shall I frame a hymn of praise to God? How shall a mortal man make a crown for the Lord where no jewels are? Let but this voice be clear, and this body full of health, and I can sing God's praise. Silence my tongue, lay me upon the bed of languishing, and how shall I then chant God's high praises unless He Himself gives me the song? No, it is not in man's power to sing when all is adverse, unless an altar-coal shall touch his lip. It was a divine song, which Habakkuk sang, when in the night he said, "Although the fig-tree shall not blossom, neither shall fruit be in the vines; the labor of the olive shall fail, and the fields shall yield no meat; the flock shall be cut off from the fold, and there shall be no herd in the stalls: yet I will rejoice in the Lord, I will joy in the God of my salvation."[621] Then, since our Maker gives songs in the night, let us wait upon Him for the music. O Thou chief musician, let us not remain songless because affliction is upon us, but tune Thou our lips to the melody of thanksgiving.

Keep not back (Isaiah 43:6).

Although this message was sent to the south, and referred to the seed of Israel, it may profitably be a summons to us. Backward we are naturally to all good things, and it is a lesson of grace to learn to go forward in the ways of God. Reader, are you unconverted, but do you desire to trust in the Lord Jesus? Then *keep not back*. Love invites you; the promises secure you success; the precious blood prepares the way. Let not sins or fears hinder you, but come to Jesus just as you are. Do you long to pray? Would you pour out your heart before the Lord? *Keep not back*. The mercy seat is prepared for such as need mercy; a sinner's cries will prevail with God. You are invited, nay, you are *commanded* to pray, come therefore with boldness to the throne of grace.[622] Dear friend, are you already saved? Then *keep not back* from union with the Lord's people. Neglect not the ordinances of baptism and the Lord's Supper. You may be of a timid disposition, but you must strive against it, lest it lead you into disobedience. There is a sweet promise made to those who confess Christ—by no means miss it, lest you come under the condemnation of those who deny Him. If you have talents keep not back from using them. Hoard not your wealth, waste not your time; let not your abilities rust or your influence be unused. Jesus kept not back; imitate Him by being foremost in self-denials and self-sacrifices. *Keep not back* from close communion with God, from boldly appropriating covenant blessings, from advancing in the divine life, and from prying into the precious mysteries of the love of Christ. Neither, beloved friend, be guilty of keeping others back by your coldness, harshness, or suspicions. For Jesus' sake, go forward yourself and encourage others to do the same. Hell and the leaguered bands of superstition and infidelity are forward to the fight. O soldiers of the cross, keep not back.

Why are ye troubled? And why do thoughts arise in your hearts (Luke 24:38).

"Why sayest thou, O Jacob, and speakest O Israel, My way is hid from the Lord, and my judgment is passed over from my God?"[623] The Lord cares for all things, and the meanest creatures share in His universal providence, but His particular providence is over His saints. "The angel of the Lord encampeth round about them that fear Him."[624] "Precious shall their blood be in His sight."[625] "Precious in the sight of the Lord is the death of His saints."[626] "We know that all things work together for good to them that love God, to them that are the called according to His purpose."[627] Let the fact that, while He is the Savior of all men, He is specially the Savior of those who believe, cheer and comfort you. You are His peculiar care, His regal treasure that He guards as the apple of His eye, and His vineyard over which He watches day and night. "The very hairs of your head are all numbered."[628] Let the thought of His special love *to you* be a spiritual painkiller, a dear quietus to your woe: "I will never leave *you*, nor forsake *you*."[629] God says that as much to you as to any saint of old. "Fear not, I am your shield, and your exceeding great reward."[630] We lose much consolation by the habit of reading His promises for the whole church, instead of taking them directly home to ourselves. Believer, grasp the divine word with a personal, appropriating faith. Think that you hear Jesus say, "I have prayed for *you* that your faith fail not."[631] Think you see Him walking on the waters of your trouble, for He is there and He is saying, "Fear not, it is I; be not afraid."[632] Oh, those sweet words of Christ! May the Holy Ghost make you feel them as spoken to *you*; forget others for awhile—accept the voice of Jesus as addressed to you, and say, "Jesus whispers consolation; I cannot refuse it; I will sit under His shadow with great delight."

∼ *October 22* ∼

He shall take of Mine, and shall show it unto you
(John 16:15).

There are times when all the promises and doctrines of the Bible
are of no avail, unless a gracious hand shall apply them to us.
We are thirsty, but too faint to crawl to the water-brook. When
a soldier is wounded in battle, it is of little use for him to know
that there are those at the hospital who can bind up his wounds
and medicines there to ease all the pains he now suffers. What
he needs is to be carried there and to have the remedies applied.
It is thus with our souls, and to meet this need there is one,
even the Spirit of truth,[633] who takes of the things of Jesus and
applies them to us. Think not that Christ has placed His joys on
heavenly shelves that we may climb up to them for ourselves,
but He draws near and sheds His peace abroad in our hearts.
O Christian, if you are tonight laboring under deep distresses,
your Father does not give you promises and then leave you to
draw them up from the Word like buckets from a well. The
promises He has written in the Word, He will write anew on
your heart. He will manifest His love to you, and by His blessed
Spirit, dispel your cares and troubles. Be it known unto you, O
mourner, that it is God's prerogative to wipe every tear from the
eye of His people. The Good Samaritan did not say, "Here is the
wine, and here is the oil for you;" he actually poured in the oil
and the wine.[634] So Jesus not only gives you the sweet wine of
the promise, but also holds the golden chalice to your lips and
pours the life-blood into your mouth. The poor, sick, way-worn
pilgrim is not merely strengthened to walk, but he is borne on
eagles' wings. Glorious gospel! Which provides everything for
the helpless, which draws near to us when we cannot reach after
it—brings us grace before we seek for grace! Here is as much
glory in the giving as in the gift. Happy people who have the
Holy Ghost to bring Jesus to them.

☜ *October 23* ☞

*Why sleep ye? Rise and pray, lest ye enter into
temptation (Luke 22:46).*

When is the Christian most liable to sleep? Is it not when his temporal circumstances are prosperous? Have you not found it so? When you had daily troubles to take to the throne of grace, were you not more wakeful than you are now? Easy roads make sleepy travelers. Another dangerous time is when all goes pleasantly in spiritual matters. Christian *[reference to John Bunyan's Pilgrim's Progress]* did not go to sleep when lions were in the way, or when he was wading through the river, or when fighting with Apollyon. But when he had climbed halfway up the Hill Difficult, and came to a delightful arbor, he sat down, and forthwith fell asleep to his great sorrow and loss. The enchanted ground is a place of balmy breezes, laden with fragrant odors and soft influences, all tending to lull pilgrims to sleep. Remember Bunyan's description: "Then they came to an arbor, warm, and promising much refreshing to the weary pilgrims; for it was finely wrought above head, beautified with greens, and furnished with benches and settles. It had also in it a soft couch, where the weary might lean." "The arbor was called the Slothful's Friend, and was made on purpose to allure, if it might be, some of the pilgrims to take up their rest there when weary."[635] Depend upon it; it is in easy places that men shut their eyes and wander into the dreamy land of forgetfulness. Old Erskine wisely remarked, "I like a roaring devil better than a sleeping devil." There is no temptation half so dangerous as not being tempted. The distressed soul does not sleep; it is after we enter into peaceful confidence and full assurance that we are in danger of slumbering. The disciples fell asleep after they had seen Jesus transfigured on the mountaintop. Take heed, joyous Christian, good frames are near neighbors to temptations: be as happy as you will—only be watchful.

He began to wash the disciples' feet (John 13:5).

The Lord Jesus loves His people so much that every day He is still doing for them much that is analogous to washing their soiled feet. He accepts their poorest actions. He feels their deepest sorrow. He hears their slenderest wish. He forgives their every transgression. He is still their servant, as well as their Friend and Master. He not only performs majestic deeds for them, as wearing the miter on His brow and the precious jewels glittering on His breastplate, and standing up to plead for them, but humbly, patiently, He yet goes about among His people with the basin and the towel. He does this when, day by day, He puts away from us our constant infirmities and sins.[636] Last night, when you bowed the knee, you mournfully confessed that much of your conduct was not worthy of your profession; and even tonight, you must mourn afresh that you have fallen again into the selfsame folly and sin from which special grace delivered you long ago. Yet Jesus will have great patience with you. He will hear your confession of sin. He will say, "I will, be thou clean."[637] He will again apply the blood of sprinkling, and speak peace to your conscience, and remove every spot. It is a great act of eternal love when Christ once and for all absolves the sinner and puts him into the family of God. What condescending patience there is when the Savior, with much long-suffering, bears the oft recurring follies of His wayward disciple day by day and hour by hour, washing away the multiplied transgressions of His erring, yet beloved child! To dry up a flood of rebellion is something marvelous, but to endure the constant dropping of repeated offences—to bear with a perpetual trying of patience—this is divine indeed! While we find comfort and peace in our Lord's daily cleansing, its legitimate influence upon us will be to increase our watchfulness, and quicken our desire for holiness. *Is it so?*

⇜ *October 25* ⇝

She gleaned in the field after the reapers: and her hap was to light on a part of the field belonging unto Boaz, who was of the kindred of Elimelech (Ruth 2:3).

Her hap was. [Hap is the archaic form of "happening" or "thing to make or have happen."] Yes, it seemed nothing but an accident, but how divinely was it overruled! Ruth had gone forth with her mother's blessing, under the care of her mother's God, to humble but honorable toil. The providence of God was guiding her every step. Little did she know that amid the sheaves she would find a husband who would make her the joint owner of all those broad acres, and that she, a poor foreigner, would become one of the progenitors of the great Messiah. God is very good to those who trust in Him, and often surprises them with unexpected blessings. Little do we know what may happen to us tomorrow, but this sweet fact may cheer us: No good thing shall be withheld. Chance is banished from the faith of Christians, for they see the hand of God in everything. The trivial events of today or tomorrow may involve consequences of the highest importance. O Lord, deal as graciously with Your servants as Thou didst with Ruth. How blessed would it be, if, in wandering in the field of meditation tonight, our hap should be to light upon the place where our next Kinsman will reveal Himself to us! O Spirit of God, guide us to Him. We would sooner glean in His field than bear away the whole harvest from any other. O for the footsteps of His flock, which may conduct us to the green pastures where He dwells! This is a weary world when Jesus is away—we could better do without sun and moon than without Him—but how divinely fair all things become in the glory of His presence! Our souls know the virtue, which dwells in Jesus, and can never be content without Him. We will wait in prayer this night until our hap shall be to light on a part of the field belonging to Jesus wherein He will manifest Himself to us.

⤙ October 26 ⤚

All the rivers run into the sea; yet the sea is not full;
unto the place from whence the rivers come, thither they
return again (Ecclesiastes 1:7).

Everything sublunary *[belonging to the material world]* is on the move; time knows nothing of rest. The solid earth is a rolling ball, and the great sun, himself a star, obediently fulfills its course around some greater luminary. Tides move the sea, winds stir the airy ocean, and friction wears the rock; change and death rule everywhere. The sea is not a miser's storehouse for a wealth of waters, for as by one force the waters flow into it, and by another, they are lifted from it. Men are born but to die. Everything is hurry, worry, and vexation of spirit. Friend of the unchanging Jesus, what a joy it is to reflect upon your changeless heritage: your sea of bliss, which will be forever full, since God Himself shall pour eternal rivers of pleasure into it. We seek an abiding city beyond the skies, and we shall not be disappointed. The passage before us may well teach us gratitude. Father Ocean is a great receiver, but he is a generous distributor. What the rivers bring him, he returns to the earth in the form of clouds and rain. That man who takes all, but makes no return, is out of joint with the universe. To give to others is but sowing seed for us.[638] He, who is so good a steward as to be willing to use his substance for his Lord, shall be entrusted with more. Friend of Jesus, are you rendering to Him according to the benefit received? Much has been given you, what is your fruit?[639] Have you done all? Can you not do more? To be selfish is to be wicked. Suppose the ocean gave up none of its watery treasure? It would bring ruin upon our race. God forbid that any of us should follow the ungenerous and destructive policy of living unto ourselves. Jesus pleased not Himself. All fullness dwells in Him, but of His fullness have all we received. O for Jesus' spirit, that henceforth we may live not unto ourselves!

❧ *October 27* ❧

We are all as an unclean thing (Isaiah 64:6).

The believer is a new creature.[640] He belongs to a holy generation and a peculiar people[641]—the Spirit of God is in him. In all respects he is far removed from the natural man, but for all that, the Christian is a sinner still. He is so from the imperfection of his nature, and will continue so to the end of his earthly life. The black fingers of sin leave smuts upon our fairest robes. Sin mars our repentance before the great Potter has finished it upon the wheel. Selfishness defiles our tears, and unbelief tampers with our faith. The best thing we ever did apart from the merit of Jesus only swelled the number of our sins, for when we have been most pure in our own sight,[642] yet, like the heavens, we are not pure in God's sight. As He charged His angels with folly, much more must He charge us with it, even in our most angelic frames of mind. The song that thrills to heaven and seeks to emulate seraphic strains has human discords in it. The prayer that moves the arm of God is still a bruised and battered prayer, and only moves that arm because the sinless One, the great Mediator,[643] has stepped in to take away the sin of our supplication. The most golden faith or the purest degree of sanctification to which a Christian ever attained on earth, has still so much alloy in it as to be only worthy of the flames, in itself considered. Every night we look in the glass we see a sinner and need to confess, "We are all as an unclean thing, and all our righteousness is as filthy rags."[644] Oh, how precious the blood of Christ to such hearts as ours! How priceless a gift is His perfect righteousness! And how bright the hope of perfect holiness hereafter! Even now, though sin dwells in us, *its power is broken.* It has no dominion; it is a broken-backed snake; we are in bitter conflict with it, but it is with a vanquished foe that we have to deal. Yet a little while and we shall enter victoriously into the city where nothing defiles.

361

☙ *October 28* ☞

*His head is as the most fine gold, His locks are bushy,
and black as a raven (Song of Solomon 5:11).*

Comparisons all fail to set forth the Lord Jesus, but the spouse uses the best within her reach. By *the head* of Jesus we may understand His deity, "for the head of Christ is God" and then the ingot of purest gold is the best conceivable metaphor, but all too poor to describe one so precious, so pure, so dear, and so glorious. Jesus is not a grain of gold, but a vast globe of it, a priceless mass of treasure such as earth and heaven cannot excel. The creatures are mere iron and clay, they all shall perish like wood, hay, and stubble,[645] but the ever-living Head of the creation of God shall shine on forever and ever. In Him is no mixture, nor smallest taint of alloy. He is forever infinitely holy and altogether divine. *The bushy locks* depict His manly vigor. There is nothing effeminate in our Beloved. He is the manliest of men. Bold as a lion, laborious as an ox, swift as an eagle. Every conceivable and inconceivable beauty is to be found in Him, though once He was despised and rejected of men.[646]

"His head the finest gold; With secret sweet perfume,
His curled locks hang all as black, As any raven's plume."

The glory of His head is not shorn away; He is eternally crowned with peerless majesty. *The black hair* indicates youthful freshness, for Jesus has the dew of His youth upon Him. Others grow languid with age, but He is forever a Priest as was Melchisedek.[647] Others come and go, but He abides as God upon His throne, world without end. We will behold Him tonight and adore Him. Angels are gazing upon Him—His redeemed must not turn away their eyes from Him. Where else is there such a Beloved? O for an hour's fellowship with Him! Away, you intruding cares! Jesus draws me, and I run after Him.

362

But their eyes were holden that they should not know Him (Luke 24:16).

The disciples ought to have known Jesus. They had heard His voice so often and gazed upon that marred face so frequently, that it is amazing that they did not discover Him. Yet is it not so with you, also? You have not seen Jesus lately. You have been to His table, and you have not met Him there. You are in a dark trouble this evening, and though He plainly says, "It is I, be not afraid," yet you cannot discern Him. Alas! our eyes are holden. We know His voice; we have looked into His face; we have leaned our head upon His bosom, and yet, though Christ is very near us, we are saying, "O that I knew where I might find Him!" We should know Jesus, for we have the Scriptures to reflect His image, and yet how possible it is for us to open that precious book and have no glimpse of the Well Beloved! Dear child of God, are you in that state?[648] Jesus feeds among the lilies of the word, and you walk among those lilies, and yet you behold Him not. He is accustomed to walking through the glades of Scripture, and to communing with His people, as the Father did with Adam in the cool of the day. Yet you are in the garden of Scripture, but cannot see Him, though He is always there. And why do we not see Him? It must be ascribed in our case, as in the disciples', to unbelief. They evidently did not expect to see Jesus, and therefore they did not know Him.[649] To a great extent in spiritual things, we get what we expect of the Lord. Faith alone can bring us to see Jesus. Make it your prayer, "Lord, open Thou mine eyes, that I may see my Savior present with me." It is a blessed thing to want to see Him; but oh! it is better far to gaze upon Him. To those who seek Him, He is kind. But to those who find Him, He is dear beyond expression!

Thou that dwellest in the gardens, the companions
hearken to Your voice: cause me to hear it
(Song of Solomon 8:13).

My sweet Lord Jesus remembers well the garden of Gethsemane, and although He has left that garden, He now dwells in the garden of His church. There He embosoms Himself to those who keep His blessed company. That voice of love with which He speaks to His beloved is more musical than the harps of heaven. There is a depth of melodious love within it that leaves all human music far behind. Ten of thousands on earth and millions above are indulged with its harmonious accents. Some whom I well know and whom I greatly envy are at this moment hearkening to the beloved voice. O that I was a partaker of their joys! It is true that some of these are poor, others bedridden, and some near the gates of death, but O my Lord, I would cheerfully starve with them, pine with them, or die with them if I might but hear Your voice. Once I did hear it often, but I have grieved Your Spirit. Return unto me in compassion, and once again say unto me, "I am your salvation." No other voice can content me. I know Your voice and cannot be deceived by another.[650] Let me hear it, I pray You. I know not what Thou wilt say, neither do I make any condition, O my Beloved, do but let me hear You speak, and if it be a rebuke, then I will bless You for it. Perhaps to cleanse my dull ear may need an operation very grievous to the flesh, but no matter what the cost, I turn not from the one consuming desire: cause me to hear Your voice. Bore my ear afresh; pierce my ear with Your harshest notes. Only do not permit me to continue deaf to Your calls. Tonight, Lord, grant Your unworthy one his desire, for I am Yours, and Thou hast bought me with Your blood. Thou hast opened mine eye to see You, and the sight has saved me. Lord, open Thou mine ear. I have read Your heart. Now let me hear Your lips.

✎ *October 31* ✎

I did know you in the wilderness,
in the land of great drought (Hosea 13:5).

Yes, Lord, Thou didst indeed know me in my *fallen state*, and Thou didst even then choose me for Yourself. When I was loathsome and self-abhorred, Thou didst receive me as Your child, and Thou didst satisfy my craving wants. Blessed forever be Your name for this free, rich, abounding mercy. Since then, my inward experience has often been a wilderness; but Thou hast owned me still as Your beloved, and poured streams of love and grace into me to gladden me and make me fruitful. Yea, when my *outward circumstances* have been at the worst, and I have wandered in a land of drought, Your sweet presence has solaced me. Men have not known me when scorn has awaited me, but Thou hast known my soul in adversities, for no affliction dims the luster of Your love. Most gracious Lord, I magnify You for all Your faithfulness to me in trying circumstances, and I deplore that I should at any time have forgotten You and been exalted in heart, when I have owed all to Your gentleness and love. Have mercy upon Your servant in this thing! My soul, if Jesus thus acknowledged You in your low estate, is sure that thou own both Himself and His cause now that you are in your prosperity. Be not lifted up by your worldly successes so as to be ashamed of the truth or of the poor church with which you have been associated. Follow Jesus into the wilderness. Bear the cross with Him when the heat of persecution grows hot. He owned you, O my soul, in your poverty and shame—never be so treacherous as to be ashamed of Him.[651] O for more shame at the thought of being ashamed of my best Beloved! Jesus, my soul cleaves to You.

> "I'll turn to You in days of light,
>   As well as nights of care,
>   Thou brightest amid all that's bright!
>   Thou fairest of the fair!"

November

☙ November 1 ☙

And knew not until the flood came, and took them all away: so shall also the coming of the Son of man be (Matthew 24:39).

Universal was the doom, neither rich nor poor escaped: the learned and the illiterate, the admired and the abhorred, the religious and the profane, and the old and the young all sank in one common ruin. Some had doubtlessly ridiculed the patriarch— where now their merry jests? Others had threatened him for his zeal, which they counted madness—where now their boastings and hard speeches? The critic who judged the old man's work is drowned in the same sea, which covers his sneering companions. Those who spoke patronizingly of the good man's fidelity to his convictions, but shared not in them, have sunk to rise no more. The workers, who for pay helped to build the wondrous ark, are all lost, also. The flood swept them *all* away and made no single exception. Even so, out of Christ, final destruction is sure to every man of woman born; no rank, possession, or character shall suffice to save a single soul who has not believed in the Lord Jesus.[652] My soul, behold this widespread judgment and tremble at it. How marvelous the general apathy! They were all eating and drinking, marrying and giving in marriage till the awful morning dawned.[653] There was not one wise man upon earth out of the ark. Folly duped the whole race: folly as to self-preservation— the most foolish of all follies, and folly in doubting the most true God—the most malignant of fooleries. Strange, my soul, is it not? All men are negligent of their souls till grace gives them reason, and then they leave their madness and act like rational beings, but not till then. *All*, blessed be God, were safe in the ark, no ruin entered there. From the huge elephant down to the tiny mouse, all were safe. The timid hare was equally secure with the courageous lion, the helpless rabbit as safe as the laborious ox. All are safe in Jesus. My soul, are you in Him?[654]

Horror has taken hold upon me because of the wicked that forsake Your law (Psalm 119:53).

My soul, do you feel this holy shuddering at the sins of others? Otherwise you lack inward holiness. David's cheeks were wet with rivers of waters because of prevailing unholiness; Jeremiah desired eyes like fountains, that he might lament the iniquities of Israel. Lot was vexed with the conversation of the men of Sodom. Those, upon whom the mark was set in Ezekiel's vision, were those who sighed and cried for the abominations of Jerusalem.[655] It cannot but grieve gracious souls to see what pains men take to go to hell. They know the evil of sin experimentally, and they are alarmed to see others flying like moths into its blaze. Sin makes the righteous shudder, because it violates a holy law, which it is to every man's highest interest to keep. It pulls down the pillars of the commonwealth. Sin in others horrifies a believer, because it puts him in mind of the baseness of his own heart. When he sees a transgressor, he cries with the saint mentioned by Bernard: "He fell today, and I may fall tomorrow." Sin to a believer is horrible, because it crucified the Savior. He sees in every iniquity the nails and spear. How can a saved soul behold that cursed kill-Christ sin without abhorrence? Say, my heart, do you sensibly join in all this? It is an awful thing to insult God to His face. The good God deserves better treatment, the great God claims it, and the just God will have it or repay His adversary to his face. An awakened heart trembles at the audacity of sin, and stands alarmed at the contemplation of its punishment. How monstrous a thing is rebellion! How direful a doom is prepared for the ungodly! My soul, never laugh at sin's fooleries, lest thou come to smile at sin itself. It is your enemy and your Lord's enemy—view it with detestation, for so only can you evidence the possession of holiness, without which no man can see the Lord.[656]

⤜ *November 3* ⤐

Their prayer came up to His holy dwelling place, even unto heaven (2 Chronicles 30:27).

Prayer is the never-failing resort of the Christian in any case, in every plight.[657] When you cannot use your sword you may take to the weapon of all-prayer. Your powder may be damp, your bowstring may be relaxed, but the weapon of all-prayer need never be out of order. Leviathan laughs at the javelin, but he trembles at prayer. Sword and spear need furbishing, but prayer never rusts, and when we think it most blunt it cuts the best. Prayer is an open door which none can shut. Devils may surround you on all sides, but the way upward is always open, and as long as that road is unobstructed, you will not fall into the enemy's hand.[658] We can never be taken by blockade, escalade, mine, or storm, so long as heavenly succors can come down to us by Jacob's ladder to relieve us in the time of our necessities. Prayer is never out of season: in summer and in winter its merchandize is precious. Prayer gains audience with heaven in the dead of night, in the midst of business, in the heat of noonday, in the shades of evening. In every condition, whether of poverty, or sickness, or obscurity, or slander, or doubt, your covenant God will welcome your prayer and answer it from His holy place. Nor is prayer ever *futile*. True prayer is evermore-true power.[659] You may not always get what you ask, but you shall always have your real wants supplied.[660] When God does not answer His children according to the letter, He does so according to the spirit. If you ask for coarse meal, will you be angered because He gives you the finest flour? If you seek bodily health, should you complain if instead He makes your sickness turn to the healing of spiritual maladies?[661] Is it not better to have the cross sanctified than removed? This evening, my soul, forget not to offer your petition and request, for the Lord is ready to grant you your desires.

☜ *November 4* ☞

In Your light shall we see light (Psalm 36:9).

No lips can tell the love of Christ to the heart till Jesus Himself shall speak within. Descriptions all fall flat and tame unless the Holy Ghost fills them with life and power; till our Immanuel reveals Himself within, the soul sees Him not. If you would see the sun, would you gather together the common means of illumination, and seek in that way to behold the orb of day? No, the wise man knows that the sun must reveal itself, and only by its own blaze can that mighty lamp be seen. It is so with Christ. "Blessed are you, Simon Bar-jona,"[662] said He to Peter, "for flesh and blood has not revealed this unto you." Purify flesh and blood by any educational process you may select, and elevate mental faculties to the highest degree of intellectual power. Yet none of these can reveal Christ. The Spirit of God must come with power, and overshadow the man with His wings. Then in that mystic holy of holies, the Lord Jesus must display Himself to the sanctified eye, as He doth not unto the completely blind sons of men. Christ must be His own mirror. The great mass of this bleary-eyed world can see nothing of the ineffable glories of Immanuel. He stands before them without form or comeliness, a root out of a dry ground,[663] rejected by the vain and despised by the proud. Only where the Spirit has touched the eye with eye-salve, quickened the heart with divine life, and educated the soul to a heavenly taste—only there is He understood. "To you that believe He is precious;" to you He is the chief corner-stone, the Rock of your salvation, and your all in all. But to others, He is "a stone of stumbling and a rock of offense."[664] Happy are those to whom our Lord manifests Himself, for His promise to such is that He will *make His abode with them*. O Jesus, our Lord, our hearts are open. Come in and go out no more forever. Show Yourself to us now! Favor us with a glimpse of Your all-conquering charms.

Be thankful unto Him, and bless His name
(Psalm 100:4).

Our Lord would have all His people rich in high and happy thoughts concerning His blessed person. Jesus is not content that His brethren should think meanly of Him; it is His pleasure that His espoused ones should be delighted with His beauty. We are not to regard Him as a bare necessary, like to bread and water, but as a luxurious delicacy, as a rare and ravishing delight. To this end He has revealed Himself as the "pearl of great price"[665] in its peerless beauty, as the "bundle of myrrh" in its refreshing fragrance, as the "rose of Sharon" in its lasting perfume, as the "lily" in its spotless purity.[666]

As a help to high thoughts of Christ, remember the estimation that Christ is had in beyond the skies, where things are measured by the right standard. Think how God esteems the Only Begotten, His unspeakable gift to us. Consider what the angels think of Him, as they count it their highest honor to veil their faces at His feet. Consider what the blood-washed think of Him, as day without night they sing His well deserved praises. High thoughts of Christ will enable us to act consistently with our relations toward Him. The more loftily we see Christ enthroned, and the more lowly we are when bowing before the foot of the throne, the more truly shall we be prepared to act our part toward Him.[667] Our Lord Jesus desires us to think well of Him, that we may submit cheerfully to His authority. High thoughts of Him increase our love. Love and esteem go together. Therefore, believer, think much of your Master's excellencies. Study Him in His primeval glory, before He took upon Himself your nature! Think of the mighty love that drew Him from His throne to die upon the cross! Admire Him as He conquers all the powers of hell![668] See Him risen, crowned, glorified! Bow before Him as the Wonderful, the Counselor, the mighty God, for only thus will your love to Him be what it should.

⊰ *November 6* ⊱

Saying, This is the blood of the testament which God has enjoined unto you (Hebrews 9:20).

There is a strange power about the very name of blood, and the sight of it is always affecting. A kind heart cannot bear to see a sparrow bleed, and unless familiarized by use, turns away with horror at the slaughter of a beast. As to the blood of men, it is a consecrated thing: it is murder to shed it in wrath; it is a dreadful crime to squander it in war. Is this solemnity occasioned by the fact that the blood is the life,[669] and the pouring of it forth the token of death? We think so. When we rise to contemplate the blood of the Son of God, our awe is yet more increased, and we shudder as we think of the guilt of sin, and the terrible penalty that the Sin-bearer endured. Blood, always precious, is priceless when it streams from Immanuel's side. The blood of Jesus seals the *covenant* of grace, and makes it forever sure.[670] Covenants of old were made by sacrifice, and the everlasting covenant was ratified in the same manner.[671] Oh, the delight of being saved upon the sure foundation of divine engagements that cannot be dishonored! Salvation by the works of the law is a frail and broken vessel whose shipwreck is sure;[672] but the covenant vessel fears no storms, for the blood ensures the whole. The blood of Jesus made His *testament* valid. Wills are of no power unless the testators die. In this light the soldier's spear is a blessed aid to faith, since it proved our Lord to be really dead. Doubts upon that matter there can be none, and we may boldly appropriate the legacies that He has left for His people. Happy they who see their title to heavenly blessings assured to them by a dying Savior. But has this blood no voice to us? Does it not bid us sanctify ourselves unto Him by whom we have been redeemed? Does it not call us to newness of life,[673] and incite us to entire consecration to the Lord? O that the power of the blood might be known, and felt in us this night!

☞ November 7 ☞

And ye shall be witnesses unto Me (Acts 1:8).

In order to learn how to discharge your duty as a witness for Christ, look at His example. He is always witnessing: by the well of Samaria, or in the Temple of Jerusalem: by the lake of Gennesaret, or on the mountain's brow. He is witnessing night and day; His mighty prayers are as vocal to God as His daily services. He witnesses under all circumstances. Scribes and Pharisees cannot shut His mouth. Even before Pilate He witnesses a good confession. He witnesses so clearly, and distinctly that there is no mistake in Him. Christian, make your life a clear testimony. Be you as the brook wherein you may see every stone at the bottom—not as the muddy creek, of which you only see the surface—but clear and transparent, so that your heart's love to God and man may be visible to all. You need not say, "I am true:" be true. Boast not of integrity, but be upright. So shall your testimony be such that men cannot help seeing it. Never, for fear of feeble man, restrain your witness. Your lips have been warmed with a coal from off the altar; let them speak as like heaven-touched lips should do. "In the morning sow your seed, and in the evening withhold not your hand."[674] Watch not the clouds, consult not the wind—in season and out of season witness for the Savior, and if it shall come to pass that for Christ's sake and the gospel's you shall endure suffering in any shape, shrink not, but rejoice in the honor thus conferred upon you, that you are counted worthy to suffer with your Lord;[675] and joy also in this—that your sufferings, your losses, and persecutions shall make you a platform, from which the more vigorously and with greater power you shall witness for Christ Jesus.[676] Study your great Exemplar, and be filled with His Spirit. Remember that you need much teaching, much upholding, much grace, and much humility, if your witnessing is to be to your Master's glory.

*The Master saith, "Where is the guestchamber, where I
shall eat the passover with My disciples?" (Mark 14:14)*

Jerusalem at the time of the Passover was one great inn. Each
householder had invited his own friends, but no one had invited
the Savior, and He had no dwelling of His own. It was by His
own supernatural power that He found Himself an upper
room in which to keep the feast. It is so even to this day—Jesus
is not received among the sons of men, except where by His
supernatural power and grace He makes the heart anew. All
doors are open enough to the prince of darkness, but Jesus must
clear a way for Himself or lodge in the streets. It was through
the mysterious power exerted by our Lord that the householder
raised no question, but at once cheerfully and joyfully opened his
guest chamber. We do not know who he was and what he was,
but he readily accepted the honor that the Redeemer proposed
to confer upon him. In like manner it is still discovered who are
the Lord's chosen and who are not. When the gospel comes to
some, they fight against it and will not have it, but where men
receive it, welcoming it, this is a sure indication that there is a
secret work going on in the soul, and that God has chosen them
unto eternal life. Are you willing, dear reader, to receive Christ?
Then there is no difficulty in the way; Christ will be your guest.
His own power is working with you, making you willing.[677]
What an honor to entertain the Son of God! The heaven of
heavens cannot contain Him, and yet He condescends to find
a house within our hearts! We are not worthy that He should
come under our roof, but what an unutterable privilege when
He condescends to enter! For then He makes a feast, and causes
us to feast with Him upon royal dainties, we sit at a banquet
where the viands are immortal, and give immortality to those
who feed thereon. Blessed among the sons of Adam is he who
entertains the angels' Lord.[678]

His place of defense shall be the munitions of rocks:
bread shall be given him; his waters shall be sure
(Isaiah 33:16).

Do you doubt, O Christian? Do you doubt as to whether God
will fulfill His promise? Shall the munitions of rock be carried
by storm? O Shall the storehouses of heaven fail? Do you think
that your heavenly Father, though He knows that you have need
of food and clothing, will yet forget you?[679] When not a sparrow
falls to the ground without your Father, and the very hairs of
your head are all numbered, will you mistrust and doubt Him?
Perhaps your affliction will continue upon you till you dare to
trust your God, and then it shall end. Full many there be who
have been tried and sore vexed till at last they have been driven
in sheer desperation to exercise faith in God, and the moment of
their faith has been the instant of their deliverance; they have seen
whether God would keep His promise or not. Oh, I pray you,
doubt Him no longer![680] Please not Satan, and vex not yourself
by indulging any more those hard thoughts of God. Think it not
a light matter to doubt Jehovah. Remember, it is a *sin*; and not
a little sin either, but in the highest degree criminal. The angels
never doubted Him, nor the devils either: we alone, out of all
the beings that God has fashioned, dishonor Him by unbelief,
and tarnish His honor by mistrust. Shame upon us for this! Our
God does not deserve to be so basely suspected; in our past life
we have proved Him to be true and faithful to His word, and
with so many instances of His love and of His kindness as we
have received, and are daily receiving, at His hands, it is base
and inexcusable that we suffer a doubt to sojourn within our
heart. May we henceforth wage constant war against doubts of
our God—enemies to our peace and to His honor; and with an
unshakable faith believe that what He has promised He will also
perform.[681] "Lord, I believe, help Thou mine unbelief."

*It is enough for the disciple that he be as His Master
(Matthew 10:25).*

No one will dispute this statement, for it would be unseemly for the servant to be exalted above his Master. When our Lord was on earth, what was the treatment He received? Were His claims acknowledged, His instructions followed, and His perfections worshipped by those whom He came to bless? No. "He was despised and rejected of men." Outside the camp was His place. Cross bearing was His occupation. Did the world yield Him solace and rest? "Foxes have holes, and the birds of the air have nests; but the Son of man has not where to lay His head."[682] This inhospitable country afforded Him no shelter. It cast Him out and crucified Him. Such—if you are a follower of Jesus and maintain a consistent, Christ-like walk and conversation—you must expect to be the lot of that part of your spiritual life which, in its outward development, comes under the observation of men. They will treat it as they treated the Savior—they will despise it. Dream not that worldlings will admire you, or that the more holy and the more Christ-like you are, the more peaceably people will act toward you. They prized not the polished gem; how should they value the jewel in the rough? "If they have called the Master of the house Beelzebub, how much more shall they call them of His household?"[683] If we were more like Christ, we should be more hated by His enemies. It was a sad dishonor to a child of God to be the world's favorite. It is a very ill omen to hear a wicked world clap its hands and shout "Well done" to the Christian man. He may begin to look to his character, and wonder whether he has not been doing wrong, when the unrighteous give him their approbation. Let us be true to our Master, and have no friendship with a blind and base world that scorns and rejects Him. Far be it from us to seek a crown of honor where our Lord found a coronet of thorn.

He shall choose our inheritance for us (Psalm 47:4).

Believer, if your inheritance is a lowly one, you should be satisfied with your earthly portion; for you may rest assured that it is the fittest *for you*. Unerring wisdom ordained your lot, and selected for you the safest and best condition. A ship of large tonnage is to be brought up the river. Now, in one part of the stream there is a sandbank. Someone might ask, "Why does the captain steer through the deep part of the channel and deviate so much from a straight line?" His answer would be, "Because I should not get my vessel into harbor at all if I did not keep to the deep channel." So, it may be, you would run aground and suffer shipwreck, if your divine Captain did not steer you into the depths of affliction where waves of trouble follow each other in quick succession. Some plants die if they have too much sunshine. It may be that you are planted where you get but little, but remember that the loving Husbandman puts you there, because only in that situation will you bring forth fruit unto perfection. Remember this, had any other condition been better for you than the one in which you are, divine love would have put you there. God places you in the most suitable circumstances, and if you had the choosing of your lot, you would soon cry, "Lord, choose my inheritance for me, for by my self-will I am pierced through with many sorrows." Be content with such things as you have, since the Lord has ordered all things for your good. Take up your own daily cross; it is the burden best suited for your shoulder, and will prove most effective to make you perfect in every good word and work to the glory of God. Down, busy self and proud impatience; it is not for you to choose, but for the Lord of Love!

"Trials must and will befall—But with humble faith to see
Love inscribed upon them all; This is happiness to me."

☙ *November 12* ❧

And it came to pass in those days, that He went out into a mountain to pray, and continued all night in prayer to God (Luke 6:12).

If ever one born of woman might have lived without prayer, it was our spotless, perfect Lord, and yet none was ever so much in supplication as He! Such was His love to His Father that He loved much to be in communion with Him. Such was His love for His people that He desired to be much in intercession for them. *The fact* of this eminent prayerfulness of Jesus is a lesson for us—He has given us an example that we may follow in His steps. *The time* He chose was admirable: it was the hour of silence, when the crowd would not disturb Him; the time of inaction, when all but Himself had ceased to labor; and the season when slumber made men forget their woes and cease their applications to Him for relief. While others found rest in sleep, He refreshed Himself with prayer. *The place* was also well selected: He was alone where none would intrude, where none could observe. Thus was He free from Pharisaic ostentation and vulgar interruption. Those dark and silent hills were a fit oratory for the Son of God. Heaven and earth in midnight stillness heard the groans and sighs of the mysterious Being in whom both worlds were blended. *The continuance* of His pleadings is remarkable: the long watches were not too long; the cold wind did not chill His devotions; the grim darkness did not darken His faith; or loneliness check His importunity. We cannot watch with Him one hour, but He watched for us whole nights. *The occasion* for this prayer is notable: It was after His enemies had been enraged—prayer was His refuge and solace. It was before He sent forth the twelve apostles—prayer was the gate of His enterprise, the herald of His new work. Should we not learn from Jesus to resort to special prayer when we are under peculiar trial, or contemplate fresh endeavors for the Master's glory? Lord Jesus, teach us to pray.[684]

Men ought always to pray (Luke 18:1).

If *men* ought always to pray and not to faint, Christian men should pray much more. Jesus has sent His church into the world on the same errand upon which He Himself came, and this mission includes intercession. What if I say that the church is the world's priest? Creation is mute, but the church is to find a mouth for it. It is the church's high privilege to pray with acceptance. The door of grace is always open for her petitions, and they never return empty-handed. The veil was rent *for her*, the blood was sprinkled upon the altar *for her*, and God constantly invites her to ask what she wills. Will she refuse the privilege that angels might envy her? Is she not the bride of Christ? May she not go in unto her King at every hour? Shall she allow the precious privilege to be unused? The church always has need for prayer. There are always some in her midst who are declining or falling into open sin. There are lambs to be prayed for, that they may be carried in Christ's bosom: the strong, lest they grow presumptuous, and the weak, lest they become despairing. If we kept up prayer-meetings four-and-twenty hours in the day, all the days in the year, we would never be without a special subject for supplication. Are we ever without the sick and the poor, the afflicted and the wavering? Are we ever without those who seek the conversion of relatives, the reclaiming of backsliders, or the salvation of the depraved? Nay, with congregations constantly gathering, with ministers always preaching, with millions of sinners lying dead in trespasses and sins; in a country over which the darkness of Romanism is certainly descending; in a world full of idols, cruelties, devilries—if the church does not pray, how shall she excuse her base neglect of the commission of her loving Lord?[685] Let the church be constant in supplication. Let every private believer cast his mite of prayer into the treasury.

And Laban said, "It must not be so done in our country,
to give the younger before the firstborn"
(Genesis 29:26).

We do not excuse Laban for his dishonesty, but we scruple not to learn from the custom that he quoted as his excuse. There are some things that must be taken in order. If we would win the second, we must secure the first. The second may be the more lovely in our eyes, but the rule of the heavenly country must stand, and the elder must be married first. For instance, many men desire the beautiful and well-favored Rachel of joy and peace in believing, but they must first be wedded to the tender-eyed Leah of repentance. Everyone falls in love with happiness, and many would cheerfully serve twice seven years to enjoy it, but according to the rule of the Lord's kingdom, the Leah of real holiness must be beloved of our soul before the Rachel of true happiness can be attained. Heaven stands not first, but second. Only by persevering to the end can we win a portion in it. The cross must be carried before the crown can be worn. We must follow our Lord in His humiliation, or we shall never rest with Him in glory. My soul, are you so vain as to hope to break through the heavenly rule? Do you hope for reward without labor, or honor without toil? Dismiss the idle expectation, and be content to take the ill-favored things for the sake of the sweet love of Jesus, which will recompense you for all. In such a spirit, laboring and suffering, you will find bitters grow sweet and hard things easy. Like Jacob, your years of service will seem unto you but a few days for the love you have to Jesus; and when the dear hour of the wedding feast shall come, all your toils shall be as though they had never been—an hour with Jesus will make up for ages of pain and labor.

Jesus, to win Yourself so fair,
Your cross I will with gladness bear:
Since so the rules of heaven ordain,
The first I'll wed the next to gain.

☞ *November 15* ☜

Strengthen, O God, that which thou hast wrought for us
(Psalm 68:28).

It is our wisdom, as well as our necessity, to beseech God continually to strengthen that which He has wrought in us. It is because of their neglect in this that many Christians may blame themselves for those trials and afflictions of spirit that arise from unbelief.[686] It is true that Satan seeks to flood the fair garden of the heart and make it a scene of desolation, but it is also true that many Christians leave open the sluice-gates themselves, and let in the dreadful deluge through carelessness and want of prayer to their strong Helper. We often forget that the Author of our faith must be the Preserver of it, also. The lamp that was burning in the temple was never allowed to go out, but it had to be daily replenished with fresh oil. In like manner, our faith can only live by being sustained with the oil of grace, and we can only obtain this from God Himself. Foolish virgins we shall prove if we do not secure the needed sustenance for our lamps. He, who built the world, upholds it or it would fall in one tremendous crash. He, who made us Christians, must maintain us by His Spirit, or our ruin will be speedy and final. Let us, then, evening by evening, go to our Lord for the grace and strength we need. We have a strong argument to plead, for it is *His own work of grace,* which we ask Him to strengthen—"that which Thou hast wrought for us." Do you think that He will fail to protect and sustain that? Only let your faith take hold of His strength; and all the powers of darkness, led on by the master fiend of hell, cannot cast a cloud or shadow over your joy and peace. Why faint when you may be strong? Why suffer defeat when you may conquer?[687] Oh! take your wavering faith and drooping graces to Him who can revive and replenish them, and earnestly pray, "Strengthen, O God, that which you have wrought for us."

November 16

Your eyes shall see the King in His beauty
(Isaiah 33:17).

The more you know about Christ, the less will you be satisfied with superficial views of Him. The more deeply you study His transactions in the eternal covenant, His engagements on your behalf as the eternal Surety, and the fullness of His grace that shines in all His offices, the more truly will you see the King in His beauty. Be much in such outlooks. Long more and more to see Jesus. *Meditation and contemplation* are often like windows of agate and gates of carbuncle, through which we behold the Redeemer. Meditation puts the telescope to the eye, and enables us to see Jesus better than we could have seen Him if we had lived in the days of His flesh. Would that our conversation were more in heaven, and that we were more taken up with the person, the work, and the beauty of our incarnate Lord. More meditation, and the beauty of the King would flash upon us with more resplendence. Beloved, it is very probable that we shall have such a sight of our glorious King as we never had before, *when we come to die.* Many saints in dying have looked up from amidst the stormy waters, and have seen Jesus walking on the waves of the sea, and heard Him say, "It is I, be not afraid."[688] Ah, yes! when the tenement begins to shake, and the clay falls away, we see Christ through the rifts and between the rafters the sunlight of heaven comes streaming in. But if we want to see face-to-face the "King in His beauty," we must go to heaven for the sight, or the King must come here in person. O that He would come on the wings of the wind! He is our Husband, and we are widowed by His absence; He is our Brother dear and fair, and we are lonely without Him. Thick veils and clouds hang between our souls and their true life: when shall the day break and the shadows flee away? Oh, long-expected day, begin![689]

384

He that cleaveth wood shall be endangered thereby
(Ecclesiastes 10:9).

Oppressors may get their will of poor and needy men as easily as they can split logs of wood, but they had better mind, for it is a dangerous business, and a splinter from a tree has often killed the woodman. Jesus is persecuted in every injured saint, and He is mighty to avenge His beloved ones. Success in treading down the poor and needy is a thing to be trembled at. If there be no danger to persecutors here, there will be great danger hereafter.[690] To cleave wood is a common everyday business, and yet it has its dangers; so then, reader, there are dangers connected with your calling and daily life, which it will be well for you to be aware of. We refer not to hazards by flood and field, or by disease and sudden death, but to perils of a spiritual sort. Your occupation may be as humble as log splitting, and yet the devil can tempt you in it. You may be a domestic servant, a farm laborer, or a mechanic, and you may be greatly screened from temptations to the grosser vices, and yet some secret sin may do you damage. Those who dwell at home and mingle not with the rough world may yet be endangered by their very seclusion. Nowhere is he safe who thinks himself so. Pride may enter a poor man's heart; avarice may reign in a cottager's bosom; uncleanness may venture into the quietest home; and anger, and envy, and malice may insinuate themselves into the most rural abode. Even in speaking a few words to a servant, we may sin. A little purchase at a shop may be the first link in a chain of temptations. The mere looking out of a window may be the beginning of evil.[691] O Lord, how exposed we are! How shall we be secured! To keep ourselves is work too hard for us. Only Thou Yourself art able to preserve us in such a world of evils. Spread Your wings over us, and we, like little chickens, will cower down beneath You, and feel ourselves safe![692]

⇜ *November 18* ⇝

Thou art from everlasting (Psalm 93:2).

Christ is EVERLASTING. Of Him we may sing with David, "Your throne, O God, is forever and ever." Rejoice, believer, in Jesus Christ, the same yesterday, today, and forever.[693] Jesus always *was*. The Babe born in Bethlehem was united to the Word, which was in the beginning, by whom all things were made. The title by which Christ revealed Himself to John in Patmos was, "Him which is, and which was, and which is to come."[694] If He were not God from everlasting, we could not so devoutly love Him; we could not feel that He had any share in the eternal love, which is the fountain of all covenant blessings. But since He was from all eternity with the Father, we trace the stream of divine love to Himself equally with His Father and the blessed Spirit. As our Lord always *was*, so also He is forevermore. Jesus is not dead. "He ever liveth to make intercession for us."[695] Resort to Him in all your times of need, for He is waiting to bless you still. Moreover, Jesus our Lord ever *shall be*. If God should spare your life to fulfill your full day of threescore years and ten, you will find that His cleansing fountain is still opened, and His precious blood has not lost its power. You shall find that the Priest, who filled the healing fount with His own blood, lives to purge you from all iniquity. When only your last battle remains to be fought, you shall find that the hand of your conquering Captain has not grown feeble—the living Savior shall cheer the dying saint. When you enter heaven you shall find Him there bearing the dew of His youth; and through eternity the Lord Jesus shall still remain the perennial spring of joy, and life, and glory to His people. Living waters may you draw from this sacred well! Jesus always was, He always is, and He always shall be. He is eternal in all His attributes, in all His offices, in all His might, and willingness to bless, comfort, guard, and crown His chosen people.

O that I knew where I might find Him! (Job 23:3)

In Job's uttermost extremity, he cried after the Lord. The longing desire of an afflicted child of God is once more to see his Father's face. His first prayer is not "O that I might be healed of the disease which now festers in every part of my body!" nor even "O that I might see my children restored from the jaws of the grave, and my property once more brought from the hand of the spoiler!" No, the first and uppermost cry is, "O that I knew where I might find HIM, who is my God! that I might come even to His seat!" God's children run home when the storm comes on. It is the heaven-born instinct of a gracious soul to seek shelter from all ills beneath the wings of Jehovah. "He that has made his refuge God," might serve as the title of a true believer. A hypocrite, when afflicted by God, resents the infliction, and like a slave, would run from the Master who has scourged him. But not so the true heir of heaven; he kisses the hand that smote him, and seeks shelter from the rod in the bosom of the God who frowned upon him. Job's desire to commune with God was intensified by the failure of all other sources of consolation. The patriarch turned away from his sorry friends, and looked up to the celestial throne, just as a traveler turns from his empty skin bottle, and betakes himself with all speed to the well. He bids farewell to earth-born hopes, and cries, "O that I knew where I might find my God!" Nothing teaches us so much the preciousness of the Creator as when we learn the emptiness of all besides. Turning away with bitter scorn from earth's hives, where we find no honey, but many sharp stings, we rejoice in Him whose faithful word is sweeter than honey or the honeycomb.[696] In every trouble we should first seek to realize God's presence with us. Only let us enjoy His smile, and we can bear our daily cross with a willing heart for His dear sake.

November 20

The conies are but a feeble folk, yet make they their houses in the rocks (Proverbs 30:26).

Conscious of their own natural defenselessness, the conies resort to burrows in the rocks, and are secure from their enemies. My heart, be willing to gather a lesson from these feeble folk. You are as weak and as exposed to peril as the timid rabbit. Be as wise to seek a shelter. My best security is within the munitions of an immutable Jehovah, where His unalterable promises stand like giant walls of rock. It will be well with you, my heart, if you can always hide yourself in the bulwarks of His glorious attributes, all of which are guarantees of safety for those who put their trust in Him. Blessed be the name of the Lord, I have so done, and have found myself like David in Adullam, safe from the cruelty of my enemy.[697] I have not now to find out the blessedness of the man who puts his trust in the Lord, for long ago, when Satan and my sins pursued me, I fled to the cleft of the rock Christ Jesus, and in His pierced side I found a delightful resting place.[698] My heart, run to Him anew tonight, whatever your present grief may be. Jesus feels for you; Jesus consoles you; Jesus will help you. No monarch in his impregnable fortress is more secure than the rabbit in his rocky burrow. The master of ten thousand chariots is not one whit better protected than the little dweller in the mountain's cleft. In Jesus, the weak are strong and the defenseless, safe.[699] They could not be stronger if they were giants or safer if they were in heaven. Faith gives to men on earth the protection of the God of heaven. More they cannot need and need not wish. The rabbits cannot build a castle, but they avail themselves of what is there already. I cannot make myself a refuge, but Jesus has provided it, His Father has given it, His Spirit has revealed it, and lo, again tonight I enter it, and am safe from every foe.

*Lazarus was one of them that sat at the table with Him
(John 12:2).*

He is to be envied. It was well to be Martha and serve, but better
to be Lazarus and commune. There are times for each purpose,
and each is comely in its season, but none of the trees of the
garden yield such clusters as the vine of fellowship. To sit with
Jesus, to hear His words, to mark His acts, and receive His
smiles was such a favor as must have made Lazarus as happy
as the angels. When it has been our happy lot to feast with our
Beloved in His banquet hall, we would not have given half a
sigh for all the kingdoms of the world, if so much breath could
have bought them. *He is to be imitated.* It would have been a
strange thing if Lazarus had not been at the table where Jesus
was, for he had been dead and Jesus had raised him.[700] It would
have been ungrateful indeed for the risen one to be absent when
the Lord who gave him life was at his house. We, too, were
once dead, yea, and like Lazarus stinking in the grave of sin,
Jesus raised us, and by His life we live. Can we be content to
live at a distance from Him? Do we omit to remember Him at
His table, where He deigns to feast with His brethren? Oh, this
is cruel! It is in our best interests to repent, and do as *He* has
bidden us, for His least wish should be law to us. To have lived
without constant relationship with one of whom the Jews said,
"Behold how He loved him,"[701] would have been disgraceful
to Lazarus. Is it excusable in us, whom Jesus has loved with an
everlasting love? To be cold to Him who wept over his lifeless
corpse, would have argued great brutishness in Lazarus. What
does it argue in us over whom the Savior has not only wept, but
also bled? Come, brethren, who read this portion, let us return
unto our heavenly Bridegroom, and ask for His Spirit, that we
may be on terms of closer intimacy with Him, and henceforth
sit at the table with Him.

The power of His resurrection (Philippians 3:10).

The doctrine of a risen Savior is exceedingly precious. The resurrection is the cornerstone of the entire building of Christianity. It is the keystone of the arch of our salvation. It would take a volume to set forth all the streams of living water that flow from this one sacred source, the resurrection of our dear Lord and Savior Jesus Christ. But it is even still more precious *to know* that He has risen[702] and to have fellowship with Him as such—communing with the risen Savior by possessing a risen life—seeing Him leave the tomb by leaving the tomb of worldliness ourselves. The doctrine is the basis of the experience, but as the flower is lovelier than the root, so is the experience of fellowship with the risen Savior lovelier than the doctrine itself. I would have you *believe* that Christ rose from the dead so as to sing of it and derive all the consolation that it is possible for you to extract from this well-ascertained and well-witnessed fact; but I beseech you, rest not contented even there. Though you cannot, like the disciples, see Him visibly, yet I bid you aspire to see Christ Jesus by the eye of faith; and though, like Mary Magdalene, you may not "touch" Him, yet may you be privileged to converse with Him and to know that He is risen, you yourselves being risen in Him to newness of life. To know a crucified Savior, as having crucified all my sins is a high degree of knowledge, but to know a risen Savior as having justified me, and to realize that He has bestowed upon me new life, having given me to be a new creature through His own newness of life,[703] this is a noble style of experience. Short of it, none ought to rest satisfied. May you both "know Him, and the power of His resurrection."[704] Why should souls who are quickened with Jesus, wear the grave-clothes of worldliness and unbelief? Rise, for the Lord is risen.

Get you up into the high mountain (Isaiah 40:9).

Each believer should be thirsting for God, for the living God, and longing to climb the hill of the Lord, and see Him face to face. We ought not to rest content in the mists of the valley when the summit of Tabor awaits us. My soul thirsts to drink deep of the cup that is reserved for those who reach the mountain's brow and bathe their brows in heaven. How pure are the dews of the hills, how fresh is the mountain air, how rich the fare of the dwellers aloft, whose windows look into the New Jerusalem! Many saints are content to live like men in coalmines, who see not the sun; they eat dust like the serpent when they might taste the ambrosial meat of angels. They are content to wear the miner's garb when they might put on king's robes; tears mar their faces when they might anoint them with celestial oil. Satisfied I am that many a believer pines in a dungeon when he might walk on the palace roof, and view the goodly land and Lebanon. Rouse you, O believer, from your low condition! Cast away your sloth, your lethargy, your coldness, or whatever interferes with your chaste and pure love to Christ, your soul's Husband. Make Him the source, the center, and the circumference of all your soul's range of delight. What enchants you into such folly as to remain in a pit when you may sit on a throne? Do not live in the lowlands of bondage now that mountain liberty is conferred upon you. Rest no longer satisfied with your dwarfish attainments, but press forward to things more sublime and heavenly. Aspire to a higher, a nobler, and a fuller life. Upward to heaven! Nearer to God!

"When wilt Thou come unto me, Lord?
Oh come, my Lord most dear!
Come near, come nearer, nearer still,
I'm blessed when Thou art near."

Yet a little sleep, a little slumber, a little folding of the hands to sleep: so shall your poverty come as one that travelleth; and your want as an armed man (Proverbs 24:33, 34).

The worst of sluggards only ask for a little slumber; they would be indignant if they were accused of thorough idleness. A little folding of the hands to sleep is all they crave, and they have a crowd of reasons to show that this indulgence is a very proper one. Yet by these "littles" the day ebbs out, and the time for labor is all gone, and the field is grown over with thorns. It is by little procrastinations that men ruin their souls. They have no intention of delaying for years—a few months will bring the more convenient season—tomorrow if you will, they will attend to serious things; but the present hour is so occupied and altogether so unsuitable that they beg to be excused. Like sands from an hourglass, time passes. Life is wasted by driblets, and seasons of grace are lost by little slumbers. Oh, to be wise, to catch the flying hour, to use the moments on the wing! May the Lord teach us this sacred wisdom, for otherwise a poverty of the worst sort awaits us: eternal poverty, which shall want even a drop of water and beg for it in vain. Like a traveler steadily pursuing his journey, poverty overtakes the slothful, and ruin overthrows the undecided. Each hour brings the dreaded pursuer nearer; he pauses not by the way,[705] for he is on his master's business and must not tarry. As an armed man enters with authority and power, so shall want come to the idle, and death to the impenitent, and there will be no escape. O that men were wise be-times, and would seek diligently unto the Lord Jesus, or before the solemn day shall dawn when it will be too late to plough and to sow, too late to repent and believe.[706] In harvest, it is vain to lament that the seedtime was neglected. As yet, faith and holy decision are timely. May we obtain them this night.

For He saith to Moses, I will have mercy on whom I will have mercy, and I will have compassion on whom I will have compassion (Romans 9:15).

In these words and in the plainest manner, the Lord claims the right to give or to withhold His mercy according to His own sovereign will. As the prerogative of life and death is vested in the monarch, so the Judge of all the earth has a right to spare or condemn the guilty, as may seem best in His sight. Men by their sins have forfeited all claims upon God; they deserve to perish for their sins—and if they all do so, they have no ground for complaint. If the Lord steps in to save any, He may do so if the ends of justice are not thwarted, but if He judges it best to leave the condemned to suffer the righteous sentence, none may arraign Him at their bar. Foolish and impudent are all those discourses about the rights of men to be all placed on the same footing. Ignorant, if not worse, are those contentions against discriminating grace, which are but the rebellions of proud human nature against the crown and scepter of Jehovah. When we are brought to see our own utter ruin and ill desert, and the justice of the divine verdict against sin, we no longer quibble at the truth that the Lord is not bound to save us. We do not murmur if He chooses to save others, as though He were doing us an injury, but feel that if He deigns to look upon us, it will be His own free act of undeserved goodness, for which we shall forever bless His name. How shall those who are the subjects of divine election sufficiently adore the grace of God? They have no room for boasting, for sovereignty most effectually excludes it. The Lord's will alone is glorified, and the very notion of human merit is cast out to everlasting contempt. There is no more humbling doctrine in Scripture than that of election, none more primitive of gratitude, and, consequently, none more sanctifying. Believers should not be afraid of it, but adoringly rejoice in it.[707]

They shall rejoice, and shall see the plummet in the hand of Zerubbabel (Zechariah 4:10).

Small things marked the beginning of the work in the hand of Zerubbabel, but none might despise it, for the Lord had raised up one who would persevere until the headstone should be brought forth with shouting. The plummet *[plumb bob]* was in good hands. Here is the comfort of every believer in the Lord Jesus. Let the work of grace be ever so small in its beginnings, the plummet is in good hands. A master builder greater than Solomon has undertaken the raising of the heavenly temple, and He will not fail nor be discouraged till the topmost pinnacle shall be raised. If the plummet were in the hand of any merely human being, we might fear for the building, but the pleasure of the Lord shall prosper in Jesus' hand. The works did not proceed irregularly and without care, for the master's hand carried a good instrument. Had the walls been hurriedly run up without due superintendence, they might have been out of the perpendicular, but the plummet was used by the chosen overseer. Jesus is evermore watching the erection of His spiritual temple, that it may be built securely and well. We are for haste, but Jesus is for judgment. He will use the plummet, and that which is out of line must come down, every stone of it. Hence the failure of many a flattering work, the overthrow of many a glittering profession. It is not for us to judge the Lord's church, since Jesus has a steady hand and a true eye, and can use the plummet well. Do we not rejoice to see judgment left to Him?[708] The plummet was in active use—it was in the builder's hand: a sure indication that he meant to push on the work to completion. O Lord Jesus, how would we indeed be glad if we could see You at Your great work. O Zion, the beautiful, your walls are still in ruins! Rise, Thou glorious Builder, and make her desolations to rejoice at Your coming.

The forgiveness of sins, according to the riches of His grace (Ephesians 1:7).

Could there be a sweeter word in any language than that word "forgiveness," when it sounds in a guilty sinner's ear like the silver notes of jubilee to the captive Israelite? Blessed, forever blessed be that dear star of pardon that shines into the condemned cell, and gives the perishing a gleam of hope amid the midnight of despair! Can it be possible that sin, such sin as mine, can be forgiven, forgiven altogether and forever? Hell is my portion as a sinner—there is no possibility of my escaping from it while sin remains upon me. Can the load of guilt be uplifted, the crimson stain removed? Can the hard and unyielding stones of my prison ever be loosed from their mortises or the doors be lifted from their hinges? Jesus tells me that I may yet be clear. Forever blessed be the revelation of atoning love that not only tells me that pardon is possible, but that it is secured to all those who rest in Jesus. I have believed in the appointed propitiation, even Jesus crucified, and therefore my sins are at this moment, and forever, forgiven by virtue of His substitutionary pains and death.[709] What joy is this! What bliss to be a perfectly pardoned soul! My soul dedicates all her powers to Him who of His own unpurchased love became my surety, and wrought out for me redemption through His blood.[710] What riches of grace does free forgiveness exhibit! To forgive at all, to forgive fully, to forgive freely, to forgive forever! Here is a constellation of wonders; and when I think of how great my sins were, how dear were the precious drops that cleansed me from them, and how gracious was the method by which pardon was sealed home to me, I am in a maze of wondering worshipping affection. I bow before the throne which absolves me, I clasp the cross which delivers me, I serve henceforth all my days the Incarnate God, through whom I am this night a pardoned soul.[711]

Seeking the wealth of his people (Esther 10:3).

Mordecai was a true patriot, and therefore, being exalted to the highest position under Ahasuerus, he used his eminence to promote the prosperity of Israel. In this he was a type of Jesus, who, upon His throne of glory, seeks not His own, but spends His power for His people. It would be well if every Christian would be a Mordecai to the church, striving according to his ability for its prosperity. Some are placed in stations of affluence and influence. Let them honor their Lord in the high places of the earth and testify for Jesus before great men. Others have what is far better: namely, close fellowship with the King of kings. Let them be sure to plead daily for the weak of the Lord's people, the doubting, the tempted, and the comfortless. It will redound to their honor if they make much intercession for those who are in darkness and dare not draw nigh unto the mercy seat. Instructed believers may serve their Master greatly if they lay out their talents for the general good, and impart their wealth of heavenly learning to others by teaching them the things of God.[712] The very least in our Israel may at least *seek* the welfare of his people. His desire, if he can give no more, shall be acceptable. It is at once the most Christ-like and the happiest course for a believer to cease from living to himself. He, who blesses others, cannot fail to be blessed himself. On the other hand, to seek our own personal greatness is a wicked and unhappy plan of life. Its way will be grievous and its end will be fatal.[713] Here is the place to ask you, my friend, whether you are to the best of your power seeking the wealth of the church in your neighborhood? I trust you are not doing it mischief by bitterness and scandal, nor weakening it by your neglect. Friend, unite with the Lord's poor, bear their cross, do them all the good you can, and you shall not miss your reward.

⤝ *November 29* ⤜

Spices for anointing oil (Exodus 35:8).

Much use was made of this anointing oil under the law, and that which it represents is of primary importance under the gospel. The Holy Spirit, who anoints us for all holy service, is indispensable to us if we would serve the Lord acceptably. Without His aid, our religious services are but a vain oblation, and our inward experience is a dead thing. Whenever our ministry is without unction, what miserable stuff it becomes! Nor are the prayers, praises, meditations, and efforts of private Christians one jot superior. A holy anointing is the soul and life of piety, its absence the most grievous of all calamities. To go before the Lord without anointing is as though some common Levite had thrust himself into the priest's office—his ministrations would rather have been sins than services. May we never venture upon hallowed exercises without sacred anointing. They drop upon us from our glorious Head. From His anointing we who are as the skirts of His garments partake of an abundant unction. Choice spices were compounded with the most rare art of the apothecary to form the anointing oil, to show forth to us how rich are all the influences of the Holy Spirit. All good things are found in the divine Comforter.[714] Matchless consolation, infallible instruction, immortal quickening, spiritual energy, and divine sanctification are all compounded with other excellencies in that sacred eye-slave, the heavenly anointing oil of the Holy Spirit. It imparts a delightful fragrance to the character and person of the man upon whom it is poured.[715] Nothing like it can be found in all the treasuries of the rich or the secrets of the wise. It is not to be imitated. It comes alone from God, and it is freely given through Jesus Christ to every waiting soul. Let us seek it, for we may have it, may have it this very evening. O Lord, anoint Your servants.

Michael and his angels fought against the dragon; and the dragon fought and his angels (Revelation 12:7).

War always will rage between the two great sovereignties until one or other is crushed. Peace between good and evil is impossibility; the very pretense of it would, in fact, be the triumph of the powers of darkness. *Michael will always fight*; his holy soul is vexed with sin and will not endure it. Jesus will always be the dragon's foe, and not in a quiet sense, but actively, vigorously, and with full determination to exterminate evil.[716] All His servants, whether angels in heaven or messengers on earth, will and must fight. They are born to be warriors—at the cross they enter into covenant, never to make truce with evil. They are a warlike company, firm in defense and fierce in attack. The duty of every soldier in the army of the Lord is daily, with all his heart, and soul, and strength to fight against the dragon.[717] *The dragon and his angels will not decline the fight*; they are incessant in their onslaughts, sparing no weapon, fair or foul.[718] We are foolish to expect to serve God without opposition. The more zealous we are, the more sure are we to be assailed by the myrmidons *[faithful, unquestioning followers]* of hell.[719] The church may become slothful, but not so her great antagonist; his restless spirit never suffers the war to pause. He hates the woman's seed, and would eagerly devour the church if he could. The servants of Satan partake much of the old dragon's energy, and are usually an active race. War rages all around, and to dream of peace is dangerous and futile.[720] Glory be to God, we know the end of the war. The great dragon shall be cast out and forever destroyed, while Jesus and they who are with Him shall receive the crown. Let us sharpen our swords tonight, and pray the Holy Spirit to nerve our arms for the conflict. Never battle so important, never crown so glorious. Every man to his post, ye warriors of the cross, and may the Lord tread Satan under your feet shortly![721]

December

❧ *December 1* ☙

O that men would praise the Lord for His goodness,
and for His wonderful works to the children of men
(Psalm 107:8).

If we complained less and praised more, we should be happier
and God would be more glorified. Let us daily praise God for
common mercies—"common" as we frequently call them, and
yet so priceless that when deprived of them, we are ready to
perish. Let us bless God for the eyes with which we behold the
sun, for the health and strength to walk abroad, for the bread we
eat, and for the clothes we wear. Let us praise Him that we are
not cast out among the hopeless, or confined among the guilty.
Let us thank Him for liberty, for friends, for family associations
and comforts. Let us praise Him, in fact, for everything, which
we receive from His bounteous hand, for we deserve little and yet
are most plentifully endowed. But, beloved, the sweetest and the
loudest note in our songs of praise should be of *redeeming love*.
God's redeeming acts toward His chosen are forever the favorite
themes of their praise. If we know what redemption means, let
us not withhold our sonnets of thanksgiving.[722] We have been
redeemed from the power of our corruptions, uplifted from the
depth of sin in which we were naturally plunged. We have been
led to the cross of Christ—our shackles of guilt have been broken
off. We are no longer slaves, but children of the living God, and
can antedate the period when we shall be presented before the
throne without spot or wrinkle or any such thing. Even now by
faith, we wave the palm-branch and wrap ourselves about with
the fair linen that is to be our everlasting array, and shall we
not unceasingly give thanks to the Lord our Redeemer? Child
of God, can you be silent? Awake, awake, ye heritors of glory,
and lead your captivity captive, as you cry with David, "Bless
the Lord, O my soul: and all that is within me, bless His holy
name." Let the new month begin with new songs.[723]

Behold, all is vanity (Ecclesiastes 1:14).

Nothing can satisfy the entire man except the Lord's love and the Lord's own self. Saints have tried to anchor in other roadsteads, but they have been driven out of such fatal refuges. Solomon, the wisest of men, was permitted to make experiments for us all, and to do for us what we must not dare to do for ourselves. Here is his testimony in his own words: "So I was great, and increased more than all that were before me in Jerusalem: also my wisdom remained with me. And whatsoever mine eyes desired I kept not from them, I withheld not my heart from any joy; for my heart rejoiced in all my labor: and this was my portion of all my labor. Then I looked on all the works that my hands had wrought, and on the labor that I had labored to do: and, behold, all was vanity and vexation of spirit, and there was no profit under the sun."[724] "Vanity of vanities, all is vanity." What! the whole of it vanity? O favored monarch, is there nothing in all your wealth? Nothing in that wide dominion reaching from the river even to the sea? Nothing in Palmyra's glorious palaces? Nothing in the house of the forest of Lebanon? In all your music and dancing, and wine and luxury, is there nothing? "Nothing," he says, "but weariness of spirit." This was his verdict when he had trodden the whole round of pleasure. To embrace our Lord Jesus, to dwell in His love, and be fully assured of union with Him—this is all in all. Dear reader, you need not try other forms of life in order to see whether they are better than the Christian's. If you roam the world around, you will see no sights like a sight of the Savior's face. If you could have all the comforts of life, and lost your Savior, you would be wretched; but if you win Christ, then if you were to rot in a dungeon, you would find it a paradise.[725] If you live in obscurity or die with famine, you will yet be satisfied with favor and full of the goodness of the Lord.

The Lord mighty in battle (Psalm 24:8).

Well may our God be glorious in the eyes of His people, seeing that He has wrought such wonders for them, in them, and by them. *For them*, the Lord Jesus upon Calvary routed every foe, breaking all the weapons of the enemy in pieces by His finished work of satisfactory obedience.[726] By His triumphant resurrection and ascension He completely overturned the hopes of hell, leading captivity captive,[727] making a show of our enemies openly, triumphing over them by His cross.[728] Every arrow of guilt that Satan might have shot at us is broken, for who can lay anything to the charge of God's elect?[729] Vain are the sharp swords of infernal malice and the perpetual battles of the serpent's seed, for in the midst of the church, the lame take the prey and the feeblest warriors are crowned. The saved may well adore their Lord for His conquests in them, since the arrows of their natural hatred are snapped and the weapons of their rebellion broken. What victories has grace won in our evil hearts![730] How glorious is Jesus when the will is subdued and sin dethroned! As for our remaining corruptions, they shall sustain an equally sure defeat. Every temptation and doubt and fear shall be utterly destroyed.[731] In the Salem of our peaceful hearts, the name of Jesus is great beyond compare.[732] He has won our love, and He shall wear it. Even thus securely may we look for victories *by us*. We are more than conquerors through Him that loved us.[733] We shall cast down the powers of darkness, which are in the world, by our faith, and zeal, and holiness. We shall win sinners to Jesus. We shall overturn false systems. We shall convert nations, for God is with us, and none shall stand before us. This evening let the Christian warrior chant the war song, and prepare for tomorrow's fight. Greater is He that is in us than he that is in the world.[734]

❧ *December 4* ❧

*Even we ourselves groan within ourselves, waiting
for the adoption, to wit, the redemption of our body
(Romans 8:23).*

This groaning is universal among the saints; to a greater or less extent we all feel it. It is not the groan of murmuring or complaint; it is the note of desire rather than of distress. Having received an earnest,[735] we desire the whole of our portion; we are sighing that our entire manhood, in its trinity of spirit, soul, and body, may be set free from the last vestige of the fall. We long to put off corruption, weakness, and dishonor, and to wrap ourselves in incorruption, in immortality, in glory, and in the spiritual body, which the Lord Jesus will bestow upon His people.[736] We long for the manifestation of our adoption as the children of God. "We groan," but it is "within ourselves." It is not the hypocrite's groan, by which he would make men believe that he is a saint because he is wretched. Our sighs are sacred things, too hallowed for us to tell abroad. We keep our longings to our Lord alone. Then the apostle says we are "waiting," by which we learn that we are not to be petulant, like Jonah or Elijah, when they said, "Let me die." Nor are we to whimper and sigh for the end of life because we are tired of work, nor wish to escape from our present sufferings till the will of the Lord is done. We are to groan for glorification, but we are to wait patiently for it, knowing that what the Lord appoints is best. Waiting implies being ready. We are to stand at the door expecting the Beloved to open it and take us away to Himself. This "groaning" is a test. You may judge of a man by what he groans after. Some men groan after wealth—they worship Mammon; some groan continually under the troubles of life—they are merely impatient; but the man who sighs after God, who is uneasy till he is made like Christ, that is the blessed man. May God help us to groan for the coming of the Lord, and the resurrection, which He will bring to us.[737]

December 5

And the Lord shewed me four carpenters
(Zechariah 1:20).

In the vision described in this chapter, the prophet saw four terrible horns. They were pushing this way and that way, dashing down the strongest and the mightiest. The prophet asked, "What are these?" The answer was, "These are the horns which have scattered Israel." He saw before him a representation of those powers, which had oppressed the church of God. There were four horns, because the church is attacked from all quarters. Well might the prophet have felt dismayed, but all of a sudden there appeared before him *four carpenters*. He asked, "What shall these do?" These are the men whom God has found to break those horns in pieces. *God will always find men for His work*, and He will find them at the right time. The prophet did not see the carpenters *first*, when there was nothing to do, but first the "horns," and then the "carpenters." Moreover, the Lord finds *enough men*. He did not find three carpenters, but *four*; there were four horns, and there must be four workmen. God finds *the right men*—not four men with pens to write, not four architects to draw plans, but four carpenters to do rough work. Rest assured, you who tremble for the ark of God, that when the "horns" grow troublesome, the "carpenters" will be found. You need not fret concerning the weakness of the church of God at any moment; there may be growing up in obscurity the valiant reformer who will shake the nations: Chrysostoms may come forth from our Ragged Schools, and Augustines from the thickest darkness of London's poverty. The Lord knows where to find His servants. He has in ambush a multitude of mighty men, and at His word they shall start up to the battle; "for the battle is the Lord's,"[738] and He shall get to Himself the victory. Let us abide faithful to Christ, and He, in the right time, will raise up for us a defense, whether it is in the day of our personal need or in the season of peril to His Church.

Girt about the paps with a golden girdle
(Revelation 1:13).

"One like unto the Son of Man" appeared to John in Patmos, and the beloved disciple marked that He wore a girdle of gold. A girdle, for Jesus never was ungirt [*without girding*] while upon earth, but stood always ready for service. Now before the eternal throne He stays—not in holy ministry, but as a priest is girt about with "the curious girdle of the ephod." Well it is for us that He has not ceased to fulfill His offices of love for us, since this is one of our choicest safeguards that He ever lives to make intercession for us.[739] Jesus is never an idler; His garments are never loose as though His offices were ended. He diligently carries on the cause of His people. *A golden girdle*, to manifest the superiority of His service, the royalty of His person, the dignity of His state, and the glory of His reward. No longer does He cry out of the dust, but He pleads with authority, a King as well as a Priest. Safe enough is our cause in the hands of our enthroned Melchisedek. Our Lord presents all His people with an example. We must never unbind our girdles. This is not the time for lying down at ease; it is the season of service and warfare. We need to bind the girdle of truth more and more tightly around our loins. It is a golden girdle, and so will be our richest ornament. We greatly need it, for a heart that is not well braced up with the truth as it is in Jesus and with the fidelity that is wrought of the Spirit, will be easily entangled with the things of this life and tripped up by the snares of temptation. It is in vain that we possess the Scriptures unless we bind them around us like girdles, surrounding our entire nature, keeping each part of our character in order, and giving compactness to our whole man. If in heaven Jesus unbinds not the girdle, much less may we upon earth. Stand, therefore, having your loins girt about with truth.[740]

I am made all things to all men, that I might by all means save some (1 Corinthians 9:22).

Paul's great object was not merely to instruct and to improve, but to save. Anything short of this would have disappointed him. He would have men renewed in heart, forgiven, sanctified, and, in fact, saved. Have our Christian labors been aimed at anything below this great point? Then let us amend our ways, for of what avail will it be at the last great day to have taught and moralized men if they appear before God unsaved? Our skirts will be blood red if, through life, we have sought inferior objects, and forgotten that men needed to be saved. Paul knew the ruin of man's natural state, and did not try to educate him, but to save him. He saw men sinking to hell, and did not talk of refining them, but of saving from the wrath to come. To compass their salvation, he gave himself up with untiring zeal to telling abroad the gospel, to warning and beseeching men to be reconciled to God.[741] His prayers were importunate and his labors incessant. To save souls was his consuming passion, his ambition, and his calling. He became a servant to all men, toiling for his race, feeling a woe within him if he preached not the gospel. He laid aside his preferences to prevent prejudice; he submitted his will in things indifferent. If men would but receive the gospel, he raised no questions about forms or ceremonies. The gospel was the one all-important business with him. If he might save some, he would be content. This was the crown for which he strove, the sole and sufficient reward of all his labors and self-denials. Dear reader, have you and I lived to win souls at this noble rate? Are we possessed with the same all-absorbing desire? If not, why not? Jesus died for sinners; cannot we live for them? Where is our tenderness? Where our love to Christ, if we seek not His honor in the salvation of men? O that the Lord would saturate us through and through with an undying zeal for the souls of men.

Thou, O God, hast prepared of Your goodness for the poor (Psalm 68:10).

All God's gifts are prepared gifts laid up in store for wants foreseen. He anticipates our needs; and out of the fullness, which He has treasured up in Christ Jesus, He provides of His goodness for the poor. You may trust Him for all the necessities that can occur, for He has infallibly foreknown every one of them. He can say of us in all conditions, "I knew that thou wouldst be this and that." A man goes a journey across the desert, and when he has made a day's advance and pitched his tent, he discovers that he wants many comforts and necessaries, which he has not brought in his baggage. "Ah!" says he, "I did not foresee this. If I had this journey to go again, I should bring these things with me, so necessary to my comfort." But God has marked with prescient eye all the requirements of His poor wandering children, and when those needs occur, supplies are ready. It is goodness, which He has prepared for the poor in heart—goodness and goodness only. "My grace is sufficient for you."[742] "As your days, so shall your strength be. Reader, is your heart heavy this evening? God knew it would be; the comfort that your heart wants is treasured in the sweet assurance of the text. You are poor and needy, but He has thought upon you, and has the exact blessing that you require in store for you. Plead the promise, believe it and obtain its fulfillment. Do you feel that you never were so consciously vile as you are now? Behold, the crimson fountain is open still, with its entire former efficacy, to wash your sin away. Never shall you come into such a position that Christ cannot aid you. No pinch shall ever arrive in your spiritual affairs in which Jesus Christ shall not be equal to the emergency, for your history has all been foreknown and provided for in Jesus.

~ *December 9* ~

My people shall dwell in quiet resting places
(Isaiah 32:18).

Peace and rest belong not to the unregenerate; they are the peculiar possession of the Lord's people, and of them only. The God of Peace gives perfect peace to those whose hearts are stayed upon Him.[743] When man was unfallen, his God gave him the flowery bowers of Eden as his quiet resting places. Alas! How soon sin blighted the fair abode of innocence. In the day of universal wrath, when the flood swept away a guilty race, the chosen family was quietly secured in the resting-place of the ark, which floated them from the old condemned world into the new earth of the rainbow and the covenant, herein typifying Jesus, the ark of our salvation. Israel rested safely beneath the blood-besprinkled habitations of Egypt when the destroying angel smote the first-born. In the wilderness the shadow of the pillar of cloud and the flowing rock, gave the weary pilgrims sweet repose.[744] At this hour, we rest in the promises of our faithful God, knowing that His words are full of truth and power. We rest in the doctrines of His word, which are consolation itself. We rest in the covenant of His grace, which is a haven of delight. More highly favored are we than David in Adullam or Jonah beneath his gourd, for none can invade or destroy our shelter. The person of Jesus is the quiet resting-place of His people, and when we draw near to Him in the breaking of the bread, in the hearing of the word, the searching of the Scriptures, prayer, or praise, we find any form of approach to Him to be the return of peace to our spirits.

"I hear the words of love, I gaze upon the blood,
I see the mighty sacrifice, and I have peace with God.
'Tis everlasting peace, sure as Jehovah's name,
'Tis stable as His steadfast throne, for evermore the same:
The clouds may go and come, and storms may sweep my sky,
This blood-sealed friendship changes not, the cross is ever nigh."

☙ *December 10* ❧

Whose heart the Lord opened (Acts 16:14).

In Lydia's conversion there are many points of interest. It was brought about by *providential circumstances*. She was a seller of purple in the city of Thyatira,[745] but we find her at Philippi—at just at the right time for hearing Paul. Providence, which is the handmaid of grace, led her to the right spot. Again, grace was preparing her soul for the blessing—grace preparing for grace. She did not know the Savior, but as a Jewess, she knew many truths that were excellent stepping-stones to knowledge of Jesus. Her conversion took place in the use of the means. On the Sabbath she went when prayer was likely to be made, and there prayer was heard. Never neglect the means of grace. God *may* bless us when we are not in His house, but we have the greater reason to hope that He *will* when we are in communion with His saints. Observe the words, "Whose heart *the Lord* opened." She did not open her own heart. Her prayers did not do it. Paul did not do it. The Lord Himself must open the heart to receive the things that make for our peace. He alone can put the key into the hole of the door and open it, and get admittance for Himself.[746] He is the heart's master as He is the heart's maker. The first outward evidence of the opened heart was *obedience*. As soon as Lydia believed in Jesus, she was baptized. It is a sweet sign of a humble and broken heart, when the child of God is willing to obey a command that is not essential to his salvation and is not forced upon him by a selfish fear of condemnation, but is a simple act of obedience and of communion with his Master. The next evidence was *love*, manifesting itself in acts of grateful kindness to the apostles. Love to the saints has ever been a mark of the true convert.[747] Those who do nothing for Christ or His church give but sorry evidence of an "opened" heart. Lord, evermore give me an opened heart.

410

❧ *December 11* ❧

Ye serve the Lord Christ (Colossians 3:24).

To what choice order of officials was this word spoken? To kings who proudly boast a right divine? Ah, no! Too often do they serve themselves or Satan, and forget the God whose sufferance permits them to wear their mimic majesty for their little hour. Then does the apostle speak to those so-called "right reverend fathers in God," the bishops, or "the venerable archdeacons"? No, indeed. Paul knew nothing of these mere inventions of man. This word was not even spoken to pastors and teachers or the wealthy and esteemed among believers, but to servants, ay, and to slaves. Among the toiling multitudes, the journeymen, the day laborers, the domestic servants, and the drudges of the kitchen, the apostle found, as we find still, some of the Lord's chosen. To them he says, "Whatsoever ye do, do it heartily, as to the Lord, and not unto men; knowing that of the Lord ye shall receive the reward of the inheritance: for ye serve the Lord Christ."[748] This saying ennobles the weary routine of earthly employments, and sheds a halo around the most humble occupations. To wash feet may be servile, but to wash His feet is royal work. To unloose the shoe-latchet is poor employ, but to unloose the great Master's shoe is a princely privilege.[749] The shop, the barn, the scullery, and the smithy become temples when men and women do all to the glory of God! Then "divine service" is not a thing of a few hours and a few places, but all life becomes holiness unto the Lord, and every place and thing, as consecrated as the tabernacle and its golden candlestick.

"Teach me, my God and King, in all things You to see;
And what I do in anything to do it as to You.
All may of You partake, nothing can be so mean,
Which with this tincture, for Your sake,
Will not grow bright and clean.
A servant with this clause makes drudgery divine;
Who sweeps a room, as for Your laws,
Makes that and the action fine."

December 12

*They have dealt treacherously against the Lord
(Hosea 5:7).*

Believer, here is a sorrowful truth! Thou art the beloved of the Lord, redeemed by blood, called by grace, preserved in Christ Jesus, accepted in the Beloved, on your way to heaven, and yet, "you have dealt treacherously" with God, your best friend; treacherously with Jesus, whose you are; treacherously with the Holy Spirit, by whom you have been quickened unto life eternal! How treacherous you have been in the matter of vows and promises. Do you remember the love of your espousals, that happy time—the springtide of your spiritual life? Oh, how closely did you cling to your Master then, saying, "He shall never charge me with indifference; my feet shall never grow slow in the way of His service; I will not suffer my heart to wander after other loves; in Him is every store of sweetness ineffable. I give all up for my Lord Jesus' sake." Has it been so? Alas! If conscience speaks, it will say, "He who promised so well has performed most ill. Prayer has oftentimes been slurred—it has been short, but not sweet; brief, but not fervent. Communion with Christ has been forgotten. Instead of a heavenly mind, there have been carnal cares, worldly vanities and thoughts of evil. Instead of service, there has been disobedience; instead of fervency, lukewarmness; instead of patience, petulance; instead of faith, confidence in an arm of flesh; and as a soldier of the cross there has been cowardice, disobedience, and desertion to a very shameful degree." "Thou hast dealt treacherously." Treachery to Jesus! What words shall be used in denouncing it? Words little avail. Let our penitent thoughts declare loathsome the sin which is so surely in us. Treacherous to Your wounds, O Jesus! Forgive us, and let us not sin again! How shameful to be treacherous to Him who never forgets us, but whom this day stands with our names engraved on His breastplate before the eternal throne.[750]

412

ᵗᵃ *December 13* ᶠᵉ

I will make your windows of agates (Isaiah 54:12).

The church is most instructively symbolized by a building erected by heavenly power and designed by divine skill. Such a spiritual house must not be dark, for the Israelites had light in their dwellings. There must therefore be windows to let the light in and to allow the inhabitants to gaze abroad. These windows are as *precious* as agates. The ways in which the church beholds her Lord and heaven, and spiritual truth in general are to be held in the highest esteem. Agates are not the most transparent of gems, they are but semi-pellucid at the best:

> "Our knowledge of that life is small,
> Our eye of faith is dim."

Faith is one of these precious agate windows, but alas! It is often so misty and beclouded that we see but darkly, and mistake much that we see. Yet if we cannot gaze through windows of diamonds and know even as we are known, it is a glorious thing to behold the altogether lovely One, even though the glass is hazy as the agate. *Experience* is another of these dim but precious windows, yielding to us a subdued religious light, in which we see the sufferings of the Man of Sorrows through our own afflictions. Our weak eyes could not endure windows of transparent glass to let in the Master's glory, but when they are dimmed with weeping, the beams of the Sun of Righteousness are tempered, and shine through the windows of agate with a soft radiance inexpressibly soothing to tempted souls. *Sanctification*, as it conforms us to our Lord, is another agate window. Only as we become heavenly can we comprehend heavenly things. The pure in heart see a pure God.[751] Those who are like Jesus see Him as He is.[752] Because we are so little like Him, the window is but agate. Because we are somewhat like Him, it is agate. We thank God for what we have, and long for more. When shall we see God and Jesus, and heaven and truth, face to face?

⇜ ᴅ *December 14* ᴘ ⇝

I am crucified with Christ (Galatians 2:20).

The Lord Jesus Christ acted in what He did as a great public representative, and His dying upon the cross was the virtual dying of all His people. Then all His saints rendered unto justice what was due, and made an expiation to divine vengeance for all their sins. The apostle of the Gentiles delighted to think that as one of Christ's chosen people, he died upon the cross in Christ. He did more than believe this doctrinally; he accepted it confidently, resting his hope upon it. He believed that by virtue of Christ's death, he had satisfied divine justice and found reconciliation with God.[753] Beloved, what a blessed thing it is when the soul can, as it were, stretch itself upon the cross of Christ, and feel, "I am dead; the law has slain me, and I am therefore free from its power, because in my Surety I have borne the curse, and in the person of my Substitute the whole that the law could do, by way of condemnation, has been executed upon me, for I am crucified with Christ."[754] But Paul meant even more than this. He not only believed in Christ's death and trusted in it, but he actually felt its power in him, causing the crucifixion of his old corrupt nature. When he saw the pleasures of sin, he said, "I cannot enjoy these: I am dead to them."[755] Such is the experience of every true Christian. Having received Christ, he is to this world as one who is utterly dead. Yet, while conscious of death to the world, he can, at the same time, exclaim with the apostle, "Nevertheless I live." He is fully alive unto God. The Christian's life is a matchless riddle. No worldling can comprehend it; even the believer himself cannot understand it. Dead, yet alive! crucified with Christ, and yet at the same time risen with Christ in newness of life![756] Union with the suffering, bleeding Savior, and death to the world and sin are soul-cheering things. O for more enjoyment of them!

And lay your foundations with sapphires (Isaiah 54:11).

Not only is that which is seen of the church of God fair and precious, but also that which is unseen. Foundations are out of sight, and so long as they are firm, it is not expected that they should be valuable. But in Jehovah's work everything is of a piece, nothing slurred, nothing mean. The deep foundations of the work of grace are as sapphires for preciousness; no human mind is able to measure their glory. We build upon the covenant of grace, which is firmer than adamant and as enduring as jewels upon which age spends itself in vain.[757] Sapphire foundations are eternal, and the covenant abides throughout the lifetime of the Almighty. Another foundation is the person of the Lord Jesus, which is clear and spotless, everlasting and beautiful as the sapphire; blending in one the deep blue of earth's ever rolling ocean and the azure of its all embracing sky. Once might our Lord have been likened to the ruby as He stood covered with His own blood, but now we see Him radiant with the soft blue of love—love abounding, deep, and eternal. Our eternal hopes are built upon the justice and faithfulness of God, which are as clear and cloudless as the sapphire. We are not saved by a compromise, by mercy defeating justice, or law suspending its operations. No, we defy the eagle's eye to detect a flaw in the groundwork of our confidence—our foundation is of sapphire and will endure the fire.[758] The Lord Himself has laid the foundation of His people's hopes. It is matter for grave enquiry whether *our* hopes are built upon such a basis. Good works and ceremonies are not foundations of sapphires, but of wood, hay, and stubble. Neither are they laid by God, but by our own conceit.[759] Foundations will all be tried before long. Woe unto him whose lofty tower shall come down with a crash, because it is based on a quicksand. He who is built on sapphires may await storm or fire with equanimity, for he shall abide the test.[760]

Yea, thou heardest not; yea, thou knewest not; yea, from that time that thine ear was not opened (Isaiah 48:8).

It is painful to remember that in a certain degree, this accusation may be laid at the door of *believers*, who too often are in a measure *spiritually insensible*. We may well bewail ourselves that *we* do not hear the voice of God as we ought, "Yea, thou heardest not." There are gentle motions of the Holy Spirit in the soul that we do not heed. There are whisperings of divine command and of heavenly love that are alike unobserved by our leaden intellects. Alas! we have been carelessly ignorant—"Yea, thou knewest not." There are matters within which we ought to have seen corruptions that have made headway unnoticed; sweet affections that are being blighted like flowers in the frost—untended by us; glimpses of the divine face which might be perceived if we did not wall up the windows of our soul. But we "have not known." As we think of it, we are humbled in the deepest self-abasement. How must we adore the grace of God as we learn from the context that all this folly and ignorance on our part *was foreknown by God*, and, notwithstanding that foreknowledge, He yet has been pleased to deal with us in a way of mercy![761] Admire the marvelous sovereign grace that could have chosen us in the sight of all this! Wonder at the price that was paid for us when Christ knew what we should be! He who hung upon the cross foresaw us as unbelieving, backsliding, cold of heart, indifferent, careless, lax in prayer, and yet He said, "I am the Lord your God, the Holy One of Israel,[762] your Savior ... Since thou were precious in My sight, you have been honorable, and I have loved you: therefore will I give men for you, and people for your life"! O redemption, how wondrously resplendent do you shine when we think how black we are! O Holy Spirit, give us henceforth the hearing ear, the understanding heart![763]

December 17

I am the door: by Me if any man enter in, he shall be saved, and shall go in and out, and find pasture (John 10:9).

Jesus, the great I AM, is the entrance into the true church and the way of access to God Himself. He gives to the man, who comes to God by Him, four choice privileges.

1. *He shall be saved.* The fugitive manslayer passed the gate of the city of refuge[764] and was safe. Noah entered the door of the ark and was secure. None can be lost who take Jesus as the door of faith to their souls. Entrance through Jesus into peace is the guarantee of entrance by the same door into heaven. Jesus is the only door, an open door, a wide door, and a safe door; and blessed is he who rests all his hope of admission to glory upon the crucified Redeemer.

2. *He shall go in.* He shall be privileged to go in among the divine family, sharing the children's bread, and participating in all their honors and enjoyments. He shall go in to the chambers of communion, to the banquets of love, to the treasures of the covenant, and to the storehouses of the promises. He shall go in unto the King of kings in the power of the Holy Spirit, and the secret of the Lord shall be with him.

3. *He shall go out.* This blessing is much forgotten. We go out into the world to labor and suffer, but what a mercy to go in the name and power of Jesus! We are called to bear witness to the truth, to cheer the disconsolate, to warn the careless, to win souls, and to glorify God. As the angel said to Gideon, "Go in this your might," even thus the Lord would have us proceed as His messengers in His name and strength.

4. *He shall find pasture.* He who knows Jesus shall never want. Going in and out shall be alike helpful to him; in fellowship with God he shall grow, and in watering others he shall be watered. Having made Jesus his all, he shall find all in Jesus. His soul shall be as a watered garden, and as a well of water whose waters fail not.[765]

Be thou diligent to know the state of your flocks, and look well to your herds (Proverbs 27:23).

Every wise merchant will occasionally hold a stock-taking, when he will cast up his accounts, examine what he has on hand, and ascertain decisively whether his trade is prosperous or declining. Every man, wise in the kingdom of heaven, will cry, "Search me, O God, and try me;"[766] and he will frequently set apart special seasons for self-examination, to discover whether things are right between God and his soul. The God whom we worship is a great heart-searcher; and of old His servants knew Him as "the Lord who searches the heart and tries the reins of the children of men."[767] Let me stir you up in His name to make diligent search and solemn trial of your state, lest you come short of the promised rest. That which every wise man does, that which God Himself does with us all, I exhort you to do with yourself this evening. Let the oldest saint look well to the fundamentals of his piety, for grey heads may cover black hearts. Let not the young professor despise the word of warning, for the greenness of youth may be joined to the rottenness of hypocrisy. Every now and then a cedar falls into our midst. The enemy still continues to sow tares among the wheat. It is not my aim to introduce doubts and fears into your mind; nay, truthfully. Rather, I shall hope that the rough wind of self-examination may help to drive them away. It is not security, but carnal security, which we would kill; not confidence, but fleshly confidence, which we would overthrow; not peace, but false peace, which we would destroy. By the precious blood of Christ, which was not shed to make you a hypocrite, but so that sincere souls might show forth His praise, I beseech you to search and look, lest at the last it be said of you, "Mene, Mene, Tekel: you are weighed in the balances, and art found wanting."[768]

☜ *December 19* ☞

And there was no more sea (Revelation 21:1).

We could scarcely rejoice at the thought of losing the glorious old ocean—the new heavens and the new earth are none the fairer to our imagination—if, indeed, literally there is to be no great and wide sea[769] with its gleaming waves and shelly shores. Is not the text to be read as a metaphor, tinged with the prejudice with which the Oriental mind universally regarded the sea in the olden times? It is mournful to imagine a real physical world without a sea. It would be an iron ring without the sapphire that made it precious. There must be a spiritual meaning here. In the new dispensation, there will be no division—the sea separates nations and sunders peoples from each other. To John in Patmos, the deep waters were like prison walls, shutting him out from his brethren and his work. There shall be no such barriers in the world to come. Leagues of rolling billows lie between us and many a kinsman whom tonight we prayerfully remember, but in the bright world to which we go, there shall be unbroken fellowship for all the redeemed family. In this sense, there shall be no more sea. The sea is the emblem of change. With its ebbs and flows, its glassy smoothness and mountainous billows, and its gentle murmurs and tumultuous roaring, it is never long the same. Slave of the fickle winds and the changeful moon, its instability is proverbial. We have too much of this in this mortal state; earth is constant only in her inconstancy, but in the heavenly state all mournful change shall be unknown, and with it all fear of *storm* to wreck our hopes and drown our joys. The sea of glass glows with a glory unbroken by a wave.[770] No tempest howls along the peaceful shores of paradise. Soon shall we reach that happy land where partings, and changes, and storms shall be ended! Jesus will waft us there. Are we in Him or not? This is the grand question.

❧ *December 20* ❧

Call your laborers, and give them their hire
(Matthew 20:8).

God is a good paymaster; He pays His servants while at work as well as when they have done it; and one of His payments is this: *an easy conscience.* If you have spoken faithfully of Jesus to one person, when you go to bed at night you feel happy in thinking, "I have this day discharged my conscience of that man's blood." There is a great comfort in doing something for Jesus. Oh, what a happiness to place jewels in His crown, and give Him to see of the hard labor of His soul! There is also very great reward in watching the first budding of conviction in a soul! To say of that girl in the class, "She is tender of heart. I do hope that there is the Lord's work within." To go home and pray over that boy, who said something in the afternoon that made you think he must know more of divine truth than you had feared! Oh, the joy of hope! But as for the joy of success! It is unspeakable. This joy, overwhelming as it is, is a hungry thing—you pine for more of it.[771] To be a soul-winner is the happiest thing in the world. With every soul you bring to Christ, you get a new heaven upon earth. But who can conceive of the bliss that awaits us above! Oh, how sweet is that sentence, "Enter thou into *the joy of your Lord!*"[772] Do you know what the joy of Christ is over a saved sinner? This is the very joy that we are to possess in heaven. Yes, when He mounts the throne, you shall mount with Him. When the heavens ring with "Well done, well done." you shall partake in the reward. You have toiled with Him and suffered with Him; you shall now reign with Him. You have sown with Him; you shall reap with Him. Your face was covered with sweat like His, and your soul was grieved for the sins of men as His soul was; now shall your face be bright with heaven's splendor as His countenance, and now shall your soul be filled with beatific joys even as is His soul.

⇜ *December 21* ⇝

I clothed you also with broidered work, and shod you with badgers' skin, and I girded you about with fine linen, and I covered you with silk (Ezekiel 16:10).

See with what matchless generosity the Lord provides for His people's apparel. They are so arrayed that the divine skill is seen producing an unrivalled *embroidered work*, in which every attribute takes its part and every divine beauty is revealed. No art like the art displayed in our salvation, no cunning workmanship like that beheld in the righteousness of the saints. Justification has engrossed learned pens in all ages of the church, and will be the theme of admiration in eternity. God has indeed "curiously wrought it." With all this elaboration there is mingled utility and durability, comparable to our being shod with badgers' skins.[773] The animal here meant is unknown, but its skin covered the tabernacle, and formed one of the finest and strongest leathers known. The righteousness that is of God by faith endures forever, and he who is shod with this divine preparation will tread the desert safely, and may even set his foot upon the lion and the adder. Purity and dignity of our holy vesture are brought out in *the fine linen*. When the Lord sanctifies His people, they are clad as priests in pure white; not the snow itself excels them; they are in the eyes of men and angels fair to look upon, and even in the Lord's eyes they are without spot. Meanwhile the royal apparel is delicate and rich as *silk*. No expense is spared, no beauty withheld, no daintiness denied. What, then? Is there no inference from this? Surely there is gratitude to be felt and joy to be expressed. Come, my heart, refuse not your evening hallelujah! Tune your pipes! Touch your chords!

> "Strangely, my soul, art thou arrayed,
> By the Great Sacred Three!
> In sweetest harmony of praise,
> Let all your powers agree."

December 22

The spot of His children (Deuteronomy 32:5).

What is the secret spot that infallibly gives evidence of the child of God? It is vain presumption to decide this upon our own judgment; but God's word reveals it to us, and we may tread surely where we have revelation to be our guide. Now, we are told concerning our Lord, "to as many as *received Him*, to them gave He power to become the sons of God, even to as many as believed on His name."[774] Then, if I have received Christ Jesus into my heart, I am a child of God. That reception is described in the same verse as *believing on the name of Jesus Christ*. If, then, I believe on Jesus Christ's name—that is, simply from my heart trust myself with the crucified, but now exalted, Redeemer, I am a member of the family of the Most High. Whatever else I may not have, if I have this, I have the privilege of becoming a child of God. Our Lord Jesus puts it in another shape: "My sheep hear My voice, and I know them, and they follow Me."[775] Here is the matter in a nutshell. Christ appears as a shepherd to His own sheep, not to others. As soon as He appears, His own sheep perceive Him—they trust Him, they are prepared to follow Him. He knows them, and they know Him—there is a mutual knowledge—there is a constant connection between them. Thus the one mark, the sure mark, the infallible mark of regeneration and adoption is a hearty faith in the appointed Redeemer. Reader, are you in doubt, are you uncertain whether you bear the secret mark of God's children? Then let not an hour pass over your head till you have said, "Search me, O God, and know my heart."[776] I implore you, do not take this lightly! If you must trifle anywhere, let it be about some secondary matter: your health, if you will, or the title deeds of your estate; but about your soul, your never-dying soul and its eternal destinies, I beseech you to be in earnest. Make sure work for eternity.

⇛ *December 23* ⇚

The night also is yours (Psalm 74:16).

Yes, Lord, Thou dost not abdicate Your throne when the sun goes down, nor dost Thou leave the world all through these long wintry nights to be the prey of evil. Your eyes watch us as the stars, and Your arms surround us as the zodiac belts the sky. The dews of kindly sleep and all the influences of the moon are in Your hand, and the alarms and solemnities of night are equally with You. This is very sweet to me when watching through the midnight hours, or tossing to and fro in anguish. There are precious fruits put forth by the moon as well as by the sun; may my Lord make me to be a favored partaker in them. The night of affliction is as much under the arrangement and control of the Lord of Love as the bright summer days when all is bliss.[777] Jesus is in the tempest. His love wraps the night about itself as a mantle, but to the eye of faith, the sable robe is scarcely a disguise. From the first watch of the night even unto the break of day, the eternal Watcher observes His saints, and overrules the shades and dews of midnight for His people's highest good. We believe in no rival deities of good and evil contending for the mastery, but we hear the voice of Jehovah saying, "I create light and I create darkness; I, the Lord, do all these things."[778] Gloomy seasons of religious indifference and social sin are not exempted from the divine purpose. When the altars of truth are defiled and the ways of God forsaken, the Lord's servants weep with bitter sorrow, but they may not despair, for the darkest eras are governed by the Lord, and shall come to their end at His bidding. What may seem defeat to us may be victory to Him.[779]

> "Though enwrapped in gloomy night,
> We perceive no ray of light;
> Since the Lord Himself is here,
> 'Tis not meet that we should fear."

*The glory of the Lord shall be revealed, and all flesh
shall see it together (Isaiah 40:5).*

We anticipate the happy day when the whole world shall be
converted to Christ; when the gods of the heathen shall be cast to
the moles and the bats; when Romanism shall be exploded, and the
crescent of Mohammed shall wane, never again to cast its baleful
rays upon the nations; when kings shall bow down before the Prince
of Peace, and all nations shall call their Redeemer blessed. Some
despair of this. They look upon the world as a vessel breaking up
and going to pieces, never to float again. We know that the world
and all therein are one day to be burned up,[780] and afterwards we
look for new heavens and for a new earth;[781] but we cannot read
our Bibles without the conviction that—

> "Jesus shall reign where'er the sun,
> Does his successive journeys run."

The length of His delays does not discourage us. We are not
disheartened by the long period that He allots to the church in
which to struggle with little success and much defeat. We believe
that God will never suffer this world, which has once seen Christ's
blood shed upon it, to be always the devil's stronghold. Christ
came here to deliver this world from the detested sway of the
powers of darkness.[782] What a shout shall that be when men
and angels will unite to cry "Hallelujah, hallelujah, for the Lord
God Omnipotent reigns!"[783] What a satisfaction will it be in that
day to have had a share in the fight, to have helped to break
the arrows of the bow, and to have aided in winning the victory
for our Lord! Happy are they who trust themselves with this
conquering Lord, and who fight side by side with Him, doing
their little in His name and by His strength! How unhappy are
those on the side of evil![784] It is a losing side, and it is a matter
wherein to lose is to lose and to be lost forever. On whose side
are you?

And it was so, when the days of their feasting were gone about, that Job sent and sanctified them, and rose up early in the morning, and offered burnt offerings according to the number of them all: for Job said, It may be that my sons have sinned, and cursed God in their hearts. Thus did Job continually (Job 1:5).

Before the believer rests tonight, it would be well to do that which the patriarch did early in the morning, after the family festivities. Amid the cheerfulness of household gatherings it is easy to slide into sinful levities, and to forget our avowed character as Christians. It ought not to be so, but so it is that our days of feasting are very seldom days of sanctified enjoyment, but too frequently degenerate into unhallowed mirth. There is a way of joy as pure and sanctifying as though one bathed in the rivers of Eden. Holy gratitude should be as purifying an element as grief. Alas! For our poor hearts, facts prove that the house of mourning is better than the house of feasting. Come, believer, in what have you sinned today? Have you been forgetful of your high calling?[785] Have you been even as others in idle words and loose speeches?[786] Then confess the sin and fly to the sacrifice. The sacrifice sanctifies. The precious blood of the Lamb slain removes the guilt, and purges away the defilement of our sins of ignorance and carelessness. This is the best ending of a Christmas day—to wash anew in the cleansing fountain.[787] Believer, come to this sacrifice continually. If it is so good tonight, it is good every night. To live at the altar is the privilege of the royal priesthood. To them sin, as great as it is, is nevertheless no cause for despair, since they draw near yet again to the sin-atoning victim, and their conscience is purged from dead works.[788]

> "Gladly I close this festive day,
> Grasping the altar's hallowed horn;
> My slips and faults are washed away,
> The Lamb has all my trespass borne."

☞ December 26 ☜

Lo, I am with you always (Matthew 28:20).

The Lord Jesus is in the midst of His church. He walks among the golden candlesticks. His promise is, "Lo, I am with you always." He is as surely with us now as He was with the disciples at the lake when they saw coals of fire, and laid thereon fish and bread.[789] Not carnally, but still in real truth, Jesus is with us. And a blessed truth it is, for where Jesus is, *love becomes inflamed.* Of all the things in the world that can set the heart burning, there is nothing like the presence of Jesus! A glimpse of Him so overcomes us that we are ready to say, "Turn away Your eyes from me, for they have overcome me."[790] Even the smell of the aloes and myrrh and cassia, which drop from His perfumed garments, causes the sick and the faint to grow strong. Let there be but a moment's leaning of the head upon that gracious bosom, and we receive His divine love into our poor cold hearts, and we are cold no longer, but glow like seraphs, equal to every labor and capable of every suffering. If we know that Jesus is with us, every power will be developed and every grace will be strengthened, and we shall cast ourselves into the Lord's service with heart and soul and strength; therefore is the presence of Christ to be desired above all things. His presence will be most realized by those who are most like Him. If you desire to see Christ, you must grow in conformity to Him.[791] Bring yourself, by the power of the Spirit, into union with Christ's desires and motives and plans of action, and you are likely to be favored with His company. Remember *His presence may be had.* His promise is as true as ever. He delights to be with us. If He does not come, it is because we hinder Him by our indifference. He will reveal Himself to our earnest prayers, and graciously suffer Himself to be detained by our entreaties and tears, for these are the golden chains that bind Jesus to His people.

❧ *December 27* ❧

And the LORD shall guide you continually
(Isaiah 58:11).

"The *Lord* shall guide you." Not an angel, but JEHOVAH shall guide you. He said He would not go through the wilderness before His people; an angel should go before them to lead them in the way, but Moses said, "If *Your* presence go not with me, carry us not up hence." Christian, God has not left you in your earthly pilgrimage to an angel's guidance. He Himself leads the van. You may not see the cloudy, fiery pillar, but Jehovah will never forsake you. Notice the word shall—"The Lord shall guide you." How certain this makes it! How sure it is that God will not forsake us! His precious "shalls" and "wills" are better than men's oaths. "I will never leave you nor forsake you." Then observe the adverb *continually*. We are not merely to be guided sometimes, but we are to have a perpetual monitor, not occasionally to be left to our own understanding and so to wander, but continually to hear the guiding voice of the Great Shepherd. If we follow close at His heels, we shall not err, but be led by a right way to a city to dwell in.[792] If you have to change your position in life; if you have to emigrate to distant shores; if it should happen that you are cast into poverty or uplifted suddenly into a more responsible position than the one you now occupy; if you are thrown among strangers or cast among foes, yet tremble not, for "the Lord shall guide you continually." There are no dilemmas out of which you shall not be delivered if you live near to God, and your heart is kept warm with holy love. He goes not amiss who goes in the company of God. Like Enoch, walk with God, and you cannot mistake your road. You have infallible wisdom to direct you, immutable love to comfort you, and eternal power to defend you. "Jehovah"—mark the word—"Jehovah shall guide you continually."[793]

427

I came not to send peace on earth, but a sword
(Matthew 10:34).

The Christian will be sure to make enemies. It will be one of his objects to make none, but if doing right and believing truth should cause him to lose every earthly friend, he will count it but a small loss, since his great Friend in heaven will be yet more friendly and reveal Himself to him more graciously than ever.[794] O ye who have taken up His cross, know ye not what your Master said? "I am come to set a man at variance against his father, and the daughter against her mother; and a man's foes shall be they of his own household."[795] Christ is the great Peacemaker, but before peace, He brings war. Where the light cometh, the darkness must retire. Where truth is, the lie must flee; or, if it abides, there must be a stern conflict, for the truth cannot and will not lower its standard, and the lie must be trodden under foot. If you follow Christ, you shall have all the dogs of the world yelping at your heels. If you would live so as to stand the test of the last tribunal, depend upon it the world will not speak well of you. He who has the friendship of the world is an enemy to God;[796] but if you are true and faithful to the Most High, men will resent your unflinching fidelity, since it is a testimony against their iniquities. Fearless of all consequences, you must do the right. You will need the courage of a lion unhesitatingly to pursue a course that shall turn your best friend into your fiercest foe; but for the love of Jesus, you must thus be courageous.[797] To hazard reputation and affection for truth's sake is such a deed that to do it constantly, you will need a degree of moral principle that only the Spirit of God can work in you; yet turn not your back like a coward, but play the man. Follow right manfully in your Master's steps, for He has traversed this rough way before you. Better a brief warfare and eternal rest, than false peace and everlasting torment.

⚜ *December 29* ⚜

What think ye of Christ? (Matthew 22:42)

The great test of your soul's health is: What do you think of Christ? Is He to you "fairer than the children of men"[798]—"the chief among ten thousand"—the "altogether lovely"?[799] Wherever Christ is thus esteemed, all the faculties of the spiritual man exercise themselves with energy. I will judge your piety by this barometer: Does Christ stand high or low with you? If you have thought little of Christ, if you have been content to live without His presence, if you have cared little for His honor, and if you have been neglectful of His laws, then I know that your soul is sick—God grant that it may not be sick unto death! But if the first thought of your spirit has been: How can I honor Jesus? If the daily desire of your soul has been, "O that I knew where I might find Him!" I tell you that you may have a thousand infirmities, and even scarcely know whether you are a child of God at all, and yet I am persuaded, beyond a doubt, that you are safe, since Jesus is great in your esteem. I care not for your rags; what do you think of *His* royal apparel? I care not for your wounds, though they bleed in torrents; what do you think of *His* wounds? Are they like glittering rubies in your esteem? I think none the less of you, although thou lie like Lazarus on the dunghill and the dogs lick you[800]—I judge you not by your poverty; what do you think of the King in His beauty? Has He a glorious high throne in your heart? Would you set Him higher if you could? Would you be willing to die if only you could add another trumpet to the strain that proclaims His praise? Ah! then it is well with you. Whatever you may think of yourself, if Christ is great to you, you shall be with Him before long.

"Though all the world my choice deride,
 Yet Jesus shall my portion be;
 For I am pleased with none beside,
 The fairest of the fair is He"

429

December 30

Knowest thou not that it will be bitterness in the latter end? (2 Samuel 2:26)

If, O my reader! you are merely a professor, and not a possessor of the faith that is in Christ Jesus, the following lines are a true ketch of your end. You are a respectable attendant at a place of worship; you go because others go, not because your heart is right with God. This is your beginning. I will suppose that for the next twenty or thirty years, you will be spared to go on as you do now, professing religion by an outward attendance upon the means of grace, but having no heart in the matter. Tread softly, for I must show you the deathbed of such a one as yourself. Let us gaze upon him gently. A clammy sweat is on his brow, and he wakes up crying, "O God, it is hard to die. Did you send for my minister?" "Yes, he is coming." The minister comes. "Sir, I fear that I am dying!" "Have you any hope?" "I cannot say that I have. I fear to stand before my God. Oh! pray for me." The prayer is offered for him with sincere earnestness, and the way of salvation is for the ten-thousandth time put before him, but before he has grasped the rope, I see him sink. I may put my finger upon those cold eyelids, for they will never see anything here again. But where is the man, and where are the man's true eyes? It is written, "In hell he lifted up his eyes, being in torment."[801] Ah! why did he not lift up his eyes before? Because he was so accustomed to hearing the gospel that his soul slept under it. Alas! if you should lift up your eyes there, how bitter will be your wailings. Let the Savior's own words reveal the woe: "Father Abraham, send Lazarus, that he may dip the tip of his finger in water, and cool my tongue, for I am tormented in this flame."[802] There is a frightful meaning in those words. May you never have to spell it out by the red light of Jehovah's wrath!

The harvest is past, the summer is ended, and we are not saved (Jeremiah 8:20).

Not *saved*! Dear reader, is this your mournful plight? Warned of the judgment to come, bidden to escape for your life, and yet at this moment *not saved*! You know the way of salvation. You read it in the Bible. You hear it from the pulpit. Friends explain it to you. And yet you neglect it, and therefore you are *not saved*. You will be without excuse when the Lord shall judge the quick and dead.[803] The Holy Spirit has given more or less of blessing upon the word, which has been preached in your hearing, and times of refreshing have come from the divine presence, and yet you are without Christ. All these hopeful seasons have come and gone—your summer and your harvest have past—and yet you are *not saved*. Years have followed one another into eternity, and your last year will soon be here. Youth has gone, manhood is going, and yet you are not saved. Let me ask you—will you ever be saved? Is there any likelihood of it? Already the most favorable seasons have left you unsaved; will other occasions alter your condition? Means have failed with you—the best of means, used perseveringly and with the utmost affection—what more can be done for you? Affliction and prosperity have alike failed to impress you; tears and prayers and sermons have been wasted on your barren heart. Are not the probabilities dead against your ever being saved? Is it not more than likely that you will abide as you are till death forever bars the door of hope? Do you recoil from the supposition? Yet it is a most reasonable one: He who is not washed in so many waters will in all probability go filthy to his end. The convenient time never has come; why should it ever come?[804] It is logical to fear that it never will arrive, and that like Felix, you will find no convenient season till you are in hell. Think of what that hell is, and of the dread probability that you will soon be cast into it![805] Reader, suppose you should die unsaved; there are not words to describe your doom no. Write out your dread estate in tears and blood; talk of it with groans and gnashing of teeth. You will be punished with everlasting destruction from the glory of the Lord and His power.[806] A brother's voice would eagerly startle you into earnestness. O be wise, be wise in time, and before another year begins, believe in Jesus, who is able to save to the utmost. Consecrate these last hours to lonely thought, and if deep repentance is bred in you, it will be well. If it leads to a humble faith in Jesus, it will be best of all. O see to it that this year passes not away, and you an unforgiven spirit. Let not the New Year's midnight peals sound upon a joyless spirit! Now, NOW, NOW believe, and live.

"ESCAPE FOR YOUR LIFE; LOOK NOT BEHIND YOU, NEITHER STAY THOU IN ALL THE PLAIN; ESCAPE TO THE MOUNTAIN, LEST THOU BE CONSUMED."

ENDNOTES

1. Psalm 95:1
2. Exodus 13:22-25
3. Matthew 9:15
4. Revelation 3:12
5. Psalm 104:30
6. Isaiah 40:31
7. 1 Samuel 40:3
8. 1 Samuel 40:4
9. Psalm 138:6
10. Psalm 139:16
11. 2 Timothy 2:19
12. Malachi 4:2
13. John 1:10
14. Matthew 7:23
15. John 14:17
16. 1 John 1:5
17. 2 Corinthians 4:7
18. 2 Timothy 2:19
19. Hebrews 12:7
20. Psalm 22:16
21. Revelation 21:2; 9; 22:17
22. Leviticus 19:10
23. John 6:31-33
24. John 19:34
25. 1 Samuel 16:7
26. Nehemiah 8:10
27. Revelation 1:7; 22:4
28. John 1:14
29. Hebrews 7:25
30. Luke 22:31
31. 1 John 3:8
32. Matthew 5:16
33. Acts 3:6
34. John 4:6-17
35. Matthew 25:15-28
36. Mark 10:27
37. Matthew 9:29
38. Hebrews 4:16
39. James 5:16
40. James 1:6-7
41. 1 Thessalonians 5:17
42. John 10:18
43. Matthew 20:28; Mark 10:45; 1 Timothy 2:16
44. Isaiah 53:5; 1 Peter 2:24
45. 1 Corinthians 1:30
46. Matthew 13:23
47. Matthew 13:22
48. Genesis 32:25
49. 2 Samuel 3:39
50. 2 Timothy 2:3
51. John 15:2
52. James 1:12-17
53. Hebrews 7:22
54. Revelation 22:20
55. Exodus 17:11-13
56. 1 Corinthians 15:22
57. Galatians 4:6-7
58. Matthew 5:48
59. John 14:15
60. John 15:12
61. Matthew 5:42
62. Matthew 5:17
63. Psalm 40:8; 119:35
64. Exodus 3:5
65. Luke 2:8-18
66. Matthew 26:7
67. John 15:4
68. Isaiah 40:15
69. Isaiah 40:12
70. Psalm 45:1
71. Matthew 11:28
72. 1 Kings 10:7; 1 Corinthians 2:9
73. Psalm 116:7
74. Genesis 8:11
75. Lamentations 3:23
76. Romans 8:17
77. Matthew 28:18
78. 1 Corinthians 1:30
79. Colossians 2:10
80. 1 Corinthians 3:23
81. Luke 8:13
82. Isaiah 40:31
83. Philippians 3:14
84. Luke 13:7
85. Matthew 11:28
86. Isaiah 1:18

87. John 17:10
88. John 16:27
89. Exodus 33:22
90. Ephesians 1:4
91. John 17:24; Hebrews 4:3; 9:26; 1 Peter 1:20; Revelation 13:8
92. Psalm 42:1
93. Numbers 35:6-32
94. Matthew 9:20; 14:36
95. Matthew 11:25
96. 1 John 4:17
97. 1 Corinthians 14:2
98. Galatians 5:22
99. Romans 8:26-27; 34
100. Revelation 21:3
101. James 1:4
102. Romans 5:9
103. Romans 4:8
104. Hebrews 9:26
105. Romans 7:14-25
106. Romans 8:2
107. Hebrews 12:14
108. 2 Timothy 2:19
109. Psalm 1:1
110. Matthew 26:41
111. Matthew 6:13
112. 1 Peter 5:8
113. Ephesians 6:10-18
114. 1 John 5:17-18
115. 1 John 1:8-9
116. 1 Corinthians 6:20; 7:23
117. Revelation 2:4
118. Acts 2:1-4
119. Romans 8:2
120. Ephesians 3:11-12; Hebrews 10:19-20; Hebrews 4:16
121. John 3:18
122. 2 Corinthians 8:9
123. Galatians 3:24; Romans 5:1
124. Song of Solomon 5:1
125. Matthew 26:7; Mark 14:3; Luke 7:37
126. John 14:16; 26; 15:26; 16:7; 16:13; 6:63
127. Ephesians 6:13-18
128. 1 John 1:9
129. Luke 15:18
130. 1 John 2:16
131. John 4:34
132. Hebrews 2:1; 4:15
133. Daniel 2:1-49
134. Revelation 5:2
135. Colossians 1:9
136. Romans 2:4
137. Hebrews 6:18-19
138. Zechariah 1:14
139. Psalm 103:13
140. Isaiah 49:16
141. Romans 8:31
142. John 16:8
143. Luke 22:44
144. Isaiah 33:16
145. 1 Peter 2:9
146. Hebrews 8:6-13
147. Romans 8:1
148. John 3:16
149. Hebrews 13:5
150. 1 Corinthians 2:2
151. Isaiah 55:10
152. Matthew 10:16
153. Genesis 1:2
154. Matthew 3:16
155. Psalm 91:4
156. Matthew 7:27-28
157. 2 Samuel 9:7
158. Ephesians 1:6
159. Luke 12:16-21
160. 1 Corinthians 1:31; 2 Corinthians 10:17
161. 1 Peter 5:7
162. Philippians 4:6
163. Luke 6:48
164. Judges 14:8
165. 1 Peter 5:7
166. Deuteronomy 33:27
167. Isaiah 43:2
168. Genesis 32:24-29
169. Ephesians 5:27
170. Psalm 30:6-8
171. 2 Timothy 3:11
172. Colossians 3:2

173. Matthew 13:46
174. Isaiah 53:6
175. John 1:12
176. Matthew 6:24
177. Jeremiah 3:12
178. 1 Peter 5:8
179. Proverbs 10:4
180. Psalm 69:9
181. Colossians 3:5
182. Jude 24
183. Isaiah 53:3
184. Jeremiah 31:3
185. 1 Timothy 2:6; Titus 2:14
186. Ephesians 3:19
187. Philippians 3:9
188. John 16:12
189. John 17:9
190. Romans 8:39
191. Psalm 8:4
192. Mark 16:3
193. Isaiah 53:3
194. Hebrews 1:9
195. Luke 10:21
196. Psalm 46:4
197. Matthew 1:23
198. Hebrews 12:2
199. 2 Thessalonians 1:7
200. Hosea 2:19
201. Luke 22:44
202. Isaiah 50:6
203. Ephesians 1:6
204. Job 10:2
205. Galatians 3:15
206. Matthew 6:11
207. Matthew 13:22
208. 1 Corinthians 11:24-26
209. Isaiah 66:2
210. Ephesians 4:10
211. Matthew 5:3
212. 1 Thessalonians 5:23
213. Romans 6:12
214. 1 John 4:4;
     Revelation 12:11
215. 2 Samuel 11:3-26; 12:9-10
216. Psalm 91
217. Hebrew 1:13-14
218. Matthew 10:30
219. Proverbs 13:15
220. Genesis 8:21
221. Genesis 3:1-7
222. Genesis 3:15
223. 2 Corinthians 5:21
224. Leviticus 16:1-10
225. Revelation 13:8
226. Romans 4:11-25
227. Luke 10:33
228. 2 Timothy 3:12
229. 2 Kings 4:8-37
230. 2 Corinthians 5:7
231. Psalm 25:1
232. John 17:15
233. 2 Corinthians 1:20
234. Luke 18:1
235. Hebrews 4:15
236. John 12:21
237. Numbers 23:19
238. Joshua 23:14
239. Matthew 11:28
240. Matthew 12:20
241. Luke 21:33
242. Proverbs 18:24
243. Matthew 28:20
244. 1 Samuel 17:47
245. Isaiah 53:3
246. Psalm 21:5
247. Romans 8:34
248. Matthew 28:18
249. Romans 8:31
250. Zechariah 13:6
251. Hebrews 10:23
252. James 1:17
253. Ephesians 3:18
254. Philippians 4:7
255. 1 Corinthians 15:31
256. 1 Peter 5:8
257. Romans 8:37
258. Colossians 1:19
259. Matthew 28:18
260. Galatians 3:13
261. Ezekiel 36:26
262. Romans 7:24
263. Luke 12:7
264. Psalm 37:23
265. Ephesians 3:8

266. 1 Corinthians 15:51-54
267. Hebrews 12:2
268. Galatians 3:29
269. 1 Peter 1:22
270. Titus 2:14
271. Galatians 4:3
272. Proverbs 16:20
273. Job 23:21
274. Genesis 1:26
275. Luke 15:11-32
276. Hebrews 1:3
277. Luke 10:38-39
278. Psalm 30:11
279. Ephesians 4:8
280. 1 Peter 1:8
281. Philippians 4:6
282. Jeremiah 33:11;
     Isaiah 61:3
283. Nehemiah 8:10
284. Psalm 126:5
285. Joshua 1:7
286. James 1:12-13
287. Hebrews 13:5
288. Psalm 139:7-8
289. Luke 12:32
290. Numbers 13:1-33; 14:1-24
291. Matthew 6:33
292. Mark 8:36
293. Philippians 4:19
294. 1 Corinthians 6:19-20
295. John 17:1-26
296. Hebrews 4:11
297. Hebrews 6:1
298. Romans 7:24
299. Ephesians 5:18
300. Ezekiel 34:26
301. Ephesians 3:20
302. Ephesians 1:4
303. Jeremiah 31:3
304. Isaiah 6:3
305. Malachi 2:16
306. James 3:17
307. Hebrews 11:34
308. 2 Kings 2:11
309. James 4:3
310. James 2:23
311. Luke 10:40

312. Psalm 81:10
313. Hebrews 4:16
314. 1 Peter 5:7
315. Ephesians 5:25
316. Genesis 41:1-57
317. 1 Kings 17:4
318. Deuteronomy 8:3
319. Song of Solomon 4:8
320. Acts 7:59-60
321. Luke 21:1-4
322. Luke 12:48
323. 1 Corinthians 6:20
324. Isaiah 42:3
325. 1 John 4:7-8
326. John 20:3-7
327. John 20:1-2
328. Ephesians 4:12-13
329. Job 2:9
330. Matthew 25:1
331. Ephesians 6:11
332. Psalm 120:5
333. Colossians 1:28
334. Hebrews 6:6
335. 1 John 1:9
336. 2 Corinthians 5:17
337. 1 John 1:7
338. Isaiah 37:24
339. Galatians 4:5-6
340. Isaiah 44:3
341. Colossians 2:9
342. Matthew 11:29
343. John 13:4
344. Psalm 22:1; Matthew
     27:46; Mark 15:34
345. Luke 7:47
346. Isaiah 53:3
347. Matthew 28:18
348. Acts 1:11
349. Revelation 19:12-13
350. Revelation 5:9
351. Matthew 25:31
352. 1 John 4:19
353. 2 Corinthians 5:14
354. Romans 5:5
355. Ephesians 3:8
356. Revelation 11:15
357. Daniel 11:28

358. Isaiah 59:17	405. 1 Corinthians 10:4
359. John 6:9	406. Psalm 103:5
360. Numbers 11:23	407. Ecclesiastes 12:8
361. John 1:14	408. Luke 24:5
362. Revelation 22:13	409. 1 Corinthians 10:21
363. Genesis 3:15	410. Revelation 5:10
364. 1 John 4:12	411. 1 John 4:4
365. Matthew 1:23	412. Ephesians 6:5-8
366. Revelation 21:3	413. 1 Corinthians 1:17-18
367. John 19:30	414. 1 John 5:4-6
368. Isaiah 53:6	415. Revelation 3:14-19
369. Romans 8:34	416. Isaiah 27:3
370. 2 Corinthians 10:4	417. Romans 8:7
371. Romans 6:9-10	418. Genesis 6:8
372. 1 Corinthians 15:22	419. Genesis 22:2
373. 2 Peter 1:4	420. Joshua 6:4
374. Hebrews 11:25; James 5:5	421. Revelation 3:20
375. Psalms 42:7	422. Malachi 4:2
376. Luke 22:34	423. Revelation 6:15-17
377. Revelation 3:8	424. Deuteronomy 24:9
378. Song of Solomon 2:1	425. 2 Corinthians 4:17
379. 1 John 1:5	426. Matthew 5:8
380. 2 Peter 3:15	427. 2 Corinthians 20:1-15
381. 1 Samuel 17:4	428. Psalm 15:4
382. Romans 8:31	429. Ephesians 4:27-30
383. Numbers 21:16	430. Psalm 77:8
384. Hebrews 10:25	431. 1 Samuel 21:9
385. 2 Peter 3:18	432. Isaiah 46:5
386. Luke 10:39	433. 1 Kings 18:19-40
387. Song of Solomon 2:4	434. John 3:16
388. James 1:22-23	435. Philippians 2:7
389. 2 Corinthians 5:19	436. Romans 8:34
390. 1 John 1:14	437. Colossians 3:1
391. 1 Peter 3:18	438. Colossians 2:13
392. 1 Peter 2:24	439. Acts 9:5
393. 1 Peter 2:24	440. Psalm 25:5
394. 2 Corinthians 5:21	441. Hebrews 12:2
395. John 1:29	442. Isaiah 40:31
396. 2 Timothy 2:19	443. Romans 7:23
397. John 14:2	444. 1 John 3:14
398. Habakkuk 3:17	445. 1 Peter 2:9
399. 1 John 3:2	446. Romans 12:2
400. 1 John 3:2	447. Romans 4:17
401. 1 Peter 6:5-6	448. Luke 18:13
402. Luke 12:31	449. 1 Timothy 5:8
403. Romans 14:17	450. 1 Corinthians 7:14
404. Proverbs 15:17	451. Revelation 22:5

1 Thessalonians 3:8
546. Romans 6:4
547. Colossians 2:13
548. John 15:4
549. Matthew 7:15
550. John 15:18
551. Matthew 5:25
552. Ephesians 5:15
553. 1 Corinthians 1:23
554. 2 Corinthians 4:14-17
555. Philippians 2:7
556. Psalm 32:3
557. Nehemiah 9:17
558. Exodus 3:5
559. Exodus 19:23
560. Ephesians 2:13
561. Matthew 11:28
562. Revelation 21:3
563. 1 Thessalonians 5:11
564. Philippians 2:13
565. 1 Corinthians 6:19-20
566. Hebrews 10:23
567. John 21:23
568. Hebrews 11:10
569. Psalm 103:17-18
570. Song of Solomon 4:8
571. Proverbs 22:6
572. Luke 2:46
573. Hosea 4:6
574. Psalm 103:12
575. Psalm 26:9
576. Matthew 13:30
577. Psalm 91:1
578. Mark 9:23
579. Judges 16:19
580. 1 Timothy 1:15
581. Proverbs 9:10
582. Psalm 111:10
583. Matthew 25:21
584. Luke 21:36
585. Haggai 2:23
586. Ephesians 2:1;
     Colossians 2:13
587. John 1:14
588. 2 Corinthians 8:9
589. Hebrews 4:15
590. Ephesians 6:13-18

591. Matthew 1:21
592. Luke 4:18
593. Romans 10:9-10
594. John 14:6
595. John 5:45-46
596. Ephesians 5:27
597. Luke 15:2
598. Numbers 12:1
599. 1 Timothy 4:9-10
600. 1 John 5:14-15
601. Hebrews 12:2
602. John 16:7-13
603. Matthew 15:26
604. Matthew 11:28
605. 1 Peter 5:6-7
606. Isaiah 40:31
607. 1 Thessalonians 4:4
608. 2 Timothy 1:9
609. 1 Peter 1:15
610. Hebrews 3:1
611. Isaiah 61:3
612. Galatians 3:13
613. 2 Corinthians 6:17
614. 1 John 2:15
615. Galatians 3:13
616. Luke 15:11-32
617. 2 Corinthians 6:10
618. Colossians 2:10
619. Matthew 18:14
620. 1 Corinthians 13:3
621. Habakkuk 3:17-18
622. Hebrews 4:16
623. Isaiah 40:27
624. Psalm 34:7
625. Psalm 72:14
626. Psalm 116:15
627. Romans 8:28
628. Luke 12:7
629. Matthew 28:20
630. Genesis 15:1
631. Luke 22:32
632. John 6:20
633. John 16:13
634. Luke 10:34
635. Hebrews 4:11
636. John 13:14
637. Luke 5:13

638. Galatians 6:7
639. Luke 12:48
640. 2 Corinthians 5:17
641. 1 Peter 2:9
642. 1 John 3:3
643. 1 Timothy 2:5;
Hebrews 8:6; 9:15; 12:24
644. Isaiah 64:6;
2 Corinthians 5:21
645. 1 Corinthians 3:12
646. Isaiah 53:3
647. Hebrews 6:20
648. John 16:13
649. Luke 24:31
650. John 10:27; 10:5
651. Luke 9:26
652. Acts 16:31
653. Matthew 24:38
654. John 15:4
655. Deuteronomy 18:9
656. Hebrews 12:14
657. Luke 18:1
658. 1 John 5:18
659. James 5:16
660. 1 John 5:14
661. 1 Peter 2:24
662. Matthew 16:17
663. Isaiah 53:2
664. Luke 20:17
665. Matthew 13:46
666. Song of Solomon 2:1
667. Isaiah 6:1
668. Ephesians 4:8
669. Leviticus 17:11
670. 1 Corinthians 11:25
671. Psalm 105:8
672. Romans 8:3
673. Romans 6:4
674. Ecclesiastes 11:6
675. Acts 5:41
676. Matthew 5:11
677. Hebrews 13:21
678. Revelation 3:20
679. Luke 12:27-28
680. Hebrews 6:13-19
681. Isaiah 46:9-11
682. Matthew 8:20

683. Luke 11:1
684. Matthew 10:25
685. Mark 16:15
686. 1 Corinthians 10:13
687. Romans 8:37
688. John 6:20
689. Revelation 22:17
690. Acts 9:5
691. 2 Samuel 11:2-3
692. Psalm 91:4
693. Hebrews 13:8
694. Revelation 1:4
695. Hebrews 7:25
696. Psalm 19:10
697. Hebrews 2:13-14
698. Psalm 61:2
699. Joel 3:11
700. John 11:39
701. John 11:36
702. Philippians 3:10
703. Romans 6:4
704. Philippians 3:10
705. Ecclesiastes 10:8
706. Proverbs 22:29
707. Matthew 11:28
708. 1 Peter 4:17
709. 1 John 4:10
710. Hebrews 9:12
711. Colossians 2:14
712. 2 Timothy 2:2
713. James 3:9-13
714. Romans 8:28
715. James 5:14
716. Hebrews 2:14
717. Ephesians 6:13
718. 2 Corinthians 10:4
719. 1 Corinthians 10:13
720. Colossians 2:15; 2 Corinthians 2:14
721. 2 Thessalonians 1:9; Romans 16:20
722. 1 Thessalonians 5:18
723. Psalm 103:1
724. Ecclesiastes 2:10-11
725. Philippians 3:8
726. John 19:30
727. Ephesians 4:8

728. Colossians 2:15
729. Romans 8:33
730. Hebrews 10:22
731. 1 Corinthians 15:53
732. Romans 14:11
733. Romans 8:37
734. 1 John 4:4
735. Ephesians 1:13-14
736. Romans 2:7
737. Romans 8:26
738. 2 Corinthians 20:15
739. Hebrews 7:25
740. Ephesians 6:14
741. Colossians 1:28
742. 2 Corinthians 12:9
743. Isaiah 26:3
744. Exodus 13:22
745. Acts 16:14
746. John 6:65
747. 1 John 3:14
748. Colossians 3:17; 1 Corinthians 10:31
749. Matthew 25:40
750. Luke 18:13
751. Matthew 5:8
752. 1 John 4:17
753. 2 Corinthians 5:19
754. Galatians 2:20
755. Romans 7:4
756. Romans 6:4
757. Hebrews 6:1
758. Isaiah 28:16
759. 1 Corinthians 3:12
760. Matthew 7:26
761. Colossians 2:14
762. Ezekiel 39:7
763. Matthew 13:23
764. Numbers 35:6
765. Jeremiah 31:12
766. Psalm 139:23
767. Hebrews 4:12
768. Daniel 5:27
769. Revelation 21:1
770. Revelation 15:2
771. 1 Peter 1:8
772. Matthew 25:21
773. Ezekiel 16:10

774. John 1:12; Romans 8:14
775. John 10:3-5; 27
776. Psalm 139.23
777. Isaiah 53:3-6
778. Isaiah 45:7
779. 2 Corinthians 2:14
780. 2 Peter 3:10
781. Revelation 21:1
782. John 10:10
783. Revelation 19:6
784. 1 John 3:8
785. Philippians 3:14
786. Matthew 12:37
787. 1 Corinthians 11:25-26
788. Hebrews 9:14
789. John 21:9
790. Song of Solomon 6:5
791. Romans 8:29; 12:2
792. John 16:13
793. Psalm 119:105
794. Philippians 3:8
795. Matthew 10:36
796. James 4:4
797. Proverbs 28:1
798. Psalm 45:2
799. Song of Solomon 5:16
800. Luke 16:21
801. Luke 16:23
802. Luke 16:24
803. 2 Timothy 4:1
804. Acts 24:25
805. Acts 24:25
806. 2 Thessalonians 1:9

SCRIPTURE TEXT

Genesis

1:4	January 5
1:4	July 9
1:5	July 10
3:8	July 1
8:9	March 13
8:9	June 25
8:11	January 29
9:14	August 12
9:15	August 13
29:26	November 14
32:12	April 18
35:18	March 8
42:2	May 21
42:8	January 4
46:3, 4	May 12

Exodus

3:7	August 14
7:12	June 28
17:12	April 16
32:6	August 24
34:20	October 15
35:8	November 29

Leviticus

1:4	April 13
3:13	February 26
19:36	September 4

Numbers

6:4	August 29
11:23	June 8
12:1	October 6
21:17	June 17
32:6	August 5

Deuteronomy

1:38	September 17
32:5	December 22

Joshua

1:7	May 11
6:26	May 29

20:3	February 4

Judges

15:18	January 21

Ruth

2:3	October 25
2:14	March 19
2:17	August 2

1 Samuel

1:27	September 19
15:22	October 18
18:17	April 20
30:13	March 12

2 Samuel

1:26	February 1
2:26	December 30
9:8	May 27
11:2	January 17
18:23	January 31
21:10	March 31

1 Kings

17:16	February 28
18:40	July 17
18:43	September 28
19:4	May 19

2 Kings

3:16, 17	May 16
6:9	January 13

1 Chronicles

4:22	February 2
9:33	July 31

2 Chronicles

30:27	November 3
31:21	March 15
32:31	June 29

Ezra

9:4	September 30
10:9	November 17
11:6	September 20

Song of Solomon
1:2	January 8
1:4	January 1
1:4	January 23
1:7	February 3
1:16	May 22
2:1	May 1
2:12	April 24
2:16, 17	June 19
3:4	September 29
4:12	January 7
5:1	June 18
5:2	September 24
5:4	September 27
5:6	March 29
5:11	October 28
7:11, 12	May 9
8:6	October 13
8:13	October 30

Isaiah
2:3	April 4
3:10	April 14
26:4	July 5
32:18	December 9
33:16	November 9
33:17	November 16
36:5	October 7
40:5	December 24
40:9	November 23
40:11	May 14
40:11	October 17
41:1	January 2
41:9	May 17
43:6	October 20
43:24	May 23
44:22	February 10
45:19	August 21
48:8	December 16
51:3	June 1
53:6	April 3
53:10	April 2
54:1	August 28

54:11	December 15
54:12	December 13
57:18	August 28
58:11	December 27
62:12	March 11
64:6	October 27

Jeremiah
2:18	July 20
15:21	October 10
17:4	August 30
32:17	June 30
49:23	September 7

Lamentations
| 3:21 | May 28 |
| 3:40 | March 30 |

Ezekiel
3:7	April 28
16:6	July 7
16:10	December 21
20:41	March 28
33:22	January 6
35:10	February 17
36:26	August 15

Daniel
3:16, 18	June 24
9:8	June 14
9:26	January 16
10:11	October 2

Hosea
5:7	December 12
5:15	July 25
10:12	April 1
11:4	May 20
13:5	October 31

Joel
1:3	July 11
2:8	July 18
2:11	July 24

Amos
No entry

5:39	June 10
6:37	July 29
6:37	July 30
10:9	December 17
10:27	September 18
11:4	August 17
12:2	November 21
12:21	April 17
13:5	October 24
14:16	February 12
14:26	October 12
15:4	March 9
15:9	March 18
16:15	October 22
17:24	March 22
19:5	July 22

Acts

1:8	November 7
8:30	February 21
8:37	August 25
10:38	July 28
14:22	May 26
16:14	December 10
27:23	April 10

Romans

3:31	January 25
6:6	May 30
8:1	February 13
8:23	June 23
8:23	August 16
8:23	December 4
8:30	October 11
8:33	July 27
8:34	April 21
9:15	November 25
12:2	October 14

1 Corinthians

1:30	September 25
2:12	February 29
7:20	June 27
9:22	December 7

2 Corinthians

11:22	June 6

Galatians

2:20	December 14
5:18	September 6

Ephesians

1:7	November 2
1:11	January 30
1:19, 20	September 8
3:8	March 2
3:8	August 22
3:17	August 23
5:25	March 20

Philippians

1:27	May 24
2:8	June 3
3:10	November 22

Colossians

3:24	December 11

1 Thessalonians

2:18	August 7

2 Thessalonians

2:16	August 11

1 Timothy

3:16	June 4

2 Timothy

1:9	June 12
2:12	July 3
2:19	June 21
4:18	July 12

Titus
No entry

Philemon
No entry

Hebrews

2:18	October 3
9:20	November 6
11:13	May 2

12:11	May 18	**3 John**	
12:23	May 15	No entry	
12:27	June 22		

James

TOPICAL INDEX

451

R

S

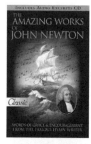
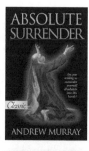
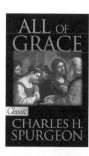
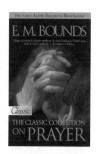
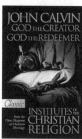

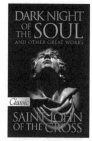

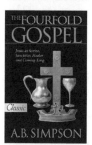

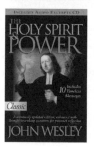
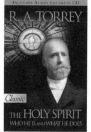
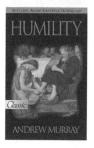

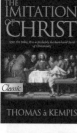
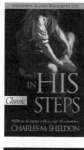

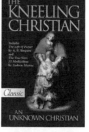

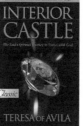

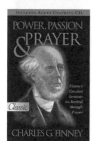

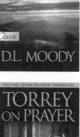
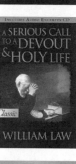
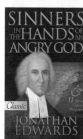

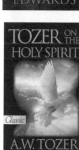

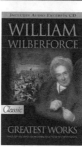
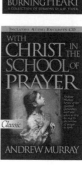

Pure Gold Classics

CHRISTIAN CLASSICS

assic is a work of enduring
llence; a Christian classic is a
k of enduring excellence that is
d with divine wisdom, biblical
lation, and insights that are
vant to living a godly life. Such
ks are both spiritual and
ctical. Our Pure Gold Classics
tain some of the finest examples
Christian writing that have ever
n published, including the works
ohn Foxe, Charles Spurgeon,
. Moody, Martin Luther, John
vin, Saint John of the Cross,
. Bounds, John Wesley, Andrew
rray, Hannah Whitall Smith, and
ny others.

The timeline on the following
es will help you to understand
context of the times in which
e extraordinary books were
tten and the historical events that
t have served to influence these
t writers to create works that
always stand the test of time.
ired by God, many of these
ors did their work in difficult
es and during periods of history
were not sympathetic to their
sage. Some even had to endure
t persecution, misunderstanding,
risonment, and martyrdom as a
ct result of their writing.

The entries that are printed in
green type will give you a good
overview of Christian history from
the birth of Jesus to modern times.

The entries in red pertain to
writers of Christian classics from
Saint Augustine, who wrote his
Confessions and *City of God*, to
Charles Sheldon, twentieth-century
author of *In His Steps*.

Entries in black provide a clear
perspective on the development of
secular history from the early days
of Buddhism (first century) through
the Civil Rights Movement.

Finally, the blue entries highlight
secular writers and artists, including
Chaucer, Michelangelo, and others.

Our color timeline will provide
you with a fresh perspective of
history, both secular and Christian,
and the classics, both secular and
Christian. This perspective will help
you to understand each author
better and to see the world through
his or her eyes.